Anthropologists and the Rediscovery of America, 1886–1965

This book examines the intersection of cultural anthropology and American cultural nationalism from 1886, when Franz Boas left Germany for the United States, until 1965, when the National Endowment for the Humanities was established. Five chapters trace the development within academic anthropology of the concepts of culture, social class, national character, value, and civilization, and their dissemination to non-anthropologists. As Americans came to think of culture anthropologically, as a complex whole far broader and more inclusive than Matthew Arnold's "the best that has been thought and known," so, too, did they come to see American communities as stratified into social classes distinguished by their subcultures, to attribute the making of the American character to socialization rather than birth, to locate the distinctiveness of American culture in its unconscious canons of choice, and to view American culture and civilization in a global perspective.

John S. Gilkeson is Associate Professor of Humanities, Arts, and Cultural Studies at Arizona State University, where his teaching focuses on history and American studies. He has been visiting professor at the John F. Kennedy Institute for North American Studies at the Freie Universität Berlin and has held fellowships from the National Endowment for the Humanities, the Woodrow Wilson International Center for Scholars, and the Charles Warren Center for Studies in American History. He is the author of *Middle-Class Providence, 1820–1940*.

'Tis the gift to be simple,
'Tis the gift to be free,
'Tis the gift to come down where you ought to be,
And when we find ourselves in the place just right,
It will be in the valley of love and delight.

When true simplicity is gained,
To bow and to bend we shan't be ashamed.
To turn, turn will be our delight,
'Til by turning, turning we come round right.

(Elder Joseph Brackett, "Simple Gifts")

Anthropologists and the Rediscovery of America, 1886–1965

JOHN S. GILKESON

Arizona State University

CAMBRIDGE
UNIVERSITY PRESS

CAMBRIDGE UNIVERSITY PRESS
Cambridge, New York, Melbourne, Madrid, Cape Town,
Singapore, São Paulo, Delhi, Tokyo, Mexico City

Cambridge University Press
32 Avenue of the Americas, New York, NY 10013-2473, USA

www.cambridge.org
Information on this title: www.cambridge.org/9780521766722

First published 2010
Reprinted 2011

A catalog record for this publication is available from the British Library.

Library of Congress Cataloging in Publication Data
Gilkeson, John S., 1948–
Anthropologists and the rediscovery of America, 1886–1965 / John S. Gilkeson.
    p. cm.
Includes bibliographical references and index.
ISBN 978-0-521-76672-2 (hardback)
1. Ethnology – United States – History. 2. United States – Civilization. 3. Social
Classes – United States – History. 4. Cultural pluralism – United States – History.
5. Subcultures – United States – History. 6. National characteristics, American. I. Title.
E184.A1G47 2010
305.800973–dc22   2010022339

ISBN 978-0-521-76672-2 Hardback

Contents

Acknowledgments

This book originated in the Summer Institute on the History of Social Scientific Inquiry, held at the Center for Advanced Study in the Behavioral Sciences and directed by George W. Stocking, Jr., and David E. Leary. I am grateful for the encouragement and helpful advice that I received from fellow participants JoAnne Brown, Walter A. Jackson, and the late David K. van Keuren, and from senior scholars James T. Patterson, David Hollinger, Daniel Horowitz, Michael Lacey, Fred Matthews, and Dorothy Ross. Fellowships from the National Endowment for the Humanities, the Woodrow Wilson International Center for Scholars, and the Charles Warren Center for Studies in American History provided release time from teaching and conducive environments in which I could learn my way around the field of anthropology and begin to frame my project. Summer travel and research grants from Arizona State University, the Rockefeller Archive Center, and the National Endowment for the Humanities supported extensive archival research. Sabbatical leaves from Arizona State University provided the large blocks of time necessary to draft chapters of the book. During a semester spent at the John F. Kennedy Institute, Free University of Berlin, I was the beneficiary of the gracious hospitality and intellectual stimulation of the late Willi Paul Adams and Knut Krakau. I benefited as well from the experience of exploring the history of the American studies movement with interested German students and of thinking comparatively about the intellectual histories of Germany and the United States.

Many archivists guided and facilitated my research. I gratefully acknowledge permission to reproduce material from the collections of the American Philosophical Society; the Bancroft Library, University of California, Berkeley; the Special Collections Research Center, University of Chicago; the Harvard University Archives; the Baker Library Historical Collections, Harvard Business School; the Manuscript Division of the Library of Congress; the Bentley Historical Library, University of Michigan; the National Academy of Sciences; the Rockefeller Archive Center; and Special Collections, Vassar College Libraries. I am also grateful to the Institute for Intercultural Studies, Inc., for permission to quote from Margaret Mead's papers at the Library of Congress, and to James M. Redfield, for permission to quote from the papers of Robert E. Park and Robert Redfield at the University of Chicago.

Drafts of this book benefited from the detailed comments and editorial advice of John Burnham, Dave Madden, Fred Beuttler, Michael Elliott, Ruth Homrighaus, Peter Iverson, Vicky Ruiz, Monica Casper, Eric Wertheimer, and anonymous reviewers for Cambridge University Press. Cliff Wilcox not only shared with me his interest in Robert Redfield but also pointed me to a number of manuscripts that I would otherwise have missed. Sharon Tiffany and Jerry Sullivan helped me to clarify my thoughts on Clyde Kluckhohn's relations to Ruth Benedict and Margaret Mead. Willow Powers enlightened me about the Comparative Study of Values in Five Cultures.

Portions of Chapter 1 appeared previously in "The Domestication of 'Culture' in Interwar America," in *The Estate of Social Knowledge*, edited by JoAnne Brown and David van Keuren, and published in 1991 by the Johns Hopkins University Press; portions of Chapter 2 in "American Social Scientists and the Domestication of 'Class,' 1929–1955," *Journal of the History of the Behavioral Sciences* 31 (1995): 331–346; and portions of Chapter 4 in "Clyde Kluckhohn and the New Anthropology: From Culture and Personality to the Scientific Study of Values," *Pacific Studies* 32 (2009): 251–272.

I am grateful to my editor at Cambridge University Press, Lewis Bateman, for maintaining his faith in me and the project over these many years. My production editor, Mary Cadette, was a delight to work with. Betsy Truax prepared a fine index. I should also like to acknowledge the subvention I received from the New College of Interdisciplinary Arts & Sciences, Arizona State University.

I regret that David van Keuren did not live to see this book's publication. He strongly believed in the project from its very inception and was a constant source of support.

I dedicate this book to Susan Gray, without whose critical advice, generosity, and love this book would never have been published.

Tempe, Arizona
March 2010

Introduction

This is the story of how a small group of anthropologists, many of them students of the German émigré Franz Boas, shaped American thought from the late nineteenth century until the mid-1960s by democratizing American conceptions of culture, putting class analysis on the agenda of American social science, rehabilitating the American character, studying American values, and reconciling American culture and civilization.

My story begins in 1886, when Franz Boas left Germany to seek his fortune in the United States. Between the time of his arrival in the United States and his death in 1942, Boas reoriented American anthropology around a broad, pluralistic, relativistic, and holistic conception of culture. The connotations of pluralism, relativism, and holism were not present in Matthew Arnold's humanistic conception of culture as "the best that has been thought and known in the world," nor were they present in E. B. Tylor's charter definition of culture in its technical, anthropological sense as a "complex whole."[1] To these connotations, anthropologists subsequently added a concern with patterning and a stress on the structural aspects of culture.[2] Although new in American usage, these connotations had long been familiar in Germany, where, from the late eighteenth century on, the educated middle classes invoked a particularistic and relativistic *Kultur* to defend their way of life from the threat posed by a

---

[1] Matthew Arnold, "Culture and Anarchy: An Essay in Political and Social Criticism," in *Culture and Anarchy and Other Writings*, ed. Stefan Collini (Cambridge: Cambridge University Press, 1999), 79; Edward Burnett Tylor, *Primitive Culture: Researches into the Development of Mythology, Philosophy, Religion, Art, and Custom* (London: J. Murray, 1871), 1, quoted in A. L. Kroeber and Clyde Kluckhohn, *Culture: A Critical Review of Concepts and Definitions* (Cambridge, Mass.: Harvard University Peabody Museum of American Archaeology and Ethnology, 1952), 43.

[2] Robert F. Berkhofer, Jr., "Clio and the Culture Concept: Some Impressions of a Changing Relationship in American Historiography," in *The Idea of Culture in the Social Sciences*, ed. Louis Schneider and Charles Bonjean (Cambridge: Cambridge University Press, 1973), 81–82.

universalistic civilization emanating from Paris.[3] In the United States, this conception of culture fell on peculiarly fertile ground.

How, I wondered, did such a broad, German-inflected conception of culture become so pervasive in American thought that, in 1948, the popular economist Stuart Chase pronounced it "the foundation stone of the social sciences"; that, in 1952, the anthropologists Alfred Kroeber and Clyde Kluckhohn claimed that it was comparable to such concepts as evolution and gravity; and that, in 1954, the educator John R. Everett identified it as "the indigenous American concept of culture"?[4] Why did the culture concept become so much more pervasive in American thought than in English or French thought? And why did culture, in the anthropological sense, come to be seen both in England and on the Continent as peculiarly American?[5]

American receptivity to a German-inflected conception of culture can be explained, in part, by the enormous influence wielded in American universities before the First World War by Boas and other German, or German-trained, scholars. It may also have been the case, as the Austrian émigré Eric Wolf once suggested, that their disdain for "artificiality and outer form" predisposed Americans to adopt the "informal and internal" German understanding of culture. But the more that I thought about American receptivity to borrowings from German thought, the more it seemed to me that the culture concept also spoke to the need of educated Americans to overcome their long-standing sense of cultural inferiority to Europe. In what follows, I examine the peculiar fit between American anthropology and American cultural nationalism, specifically, how anthropological concepts helped to meet the "need," as the literary historian Alfred Kazin put it in 1942, "to chart America and to possess it."[6]

Beginning in the 1920s, American anthropologists embarked on a campaign to make Americans culture-conscious. Becoming "culture-conscious," as Ruth Benedict explained in 1929, meant learning how to detach oneself from the taken-for-granted conventions of one's own culture, to appreciate "the intriguing variety of possible forms of behavior" manifested by other cultures, and to

[3] Norbert Elias, *The Civilizing Process.* Vol. 1: *The History of Manners*, trans. Edmund Jephcott (1978; repr., New York: Pantheon, 1982), 3–50.

[4] Stuart Chase, *The Proper Study of Mankind: An Inquiry into the Science of Human Relations* (New York: Harper, 1948), 59; Kroeber and Kluckhohn, *Culture*, 3; John R. Everett, "American Culture in the World To-Day: Reflections on a UNESCO Meeting," *American Quarterly* 6 (1954): 247.

[5] Kenelm Burridge, "The Concept of Culture Revisited: A Personal Retrospective," *Social Analysis* 41 (1997): 58; Barbara Duden, "Rereading Boas: A Woman Historian's Response to Carl N. Degler," in Carl N. Degler, *Culture versus Biology in the Thought of Franz Boas and Alfred L. Kroeber* (New York: Berg, 1989), 25.

[6] Eric R. Wolf, *Anthropology* (1964; repr., New York: Norton, 1974), 19; Anthony Molho and Gordon S. Wood, introduction to *Imagined Histories: American Historians Interpret the Past*, ed. Anthony Molho and Gordon S. Wood (Princeton, N.J.: Princeton University Press, 1998), 5; Alfred Kazin, *On Native Grounds: An Interpretation of Modern American Prose Literature* (1942; repr., New York: Harcourt, 1982), 486.

develop tolerance for other people's values.[7] In 1946, Benedict told Clyde Kluckhohn that it was "a really crucial matter whether" Americans could become culture-conscious about other peoples. For it would be "fatal to all peace" if Americans continued to "see every evidence of other nations' different cultural assumptions as examples of moral perfidy," without understanding that "a piece of unfamiliar behavior" was "really an expression of their total cultural experience."[8] Was it possible, asked Margaret Mead in 1951, "to make self-consciousness bearable to Americans?"[9] For Mead, becoming culture-conscious meant getting into the habit of invoking the phrase "in our culture" to qualify one's generalizations about human nature. By 1959, Mead could report that "the words 'in our culture' slipped from the lips of educated men and women almost as effortlessly as do the phrases that refer to period and to place."[10]

My book examines the intersection between anthropologists' campaign to make Americans culture-conscious and American cultural nationalism by tracing the dissemination – first to social scientists in cognate disciplines, then to other intellectuals, and finally to educated Americans – of the culture concept and the corollary concepts of social class, national character, value, and civilization. By concept, I mean concept in the strong philosophical sense established in the seventeenth century: concept as "an idea of a class of objects, a general notion." A concept serves, in Robert Redfield's words, as a "form of thought" that guides "the investigator's choice and arrangement of facts." But a concept can also be what Raymond Williams called a keyword. Keywords, Williams explains, register the larger "formations of meaning" that people devise to come to terms with "central experiences" in their lives. Indeed, they matter enough, as Daniel Rodgers reminds us, that persons "fight for control *over* them."[11]

I trace the development of these concepts within intellectual and social networks that linked anthropologists to social scientists in neighboring disciplines and to nonspecialist intellectuals. To reconstruct these networks, I have made extensive use of unpublished correspondence in which anthropologists and their correspondents tried out ideas, enlisted financial patrons, and, in the process, formed what David Hollinger has called a "discourse community." The correspondence also allows me to trace anthropological concepts

[7] Ruth Benedict, "The Science of Custom: The Bearing of Culture on Contemporary Thought," *Century Magazine*, April 1929, 642, 648, 649.
[8] Ruth Benedict to Clyde Kluckhohn, 16 May 1946, HUG 4490.3, Clyde Kay Maben Kluckhohn Papers, courtesy of the Harvard University Archives (hereafter Kluckhohn Papers).
[9] Margaret Mead, quoted in Eric Larrabee, *The Self-Conscious Society: The State of American Culture at Mid-Century* (Garden City, N.Y.: Doubleday, 1960), 19.
[10] Margaret Mead, "A New Preface," in Ruth Benedict, *Patterns of Culture* (1934; repr., Boston: Houghton Mifflin, 1959), vii.
[11] Q. v. "Concept," *The New Fowler's Modern English Usage*, 3rd ed., ed. R. W. Burchfield (Oxford: Clarendon Press, 1996), 169; Robert Redfield, *The Little Community* (1955; repr., Chicago: University of Chicago Press, 1960), 151; Raymond Williams, *Keywords: A Vocabulary of Culture and Science* (New York: Oxford University Press, 1976), 13; Daniel T. Rodgers, "Keywords: A Reply," *Journal of the History of Ideas* 49 (1988): 671.

as they developed over time in a way that reliance on published work alone does not.[12]

That there was an intimate association between the culture concept and American cultural nationalism is hardly surprising. For the culture concept, as Eric Wolf reminds us, emerged in late eighteenth- and early nineteenth-century Europe at a moment when a people's claim to possess a distinctive culture, or way of life, strengthened that people's claim to recognition to constituting a nation-state. What was different about the United States was that Americans achieved political independence long before they achieved cultural independence from Europe. As we shall see, the notion of separate and integral cultures that anthropologists popularized lent itself to the "rediscovery" of America in the years after the First World War. It also informed the American studies programs that proliferated after 1945 and were dedicated to "the study of American culture, past and present, as a whole."[13]

Five distinctive features of American anthropology also help to explain why anthropological concepts enjoyed so much currency in twentieth-century American thought. First and foremost, only American anthropologists made culture their "master term," or core concept. In contrast, British anthropologists were preoccupied with social structure, German anthropologists studied race, and French anthropologists evinced little interest in culture until after the Second World War.[14]

Second, the distinctive four-field orientation of American anthropology that Boas institutionalized at Columbia – instruction in cultural (or cultural/social) anthropology, physical (or biological) anthropology, archaeology, and linguistics – endowed the discipline with unusual breadth. Although few American anthropologists commanded all four fields, they admired "generalists" who did. This breadth helps to explain why Clyde Kluckhohn construed anthropology as an "intellectual poaching license."[15]

[12] David A. Hollinger, "Historians and the Discourse of Intellectuals," in *New Directions in American Intellectual History*, ed. John Higham and Paul K. Conkin (Baltimore: Johns Hopkins University Press, 1979), 42–63.
[13] Henry Nash Smith, "Can 'American Studies' Develop a Method?" *American Quarterly* 9 (1957): 197–208; reprinted in *Locating American Studies: The Evolution of a Discipline*, ed. Lucy Maddox (Baltimore: Johns Hopkins University Press, 1999), 1–12, on 1.
[14] Robert Redfield, "Social Science among the Humanities," in *Human Nature and the Study of Society: The Papers of Robert Redfield*, vol. 1, ed. Margaret Park Redfield (Chicago: University of Chicago Press, 1962), 55; Marshall Sahlins, "'Sentimental Pessimism' and Ethnographic Experience; or, Why Culture Is Not a Disappearing 'Object,'" in *Biographies of Scientific Objects*, ed. Lorraine Daston (Chicago: University of Chicago Press, 2000), 166–167; Matti Bunzl and H. Glenn Penny, "Introduction: Rethinking German Anthropology, Colonialism, and Race," in *Worldly Provincialism: German Anthropology in the Age of Empire*, ed. H. Glenn Penny and Matti Bunzl (Ann Arbor: University of Michigan Press, 2003), 1–30.
[15] George W. Stocking, Jr., "The Basic Assumptions of Boasian Anthropology," in *Delimiting Anthropology: Occasional Inquiries and Reflections* (Madison: University of Wisconsin Press, 2001), 40–41; Sydel Silverman, "The United States," in Fredrik Barth et al., *One Discipline, Four Ways: British, German, French, and American Anthropology* (Chicago: University of Chicago Press, 2005), 331; Clifford Geertz, "Blurred Genres: The Refiguration of Social Thought," in *Local Knowledge: Further Essays in Interpretive Anthropology* (New York: Basic Books, 1983), 21.

Because of its breadth, anthropology did not fit neatly into the threefold division of the natural sciences, social sciences, and humanities that became institutionalized in the American academy after 1945. Anthropologists also resisted assignment to one or the other of the "Two Cultures" of literary intellectuals and scientists that the English scientist-turned-novelist C. P. Snow discerned in 1959.[16] Although commonly classified as a social science, and therefore represented in the Social Science Research Council, anthropology also sent representatives to the National Research Council and the American Council of Learned Societies.[17] Alfred Kroeber may have been unusual in refusing to identify himself as a social scientist, but he spoke for many anthropologists when he defined himself as a scientific humanist and extolled anthropology's mixed parentage of "natural science" and "aesthetically tinged humanities."[18] Robert Redfield, who, as we shall see, worked on the margins of anthropology and sociology, famously depicted anthropology as "pulled toward" the natural sciences in its methodology, but "held back" by the subject matter – culture – that it shared with the humanities.[19] As what Eric Wolf described as "the most scientific of the humanities, the most humanist of the sciences," anthropology was nothing if not interdisciplinary, "a discipline between disciplines."[20]

Third, anthropology came into its own after 1945 as one of the so-called behavioral sciences institutionalized in the Harvard Department of Social Relations, the Harvard Russian Research Center, the Behavioral Sciences Division of the Ford Foundation, and the Center for Advanced Study in the Behavioral Sciences.[21] Devoted, as Clyde Kluckhohn put it, to "finding out what makes people tick," the behavioral sciences went "scientific in a big way" by demonstrating that "the data of culture and social life" were "as susceptible to exact scientific treatment as one of the facts of the physical and social sciences."[22] In so doing, they helped to bring about what Kluckhohn's Harvard colleague, the sociologist Talcott Parsons, called a "shift away from economics" and from

---

[16] John Higham, "The Schism in American Scholarship," in *Writing American History: Essays on Modern Scholarship* (Bloomington: Indiana University Press, 1970), 14–23; C. P. Snow, *The Two Cultures* (1959; repr., Cambridge: Cambridge University Press, 1998). See also Wolf Lepenies, *Between Literature and Science: The Rise of Sociology*, trans. R. J. Hollingdale (Cambridge: Cambridge University Press, 1988).

[17] Redfield, "Social Science among the Humanities," 44.

[18] A. L. Kroeber, "The Personality of Anthropology," in *An Anthropologist Looks at History* (Berkeley: University of California Press, 1963), 177; A. L. Kroeber, "Concluding Review," in *An Appraisal of Anthropology Today*, ed. Sol Tax, Loren C. Eiseley, Irving Rouse, and Carl F. Voegelin (1953; repr., Chicago: University of Chicago Press, 1976), 361.

[19] Robert Redfield, "Relation of Anthropology to the Social Sciences and the Humanities," in *Human Nature and the Study of Society*, 109–110.

[20] Wolf, *Anthropology*, 88, x.

[21] John Gillin, ed., *For A Science of Social Man: Convergences in Anthropology, Psychology and Sociology* (New York: Macmillan, 1954); Bernard Berelson, "Behavioral Sciences," *International Encyclopedia of the Social Sciences*, ed. David L. Sills (New York: Macmillan, 1968), 2:41–44; Peter S. Senn, "What Is 'Behavioral Science'? – Notes toward a History," *Journal of the History of the Behavioral Sciences* 2 (1966): 107–122.

[22] Clyde Kluckhohn, "Anthropology," *Saturday Review of Literature*, 4 April 1953, 25, 49–50.

economists' rational, self-interested conception of human behavior toward recognition of the nonrational, even irrational, aspects.[23] The behavioral sciences thus continued the transatlantic revolt against positivism that had begun in the 1890s when European theorists first began to pay attention to "the nonlogical, the uncivilized, [and] the inexplicable" in an attempt to "exorcise" the irrational.[24]

Yet a fourth distinctive feature of American anthropology was that so many of its leading figures were, in one sense or another, outsiders. Not only Franz Boas but also his students Robert Lowie, Alexander Goldenweiser, and Edward Sapir were foreign-born. Although American-born, Alfred Kroeber spoke German as his first language. Even the old-stock Americans Clyde Kluckhohn and Robert Redfield never felt completely at home in America.[25] As women, Ruth Benedict and Margaret Mead had to overcome formidable obstacles in forging their careers. There was also the matter of religion, or the lack thereof; anthropologists were an unusually secular lot, many either secular Jews or lapsed Protestants. Thus the ethnicity, temperament, gender, and religion of leading anthropologists between the world wars gave anthropology an unusual profile in the American academy at a time when American-born Protestant males dominated most of the humanities and the social sciences.[26]

This unusual profile also helps to explain why anthropologists were charter members of the American liberal intelligentsia that coalesced between the First World War and the 1950s. David Hollinger has traced the roots of this intelligentsia to the cosmopolitanism – or anti-provincialism – of lapsed Protestants, many of whom were Midwesterners rebelling against "the village virus" of small-town America, and secular Jews, many of them Eastern Europeans, breaking out of the *shtetl*.[27] From the First World War into the 1950s, its members waged a culture war to open up the academy, and American culture in general, to non-Christians. As their rallying cry, they invoked "the scientific ethos," which held that scientists belonged to a community that transcended ethnic, religious, and even national identities. Their imagined community

[23] Howard Brick, "Talcott Parsons's 'Shift Away from Economics,' 1937–1946," *Journal of American History* 87 (2000): 490–514.
[24] H. Stuart Hughes, *Consciousness and Society: The Reorientation of European Social Thought, 1890–1930*, rev. ed. (New York: Vintage, 1977), 35–36.
[25] Clyde Kluckhohn, *Mirror for Man: The Relation of Anthropology to Modern Life* (1949; repr., Tucson: University of Arizona Press, 1985), 4.
[26] David A. Hollinger, "Cultural Relativism," in *Cosmopolitanism and Solidarity: Studies in Ethnoracial, Religious, and Professional Affiliation in the United States* (Madison: University of Wisconsin Press, 2006), 174.
[27] David A. Hollinger, "Ethnic Diversity, Cosmopolitanism, and the Emergence of the American Liberal Intelligentsia," in his *In the American Province: Studies in the History and Historiography of Ideas* (Bloomington: Indiana University Press, 1985), 56–57. In a 1970 survey of some sixty thousand American academics, anthropologists were the most secular of the disciplinary practitioners surveyed. George W. Stocking, Jr., "Animism in Theory and Practice: E. B. Tylor's Unpublished Notes on 'Spiritualism,'" in *Delimiting Anthropology*, 117.

subjected research findings to exacting scrutiny, treated ideas as communal property, and refused to bend to sacred or supernatural authority.[28]

As we shall see, anthropologists made their biggest contribution to the culture war waged by the liberal intelligentsia by developing "cultural relativism" as both a methodological axiom and a polemical weapon. As a methodological axiom, cultural relativism enjoined researchers to strive to understand other cultures on their own terms by breaking free, as Franz Boas put it, of the "shackles," or conventions, of their own culture.[29] As a polemical weapon, cultural relativism called into question, as Clifford Geertz once put it, "the familiar, the received, and the near at hand."[30]

Anthropologists' iconoclasm also derived from fieldwork, which early in the twentieth century became their discipline's *rite de passage*. Fieldwork, which Clifford Geertz defined as "localized, long-term, close-in, vernacular field research," could produce a "dislocatory effect" that, as the editors of the monumental *Encyclopedia of the Social Sciences* put it in 1930, enabled the field-worker to view any culture, his or her own included, not "as endowed with an unyielding and inherent place in the scheme of things," but rather as "mutable" and a "variant."[31]

Fifth and finally, anthropology was notable for the sizable number of prominent public intellectuals that it produced. Why so many American anthropologists became public intellectuals is not entirely clear. One reason may have been the example of Franz Boas, who from early in the twentieth century until his death campaigned against nativism, hostility to immigrants, persecution of German-Americans, and racialist thought.[32] A second reason could be that a number of anthropologists had literary aspirations: Edward Sapir, Ruth Benedict, and Robert Redfield were published poets; Clyde Kluckhohn wrote travelogues before he became an anthropologist. Sapir, Benedict, Redfield, Kluckhohn, Robert Lowie, and Margaret Mead all contributed book reviews and articles to mass-circulation magazines, the *New York Times*, and the *New York Herald Tribune*. Then, too, there was the commercial success that

---

[28] David A. Hollinger, "The Defense of Democracy and Robert K. Merton's Formulation of the Scientific Ethos," in *Science, Jews, and Secular Culture: Studies in Mid-Twentieth-Century American Intellectual History* (Princeton, N.J.: Princeton University Press, 1996), 80–96; David A. Hollinger, "Science as a Weapon in *Kulturkämpfe* in the United States during and after World War II," ibid., 155–174.

[29] Franz Boas, "The Aims of Ethnology," in *Race, Language and Culture* (1940; repr., New York: Free Press, 1966), 636.

[30] Hollinger, "Cultural Relativism," 169–170; Clifford Geertz, "The World in Pieces: Culture and Politics at the End of the Century," in *Available Light: Anthropological Reflections on Philosophical Topics* (Princeton, N.J.: Princeton University Press, 2000), 251.

[31] Clifford Geertz, "Deep Hanging Out," *New York Review of Books*, 22 October 1998, 69; "War and Reorientation," *Encyclopedia of the Social Sciences*, ed. Edwin R. A. Seligman (New York: Macmillan, 1930), 1:203.

[32] George W. Stocking, Jr., "Anthropology as *Kulturkampf*: Science and Politics in the Career of Franz Boas," in *The Ethnographer's Magic and Other Essays in the History of Anthropology* (Madison: University of Wisconsin Press, 1992), 92–113.

Margaret Mead's trilogy of works on the South Seas (*Coming of Age in Samoa, Growing Up in New Guinea,* and *Sex and Temperament in Three Primitive Societies*) and Ruth Benedict's *Patterns of Culture* enjoyed. Last but certainly not least, in passing judgment on their own civilization, anthropologists convinced educated Americans that if they could not prescribe cures for American ailments, they could help to diagnose those ailments.[33]

As public intellectuals, anthropologists "repatriated" anthropology by applying anthropological techniques fashioned for the study of "primitive" cultures to many aspects of American life. The material that they collected in their fieldwork warranted both cultural critique and social engineering.[34] Yet anthropologists were slow to study American culture itself. As late as 1950, Clyde Kluckhohn complained that social scientists' "discovery of America" was far from complete, that educated Americans knew more about the "manners and morals" of South Pacific islanders than about their own. Within a decade, however, anthropologists rivaled social novelists and foreign visitors as authoritative commentators on American life.[35] When, in his 1957 tome, *America as a Civilization,* the journalist-turned-American-studies-scholar Max Lerner attempted "to grasp – however awkwardly – the pattern and inner meaning of contemporary American civilization and its relation to the world of today," his publisher, Simon and Schuster, placed his book squarely in "the great tradition of [Alexis] De Tocqueville and [James] Bryce." Lerner himself said that Tocqueville, Bryce, and other foreign observers could "now be read as amateur anthropologists of American behavior." Although Lerner did not claim to possess an anthropologist's detachment, he nonetheless drew on the substantial authority that anthropologists had garnered by the late 1950s.[36]

That authority rested on the widespread acceptance by non-anthropologists of three claims to objectivity that anthropologists had advanced since the 1920s. The first claim rooted objectivity in fieldwork by trained investigators who, in the words of the consummate fieldworker Bronislaw Malinowski, lived as participant-observers among the people they were studying for the purpose of grasping the native "point of view."[37] The second claim rooted objectivity in

[33] Raymond Firth, "The Study of Values by Social Anthropologists," *Man* 53 (1953): 149.

[34] George E. Marcus and Michael M. J. Fischer, *Anthropology as Cultural Critique: An Experimental Moment in the Human Sciences* (Chicago: University of Chicago Press, 1986), 111.

[35] Clyde Kluckhohn, "Mid-century Manners and Morals" (1950), in *Culture and Behavior: Collected Essays of Clyde Kluckhohn,* ed. Richard Kluckhohn (New York: Free Press, 1962), 323–335, on 323. Here Kluckhohn reiterated a point made by John Sirjamaki in "A Footnote to the Anthropological Approach to the Study of American Culture," *Social Forces* 25 (1947): 253–263.

[36] Max Lerner, *America as a Civilization* (New York: Simon and Schuster, 1957), xi, 639, 951–952; M. Lincoln Schuster to Leslie A. White, 17 July 1957, box 5, Leslie A. White Papers, Bentley Historical Library, University of Michigan (hereafter White Papers).

[37] Bronislaw Malinowski, *Argonauts of the Western Pacific* (1922; repr., Prospect Heights, Ill.: Waveland Press, 1984), 6, 25.

the fact that anthropologists necessarily approached other cultures as outsiders.[38] The third and final claim rooted objectivity in anthropologists' detachment from their own culture. In 1928, Alfred Kroeber ascribed "the anthropological attitude" to Europeans and Americans becoming culturally introspective in the aftermath of the First World War and thereby acquiring the ability to dissect their own cultures as they would "foreign" or "dead" cultures. Along with this detachment, Kroeber claimed, came "the ability to conceive of culture as such."[39]

By meticulously describing the mundane, ordinary, and everyday aspects of American life, anthropologists filled in the so-called Jamesian void, the invidious contrast that intellectuals since Henry James had drawn between the "barrenness" of the American scene and the much denser texture of European life.[40] The popular success of Robert S. and Helen Merrell Lynd's 1929 community study *Middletown* prompted the literary critic Malcolm Cowley to wonder whether such ethnographies of the American scene would eventually usurp "the place held by documentary novels," for the Lynds had access to "all sorts of facts . . . that a novelist could not supply out of his notebooks or his imagination."[41] In the early 1950s, the literary critic Lionel Trilling praised the "sense of social actuality" evoked by David Riesman's *Lonely Crowd* (which is discussed in Chapter 3). Were ethnographic works such as *The Lonely Crowd*, Trilling asked, taking over "the investigation and criticism of morals and manners" that had been, ever since Matthew Arnold, "one of literature's most characteristic functions"?[42]

In what follows, I look at how the anthropological attitude was disseminated to American audiences, and how its dissemination opened up new ways of charting and possessing American culture. Chapter 1 rehearses the career of the cultural concept from its inception in the work of Franz Boas in the late nineteenth century through the early 1950s, by which time anthropologists had come very close to capturing for the social sciences the term "culture." By then, social scientists in other disciplines, intellectuals, and even educated Americans not only construed culture in a broad, pluralistic, relativistic, holistic manner, but also identified this conception as a peculiarly American one.

Chapter 2 traces the development of a distinctive American understanding of social class in which classes came to be seen as subcultures distinguished by their cultural attributes. Key figures in calling into question the axiom of

---

[38] Clark Wissler, foreword to *Middletown: A Study in Modern American Culture*, by Robert S. Lynd and Helen Merrell Lynd (1929; repr., New York: Harcourt, 1957), vi.

[39] A. L. Kroeber, "The Anthropological Attitude," *American Mercury*, April 1928, 491.

[40] Clifford Geertz, "The State of the Art," in *Available Light*, 119; Henry James, *Hawthorne* (London: Macmillan, 1879), 42–44; Philip Rahv, quoted in *America and the Intellectuals* (New York: Partisan Review, 1953), 89.

[41] Malcolm Cowley, "Muddletown," review of *Greenwich Village, 1920–1930*, by Caroline F. Ware, *New Republic*, 15 May 1935, 23.

[42] Lionel Trilling, "Two Notes on David Riesman," in *A Gathering of Fugitives* (London: Secker and Warburg, 1957), 85, 86, 93–94.

America classlessness were Robert and Helen Lynd, the self-trained field-workers who subjected Muncie, Indiana, to anthropological scrutiny, and the entrepreneurial anthropologist W. Lloyd Warner, who brought to bear many of the same techniques he had used earlier in fieldwork among Australian aborigines in long-term studies of Newburyport, Massachusetts, and Morris, Illinois. On the strength of these "ethnographies of the American scene" anthropologists' cultural authority came to rival that of social novelists and foreign visitors. For the detail marshaled in these ethnographies thickened the texture that many American intellectuals had long felt was missing from American life.

Chapter 3 focuses on anthropologists' collaboration in the 1930s and 1940s with psychiatrists and other students of the relationship between culture and personality. In so doing, they became parties to the long-standing debate about the making of Americans. What they contributed to this debate were an emphasis on socialization and a broad definition of American nationality. At the heart of their inquiries into the relationship between culture and personality was curiosity about what made a Frenchman a Frenchman, a Russian a Russian, and an American an American. National character studies thus represented a significant expansion of anthropologists' horizons beyond "primitive isolates" to the developed and developing world. Hereafter, anthropologists would figure prominently as transatlantic intellectuals. Although the controversy aroused by some postwar studies of national character tarnished culture-and-personality research in the eyes of many social scientists, interest in delineating the American character spilled over into American history and American studies in the 1950s and early 1960s.

Chapter 4 discusses anthropologists' efforts after the Second World War to study values scientifically, despite the resurgent positivism of American social science. Inspired by Edward Sapir and Ruth Benedict, Clyde Kluckhohn investigated the "implicit culture," the unconscious canons of choice that distinguished Americans from other peoples. As a prophet of the "New Anthropology," Kluckhohn urged that as much attention be paid to the similarities of cultures as to the differences. Modeling anthropology on linguistics, he searched for the cultural equivalent of the phoneme, the basic unit of language. As an active participant in the postwar American quest for national purpose, Kluckhohn envisioned a new American ideology, a scientifically informed "faith" that would "give meaning and purpose to living" as it supplanted "supernatural" religion.

Chapter 5 shows how the convergence between Alfred Kroeber's "natural history of civilizations" and Robert Redfield's "social anthropology of civilizations" paved the way for the development of both global anthropology and world history. As anthropologists took up the study of "peasants," of peoples engaging modernity, and of civilizations, both living and historic, they narrowed the long-standing gap between "culture" and "civilization." In so doing, they helped to convince American intellectuals, if not educated Americans, that the United States did indeed possess a creative high culture commensurate with a technologically advanced civilization. Anthropologists' turn to civilization culminated their long campaign to make Americans culture-conscious, not only about their own manners and morals, but also about those of other peoples.

The Epilogue examines how culture in its anthropological sense informed the drive for a national humanities foundation and how anthropologists staked their claim to anthropology being a discipline between disciplines. After 1965, however, the notion of separate and integral cultures, which underwrote belief in the existence of a single American culture, fell apart in a post-colonial, globalizing world. As emphasis on what Americans and other peoples had in common gave way to celebration of difference, anthropologists lost control over their master term, culture, and no longer owned ethnography.

I

Culture in the American Grain

In 1952, two leading American anthropologists, Alfred Kroeber and Clyde Kluckhohn, took stock of the idea of culture in its "technical anthropological sense." By then, the so-called culture concept, long the master concept of American anthropology, had become a key notion in American thought, comparable in both "explanatory importance" and "generality of application" to "categories such as gravity in physics, disease in medicine, [and] evolution in biology." Not only had the culture concept become pervasive in the social sciences, it was also quickly becoming part of the vocabulary of educated Americans. Yet the proliferation of formal definitions of culture had so muddled the concept's meaning that Kroeber and Kluckhohn felt the need for conceptual clarification. To this end, they canvassed some 164 definitions, factored out the common elements, and arrived at what they hoped would prove to be a consensual definition of culture: "culture," they wrote, "consists of patterns, explicit and implicit, of and for behavior acquired and transmitted by symbols, constituting the distinctive achievement of human groups, including their embodiments in artifacts." Kroeber and Kluckhohn located the "essential core" of culture in "traditional (i.e., historically derived and selected) ideas and especially their attached values."[1]

To Kroeber and Kluckhohn, the wide currency that the culture concept had gained by the early 1950s seemed all the more remarkable considering how recently the concept had been formulated. Although they traced the "modern meaning" of the word to the German scholar and collector Gustav Klemm in the 1840s, this German-inflected meaning did not enter English usage until 1871, when the English anthropologist E. B. Tylor defined "culture or civilization" as "that complex whole which includes knowledge, belief, art, law, morals, custom, and any other capabilities and habits acquired by man as a member of society." Tylor's conception of culture as a complex whole, however,

[1] A. L. Kroeber and Clyde Kluckhohn, *Culture: A Critical Review of Concepts and Definitions* (Cambridge, Mass.: Harvard University Peabody Museum of American Archaeology and Ethnology, 1952), 3–5, 181.

was slow to enter American usage. Indeed, Kroeber and Kluckhohn did not find another formal definition of culture until 1903, and they counted only five more formal definitions before 1920. Since then, however, formal definitions of culture had proliferated, the culture concept had entered standard English-language dictionaries, and references to such things as "Eskimo culture" had appeared in comic books.[2]

By the early 1950s, the culture concept had gained wide enough currency in American usage to coexist, albeit somewhat uneasily, with a venerable humanistic conception that identified culture with refinement and sophistication. This humanistic conception of culture had found classic expression in 1869 when the English poet and literary critic Matthew Arnold, in a critique of industrialism entitled *Culture and Anarchy*, defined culture as "the best that has been thought and known in the world." Tylor's definition of culture was, as Kroeber and Kluckhohn pointed out, much broader in scope and more catholic than Arnold's "ethnocentric" and "absolutistic" definition. It brought into the realm of culture the "outward set[s] of circumstances" – behavior and artifacts of material culture – that Arnold excluded. Tylor's definition, moreover, rendered all men and women "cultured" by placing "primitive" man on the same continuum as "civilized" man. Indeed, culture was, for Tylor, a "state or condition" common to "all human societies" rather than "the process of cultivation or the degree to which it has been carried." For Arnold, becoming cultured required years of strenuous self-cultivation on the individual's part; Tylor detached culture from "cultivation" and made it a birthright. In addition, by making culture contingent on membership in society, Tylor shifted the locus of culture from the individual to the group. Finally, by making "culture" anthropology's "subject matter," Tylor vested its custody in the hands not of men of letters but of "reformers," scientists he charged with exposing "survivals" – "the remains of crude old culture which have passed into harmful superstition" – and marking these "out for destruction." Thus, in Kroeber and Kluckhohn's considered opinion, Tylor "deliberately established a science" by "extricat[ing]" from *belles lettres* a conception of culture that was "non-instinctive, non-genetic, and acquired by social process."[3]

These conspicuous differences notwithstanding, Kroeber and Kluckhohn detected signs that, by the early 1950s, the anthropological and humanistic conceptions of culture were converging. As an example of this convergence, they cited the Anglo-American poet and literary critic T. S. Eliot's appropriation of the culture concept in his 1948 *Notes towards the Definition of Culture*.[4]

In their history of the culture concept, Kroeber and Kluckhohn noted how usage of the term varied by nationality. Specifically, culture in its technical anthropological sense enjoyed much greater currency in German and American usage than it did in either French or English usage. In German usage the term

[2] Kroeber and Kluckhohn, *Culture*, 9–10, 43.
[3] Kroeber and Kluckhohn, *Culture*, 29, 32, 146–147.
[4] Kroeber and Kluckhohn, *Culture*, 32–33.

Kultur denoted an interior, spiritual, and particularistic entity antithetical to *Civilisation*, which in French usage denoted civility and sophistication and knew no national boundaries. Although both culture and civilization were commonly employed in English usage, English anthropologists, perhaps put off by the German provenance of the culture concept, made "social structure," and not "culture," their master term. In any event, American anthropologists "scrupled much less" than English anthropologists "to borrow from the Germans."[5]

This American receptivity to this German term becomes more understandable when the long American struggle to achieve cultural independence from Europe is considered. Concerned about the prospects for culture in the first new nation, American men of letters rallied to Matthew Arnold's cult of the best. But as humanistic culture became increasingly remote from American conditions, intellectuals reappraised their Arnoldian inheritance and gravitated to a more pluralistic, relativistic, historicist, and holistic conception of culture emanating from the social sciences. The wide currency the anthropological conception of culture enjoyed by the early 1950s not only reflected the success with which anthropologists and social scientists in cognate fields had made Americans "culture-conscious," but also reflected the concept's varied appeal as a foil of the concept of race, a tool in social scientists' struggle for disciplinary autonomy, a weapon in American intellectuals' culture war against provincialism, and a warrant for the rediscovery of American culture.

CULTURE AND CIVILIZATION IN THE OLD WORLD

Both "culture" and "civilization" have long been keywords in French, German, and English usage. As Norbert Elias observed, the term civilization expressed the "self-consciousness of the West" by "summ[ing] up everything in which Western society of the last two or three centuries believes itself superior to earlier societies or 'more primitive' contemporary ones." Elias traced the origin of the term to seventeenth-century France, where civilization distinguished the refinement and sophistication of the courtiers around the French monarch from their "barbarian" peers in the provinces. During the Enlightenment, French *philosophes* viewed all humanity as following a set path toward civilization. Following its appropriation by the "rising [French] middle class," the word civilization came to mean "liberation" from religious superstition and political reaction. By the middle of the nineteenth century, civilization, synonymous with progressive human achievement, distilled the "self-assurance" of the French, for whom national boundaries and national identity were not problematic.[6]

[5] Kroeber and Kluckhohn, *Culture*, 35-36; George Peter Murdock, "British Social Anthropology," *American Anthropologist* 53 (1951): 471; Clyde Kluckhohn, "Culture," in *A Dictionary of the Social Sciences*, ed. Julius Gould and William L. Kolb (New York: Free Press, 1964), 165-168.
[6] Norbert Elias, *The Civilizing Process*. Vol. I: *The History of Manners*, trans. Edmund Jephcott (New York: Pantheon Books, 1982), esp. 5, 35-50; Adam Kuper, *Culture: The Anthropologists' Account* (Cambridge, Mass.: Harvard University Press, 1999), 23-29.

"Civilization" never enjoyed the same currency in German usage that it did in French. In the late eighteenth century, Johann Gottfried von Herder and other spokesmen for the German Counter-Enlightenment reacted against the *philosophes'* universal histories by proclaiming the existence of a plurality of cultures, all of them of equal worth and incommensurable. For Herder, more-over, the words "people," "culture," and "nation" were largely synonymous. Over the course of the nineteenth century, an interior, spiritual, and particularly German conception of *Kultur* developed in opposition to what the Germans saw as an exterior, mechanical, and French civilization. As the term came to be associated with *Bildung* (self-education or mental cultivation), *Kultur* distin-guished the intellectual, scientific, and artistic accomplishments of the educated German middle classes.[7] After the abortive revolutions of 1848, "cultural sci-ences" such as geography, ethnology (the study of cultural origins), and folklore arose in response to the perceived limitations of the liberal emphasis on the rational, self-interested individual. The German affinity for a particularistic and delimiting concept of culture thus reflected the historical experience of a people who, as Elias put it, had "to constantly seek out and constitute [their] national boundaries anew, in a political as well as a cultural sense."[8]

English usage followed yet a third course. Raymond Williams traced the word "civilization" in English usage to the late eighteenth century, when Enlightenment thought spread from France to Scotland and England. Over time, civilization, which originally referred to a process and was more or less synonymous with "culture," came to describe "an achieved condition of refine-ment and order." The meaning of "culture," which originally designated culti-vation, or the "tending of natural growth" (as in agriculture), was extended, by analogy, to human development, or "process of human training." In the nine-teenth century, what had been "a culture *of* something" changed "to *culture* as such, a thing in itself," meaning, first, "a general state or habit of the mind"; second, "the general state of intellectual development in a society as a whole"; and third, "the general body of the arts." As this happened, culture acquired class connotations through its association with the derivative terms "cultiva-tion" and "cultivated." Culture became a keyword in English thought when romantic writers invoked it to criticize the mechanical character and

---

[7] Elias, *The History of Manners*, 3–34; Alan Barnard and Jonathan Spencer, "Culture," *Ency-clopedia of Social and Cultural Anthropology*, ed. Alan Barnard and Jonathan Spencer (London: Routledge, 1996), 137; Gerald Broce, "Discontent and Cultural Relativism: Herder and Boasian Anthropology," *Annals of Scholarship* 2 (1981): 1–13; Matti Bunzl, "Franz Boas and the Humboldtian Tradition: From *Volksgeist* and *Nationalcharakter* to an Anthropological Concept of Culture," in *"Volksgeist" as Method and Ethic: Essays on Boasian Ethnography and the German Anthropological Tradition*, ed. George W. Stocking, Jr. (Madison: University of Wisconsin Press, 1996), 17–78; Kuper, *Culture*, 29–36.

[8] Woodruff D. Smith, *Politics and the Sciences of Culture in Germany, 1840–1920* (New York: Oxford University Press, 1991), 3–4, 10, 35; J. W. Burrow, *The Crisis of Reason: European Thought, 1848–1914* (New Haven, Conn.: Yale University Press, 2000), 88, 90; Elias, *The History of Manners*, 5–6.

"inhumanity" of what Thomas Carlyle dubbed "industrialism." Thus, in 1830, Samuel Taylor Coleridge proclaimed "the permanent distinction, and occasional contrast, between cultivation and civilization."[9]

It was against the backdrop of aesthetic recoil from industrialism that Matthew Arnold defined culture as the "the study and pursuit of perfection," which involved getting to know the best that has been thought and known." By perfection, Arnold did not have in mind an "outward set of circumstances," but rather an "inward condition of mind and spirit." When conceived of as an inward condition, culture promised to redeem the English from the anarchy that threatened to ensue from everyone's "doing as one likes." Because Arnold held that perfection was not possible as long as the individual remained "isolated," the pursuit of culture promised to bridge the rifts that had arisen in England as the "Barbarians" (aristocrats) yielded power to the "Philistines" (middle-class Englishmen reaping the material rewards of industrialism), who were themselves fending off the claims of the "Populace" (workingmen agitating for an extension of the suffrage). To Arnold, his fellow Englishmen urgently needed culture because their civilization was mechanical and external and because they themselves were preoccupied with wealth, progress, and other "stock notions." Identifying literature with the "criticism of life," he exhorted English men of letters to make culture prevail from one end of England to the other by setting aside all "prepossessions," practicing "disinterestedness," and endeavoring to "see the object as in itself it really is."[10]

CULTURE AND CIVILIZATION IN THE FIRST NEW NATION

It was far easier for Americans to achieve their political independence from England and to develop a flourishing and largely self-sufficient domestic economy than to free themselves from European cultural and intellectual dominion and from a pervasive sense of cultural inferiority. Acutely aware of their provincialism, members of the colonial gentry that coalesced after 1680 aped the latest European fashions and manners. Although the American Revolution raised hopes of "the rising glory of America" in which transplanted European arts and sciences would flourish on American soil, Americans remained vulnerable to the taunts of European critics such as the Reverend Sydney Smith, who asked in 1820: "In the four quarters of the globe, who reads an American book? or goes to an American play? or looks at an American picture or statue?" To

---

[9] Raymond Williams, *Culture and Society, 1780–1950* (1958; repr., New York: Harper, 1966), xiv (emphasis in original); Raymond Williams, "Culture," in *Keywords: A Vocabulary of Culture and Society* (New York: Oxford University Press, 1976), 76–82; Raymond Williams, *Marxism and Literature* (Oxford: Oxford University Press, 1977), esp. 11–20; Raymond Williams, "Culture and Civilization," in *The Encyclopedia of Philosophy*, ed. Paul Edwards (New York: Free Press, 1992), 1:273–276; Kuper, *Culture*, 36–46.

[10] Matthew Arnold, *Culture and Anarchy and Other Writings*, ed. Stefan Collini (Cambridge: Cambridge University Press, 1999), 61, 79; Williams, *Culture and Society*, 110–129; Stefan Collini, *Arnold* (Oxford: Oxford University Press, 1988).

Europeans such as Smith, American culture lacked historical depth, spirituality, and organic coherence.[11]

Instead of ushering in the republic of classical virtue envisioned by the Founding Fathers, the American Revolution accelerated forces of democratic leveling that soon stripped members of the gentry of much of their cultural authority. At the same time, democratization unleashed a mad scramble after wealth in which swelling numbers of self-made men claimed the perquisites of gentility on the strength of their material achievements. When the French aristocrat Alexis de Tocqueville visited the United States in 1831–32, he saw an "excited community," full of "restless" Americans, their ambition fired by the ideals of "equality" and "individualism," pursuing physical comforts in place of refinement and sophistication. Boasting few "great artists, distinguished poets, or celebrated writers," the young republic possessed no literature or poetry worthy of the name. Indeed, American authors "live[d] rather in England than in their own country." Perhaps not surprisingly, democracy in America seemed to Tocqueville to be inseparable from cultural leveling: for all their ambition, precious few Americans appeared to be pursuing "very lofty aims."[12]

It was precisely to counter these charges of materialism and mediocrity that antebellum public moralists championed "self-culture," or self-improvement, as the American equivalent of *Bildung*. Thus the Unitarian divine William Ellery Channing defined self-culture as "the care which every man owes to himself, to the unfolding and perfecting of his nature." In the first salvo of the long American struggle to achieve cultural independence, Ralph Waldo Emerson declared in 1837 that Americans had "listened too long to the courtly muses of Europe." Prophesying that "our long day of dependence, our long apprenticeship to the learning of other lands, draws to a close," Emerson urged American scholars to reject "the great, the remote, the romantic" in favor of "the common," "the familiar," and "the low."[13]

[11] Gordon S. Wood, introduction to *The Rising Glory of America, 1760–1820*, ed. Gordon S. Wood (New York: George Braziller, 1976), 1–22; Howard Mumford Jones, *O Strange New World. American Culture: The Formative Years* (New York: Viking, 1964), 394; Sydney Smith, quoted in Lawrence W. Levine, "Jazz and American Culture," in *The Unpredictable Past: Explorations in American Cultural History* (New York: Oxford University Press, 1993), 175.

[12] Gordon S. Wood, "Middle Class Order," in *The Radicalism of the American Revolution* (New York: Random House, 1991), 347–369; Joyce Appleby, *Inheriting the Revolution: The First Generation of Americans* (Cambridge, Mass.: Harvard University Press, 2000); Jon Butler, *Becoming America: The Revolution before 1776* (Cambridge, Mass.: Harvard University Press, 2000); Alexis de Tocqueville, *Democracy in America*, trans. Phillips Bradley, 2 vols. (New York: Viking, 1990), 2:137, 59, 68, 256.

[13] William Ellery Channing, quoted in Lewis Perry, *Intellectual Life in America: A History* (1984; repr., Chicago: University of Chicago Press, 1989), 265; Ralph Waldo Emerson, "The American Scholar," quoted in Alan Trachtenberg, *The Incorporation of America: Culture and Society in the Gilded Age* (New York: Hill and Wang, 1982), 156; Richard F. Teichgraeber III, "'Culture' in Industrializing America," *Intellectual History Newsletter* 21 (1999): 11–23.

In the years before the Civil War, Americans buttressed their claims to the possession of a distinctive national culture by fashioning a peculiarly American orthography and idiom, searching for a particularly American voice in literature and poetry, and celebrating their democratic polity and society.[14] They also established an impressive array of institutions – everything from libraries and mechanics' institutes to museums and lyceums – designed to multiply opportunities for self-culture while they promoted the arts.[15] Yet American artists remained sensitive to the cultural deficiencies of the new nation. In 1860, Nathaniel Hawthorne asked whether America, "a country where there is no shadow, no antiquity, no mystery, no picturesque and gloomy wrong, nor anything but a common-place prosperity," could nurture "romance and poetry," which needed "ruin [that is, historic depth] to make them grow"?[16]

CUSTODIANS OF CULTURE

If educated Americans were quick to defend their nascent culture from European animadversion before the Civil War, they nursed a stronger sense of cultural inferiority after 1865. As their wealth grew, their taste became more cosmopolitan, and more of them embarked on grand tours of Europe, they became increasingly sensitive to European criticism that Americans were a people without culture.[17] Although a few public moralists like Walt Whitman continued to champion the democratization of culture, many more invested their hopes for the "domestication" of culture in the hands of a cultivated minority. Thus, in 1867, Ralph Waldo Emerson urged the formation of a "knighthood of virtue" that, comprising a "few superior and attractive" men, would "calm and guide" an otherwise "barbarous age."[18]

Heeding the calls of Emerson and others, a small group of cosmopolitan gentry, mostly elderly Anglophiles, installed culture alongside moralism and

[14] Kenneth Cmiel, "'A Broad Fluid Language of Democracy': Discovering the American Idiom," in *Discovering America: Essays on the Search for an Identity,* ed. David Thelen and Frederick E. Hoxie (Urbana: University of Illinois Press, 1994), 79–102; Neil Harris, *The Artist in American Society: The Formative Years, 1790–1860* (New York: George Braziller, 1966).

[15] Neil Harris, "Four Stages of Cultural Growth: The American City," in *Cultural Excursions: Marketing Appetites and Cultural Tastes in Modern America* (Chicago: University of Chicago Press, 1990), 17–19.

[16] Nathaniel Hawthorne, preface to *The Marble Faun,* quoted in Howard Mumford Jones, *The Age of Energy: Varieties of American Experience, 1865–1915* (New York: Viking, 1971), 259.

[17] John Higham, "From Boundlessness to Consolidation: The Transformation of American Culture, 1848–1860," in *Hanging Together: Unity and Diversity in American Culture,* ed. Carl J. Guarneri (New Haven, Conn.: Yale University Press, 2001), 149–165; Jones, *The Age of Energy,* 259–300.

[18] Walt Whitman, *Democratic Vistas* (1871; repr., New York: Liberal Arts Press, 1949), 2, 35–36; Ralph Waldo Emerson, quoted in Trachtenberg, *The Incorporation of America,* 156; Lewis Perry, "The Ideology of Culture," in *Intellectual Life in America,* 263–276.

belief in progress in what Henry May called "the standard American credo." To "custodians of culture" such as Thomas Higginson, E. L. Godkin, and Charles Eliot Norton, culture was prescriptive: it was "an idea of how [people] ought to behave and did not." Its pursuit required training and self-discipline. Thus Higginson, the editor of the *Atlantic Monthly*, associated culture with "the training and finishing of the whole man"; Godkin, the editor of the *Nation*, with the "breaking-in of the powers to the service of the will"; and Norton, the Harvard art historian, with "whatever discipline or training fits a man to make the best use of his faculties."[19]

American custodians of culture welcomed the reinforcement they received from Matthew Arnold when he toured America in 1883–84. Arnold came away from his American travels convinced that Americans were in even greater need of culture than his fellow Englishmen. Much more interested in the pursuit of comforts and conveniences than in the pursuit of perfection, they lacked "distinction." Hence the American need for men of letters who would practice "cool and sane criticism."[20] As the American expatriate Henry James remarked, Arnold might not have "invented" culture, "but he made it more definite than it had been before." Arnold "vivified and lighted [culture] up" by voicing concern about the impact of democratic leveling, propounding an interior conception of culture as a counter to materialism, and designating the "great men of culture" as the "true apostles of equality" at a time when class, ethnic, and racial distinctions were growing ever more salient in American society.[21]

Yet in their campaign to make culture prevail from one end of America to the other, the custodians of culture faced a number of formidable obstacles. First and foremost was the problem of democratic leveling. There were simply too many new men and women claiming the perquisites of gentility. Indeed, E. L. Godkin worried that the diffusion of useful knowledge, by means of "common schools, magazines, [and] newspapers," was producing a "pseudo-culture" in which "slenderly equipped" Americans, blithely ignoring the years of strenuous self-discipline required to become cultured, mistook "a smattering of all sorts of knowledge, a taste for reading, and for 'art'" for genuine culture. Had not "the ancient aristocracy of thought" been leveled? asked the poet James Russell Lowell. Had not "a loose indolence of reading"

---

[19] Henry F. May, *The End of American Innocence: A Study of the First Years of Our Own Time, 1912–1917* (1959; repr., Chicago: Quadrangle Books, 1964), 6, 30–31; Thomas Higginson, E. L. Godkin, and Charles Eliot Norton, quoted in Joan Shelley Rubin, *The Making of Middlebrow Culture* (Chapel Hill: University of North Carolina Press, 1992), 12–13.

[20] Matthew Arnold, quoted in John Henry Raleigh, *Matthew Arnold and American Culture* (1957; repr., Berkeley: University of California Press, 1961), 12, 26, 78; Howard Mumford Jones, "Arnold, Aristocracy, and America," *American Historical Review* 49 (1944): 393–409; Jaap Verheul, "Wandering between Two Worlds: Matthew Arnold and American Civilization," in *Dynamics of Modernization: European-American Comparisons and Perceptions*, ed. Tity de Vries (Amsterdam: VU University Press, 1998), 33–46.

[21] Henry James, quoted in Raleigh, *Matthew Arnold and American Culture*, 37.

replaced the "strenuous habit of thinking"? So eager did Americans appear for a smattering of all sorts of useful knowledge that one wit suggested that it be put "in small capsules" and sold in "in boxes containing one dozen each."[22]

A second obstacle to making culture prevail in America was that culture was becoming ever more exclusive. Before the Civil War, American cultural institutions had been inclusive, but the museums, theaters, and orchestras founded after 1865 emphasized "certification" of their holdings and the good taste of their patrons. A world in which Shakespeare's plays had been common currency gave way to a more hierarchical, "European" world in which high culture became the exclusive property of elites who flaunted it as a badge of status. In the meantime, "entrepreneurs of leisure" purveyed popular culture to workers, immigrants, and nonwhite Americans. Far from blurring class distinctions, as Arnold had so fervently hoped, the pursuit of culture appeared only to reinforce them.[23]

Then, too, the pursuit of culture in late nineteenth-century America increasingly came to be regarded as a feminine pursuit. Even before the Civil War, middle-class white women had "seized the reins of national culture" by becoming the arbiters of American morality. Thanks to their dominance of Protestant churches and moral reform societies, they extended their moral influence from their homes throughout society. At the same time, the ability of "scribbling women" to tap middle-class sentimentalism threatened to marginalize serious male writers. The feminization of American culture proceeded apace after 1865 as women's colleges, coeducational land-grant universities, and women's study clubs all strengthened women's claims to being America's cultural arbiters. "Step by step," one observer remarked in 1912, women were "steadily monopolizing learning, teaching, literature, the fine arts, music, the church, and the theatre."[24]

Until the founding of Johns Hopkins, the first American research university, in 1876, culture had been the property of generalists who shared Matthew Arnold's ideal of a broad general culture and who, like Arnold, viewed

---

[22] Edwin Lawrence Godkin, "Chromo-Civilization" (1874), in *Reflections and Comments, 1865–1895* (New York: Scribner, 1895), 201–204; James Russell Lowell, "The Five Indispensable Authors," *Century*, December 1893, 223–224; James L. Ford, "The Fad of Imitation Culture," *Munsey's*, October 1900, 153–157; Rubin, *The Making of Middlebrow Culture*, 11–33.

[23] Harris, "Four Stages of Cultural Growth," 19–24; Lawrence W. Levine, *Highbrow/Lowbrow: The Emergence of Cultural Hierarchy in America* (Cambridge, Mass.: Harvard University Press, 1988), 231, 235; Rob Kroes, *If You've Seen One You've Seen the Mall: Europeans and American Mass Culture* (Urbana: University of Illinois Press, 1996), 46.

[24] Ann Douglas, *The Feminization of American Culture* (New York: Knopf, 1977); Nancy F. Cott, *The Bonds of Womanhood: "Woman's Sphere" in New England, 1780–1835* (New Haven, Conn.: Yale University Press, 1977); Henry Nash Smith, *Democracy and the Novel: Popular Resistance to Classic American Writers* (New York: Oxford University Press, 1978), esp. 3–15; Earl Barnes, "The Feminizing of Culture," *Atlantic Monthly*, June 1912, 770.

literature as the criticism of life. But the founding of universities modeled on German lines, the introduction of electives, and the increasing emphasis placed on specialization resulted in both the replacement of a broad, synthetic conception of truth by a narrower, more specialized one and the separation of knowledge from morality and of "fact" from "value." A crisis of authority ensued. By 1890, the genteel amateurs who had founded the American Social Science Association in 1865 had ceded their authority to professional social scientists armed with new historical and philological techniques. Cultural authority now rested more on the investigator's training and expertise than on his social standing.[25]

As the pursuit of culture became more segmented, feminized, and specialized, inherited notions of culture grew increasingly remote from the commonplace facts of American life. Indeed, it was precisely to overcome the "genteel cult of ideality," the expectation that literature would embody high moral ideals, that Mark Twain turned to the vernacular in *The Adventures of Huckleberry Finn* (1884).[26]

THE YOUNG INTELLECTUALS

In 1911, the Spanish-born philosopher George Santayana pictured America as a young country split on generational lines between "two mentalities" – the "Genteel Tradition" of the custodians of culture and "the instincts, practices, and discoveries" of a new generation of self-conscious intellectuals.[27] The older generation, who identified American civilization with Anglo-Saxon civilization, did not acknowledge the existence of an autonomous American culture. The new generation consisted of native-born, Anglo-Saxon Protestants, many of them from the Midwest, rebelling against the provincialism of the small town, and of Eastern European Jews rebelling against the provincialism of the *shtetl*. In the pages of the *Nation*, the *New Republic*, and "little magazines" such as

---

[25] Julie A. Reuben, *The Making of the Modern University: Intellectual Transformation and the Marginalization of Morality* (Chicago: University of Chicago Press, 1996); Gerald Graff, *Professing Literature: An Institutional History* (Chicago: University of Chicago Press, 1987); Thomas L. Haskell, *The Emergence of Professional Social Science: The American Social Science Association and the Nineteenth-Century Crisis of Authority* (1977; repr., Baltimore: Johns Hopkins University Press, 2000); Hugh Hawkins, "The Ideal of Objectivity among American Social Scientists in the Era of Professionalization, 1876–1916," in *Controversies and Decisions: The Social Sciences and Public Policy*, ed. Charles Frankel (New York: Russell Sage Foundation, 1976), 89–102.

[26] Smith, *Democracy and the Novel*, 78; Henry Nash Smith, *Mark Twain: The Development of a Writer* (Cambridge, Mass.: Harvard University Press, 1962).

[27] George Santayana, "The Genteel Tradition in American Philosophy," in *Critics of Culture: Literature and Society in the Early Twentieth Century*, ed. Alan Trachtenberg (New York: Wiley, 1976), 15–16; Thomas Bender, *New York Intellect: A History of Intellectual Life in New York City, from 1750 to the Beginnings of Our Own Time* (New York: Knopf, 1987), 241–243.

Seven Arts and the *Dial*, these Protestant and Jewish intellectuals repudiated the Genteel Tradition, reassessed Matthew Arnold's legacy, searched for a "usable past," and rediscovered America.[28]

Van Wyck Brooks sounded the tocsin of this rebellion in 1915 when he emphasized the necessity of finding a "genial middle ground" between the extremes of highbrow and lowbrow, between Americans' almost religious worship of "culture" and their "catchpenny opportunism." Invoking Arnold's injunction "to see the object as in itself it really is," Brooks challenged American men of letters to "open their minds to the facts of American life" and to understand that "creative power" sprang from an "organic" culture. By organic, Brooks had in mind a deeply rooted culture capable of nurturing individual talent and creativity – or, as F. O. Matthiessen put it, "a culture adequate to our needs."[29]

In a series of articles published before his untimely death in the influenza pandemic of 1918, Randolph Bourne condemned the "unregenerate cult of the best" that he traced to Matthew Arnold's writings. This cult, he charged, abetted Americans' "cultural humility" by focusing their attention on the "antique and foreign" rather than on the contemporary and indigenous. Thus educated Americans looked to Europe for culture "to be imbibed." American culture, Bourne predicted, would never "take its rightful place among the cultures of the world" until Americans began to look for culture closer to home.[30]

In 1922, thirty American intellectuals contributed to a symposium, *Civilization in the United States*, the aim of which was to "see the problem of modern American civilization as a whole" and "speak the truth about [it]" to bring about "a real civilization." In editing the symposium papers, Harold Stearns summed up the contributors' criticisms of American life under the three broad headings of hypocrisy, colonial mentality, and pervasive maladjustment. A "sharp dichotomy between teaching and practice," he said, existed "in almost every branch of American life"; the insidious notion, propagated by "certain financial and social minorities," that America was "still an English colony" prevented Americans from achieving "any genuine nationalistic self-consciousness"; and, finally, the

[28] David R. Shumway, *Creating American Civilization: A Genealogy of American Literature as an Academic Discipline* (Minneapolis: University of Minnesota Press, 1994), 37; David A. Hollinger, "Ethnic Diversity, Cosmopolitanism, and the Emergence of the American Liberal Intelligentsia," in his *In the American Province: Studies in the History and Historiography of Ideas* (Bloomington: Indiana University Press, 1985), 56–73.
[29] Van Wyck Brooks, "America's Coming-of-Age" (1915), in *America's Coming-of-Age* (Garden City, N.Y.: Doubleday, 1958), esp. 1–19; James Hoopes, *Van Wyck Brooks: In Search of American Culture* (Amherst: University of Massachusetts Press, 1977); Casey Nelson Blake, *Beloved Community: The Cultural Criticism of Randolph Bourne, Van Wyck Brooks, Waldo Frank, and Lewis Mumford* (Chapel Hill: University of North Carolina Press, 1990); F. O. Matthiessen, *American Renaissance: Art and Expression in the Age of Emerson and Whitman* (New York: Oxford University Press, 1941), xvii.
[30] Randolph S. Bourne, "Our Cultural Humility," *Atlantic Monthly*, October 1914, 503–507.

"maladjustment" between "the whole industrial and economic situation" and "the primary and simple needs of men and women" impoverished American intellectuals and artists.[31]

The rise of a standardized mass-production, mass-consumption economy appeared to many observers at home and abroad to be yet a fourth source of Americans' spiritual poverty. America had "once again become a new world," the French observer André Siegfried announced in 1927. In the new American social structure, which bore "only a superficial resemblance to the European," standardization was no longer confined to industry but was quickly expanding to "human nature," in the process rendering unrecognizable "the individual, so dear to us in Europe." The Dutch historian Johan Huizinga shared Siegfried's foreboding. Standardization was "not just an industrial necessity" for Americans, Huizinga declared, "but an ideal of civilization." Similarly, the German philosopher of history Oswald Spengler was struck by the "standardized type of American" – in particular, the American woman, standardized "in body, clothes, and mind." To Spengler, American life "lack[ed] depth" because it was "organized exclusively from the economic side." Standardization, the "tendency to buy ready-made thoughts and ideas" that produced what an American observer called "the chain-store mind," thus militated against individuality and originality.[32]

THE REDISCOVERY OF AMERICAN CULTURE

When Frederick Jackson Turner delivered his famous paper, "The Significance of the Frontier in American History," at the World's Columbian Exposition in 1893, he reoriented American history away from tracing the transplantation of European institutions to appreciating its distinctive features. The reorientation of American literature, however, took longer. As late as 1913, the English poet Rupert Brooks looked on America as "still [a] colony" in which writers remained "utterly dependent" on England and in which magazines were "filled with English writers." Although American literature was taken as a measure of

[31] Harold E. Stearns, preface to *Civilization in the United States: An Inquiry by Thirty Americans*, ed. Harold E. Stearns (New York: Harcourt, 1922), iii–viii; Malcolm Cowley, *Exile's Return: A Literary Odyssey of the 1920s* (1934; repr., New York: Penguin, 1976), 74–79.
[32] André Siegfried, *America Comes of Age: A French Analysis* (1927), quoted in "European vs. American Culture," *New Republic*, 6 July 1927, 161–162; Johan Huizinga, "Life and Thought in America: Stray Remarks," in *America: A Dutch Historian's Vision, from Afar and Near*, trans. Herbert H. Rowen (New York: Harper, 1972), 237; Oswald Spengler, *The Hour of Decision: Part One: Germany and World-Historical Evolution*, trans. Charles Francis Atkinson (New York: Scribner, 1934), 67–68, quoted in H. Stuart Hughes, *Oswald Spengler* (1952; repr., New Brunswick, N.J.: Transaction Publishers, 1992), 150; Jesse Rainsford Sprague, "The Chain-Store Mind: Reflections of a Shopkeeper," *Harper's*, February 1929, 359; Daniel T. Rodgers, *Atlantic Crossings: Social Politics in a Progressive Age* (Cambridge, Mass.: Harvard University Press, 1998), 372–376.

American civilization, few American writers' works were then taught in universities and colleges.[33]

The First World War shattered American provincialism and fueled cultural nationalism. When Malcolm Cowley made his pilgrimage to Europe in 1921 in quest of culture, he discovered that European intellectuals "were [even] more defeated and demoralized than those at home." Upon his return from this "exile" in 1923, Cowley was "ready to find that [his] own nation had every attribute that [he] had been taught to admire in Europe" – "a folklore, and traditions, and the songs that embodied them."[34] Amid a fierce debate over the "Americanness" of American art, "machine-age modernists" such as Alfred Stieglitz and Charles Sheeler experimented with an indigenous art featuring skyscrapers, factories, and machine-made objects.[35] In colleges and universities across the land, young Turks, chafing at the fact that "English departments remained bastions of Anglophilia," organized an American Literature Group (ALG) within the Modern Language Association in 1921. Its aim was to invent an American tradition at the same time that it refuted the notion that American literature was a derivative literature.[36] In 1923, the ALG urged that American literature be presented "as expression of *national* (historical) consciousness and not as aesthetic offshoot of English literature." American literature found its historian in 1927 when the publication of the first two volumes of Vernon L. Parrington's *Main Currents in American Thought* "cut the umbilical cord that had bound American literary theory to the literary tradition of Great Britain alone." Although Parrington focused more on political and economic life than on aesthetic evaluation, later students of American literature emphasized evaluation. By 1941, with the publication of F. O. Matthiessen's *American Renaissance*, American literature had its canon of masterpieces.[37]

In their search for a usable past and an organic culture, American intellectuals were looking for a conception of culture that would bridge the gap between inherited, largely European, ideals of culture and actual American conditions by focusing attention on the indigenous and the commonplace. Emanating from university seminars, this new conception of culture would reflect the increasing specialization and academic institutionalization of

---

[33] Rupert Brooks, quoted in Ann Douglas, *Terrible Honesty: Mongrel Manhattan in the 1920s* (New York: Farrar, 1995), 159; Claudia Stokes, *Writers in Retrospect: The Rise of American Literary History, 1875–1910* (Chapel Hill: University of North Carolina Press, 2006), 22; Shumway, *Creating American Civilization*, 25.

[34] Cowley, *Exile's Return*, 95–96.

[35] Wanda M. Corn, *The Great American Thing: Modern Art and National Identity, 1915–1935* (Berkeley: University of California Press, 1999).

[36] Shumway, *Creating American Civilization*, 149, 193, 133, 143; Robert E. Spiller, "History of a History: A Study in Cooperative Scholarship," *PMLA* 89 (1974): 604–608.

[37] Spiller, "History of a History," 604 (emphasis in original); Shumway, *Creating American Civilization*, 168–171, 195, 243. See also Richard Ruland, *The Rediscovery of American Literature: Premises of Critical Taste, 1900–1940* (Cambridge, Mass.: Harvard University Press, 1967); and Kermit Vanderbilt, *American Literature and the Academy: The Roots, Growth, and Maturity of a Profession* (Philadelphia: University of Pennsylvania Press, 1986).

knowledge. By making culture a respectable pursuit for men, it would counter the feminization of American culture. Pluralistic rather than singular, it would accommodate the heterogeneity of a society that was no longer predominantly Anglo-Saxon. Above all, it would nurture talent. But this new conception of culture would retain the Arnoldian goal of cutting across the class, ethnic, racial, and regional divisions of a heterogeneous society to emphasize what Americans held in common. Ultimately, its function was to convince educated Americans, if not skeptical Europeans, that a technologically advanced civilization did indeed possess a commensurate high culture. American anthropology would be the source of this new conception of culture.

THE ORIGINS OF AMERICAN ANTHROPOLOGY

From its very beginnings in the early nineteenth century, American anthropology was, in the words of Raymond Fogelson, "a ward of nationalism." For America, as a new nation, required a "distinctive identity" of its own. Growing out of natural history – the study of the plants, animals, and other organisms of the New World – American anthropology was dedicated to "salvaging" the artifacts, customs, and languages of Native Americans before they "vanished." From Thomas Jefferson and Albert Gallatin on, learned amateurs collected Native American artifacts, speculated about the origins of Indian languages, and investigated the mounds of the eastern United States and the Pueblo ruins of the Southwest. Early centers of anthropological activity included the American Philosophical Society in Philadelphia, the American Antiquarian Society in Worcester, and the American Ethnological Society in New York. A new center arose in 1846 with the founding of the Smithsonian Institution. Under the energetic direction of the physicist Joseph Henry, the Smithsonian sponsored a number of collecting expeditions designed to diffuse "useful knowledge" about the United States. The specimens collected formed the nucleus of the United States National Museum.[38]

---

[38] Raymond D. Fogelson, "Nationalism and the Americanist Tradition," in *Theorizing the Americanist Tradition*, ed. Lisa Philips Valentine and Regna Darnell (Toronto: University of Toronto Press, 1999), 75–83, at 75, 79; David K. Van Keuren, *"The Proper Study of Mankind": An Annotated Bibliography of Manuscript Sources on Anthropology & Archeology in the Library of the American Philosophical Society* (Philadelphia: American Philosophical Society, 1986), 1–10; A. Irving Hallowell, "The Beginnings of Anthropology in America," in *Selected Papers from the "American Anthropologist," 1888–1920*, ed. Frederica de Laguna (1960; repr., Washington, D.C.: American Anthropological Association, 1976), 1–90; Joan Mark, *Four Anthropologists: An American Science in its Early Years* (New York: Science History Publications, 1980), 5–8; Curtis M. Hinsley, Jr., *Savages and Scientists: The Smithsonian Institution and the Development of American Anthropology, 1846–1910* (Washington: Smithsonian Institution Press, 1981), 15–79; Simon J. Bronner, "Object Lessons: The Work of Ethnological Museums and Collections," in *Consuming Visions: Accumulation and Display of Goods in America, 1880–1920*, ed. Simon J. Bronner (New York: Norton, 1989), 217–251; Steven Conn, *Museums and American Intellectual Life, 1876–1926* (Chicago: University of Chicago Press, 1998).

In 1879, the founding of the Bureau of Ethnology (later called the Bureau of American Ethnology) within the Smithsonian inaugurated the slow transformation of American anthropology from the hobby of learned amateurs into a profession pursued by university-trained specialists. Directed until 1902 by John Wesley Powell, the one-armed geologist and intrepid explorer of the Colorado River, the bureau set out to "organize anthropologic research in America" by providing full-time employment to self-trained fieldworkers who were wholly concerned with the collection of specimens rather than with the formulation of theory.[39] This was in accordance with the Victorian division of labor among natural historians; amateurs collected specimens in the field, from which armchair scholars, almost all of whom were European, deduced the laws of human development.[40]

The attorney, gentleman scholar, and homegrown theorist Lewis Henry Morgan, however, was a conspicuous exception to American anthropology's "colonial relationship to Europe" in which American fieldworkers relied upon European armchair theorists for their interpretative frameworks. Becoming interested in the ways of the Seneca near Rochester, New York, Morgan pioneered the scientific study of kinship and advanced a theory of human evolution from savagery through barbarism to civilization in which successive stages were marked by progressively more complex modes of technology, methods of subsistence, and social institutions.[41]

In the 1880s, two academic centers arose in American anthropology, the first, briefly, in Philadelphia, the second, permanently, in Cambridge. Although Daniel Garrison Brinton, a physician and gentleman scholar, held a chair in Archaeology and Linguistics at the University of Pennsylvania from 1886 until his death in 1899, he left no students or intellectual heirs.[42] At Harvard, Frederic Ward Putnam was Peabody Professor of American Archaeology and Ethnology from 1887 until his retirement in 1904. Trained as a natural historian by the zoologist Louis Agassiz, Putnam built the Peabody Museum, which had been established in 1866, into the first exclusively anthropological museum in North America and made Harvard a center for specialized training in physical anthropology and archaeology. A formidable academic entrepreneur, Putnam mounted displays of anthropological specimens at the World's Columbian

[39] Hinsley, *Savages and Scientists*, 83–230; Donald Worster, *A River Running West: The Life of John Wesley Powell* (Oxford: Oxford University Press, 2001); Elizabeth McFeely, *Zuñi and the American Imagination* (New York: Hill and Wang, 2001).

[40] Henrika Kuklick, *The Savage Within: The Social History of British Anthropology, 1885–1945* (Cambridge: Cambridge University Press, 1993), 91–92; Henrika Kuklick, "After Ishmael: The Fieldwork Tradition and Its Future," in *Anthropological Locations: Boundaries and Grounds of a Field Science*, ed. Aktil Gupta and James Ferguson (Berkeley: University of California Press, 1997), 58.

[41] Hinsley, *Savages and Scientists*, 47; Thomas R. Trautmann, *Lewis Henry Morgan and the Invention of Kinship* (Berkeley: University of California Press, 1987).

[42] Regna Darnell, *Daniel Garrison Brinton: The "Fearless Critic" of Philadelphia* (Philadelphia: University of Pennsylvania Department of Anthropology, 1988).

Exposition in Chicago in 1893 and directed the anthropological department of the American Museum of Natural History and the Museum of Anthropology of the University of California.[43]

As Robert Redfield pointed out, evolutionary anthropologists such as Tylor, Morgan, Brinton, and Putnam "studied culture not cultures, all society but no particular society."[44] They did not yet conceive of culture as pluralistic, relativistic, integrated, or a precipitate of history – connotations that the culture concept was to acquire by 1952. Rather, culture was, for them singular, embedded in a unilinear evolutionary framework. Culture was also hierarchical. Although Tylor considered all human groups "cultured," neither he nor his fellow evolutionists expected all, or even most, of them to attain "civilization." Far from conceiving of cultures as integral wholes, evolutionary anthropologists atomized cultures into component traits, which they proceeded to arrange in developmental sequences designed to recapitulate the advance of civilization. Finally, as practitioners of the so-called comparative method, evolutionary anthropologists compensated for the absence of written records documenting the pasts of civilized societies by studying contemporary "primitive" societies that, they believed, exhibited prior evolutionary stages.[45]

Cultures and particular societies did not become the subject matter of American anthropology until Franz Boas installed a pluralistic, relativistic, holistic, integrated, and historically conditioned conception of culture at the core of the discipline in the late nineteenth and early twentieth century. Indeed, as George W. Stocking, Jr., has shown, the roots of the culture concept that Kroeber and Kluckhohn sought to codify in 1952 lay more in Boas's critique of evolutionary anthropology than in Tylor's 1871 omnibus definition of culture.

THE REORIENTATION OF AMERICAN ANTHROPOLOGY

Franz Uri Boas was born in the Prussian town of Minden, Westphalia, in 1858. Although he received religious instruction from a rabbi, Boas grew up without religious faith. Both his father, a prosperous merchant, and his mother, a

[43] Mark, *Four Anthropologists*, 14–61; David L. Browman, "The Peabody Museum, Frederic W. Putnam, and the Rise of U.S. Anthropology, 1866–1903," *American Anthropologist* 104 (2002): 508–519; Robert W. Rydell, *All the World's a Fair: Visions of Empire at American International Expositions, 1876–1916* (Chicago: University of Chicago Press, 1984), 55–60.

[44] Robert Redfield, *Peasant Society and Culture* (1956; repr., Chicago: University of Chicago Press, 1960), 6.

[45] George W. Stocking, Jr., "Matthew Arnold, E. B. Tylor, and the Uses of Invention," in *Race, Culture, and Evolution: Essays in the History of Anthropology* (New York: Free Press, 1968), 86–90; George W. Stocking, Jr., "Tylor, Edward Burnett," *International Encyclopedia of the Social Sciences* (New York: Macmillan, 1979), 16:170–177; George W. Stocking, Jr., *Victorian Anthropology* (New York: Free Press, 1987), 169–170; Kuklick, *The Savage Within*, 75–81.

founder of Minden's Froebel kindergarten, had broken "the shackles of [Judaic] dogma," and, like so many other assimilated German Jews of that time, subscribed to the liberal ideals of the abortive revolutions of 1848. Growing up, Boas pursued the intellectual and aesthetic cultivation prescribed by *Bildung* – natural history as a boy, literature and music as extramural pursuits, and physics and mathematics in Gymnasium. At the universities of Heidelberg, Bonn, and Kiel, where he studied successively from 1877 until 1881, Boas's interests shifted from physics, which stimulated him intellectually, to geography, which appealed to his "intensive, emotional interest in the phenomena of the world." At Kiel, where he investigated the optical qualities of water in a dissertation directed by the geographer Theobald Fischer, Boas discovered "domains" in which his "materialistic *Weltanschauung*," the worldview of a physicist, no longer seemed appropriate. Also at Kiel, the lectures of the neo-Kantian philosopher Benno Erdmann shattered his "materialism."[46]

After performing compulsory military service, Boas went to Berlin, where he learned how to take anthropological measurements from the pathologist and political liberal Rudolf Virchow. From Virchow he derived a "commitment to science and rational thought against the institutional authority of tradition." A boyhood desire to see the world, whetted by the novel *Robinson Crusoe*, and curiosity about the relationship between the "objective" and the "subjective" worlds, heightened by Gustav Fechner's psychophysics, impelled Boas to live for a year in 1883–84 among the Eskimo of Baffin Island. At the same time that his investigation of the ways in which the Eskimo adapted to their harsh natural environment disabused him of any lingering belief in environmental determinism, his exposure to the Eskimo *Herzensbildung* (inner character) revealed to him the ethnocentrism of European conceptions of cultivation.[47]

Upon his return to Germany, Boas qualified in geography at the University of Berlin while helping Adolf Bastian mount exhibits at the Royal Ethnological Museum. From Bastian he derived an "antievolutionist orientation and empirical emphasis, with certain historical and moderate diffusionist priorities." Yet Boas decided to seek his fortune in the United States, where anti-Semitism appeared less rife and academic opportunities more plentiful than in Germany. Besides, his maternal uncle by marriage, the pediatrician Abraham Jacobi, and his fiancée, Marie Krackowizer, the daughter of an Austrian Catholic physician, already made their homes in New York. In 1886, following three months of

[46] Franz Boas, "An Anthropologist's Credo," *Nation*, 27 August 1938, 201–204. On Boas's life, see Douglas Cole, *Franz Boas: The Early Years, 1858–1906* (Seattle: University of Washington Press, 1999); George W. Stocking, Jr., "Boas, Franz," *Dictionary of American Biography. Supplement Three, 1941–1945*, ed. Edward T. James et al. (New York: Scribner, 1973), 81–86.
[47] George W. Stocking, Jr., "From Physics to Ethnography," in *Race, Culture, and Evolution*, 133–160; Cole, *Franz Boas*, 63–82.

fieldwork in the Pacific Northwest (the first of thirteen field trips, the last made in 1931, in which he collected more than 10,000 pages of material), Boas settled in New York.[48]

In emigrating to the United States, Boas unwittingly condemned himself to nine years as a gypsy scholar. While serving as a geographical editor for *Science* magazine from 1887 until 1889, he learned that his German conception of geography as a human science differed from the prevailing American conception of geography, which Harvard's William Morris Davis had defined along geomorphological lines. In 1889, Boas left geography for anthropology when he was appointed docent in anthropology at Clark University. In Worcester, until he left Clark in the faculty hegira of 1892, Boas conducted anthropometric measurements among schoolchildren and trained the first American graduate student to receive a Ph.D. in anthropology. Next, Boas helped Frederic Ward Putnam to mount "living exhibits" of the world's peoples at the Columbian Exposition in Chicago, but his failure to secure a permanent curatorial position at the new Columbian Museum condemned him to more than a year of unemployment. Finally, late in 1896, Putnam engineered Boas's appointment to the curatorial staff at New York's American Museum of Natural History. Early in 1897, with the help of a subvention from Abraham Jacobi, Boas began lecturing on anthropology at Columbia. Promoted to professor in 1899, after Columbia established the first anthropology department in America, Boas trained several generations of anthropologists before his retirement in 1936. Despite poor health, he remained professionally active until his death in December 1942.[49]

Soon after moving to America, Boas began to import into American thought the historicism (without any "teleological ingredient") and the emphasis on empathy of German geography and ethnology. In 1887, he contrasted the "idiographic" (particularizing) method of the "cosmographer," who, like the explorer Alexander von Humboldt, considered the individual phenomenon "worthy of being studied for its own sake," with the "nomothetic" (generalizing) method of the physicist, for whom the individual phenomenon had no intrinsic value except as a datum from which to deduce the laws governing the physical world. Although Boas, like the contemporary German philosopher of history Wilhelm Windelband, considered both the "historical" and "scientific" methods to be of equal value, he aligned himself with the historical

[48] Cole, *Franz Boas*, 83–104; Ronald P. Rohner, "Franz Boas: Ethnographer on the Northwest Coast," in *Pioneers of American Anthropology: The Uses of Biography*, ed. June Helm (Seattle: University of Washington Press, 1966), 149–212.
[49] William A. Koelsch, "Franz Boas, Geographer, and the Problem of Disciplinary Identity," *Journal of the History of the Behavioral Sciences* 40 (2004): 1–22; Susan Schulten, *The Geographical Imagination in America, 1880–1950* (Chicago: University of Chicago Press, 2001), 170, 72–75; Neil Smith, *American Empire: Roosevelt's Geographer and the Prelude to Globalization* (Berkeley: University of California Press, 2003), 41–43; Curtis M. Hinsley, Jr., and Bill Holm, "A Cannibal in the National Museum: The Early Career of Franz Boas in America," *American Anthropologist* 78 (1976): 306–316; Cole, *Franz Boas*, 105–184.

method, which appealed to his "affective" impulse to study the individual phenomenon.[50]

Also in 1887, Boas advocated the adoption of the geographically oriented practice of German curators instead of the typological arrangements preferred by American curators. In an exchange of letters with Otis T. Mason, curator-in-chief of the United States National Museum, Boas criticized the practice of classifying ethnological specimens as though they were biological specimens and then arranging them in developmental sequences. Such sequences, he explained, rested on the questionable assumption that "under the same stress and resources" the same human inventions would arise. Yet, as Boas put it in his still rather awkward English, "though like causes have like effects, like effects have not like causes." Since phenomena that at first glance appeared similar might have different antecedents, the researcher had to study every phenomenon "individually," in its "historical development" and its "geographical distribution."[51]

Boas's fieldwork in the Pacific Northwest soon convinced him that similarities of culture were more commonly the products of diffusion (or cultural borrowing) than they were of parallel development or independent invention, explanations favored by evolutionary anthropologists. Calling into question the evolutionary framework then prevailing in American anthropology, Boas declared in 1896 that any attempt to construct "a grand system" of evolution was doomed to failure. Even a cursory review revealed that similar phenomena often had different antecedents. The history of any phenomenon required "actual historical proof"; only the inductive study of customs in the context of the "total culture of the tribe practicing them" and the distribution of those customs among neighboring tribes would enable fieldworkers to sort out the differential impact of "environmental conditions," "psychological factors," and "historical connections." While not ruling out comparisons, Boas insisted that they be limited to a "well-defined, small geographical territory," that is,

---

[50] Franz Boas, "The Study of Geography," *Science*, 11 February 1887, 137–141; reprinted in Boas, *Race, Language, and Culture* (1940; repr., New York: Free Press, 1966), 639–647. On Boas's debts to German thought, see Bunzl, "Franz Boas and the Humboldtian Tradition"; Julia E. Liss, "German Culture and German Science in the *Bildung* of Franz Boas," in *"Volksgeist" as Method and Ethic*, 155–184. In 1956, Boas's daughter Helen wrote to Alfred Kroeber: "the 'aesthetic' was an important part of my father's nature. . . . [H]e was a man with strong emotions, and great sensitivity, repressed because of his great fear of being subjective." Helen Boas Yampolsky to Alfred Kroeber, 18 May 1956, A. L. Kroeber Papers, BANC MSS C-B 925, The Bancroft Library, University of California, Berkeley (hereafter Kroeber Papers), reel 49.

[51] Franz Boas, "The Occurrence of Similar Inventions in Areas Widely Apart," *Science*, 20 May 1887, 485–486; Franz Boas, "Museums of Ethnology and Their Classification," *Science*, 17 June 1887, 587–589; both reprinted in *The Shaping of American Anthropology, 1883–1911: A Franz Boas Reader*, ed. George W. Stocking, Jr. (New York: Basic Books, 1974), 61–67. On German curatorial practices, see H. Glenn Penny, *Objects of Culture: Ethnology and Ethnographic Museums in Imperial Germany* (Chapel Hill: University of North Carolina Press, 2002).

to what Bastian called "culture provinces." Although he still expected anthropologists eventually to arrive at "general laws of human development," Boas deferred their formulation until after the compilation of "histories of diverse tribes."[52]

Boas's studies of myths and folklore in the Pacific Northwest also convinced him of the relativity of culture. The fieldworker's knowledge and emotions, he explained in 1889, were shaped by the "form of social life" and the "people" to whom he belonged. Until the fieldworker broke free from the norms of his own culture, he would not be able to grasp, and would have little sympathy for, "the strange ways of thinking and feeling of primitive people." Also in 1889, Boas extended his relativistic point of view to linguistics when he showed that the different sounds a fieldworker heard speakers utter for the same word in a "primitive" language did not indicate the primitiveness of the language, but rather reflected the fieldworker's tendency to transcribe different approximations of what he heard. Later, in 1904, Boas extolled the power of the anthropological method to impress upon the researcher "the relative value of all forms of culture," to uncover the "roots" from which his own culture had "sprung," and to curb any impulse to regard his own standpoint as "the ultimate goal of human evolution."[53]

By the early 1890s, Boas was challenging the racialist concomitants of evolutionism. In 1894, he warned against conflating the "achievement" of a people with its "aptitude for achievement" on the grounds that "historical events" were far more important than its "faculty" in accounting for why a particular "race" attained "civilization." Although he conceded that some races might not produce as many "great men" as Europeans had produced, Boas called attention to the range of individual variation within any particular race. Because of this variation, races "overlap[ped]" each other more than they differed. Moreover, Boas saw no reason why "low" aptitude for achievement would keep any race from attaining civilization. It followed, then, that their "achievements" did not warrant any assumption that one race was "more highly gifted" than another.[54]

After the turn of the century, Boas carried his campaign against racialist thought into the public arena. "The achievements of the [N]egro in Africa," he asserted in the *Ethical Record* in 1904, "justify us in maintaining that the

[52] Franz Boas, "The Limitations of the Comparative Method of Anthropology," *Science*, 18 December 1896, 901–908; reprinted in Boas, *Race, Language, and Culture*, 270–280, on 275–277.

[53] Franz Boas, "Die Ziele der Ethnologie" (1889); reprinted as "The Aims of Ethnology" in Boas, *Race, Language and Culture*, 626–638, on 636; Franz Boas, "On Alternating Sounds," *American Anthropologist* 2 (1889): 47–53; reprinted in *The Shaping of American Anthropology*, 72–77; Franz Boas, "The History of Anthropology," *Science*, 21 October 1904, 513–524; reprinted in *The Shaping of American Anthropology*, 23–36, on 36.

[54] Franz Boas, "Human Faculty as Determined by Race," *Proceedings of the American Association for the Advancement of Science* 43 (1894): 301–327; reprinted in *The Shaping of American Anthropology*, 221–242; George W. Stocking, Jr., "The Critique of Racial Formalism," in *Race, Culture, and Evolution*, 161–194.

race is capable of social and political achievements." As he pointed out in *Charities* magazine in 1905, no "anthropological evidence" had yet been adduced that demonstrated the Negro's innate inferiority. Invited by W. E. B. Du Bois to deliver the commencement address at Atlanta University in 1906, Boas celebrated the contributions that African peoples had made to the "development of human culture." These contributions suggested that "all the alleged faults" of African Americans were not innate but were rather the products of such historical events as their enslavement and subsequent "disorganization," and, following emancipation, their "severe economic struggle against heavy odds." Although he admitted in *Van Norden's* magazine in 1907 that the "somewhat larger size of the white brain" could result in "a slightly greater ability" in white intelligence, Boas insisted that there was no relation between brain size and mental capacity. Then, in an article published in the *Crisis* magazine in 1910, he suggested that intermarriage between white men and black women was the best means of countering racial prejudice.[55]

In 1911, Boas synthesized his heterodox views on race, language, and culture in three seminal publications. In *Changes in Bodily Form of Descendants of Immigrants*, he summarized findings from the thousands of anthropometric measurements he had taken of immigrants and their children for the U.S. Immigration Commission from 1908 until 1910. His discovery that the "head forms," or shapes of the heads, of American-born children varied from those of their parents and their foreign-born siblings, and that variations correlated with length of residence in America, suggested the "relative plasticity" of "physical type" (or race) owing to environmental influence. Boas's findings thus called into question the reliability of the cephalic index, the ratio of the width of the head to its length, which physical anthropologists had previously seen as stable. Even more important, they shifted the burden of proof to those claiming "the absolute permanence of other forms and functions of the body."[56]

In the introduction to the *Handbook of American Indian Languages*, a collaborative project that he supervised for the Bureau of American Ethnology, Boas urged that Native American languages be analyzed in their own terms –

---

[55] Franz Boas, "What the Negro Has Done in Africa," *Ethical Record* 5 (1904): 109; Franz Boas, "The Negro and the Demands of Modern Life," *Charities*, 7 October 1905, 85, 87; Franz Boas, "The Outlook for the American Negro," Commencement Address at Atlanta University, May 31, 1906; reprinted in *The Shaping of American Anthropology*, 310–316, on 313; Franz Boas, "The Anthropological Position of the Negro," *Van Norden's*, April 1907, 40–47; Franz Boas, "The Real Race Problem," *Crisis* 1 (1910): 25; Edward H. Beardsley, "The American Scientist as Social Activist: Franz Boas, Burt G. Wilder, and the Cause of Racial Justice, 1900–1915," *Isis* 64 (1973): 50–66; Marshall Hyatt, *Franz Boas, Social Activist: The Dynamics of Ethnicity* (Westport, Conn.: Greenwood, 1990), chap. 5.

[56] Franz Boas, *Changes in Bodily Form of Descendants of Immigrants* (Washington: U.S. Government Printing Office, 1911); Franz Boas to Gustaf Retzius, 3 May 1910, Professional Correspondence of Franz Boas, American Philosophical Society (B/B61) (hereafter Boas Papers). Boas summarized his findings in "Changes in Bodily Form of Descendants of Immigrants," *American Anthropologist* 14 (1912): 530–562; reprinted in Boas, *Race, Language, and Culture*, 60–75.

"as though an intelligent Indian was going to develop the forms of his own thought by an analysis of his form of speech" – rather than in terms of Indo-European linguistic categories. He also urged anthropologists to study linguistics for the light it would throw on the mysteries of culture. Although the origins of linguistic phenomena were just as unconscious as the origins of cultural phenomena, they were less likely to "rise into consciousness," and therefore less likely to be distorted by rationalization after the fact.[57]

Finally, in *The Mind of Primitive Man*, Boas rehearsed a number of points that he had made since migrating to the United States: that the mental aptitudes of various races should not be inferred from their cultural achievements; that human nature was relatively plastic; that the differences between races paled in comparison with the variations within a single race; and that the "mental characteristics" of mankind were largely "the same all over the world." Boas went on to call into question unilinear cultural evolution, to dispute the widespread belief that the immigration of millions of Southern and Eastern Europeans was degrading American "racial types," and to deny the innate inferiority of African-Americans. He ended *The Mind of Primitive Man* with the plea that "foreign races" be treated "with greater sympathy." Just "as all races have contributed in the past to cultural progress in one way or another," so too would they advance "the interests of mankind" if given "a fair opportunity."[58] Later, *The Mind of Primitive Man* would be hailed as a "Magna Carta of self-respect for the 'lower' races."[59]

By 1911, Boas had re-examined the basis of physical anthropology, tried "to present languages as far as possible from their own point of view, not from that of an outsider," and demanded "a more thorough empirical understanding of cultural life."[60] By then, too, he had reoriented American anthropology away from the evolutionary search for the laws of culture toward the detailed study of cultures in their specific settings. As a champion of historicism, explaining "facts" by referring them "to earlier facts," he joined John Dewey, Thorstein Veblen, Charles Beard, James Harvey Robinson, and Oliver Wendell Holmes, Jr., in the revolt against formalism, against abstract and deductive approaches to the study of philosophy, economics, history, and the law. Unlike the others, however, Boas rejected the evolutionary framework within which "liberal ideology" then operated.[61]

---

[57] Franz Boas, introduction to *Handbook of American Indian Languages* (1911; repr., Lincoln: University of Nebraska Press, 1966), 77, 63.

[58] Franz Boas, *The Mind of Primitive Man* (New York: Macmillan, 1911).

[59] "Environmentalist," *Time*, 11 May 1936, 39.

[60] Franz Boas to Robert H. Lowie, 30 December 1937, Robert Harry Lowie Papers, BANC MSS C-B 927, The Bancroft Library, University of California, Berkeley (hereafter Lowie Papers), box 5.

[61] Morton G. White, *Social Thought in America: The Revolt against Formalism* (1949; repr., Boston: Beacon, 1957), 12, 107. On the transatlantic revolt against positivism, see H. Stuart Hughes, *Consciousness and Society: The Reorientation of European Social Thought, 1800–1930*, rev. ed. (New York: Vintage, 1977).

Boas also presided over the gradual movement of anthropology out of the museum into the university – a shift accelerated by his resignation from the American Museum of Natural History in 1905 in a dispute over how anthropological specimens should be exhibited. In the meantime, the rise of fieldwork, the detailed study of "circumscribed natural communities" by university-trained fieldworkers, became the rite of passage for aspiring anthropologists as part and parcel of a larger shift in the "ecology" of natural history. Previously separated, collection and interpretation were now joined in the same person.[62]

Since his ambitious program to create a well-organized school of anthropology required that he exercise "a certain amount of control" over the discipline, Boas took the lead in reorganizing the American Anthropological Association in 1902 from a Victorian learned society that welcomed amateurs and professionals alike into a professional and, increasingly, academically based organization. Even though he initially lost his battle to exclude amateurs, Boas soon gained control over the association, serving as its president from 1907 until 1909, relocating its offices from Washington to New York, and upgrading its journal, the *American Anthropologist*.[63]

After 1911, Boas became ever more outspoken in his criticism of Nordic supremacy, intelligence testing, immigration restriction, and American intervention in the First World War. Shocked by the intensity of patriotic sentiment, anti-German feeling, and the reluctance of American intellectuals to criticize the war, he publicly denounced four anthropologists who had used their science as a cloak for espionage in Mexico. This denunciation provoked Boas's censure at the annual meeting of the American Anthropological Association in 1919. At stake was less his outspoken opposition to American intervention in the war than the direction in which he was leading American anthropology – away from race toward the study of culture, away from evolutionary toward historicist models, away from racial toward cultural determinism, and away from "fixed types" toward "plasticity." Moreover, Boas had recruited into anthropology a number of hyphenated Americans who were then challenging the dominance of native-born, Anglo-Saxon Protestants.[64]

Although he was reluctant to popularize anthropology, Boas did publish *Anthropology and Modern Life*, a book for "popular consumption," in

[62] Kuklick, "After Ishmael," 50. Although given its charter in 1922 by Bronislaw Malinowski in the introduction to *Argonauts of the Western Pacific*, fieldwork had gradually developed in both English and American anthropology since the 1890s. Bronislaw Malinowski, introduction to *Argonauts of the Western Pacific* (1922; repr., Prospect Heights, Ill.: Free Press, 1984), 1–25; George W. Stocking, Jr., "The Ethnographer's Magic: Fieldwork in British Anthropology from Tylor to Malinowski," in *The Ethnographer's Magic and Other Essays in the History of Anthropology* (Madison: University of Wisconsin Press, 1992), 12–59.
[63] Franz Boas to Zelia Nuttall, 16 May 1901; reprinted as "The Boas Plan for American Anthropology," in *The Shaping of American Anthropology*, 286–289; George W. Stocking, Jr., "The Scientific Reaction against Cultural Anthropology," in *Race, Culture, and Evolution*, 270–307.
[64] Stocking, "The Scientific Reaction against Cultural Anthropology, 1917–1920."

1928. Hailed by the *Nation*'s Freda Kirchwey for the way in which it applied "the spectacle of intelligence" to "the bases of almost all the prejudices and passions on which modern society rests," *Anthropology and Modern Life* rehearsed what were by then a number of familiar points: that culture did not follow racial lines; that all races would be included if "the most intelligent, imaginative, energetic, and emotionally stable third of mankind" were selected; and that any attempt to construct "an historical sequence that would express laws of cultural development" was doomed to failure. In addition to pouring cold water on the then-fashionable eugenics movement, Boas deplored the dismemberment of the multiethnic Habsburg Empire into a number of parochial nation-states. Boas's principal purpose in writing *Anthropology and Modern Life*, however, was to show that anthropology was no longer merely a "collection of curious facts" or an "entertaining diversion." Rather, a clear understanding of anthropology's principles could illuminate "the social processes of our own times" by showing "what to do and what to avoid."[65]

THE BOASIANS

If Boas was to create a well-organized school of American anthropology, he had to recruit students who would supplement his own efforts. His "cold enthusiasm for the truth," "highly critical objectivity," and "undisputed eminence in every phase of anthropological inquiry" quickly attracted a small group of talented men and women. Although Alfred Kroeber denied the existence of a "Boas school" organized around "a definable, selective program," these students largely subscribed to the same methodological principles and generally worked along the lines Boas had already laid out. In seminars at Columbia they were exposed to Boas's exacting standards and repeated warnings against premature generalization, imbued with a sense of the urgency of salvaging what was left of vanishing aboriginal cultures, and recruited for his culture war against evolutionism and racial formalism. As hyphenated Americans of German or Jewish origin, as women, and as cosmopolitan intellectuals, they, like Boas, viewed anthropology as an international science that rose above tribal – ethnic, religious, and even national – loyalties.[66]

---

[65] Freda Kirchwey, "Franz Boas," review of *Anthropology and Modern Life*, *Nation*, 19 December 1928, 689; Franz Boas, *Anthropology and Modern Life* (1928; repr., New York: Dover, 1986), 79, 212, 11.

[66] A. L. Kroeber, "Franz Boas: The Man," in *Franz Boas, 1858–1942* (Menasha, Wis.: American Anthropological Association, 1943), 24; George W. Stocking, Jr., "The Basic Assumptions of Boasian Anthropology," in *Delimiting Anthropology: Occasional Inquiries and Reflections* (Madison: University of Wisconsin Press, 2001), 45; George W. Stocking, Jr., "Anthropology as *Kulturkampf*: Science and Politics in the Career of Franz Boas," in *The Ethnographer's Magic*, 92–113; George W. Stocking, Jr., "Essays on Culture and Personality," in *Malinowski, Rivers, Benedict and Others: Essays on Culture and Personality*, ed. George W. Stocking, Jr. (Madison: University of Wisconsin Press, 1986), 3–12.

Boas's students were dismayed by his reluctance to popularize anthropology. Robert Lowie complained about Boas's failure to develop many subjects at greater length in *The Mind of Primitive Man* or to provide a "solid base of elementary fact" in a textbook. Similarly, Edward Sapir lamented Boas's failure in *Anthropology and Modern Life* to deal "with things in a more complete and rounded manner," summarize "the methodology of his science," and distill his "philosophy of culture." Boas, who, Alfred Kroeber thought, took culture "as given," waited until 1930 to issue his first formal definition of culture. Culture, he wrote, "embraces all the manifestations of social habits of a community, the reactions of the individual as affected by the habits of the group in which he lives, and the products of human activities as determined by these habits." Boas's definition did not satisfy Clyde Kluckhohn, who criticized its failure to throw more light on anthropologists' "presuppositions" and "the operations they follow in extracting their evidence."[67]

To supplement Boas's efforts and to popularize anthropology, Boas's students promoted what Robert Lowie called the "American view" of anthropology, based on methodological principles that were "the common property of all the active younger American students." Avoiding "false analogies borrowed from the biological sciences," they set out "to separate scientific fact from its envelope of scientific folklore."[68] In addition to minimizing the impact of the physical environment on culture, they distinguished anthropological explanations of group behavior from psychological explanations of the individual mind.[69] They also construed cultures as "historical complexes," composed of both independently invented and borrowed traits.[70] Finally, they characterized anthropology as an "historical" discipline that, in Alfred Kroeber's words, was not only free of the "determinants" and "methods" of the natural sciences but did not seek "laws."[71]

[67] Robert H. Lowie, review of *The Mind of Primitive Man*, *American Journal of Sociology* 17 (1912): 835; Robert H. Lowie, *Robert H. Lowie, Ethnologist* (Berkeley: University of California Press, 1959), 138; Edward Sapir, "Franz Boas," review of *Anthropology and Modern Life, New Republic*, 23 January 1929, 278–279; Alfred Kroeber to Clyde Kluckhohn, 10 March 1950, HUG 4490.9, Kluckhohn Papers; Franz Boas, "Anthropology," in *Encyclopedia of the Social Sciences*, ed. Edwin R. A. Seligman (New York: Macmillan, 1930), 2:79; Clyde Kluckhohn, "Bronislaw Malinowski, 1884–1942," *Journal of American Folklore* 56 (1943): 210–211.

[68] Robert H. Lowie, "A New Conception of Totemism," *American Anthropologist* 13 (1911): 189–207; reprinted in *Lowie's Selected Papers in Anthropology*, ed. Cora Du Bois (Berkeley: University of California Press, 1960), 293–311, on 293.

[69] Clark Wissler, "The Psychological Aspects of the Culture-Environment Relation," *American Anthropologist* 14 (1912): 217–225; Clark Wissler, "Psychological and Historical Interpretations for Culture," *Science*, 11 February 1916, 193–201; Clark Wissler, "Opportunities for Coordination in Anthropological and Psychological Research," *American Anthropologist* 22 (1920): 1–12. See also Edward Sapir, "Language and Environment," *American Anthropologist* 14 (1912): 226–242.

[70] Alexander Goldenweiser, "Culture and Environment," *American Journal of Sociology* 21 (1916): 628–633, on 632.

[71] A. L. Kroeber, "Eighteen Professions," *American Anthropologist* 17 (1915): 283–288.

By 1917, according to Lowie, anthropology was "claiming and gaining her rightful place in the sun" and "justifying" its disciplinary "independence" on the strength of "the unique, irreducible character of" its subject matter, culture.[72] Neither psychology nor "social differences" (race) nor physical environment, Lowie added, could explain culture. For culture was "a thing *sui generis*," which could be "explained only in terms of itself." Accordingly, explanations of cultural phenomena must take the form of searches for "antecedents."[73]

Although all the Boasians agreed upon the significance of culture, they disagreed over its ontological status. Alfred Kroeber famously viewed culture as a "superorganic" phenomenon. Although "carried" by men and "existing through them," it was "an entity in itself," and "another order of life." Hence the individual did not figure in culture history except as "illustration."[74] Edward Sapir and Alexander Goldenweiser, however, refused to consider culture apart from individuals who embodied it. Vehemently objecting to Kroeber's treatment of Shakespeare and Goethe as mere "cat's-paws of general cultural drifts," Sapir reminded him that it was "always the individual who thinks and acts and dreams and revolts." Similarly, Goldenweiser deplored Kroeber's lack of interest in "the concrete individual of historical society," without whom "culture change could not occur." Kroeber, however, continued to maintain throughout his long career that "culture history proper" could begin only after the individual had been "totally subtracted."[75]

As late as 1919, Kroeber worried that the nature of culture remained unclear. Unable to "see what culture is" or to get "a real feeling for its existence," the practitioners of other disciplines suspected anthropologists of "doing something vain and unscientific." Textbooks were therefore necessary to establish anthropology as a science, but Boas himself was reluctant to write one. To fill the vacuum, Boas's students published four textbooks in the early 1920s, all of which were designed to illuminate the "workings of culture."[76]

In *Primitive Society* (1920), Robert Lowie said the last word in the Boasian critique of evolutionary anthropology when he declared that "cultures develop mainly through borrowings due to chance contact." Not only did diffusion

[72] Robert H. Lowie, "The Universalist Fallacy," *New Republic*, 17 November 1917, 5–6.

[73] Robert H. Lowie, *Culture and Ethnology* (1917; repr., New York: Basic Books, 1966), 66.

[74] A. L. Kroeber, "Eighteen Professions," *American Anthropologist* 17 (1915): 283–288. See also A. L. Kroeber, "The Superorganic," *American Anthropologist* 19 (1917): 163–213.

[75] Edward Sapir to Alfred Kroeber, 29 October 1917, in *The Sapir-Kroeber Correspondence: Letters between Edward Sapir and A. L. Kroeber, 1905–1925*, ed. Victor Golla (Berkeley: University of California Survey of California and Other Indian Languages, 1984), 258; Edward Sapir, "Do We Need a 'Superorganic'?" *American Anthropologist* 19 (1917): 441–447; Alexander Goldenweiser, "The Autonomy of the Social," *American Anthropologist* 19 (1917): 447–449; A. L. Kroeber to Edward Sapir, 24 July 1917, in *The Sapir-Kroeber Correspondence*, 245–246.

[76] A. L. Kroeber to Franz Boas, 11 January 1919, Boas Papers; Regna Darnell, *And Along Came Boas: Continuity and Revolution in Americanist Anthropology* (Amsterdam: John Benjamins, 2000), 294; Melville J. Herskovits, "Prehistory," review of *Anthropology*, *New Republic*, 27 February 1924, 25.

render "hopeless" all attempts "to embody the exuberant variety of phenomena in a single chronological sequence," but the "order of events" by which "our own modern civilization," itself "a complex of borrowed traits," had come into existence "provide[d] no schedule for the itinerary of alien cultures." In pronouncing Western civilization a "planless hodgepodge," a "thing of shreds and patches," to which the historian could "no longer yield superstitious reverence," Lowie opened his readers' eyes to "the overwhelmingly artificial cast" of their own lives.[77]

In *Early Civilization* (1922), Alexander Goldenweiser made the point that "man is one" but "civilizations [or cultures] are many." By showing that the cultures of the Eskimo, Tlingit, and Haida of North America, the Negroes of Uganda, and the aborigines of Australia not only possessed "all the elements or aspects that characterize human civilization" but also had "achieved things of genuine and unique worth," Goldenweiser relativized civilization by placing "primitive" and "complex" societies on the same continuum. According to Margaret Mead, *Early Civilization* was the first book by an American anthropologist that treated "cultures as wholes" and conveyed "a sense of what a culture was."[78]

In *Anthropology* (1923), Alfred Kroeber staked anthropology's claim to constitute a third field between biology and history. "The specific task and place in the sun for anthropology," according to Kroeber, was to interpret "those phenomena into which both organic and social causes enter." Kroeber cited the example of the "Louisiana [N]egro," whose dark skin and thick lips were biological traits but whose alleged indolence and fondness for singing were cultural traits. Neither biology nor history alone could sort out this "blending of nature and nurture" because biology did not "operate" with "tradition" and history did not concern itself with "heredity."[79]

In *Man and Culture* (1923), Clark Wissler instructed social scientists on the nature of culture, on "the processes by which it changes," and on "its relations to geographic environment," and to "man's innate biological and psychological equipment." By showing how American culture could be broken down into three distinctive "super-characteristics" or "trait-complexes" – mechanical invention, mass education, and universal suffrage – Wissler "Americanize[d] the culture concept and [made] it acceptable to the wider scientific community." American culture was, in turn, part of a vast "culture province," the "Euro-American type of culture," then spreading to "the most outlying corners of the earth." Wissler looked forward to the day when Americans, who exhibited all

[77] Robert H. Lowie, *Primitive Society* (1920; repr., New York: Liveright, 1947), 10, 441; Edward Sapir, review of *Primitive Society*, *Dial*, November 1920, 531–532.
[78] Alexander Goldenweiser, *Early Civilization: An Introduction to Anthropology* (New York: Knopf, 1922), 14–15, 31, 131, 115, 123, 328; *An Anthropologist at Work: Writings of Ruth Benedict*, ed. Margaret Mead (Boston: Houghton, 1959), 8. The expansion of the province of civilization to include "primitive" peoples, reflected in *Early Civilization*, occurred in European thought as well. In 1929, the French historian Lucien Febvre remarked that "for a long time now the concept of a civilization of non-civilized peoples has been current." Febvre, quoted in Kuper, *Culture*, 24.
[79] A. L. Kroeber, *Anthropology* (New York: Harcourt, 1923), 1–10.

the "initiative" and "originality" characteristic of "wilder peoples," would "carry forth the lamp of civilization."[80]

THE SCIENCE OF THE "NON-EUCLIDEAN"

As social scientists in cognate disciplines began to make use of comparative anthropological material, to insist upon the necessity of "close empirical study," to emphasize the plasticity of human nature, to disprove the existence of "absolutes of any kind," and to puncture Western ethnocentrism, anthropology became the science of the "non-Euclidean" – the "not-in-the-tradition-of-Western-civilization" – in the 1920s and 1930s.[81]

By 1928, according to Alfred Kroeber, sociologists had begun to see "most anthropological material as [their] own."[82] Sociologists' appropriation of anthropological material was hardly surprising. They were frequently colleagues of anthropologists in joint departments or taught courses in anthropology offered at schools without anthropologists, and their journals published articles written by anthropologists. Moreover, many of them had been influenced by Boas's critique of the racial formalism. In 1906, Charles A. Ellwood, who had once attributed differences in achievement between white and black schoolchildren to "innate tendencies," cited Boas's work in maintaining that "mental and moral differences between the races" were products of differences in "social equipment" or "machinery" rather than "innate qualities or capacities."[83] After reading *The Mind of Primitive Man*, Carl Kelsey repudiated his belief that "thousands of generations in Africa have produced a being very different from him whose ancestors lived an equal time in Europe" in favor of the view that racial differences were "largely superficial."[84] Discarding his earlier belief in inherent racial differences, Howard W. Odum invoked Boas's authority on the "great plasticity of the mental make-up of human types."[85]

---

[80] George Peter Murdock, "Clark Wissler, 1870–1947," *American Anthropologist* 50 (1948): 295; A. L. Kroeber to Elsie Clews Parsons, [June?] 1923, quoted in Desley Deacon, *Elsie Clews Parsons: Inventing Modern Life* (Chicago: University of Chicago Press, 1997), 248; Clark Wissler, *Man and Culture* (New York: Crowell, 1923), 1–12, 23–31, 356–359.

[81] Edward A. Purcell, Jr., *The Crisis of Democratic Theory: Scientific Naturalism and the Problem of Value* (Lexington: University Press of Kentucky, 1973), 20–21, 66–67. Robert Lowie spoke of the "non-Euclidean" nature of Boasian anthropology in *The History of Ethnological Theory* (New York: Holt, 1937), 138.

[82] A. L. Kroeber, "The Anthropological Attitude," *American Mercury*, April 1928, 491.

[83] Charles A. Ellwood, review of *The Color Line*, by William Benjamin Smith, *American Journal of Sociology* 11 (1906): 571–572; Charles A. Ellwood, "The Theory of Imitation in Social Psychology," *American Journal of Sociology* 6 (1901): 735.

[84] Carl Kelsey, *The Negro Farmer* (1903; repr., New York: AMS Press, 1977), 6–7; Carl Kelsey, review of *The Mind of Primitive Man*, *Annals of the American Academy of Political and Social Science* 46 (1913): 203.

[85] Howard W. Odum, *Social and Mental Traits of the Negro* (New York: Columbia University Press, 1910), 294, 47; Howard W. Odum, "Negro Children in the Public Schools of Philadelphia," *Annals of the American Academy of Political and Social Science* 49 (1913): 205–206.

When Edward A. Ross revised his textbook *Principles of Sociology* in 1930 (the first edition of which had been published in 1920), he incorporated "the chief findings of the cultural anthropologists," replacing a chapter on "The Race Factor" with one on "Culture." "Giving school children the view of race differences common among anthropologists," Ross predicted, "would do much to forestall race prejudice."[86]

Particularly receptive to anthropological techniques and concepts were the sociologists who, until 1929, rubbed elbows with anthropologists in the University of Chicago's joint department of sociology and anthropology. Under Boas's influence, W. I. Thomas moved away from unilinear cultural evolutionism, deemphasized innate differences in racial temperament, abandoned the idea of racial hierarchy, asserted the equipotentiality of Asians and African Americans with white Americans, separated the cultural from the racial, and insisted that individual variation was more important than differences between races.[87] When in 1925 Robert E. Park revised his programmatic essay "The City" (first published in 1915), he urged that "the same patient methods of observation" employed by anthropologists to study "the life and manners of the North American Indian" be applied to investigating "the customs, beliefs, social practices, and general conceptions of life prevalent in Little Italy" or "the more sophisticated folkways of the inhabitants of Greenwich Village." After being encouraged by Park, his father-in-law, to enroll in Chicago's joint program, Robert Redfield strove throughout his career to combine anthropological techniques with sociological concepts.[88] Ellsworth Faris drew on anthropological studies of "human nature" and "the collective life of societies" as well as on his own experience as a missionary in the Belgian Congo to lead a

[86] Edward A. Ross, *Principles of Sociology*, rev. ed. (New York: Century, 1930), ix, 79–89, 206.
[87] W. I. Thomas to Franz Boas, 27 March, 14 May 1907, Boas Papers; W. I. Thomas, *Source Book for Social Origins* (Chicago: Richard G. Badger, 1909), 143–154, 303–317; W. I. Thomas, "Life History," *American Journal of Sociology* 79 (1973): 250; George W. Stocking, Jr., "Lamarckianism in American Social Science, 1890–1915," in *Race, Culture, and Evolution*, 260–263. Alfred Kroeber praised Thomas as a knowledgeable intermediary between anthropology and sociology. A. L. Kroeber, review of *The Polish Peasant in Europe and America*, by W. I. Thomas and Florian Znaniecki, *American Anthropologist* 32 (1930) 321. As Robert Lowie added in 1938, "probably no sociologist in the world – certainly none of English speech – has so systematically kept abreast of ethnological progress as Dr. Thomas." Robert H. Lowie, review of *Primitive Behavior*, by W. I. Thomas, *American Anthropologist* 40 (1938): 144.
[88] Robert E. Park, "The City: Suggestions for the Investigation of Human Behavior in the Urban Environment," in Robert E. Park, Ernest W. Burgess, and Roderick D. McKenzie, *The City* (1925; repr., Chicago: University of Chicago Press, 1984), 3. On the Chicago school, see Robert E. L. Faris, *Chicago Sociology, 1920–1932* (1967; repr., Chicago: University of Chicago Press, 1979); Fred H. Matthews, *Quest for an American Sociology: Robert E. Park and the Chicago School* (Montreal: McGill-Queen's University Press, 1977); George W. Stocking, *Anthropology at Chicago: Tradition, Discipline, Department* (Chicago: Joseph Regenstein Library, University of Chicago, 1979); Ulf Hannerz, *Exploring the City: Inquiries toward an Urban Anthropology* (New York: Columbia University Press, 1980); Andrew Abbott, *Department and Discipline: Chicago Sociology at One Hundred* (Chicago: University of Chicago Press, 1999).

revolt against "instinct theory" or "instinctivism" in the new field of social psychology.[89]

The influence of anthropology, moreover, spawned a group of self-described "culturalists" in American sociology.[90] Charles A. Ellwood cited anthropologists' studies of "primitive" peoples to affirm the plasticity of human nature, "indefinitely modif[iable] by social institutions and the social environment."[91] Clarence M. Case was convinced not only that culture was "the unique, distinctive, and exclusive possession of man," but that it could be explained "only in terms of itself."[92] Emory S. Bogardus announced that sociology "begins where culture appears."[93] F. Stuart Chapin drew on anthropology to construct a theory of "synchronous cultural change."[94] Sometimes with the help of the anthropologist Melville Herskovits, Malcolm M. Willey explicated "culture," "trait," "pattern," and other anthropological terms in publications directed at sociologists and psychologists.[95]

[89] Ellsworth Faris, "Ethnological Light on Psychological Problems," *Publications of the American Sociological Society* 16 (1921): 113–120; Ellsworth Faris, "Are Instincts Data or Hypotheses?" *American Journal of Sociology* 27 (1921): 184–196; Ellsworth Faris, "The Subjective Aspect of Culture," *Publications of the American Sociological Society* 19 (1924): 37–46; Ellsworth Faris, "The Nature of Human Nature," *Publications of the American Sociological Society* 20 (1925): 15–29; Ellsworth Faris, "Preliterate People: Proposing a New Term," *American Journal of Sociology* 30 (1925): 710–712; Robert Faris, *Chicago Sociology, 1920–1932*, 69; Roscoe C. Hinkle, *Developments in American Sociological Theory, 1915–1950* (Albany: State University of New York Press, 1994), 253–261.

[90] Floyd N. House, *The Development of Sociology* (New York: McGraw-Hill, 1936), 270–271; Dorothy Gary, "The Developing Study of Culture," in *Trends in American Sociology*, ed. George Lundberg, Read Bain, and Nels Anderson (New York: Harper, 1929), 172–220; Henrika Kuklick, "A 'Scientific Revolution': Sociological Theory in the United States, 1930–1945," *Sociological Inquiry* 43 (1973): 11–12.

[91] Charles A. Ellwood, "The Modifiability of Human Nature and Human Institutions," *Journal of Applied Sociology* 7 (1923): 229.

[92] Clarence M. Case, "Culture as a Distinctive Human Trait," *American Journal of Sociology* 32 (1927): 920; Clarence M. Case, "The Culture Concept in Social Science," *Journal of Applied Sociology* 8 (1924); 146–155; Clarence M. Case, *Outlines of Introductory Sociology: A Textbook of Readings in Social Science* (New York: Harcourt, 1924), xxix–xxxvi.

[93] Emory S. Bogardus, "Tools in Sociology," *Sociology and Social Research* 14 (1930): 336.

[94] F. Stuart Chapin, "A Theory of Synchronous Culture Cycles," *Social Forces* 3 (1925): 596–604; F. Stuart Chopin, *Cultural Change* (New York: Century, 1928); Robert C. Bannister, *Sociology and Scientism: The American Quest for Objectivity, 1880–1940* (Chapel Hill: University of North Carolina Press, 1987), 148, 156.

[95] Melville J. Herskovits and Malcolm M. Willey, "The Cultural Approach to Sociology," *American Journal of Sociology* 29 (1923): 188–199; Malcolm M. Willey and Melville J. Herskovits, "Psychology and Culture," *Psychological Bulletin* 24 (1927): 253–283; Malcolm M. Willey, "Society and Its Cultural Heritage," in *An Introduction to Sociology*, ed. Jerome Davis and Harry Elmer Barnes (Boston: Heath, 1927), 495–589; Malcolm M. Willey, "The Validity of the Culture Concept," *American Journal of Sociology* 35 (1929): 204–219. As Kroeber and Kluckhohn pointed out, Lowie's *Culture and Ethnology* and Wissler's *Man and Culture* were the anthropological sources most frequently cited by sociologists writing on "culture" and "cultural sociology." Kroeber and Kluckhohn, *Culture*, 15.

Undoubtedly the best-known culturalist was William F. Ogburn, close friend of Robert Lowie and, until 1927, Boas's colleague at Columbia. Ogburn was just as interested in anthropological fieldwork as he was in psychoanalysis. Recognizing that human nature had changed too slowly since the dawn of recorded history to account for the accelerating "march" of civilization, Ogburn rooted his explanation of the "maladjustments" then plaguing Americans in "social evolution" (culture). In *Social Change with Respect to Culture and Original Nature* (1922), he pictured American culture as consisting of correlated parts. Change in one part required the "harmonious" adjustment of the other parts. What Ogburn christened "cultural lag" occurred whenever "adaptive culture" – that is, "customs, beliefs, philosophies, laws, [and] governments" – failed to keep pace with changes in material culture stemming from invention. Alfred Kroeber likened reading *Social Change* to "meeting a fellow countryman in a strange land." To Robert Lowie, there was "probably no clearer elementary exposition" of the culture concept.[96]

Few American sociologists, however, became full-fledged culturalists. Before the culture concept could become part and parcel of American sociology, sociologists had to square it with their "evolutionary naturalism" – with their emphasis on adaptation and atomistic treatment of culture. As "social nominalists" who treated groups as aggregates of individuals, sociologists balked at what they considered the "group fallacy" – that is, substitution of "the group as a whole" as "a principle of explanation" for "the individuals of the group." Finally, many American sociologists were instrumental positivists who modeled their discipline on the natural sciences and strove to make sociology "objective" and "value-free."[97] It was hardly surprising, then, that a questionnaire circulated among sociologists in the mid-1920s revealed that although increased interest in anthropology had become "one of the most notable trends in American sociology," sociologists rarely discussed anthropological works in their courses or cited those works in their textbooks. But sociologists did modify their terminology in response to anthropological influence. By 1929, many of them spoke of *change* rather than *evolution*, all the while clinging to their belief in progress, which they traced, as did Ogburn, to the cumulative impact of invention.[98]

[96] William Fielding Ogburn, *Social Change with Respect to Culture and Original Nature* (New York: Huebsch, 1922), esp. 200–213; Roscoe C. Hinkle and Gisela J. Hinkle, *The Development of Modern Sociology* (New York: Random House, 1954), 38; Dorothy Ross, *The Origins of American Social Science* (Cambridge: Cambridge University Press, 1991), 442–445; Fred H. Matthews, "Social Scientists and the Culture Concept, 1930–1950: The Conflict between Processual and Structural Approaches," *Sociological Theory* 7 (1989): 90; A. L. Kroeber, review of *Social Change*, by W. F. Ogburn, *American Anthropologist* 25 (1923): 265; Robert H. Lowie, review of *Social Change*, by W. F. Ogburn, *Freeman*, 11 July 1923, 431.

[97] Willey, "The Validity of the Culture Concept," 212; Christopher G. A. Bryant, *Positivism in Social Theory and Research* (New York: Macmillan, 1985), 133–173; Ross, *The Origins of American Sociology*, 428–437; Hinkle, *Developments in American Sociological Theory*, 174–177, 196–197, 305.

[98] Jessie Bernard, "The History and Prospects of Sociology in the United States," in *Trends in American Sociology*, 68.

Historians also became, in Edward Sapir's words, "pretty thoroughly anthropologized." Indeed, "the New History," as Alfred Kroeber put it in 1928, "proclaims that it will never be properly remade until it absorbs the whole range of anthropological data."[99] Yet, until the late 1930s, historians were influenced more by evolutionary anthropologists and by archaeologists than they were by the Boasians. Many of them also clung to their belief in progress.

Frederick Jackson Turner's frontier hypothesis was informed by the evolutionary notion that societies resembled living organisms that evolved gradually and continuously, through a fixed series of stages, from the simple to the complex.[100] For James Harvey Robinson, "evolutionary intellectual history necessitated an alliance between history and the social sciences." In his manifesto *The New History* (1912), Robinson deemed anthropology "first and foremost" among the cognate sciences that he hoped to enlist as "auxiliary sciences of history." These auxiliaries would widen the scope of history by paying more attention to "common, mundane experience" and by shifting attention from institutions to context, environment, and "social forces." In the process, Robinson hoped to reveal "the technique of progress," for he and other New Historians had an "underlying faith in the progress of reason in human affairs."[101] Harry Elmer Barnes, the New History's chief propagandist, credited Boas and his students with having raised anthropology "to the level of the science" by supplanting the "arbitrary deductions" of the evolutionists with "critical and discriminating analysis of adequate collections of representative data." Anthropologists' studies, moreover, promised to free historians "from chauvinism and bigotry." Yet archaeological findings greatly lengthening man's prehistory made an even greater impression on Barnes. If there was "little evidence for biological and neurological improvement since the time of the appearance of the Cro-Magnon type," human progress now seemed to Barnes to be "more and more dependent upon advances in culture and ideas." Accordingly, Barnes urged his fellow historians "to rely more and more on *nurture* and less and less on *nature*" in their explanations.[102]

[99] Sapir, review of *Primitive Society*, 532; Kroeber, "The Anthropological Attitude," 491.

[100] Robert F. Berkhofer, Jr., "Space, Time, Culture and the New Frontier," *Agricultural History* 28 (1964): 21–22.

[101] James Harvey Robinson, *The New History* (1912; repr., Springfield, Mass.: Walden Press, 1958), 83–84; John Higham, *History: Professional Scholarship in America* (1965; repr., Baltimore: Johns Hopkins University Press, 1983), 111–115; Ernst A. Breisach, *American Progressive History: An Experiment in Modernization* (Chicago: University of Chicago Press, 1993), 66–77. See also Daniel Segal, "'Western Civ' and the Staging of History in American Higher Education," *American Historical Review* 105 (2000): 770–805.

[102] Harry Elmer Barnes, "Our Primitive Heritage," review of *Early Civilization*, by Alexander Goldenweiser, *New Republic*, 29 October 1922, 17; Harry Elmer Barnes, "Recent Developments in History," in *Recent Developments in the Social Sciences*, ed. Edward Cary Hayes (Philadelphia: Lippincott, 1927), 355, 365 (emphasis in original); Breisach, *American Progressive History*, 133–134. See also Leslie A. White, "Harry Elmer Barnes as a Contemporary Encyclopedist," in *Harry Elmer Barnes, Learned Crusader: The New History in Action*, ed. Arthur Goddard (Colorado Springs: Ralph Myles, 1968), 43–45.

Perhaps the most influential historical work influenced by anthropology between the world wars was Walter Prescott Webb's 1931 classic *The Great Plains*. Drawing on Wissler's *Man and Culture* and Kroeber's *Anthropology*, Webb traced the diffusion of "culture complexes" from the humid Eastern woodlands into the more arid Great Plains. Defining "culture" as "the ways of life of a group," and using the windmill, the six-shooter, barbed wire, and other tools as indices of cultural growth, Webb concluded that "Anglo-American civilization" had been drastically "modified" by the physical environment of the Great Plains. Indeed, Webb described *The Great Plains* as "the application of the principles of cultural anthropology to fairly recent history."[103]

Yet most American historians clung to their belief in progress while resisting the implications of cultural relativism.[104] Some of them, moreover, were slow to repudiate their belief in the innate inferiority of African Americans. As late as 1952, Kenneth Stampp felt compelled to remind his fellow historians that not only had "the generalization that the great majority of Negroes were contented as slaves" never been proved, but that it rested "on the assumption that certain racial traits caused [Negroes] to adapt to the system with peculiar ease." Indeed, "no historian of [slavery] can be taken seriously any longer unless he begins with the knowledge that there is no valid evidence that the Negro race is innately inferior to the white." Far from it. There was actually "growing evidence that both races have approximately the same potentialities."[105]

DISSEMINATING THE ANTHROPOLOGICAL ATTITUDE

Boas's students, however, wanted to disseminate what Alfred Kroeber called "the anthropological attitude" beyond sociologists and historians to educated Americans. "The important thing about anthropology," Kroeber explained in the *American Mercury* in 1928, was not the "science" itself but rather the "attitude" that informed its practice. Insofar as educated Americans and

[103] Walter Prescott Webb, *The Great Plains* (New York: Grossett and Dunlap, 1931), vi, 48; Fred A. Shannon, *An Appraisal of Walter Prescott Webb's "The Great Plains: A Study in Institutions and Environment"* (1940; repr., Westport, Conn.: Greenwood, 1979), 151–152; Peter Novick, *That Noble Dream: The "Objectivity Question" and the American Historical Association* (Cambridge: Cambridge University Press, 1988), 201–202.
[104] Breisach, *American Progressive History*, 197–198.
[105] Kenneth M. Stampp, "The Historian and Southern Negro Slavery," *American Historical Review* 57 (1952): 616, 620. See also Francis B. Simkins, "New Viewpoints of Southern Reconstruction," *Journal of Southern History* 5 (1939): 58. As David Brion Davis recalls, until the publication of Stampp's book, *The Peculiar Institution*, in 1956, Ulrich B. Phillips's "openly racist" *American Negro Slavery*, published in 1918, "was still the standard work on the subject of slavery." In it "Phillips frankly affirmed that blacks were inferior to whites and the southern slavery had been a benign civilizing force for 'easy going, amiable sturdy light-hearted savages from Africa.'" David Brion Davis, "Intellectual Trajectories: Why People Study What They Do," *Reviews in American History* 37 (2009): 154–155.

Europeans had become able to conceive of culture as such, they had begun "to think and act anthropologically." Although anthropologists could hardly claim full credit for the spread of this "inquiring attitude to culture," they nonetheless profited from their growing authority as those experts who sharpened this attitude and applied it to new situations. Anthropologists, in short, had become the principal custodians of culture.[106]

In 1930, the editors of the monumental *Encyclopedia of the Social Sciences* echoed Kroeber when they assessed the impact of "war and reorientation" on Western civilization. On both sides of the Atlantic they discerned a "heroic and concerted effort to understand contemporary culture," especially in Germany, "a defeated group seeking a new orientation," and in America, "a new culture inviting definition." Amid this "outburst of national introspection," anthropologists were staking their claim to being the "anatomists and biographers of culture" on the strength of "meticulous" fieldwork and "unyielding critical austerity." Thanks to their efforts, "the anthropological attitude" was entering the main stream of twentieth-century social thought.[107]

The resurgence of cultural primitivism, popularization of Freudian theory, and growth of middlebrow audiences all enhanced anthropologists' ability to reach educated Americans between the world wars. The contemporary appeal of the exotic on both sides of the Atlantic was reflected in the reclassification of anthropological specimens as works of art and the enormous impact these works had on modernist artists.[108] In their revolt against repression and embrace of sexual openness, younger Americans saw in Sigmund Freud's work a warrant to slough off the repressive mandates of civilization. (So, too, did several prominent anthropologists, as we shall see in Chapter 3.)[109] The surge of enrollment in high school and college, proliferation of white-collar jobs requiring a high-school diploma, and substantial increase in both discretionary income and leisure time fueled the growth of middlebrow audiences whose

---

[106] Kroeber, "The Anthropological Attitude," 491.

[107] "War and Reorientation," *Encyclopedia of the Social Sciences*, ed. Edwin R. A. Seligman (New York: Macmillan, 1930), 1:199–203.

[108] James Clifford, *The Predicament of Culture: Twentieth-Century Ethnography, Literature, and Art* (Cambridge, Mass.: Harvard University Press, 1988), 189–214; George W. Stocking, Jr., "The Ethnographic Sensibility of the 1920s and the Dualism of the Anthropological Tradition," in *The Ethnographer's Magic*, 284–288; Corn, *The Great American Thing*, 326–327.

[109] William E. Leuchtenburg, *The Perils of Prosperity, 1914–1932* (Chicago: University of Chicago Press, 1958), 167–170; Frederick J. Hoffman, *The Twenties: American Writing in the Postwar Decade*, rev. ed. (New York: Free Press, 1965), 229–235; John C. Burnham, "From Avant-Garde to Specialism: Psychoanalysis in America," *Journal of the History of the Behavioral Sciences* 15 (1979): 128–134; John C. Burnham, "The New Psychology," in *1915, the Cultural Moment: The New Politics, the New Woman, the New Psychology, the New Art and the New Theatre in America*, ed. Adele Heller and Louis Rudnik (New Brunswick, N.J.: Rutgers University Press, 1991), 117–127; Fred H. Matthews, "The Americanization of Sigmund Freud: Adaptation of Psychoanalysis before 1917," *Journal of American Studies* 1 (1967): 39–62; George W. Stocking, Jr., "Essays on Culture and Personality," 6–8.

members avidly consumed fiction, biographies, popularizations of science, and outlines of history and philosophy. Eager for useful knowledge, yet unsure of their own critical judgment, middlebrow readers turned for guidance to the judges of the Book-of-the-Month Club, promoters of Great Books schemes, and other "middlemen of culture."[110]

The Boasians reached out to educated Americans by means of articles and book reviews published in influential journals of public opinion such as the *Nation*, the *New Republic*, the *American Mercury*, in little magazines such as the *Dial* and the *Freeman*, in newspapers such as the *New York Times* and the *New York Herald Tribune*, in the published papers of symposiums such as *Civilization in the United States*, and in books written for educated Americans.

THE WORK OF POPULAR ENLIGHTENMENT

As a self-described *Aufklärer* (agent of enlightenment) and advocate of "reasoned nonconformism," Robert Lowie took the lead in popularizing anthropologists' findings. Born in Vienna, Austria, in 1883, Lowie had come with his family to New York in 1893. After growing up in a German-American neighborhood where he was nurtured on "the classic German tradition of liberalism," Lowie studied biology at the College of the City of New York, flirted with chemistry, and tried his hand at psychology before he was "corralled" into Boas's seminars on statistics and Indian languages. In Boas, Lowie found the nearest American equivalent to Ernst Mach, the Austrian physicist and philosopher of science whose "positivistic chastity," tough-mindedness, and opposition to systems and the supernatural he revered. From Boas, Lowie derived a conception of anthropology as "a science which requires the same logical and psychological processes as any of the supposedly more exact sciences."[111]

As one of the thirty American intellectuals who appraised American civilization in *Civilization in the United States*, Lowie characterized American science as more of "a hothouse growth" than "an organic product of our soil" – a condition that he blamed on the relative scarcity of "cultivated [American] laymen" interested in "scientific books requiring concentrated thought or supplying large bodies of fact."[112] Yet, even as he regretted the small size of

[110] James Steel Smith, "The Day of the Popularizers: The 1920s," *South Atlantic Quarterly* 62 (1963): 297–309; Higham, *History*, 73–75; Rubin, *The Making of Middlebrow Culture*; Janice Radway, "The Scandal of the Middlebrow: The Book of the Month Club, Class Fracture, and Cultural Authority," *South Atlantic Quarterly* 89 (1990): 703–736.
[111] Robert H. Lowie, "Autobiographical Data by Robert H. Lowie," in *Lowie's Selected Papers in Anthropology*, 13; Lowie, *Robert H. Lowie, Ethnologist*, 1–3; Robert H. Lowie to Wilbur K. Thomas, 14 November 1935, Lowie Papers, box 2; Robert H. Lowie, "Ernst Mach," *New Republic*, 9 April 1916, 335–337; Paul Radin, "Robert H. Lowie, 1883–1957," *American Anthropologist* 60 (1958): 358–361; Robert F. Murphy, *Robert H. Lowie* (New York: Columbia University Press, 1972), 10, 42–43.
[112] Robert H. Lowie, "Science," in *Civilization in the United States*, 151–161, on 155, 160.

the cultivated minority in America, Lowie condemned the European "spirit of caste." Writing in *Century* magazine in April 1925, he asked "Is America So Bad, After All?" His answer was no, decidedly not. In Europe, Lowie explained, Matthew Arnold's "sweetness and light" for the cultivated was "accompanied by squalor and misery for the many." The difference between Europe and America thus boiled down to the difference between aristocracy and standardization. Those Americans who fled standardization at home by going to Europe in quest of "respect for the individual as such" were "bound for a rude awakening." For in Europe they would encounter "a spirit of snobbishness and a servility bred by ages of forced hallelujahs to the upper classes."[113]

In addition to publishing a dozen brief articles on anthropology in the *American Mercury* between 1924 and 1933, Lowie wrote three books for popular audiences. In *Primitive Religion* (1924), he substituted "a genial attitude toward" religion for his youthful "anticlericalism."[114] In *The Origin of the State* (1927), his delineation of political and cultural continuities from primitive society to civilization convinced the English observer Harold Laski that "the sooner we seek to grasp the central results of anthropological research, the better for understanding [the problems we confront]."[115] In *Are We Civilized?* (1929), Lowie's marshaling of examples of the "irrationalism" of scientists and other "non-clerical writers" convinced one reviewer that "the difference between savagery and civilization is merely one of degrees, not of principle." Another reviewer admired the way in which Lowie's "close juxtaposition" of "savage and civilized practices" pierced "the clannish provincialisms and shallow, swaggering ethnocentrisms of civilized man."[116]

THE DRIFT OF AMERICAN CULTURE

Edward Sapir was not only an accomplished musician and a published poet; he was also a trenchant critic of American culture, sensitively attuned to the "fundamental conflict" between inherited European notions and "the actual conditions of life in America." The son of a cantor, Sapir was born in Pomerania in 1884. Brought to the United States in 1889, Sapir was raised in Richmond, Virginia, and New York City. As the winner of a scholarship to Columbia, Sapir earned a B.A. and M.A. in German. While taking courses in linguistics from

---

[113] Robert H. Lowie, "Is America So Bad After All?" *Century*, April 1925, 723–729, on 726–727.
[114] Robert H. Lowie, *Primitive Religion* (New York: Boni and Liveright, 1924); Lowie, *Robert H. Lowie, Ethnologist*, 134.
[115] Robert H. Lowie, *The Origin of the State* (New York: Harcourt, 1927); Harold J. Laski, "The Primitive State," review of *The Origin of the State*, *Nation*, 7 December 1927, supplement, 658.
[116] Robert H. Lowie, *Are We Civilized?* (New York: Harcourt, 1929); Berthold Laufer, review of *Are We Civilized?*, *American Anthropologist* 32 (1930): 161–162; Bernhard J. Stern, "The History of Human Culture," review of *Are We Civilized?*, *Current History* 31 (1929): 218.

Boas, Sapir became convinced of the urgency of salvage ethnology. He would eventually record the grammars of some thirty-nine Native American languages.[117]

In 1916, Sapir responded to John Dewey's call for a "specifically American revision of our ideal of culture" by condemning the "readiness" with which American intellectuals deplored the absence of "specifically American traits" in their own culture. This pathetic readiness, according to Sapir, rested on the "geographical fallacy" that America, because it was geographically separate from Europe, must necessarily possess a culture of its own. What many American intellectuals ignored was the dependence of American culture on both "historical antecedents" and "foreign influences." As long as most Americans continued to come from Europe and to speak English as their first language, American culture would remain a variant of English culture. Accordingly, Sapir urged his fellow intellectuals to renounce their vain efforts "to create an exclusively American product" and, instead, to dedicate themselves to revising "the cultural standards of the Occidental world, and more particularly of the English-speaking part of it."[118]

Sapir published his most searching analysis of American culture, "Culture, Genuine and Spurious," in the pages of the *American Journal of Sociology* in 1924, after segments had appeared in the *Dial* and the *Dalhousie Review,* in 1919 and 1922, respectively.[119] He began by distinguishing among three common meanings of the word culture: the anthropological meaning, which conceived of culture as the totality of "socially inherited element[s] in the life of man, material or spiritual"; the humanistic meaning, which identified culture with "individual refinement"; and the romantic nationalistic meaning, which made culture "nearly synonymous with the 'spirit' or 'genius' of a people." By combining the humanistic and the romantic nationalistic meanings, Sapir arrived at a literary-tinged conception of culture comprising "those general attitudes, views of life, and specific manifestations of civilization that give a particular people its distinctive place in the world." Yet culture, Sapir reminded

[117] Regna Darnell, *Edward Sapir: Linguist, Anthropologist, Humanist* (Berkeley: University of California Press, 1990); A. L. Kroeber, "Reflections on Edward Sapir, Scholar and Man," in *Edward Sapir: Appraisals of His Life and Work,* ed. Konrad Koerner (Amsterdam: John Benjamins, 1984), 131–132; Edgar E. Siskin, "The Life and Times of Edward Sapir," *Jewish Social Studies* 48 (1986): 283–293; Regna Darnell and Judith T. Irvine, "Edward Sapir: January 26, 1884-February 4, 1939," *Proceedings of the National Academy of Sciences* (1997): 281–300.

[118] Edward Sapir, "Culture in the Melting-Pot," *Nation,* supplement, 21 December 1916, 1–2. On Sapir, see Richard Handler, "Vigorous Male and Aspiring Female: Poetry, Personality, and Culture in Edward Sapir and Ruth Benedict," in *Malinowski, Rivers, Benedict and Others,* 127–155; Richard Handler, "Anti-Romantic Romanticism: Edward Sapir and the Critique of American Individualism," *Anthropological Quarterly* 62 (1989): 1–13.

[119] Edward Sapir, "Civilization and Culture," *Dial,* 20 September 1919, 233–236; Edward Sapir, "Culture, Genuine and Spurious," *Dalhousie Review* 2 (1922): 165–178; Edward Sapir, "Culture in New Countries," *Dalhousie Review* 2 (1922): 358–368.

his readers, was not synonymous with civilization: civilization "moves on," but culture "comes and goes."[120]

Sapir went on to distinguish a "genuine" culture from a "spurious" one. Echoing Van Wyck Brooks's call for locating a genial middle ground between the highbrow and the lowbrow in American culture, he defined a genuine culture as neither high nor low, but "inherently harmonious, balanced, self-satisfactory." As a "healthy spiritual organism" without "the dry rot of social habit," a genuine culture precluded any "sense of frustration" by eliciting "the creative participation of the members of a community."[121]

When appraised by the standards of a genuine culture, American culture was "superficial, discordant, [and] empty" – in a word, spurious. A ramifying division of labor and American worship of efficiency condemned the vast majority of Americans to "boring, mechanized, and unfulfilling work." In a move reminiscent of Matthew Arnold, Sapir cited the "telephone girl" as an illustration of "the great cultural fallacy of industrialism," the "harnessing" of the "majority of mankind to its machines." However efficient her routinized work, it answered "to no spiritual needs of her own." Left unfulfilled by her work, the telephone girl sought escape in the acquisition of "cultural goods" that she could flaunt as badges of status. Yet whenever a culture became more of a "manner" than a "way of life," it ceased to be genuine. No wonder that the "spiritual selves" of millions of Americans were going "hungry, for the most part, pretty much all the time."[122]

As a foil of Americans' spurious culture, Sapir celebrated the "well-rounded" life of the Native American who solved "the economic problem with salmon-spear and rabbit snare." The Native American might operate "on a relatively low level of civilization," yet Sapir deemed his solution to the problem of culture "incomparably higher" than that of the telephone girl; unlike her, he experienced no "spiritual frustration." Instead of "standing out as a desert patch of merely economic effort in the whole of life," the Native American's work fitted in "naturally with all the rest of [his] activities."[123]

When it came time to assay the prospects for "build[ing] a genuine American culture," Sapir was less optimistic than Van Wyck Brooks and Randolph Bourne, both of whom he admired. Although he conceded that "great cultures,"

---

[120] Edward Sapir, "Culture, Genuine and Spurious," *American Journal of Sociology* (1924): 401–429; reprinted in *Selected Papers of Edward Sapir in Language, Culture and Personality*, 308–331, on 308, 311. Sapir's move dismayed Robert Lowie, who complained that Sapir "explicitly set aside the accepted technical definition of culture." Robert H. Lowie, "Comments on Edward Sapir, His Personality and Scholarship," in *Edward Sapir: Appraisals of His Life and Work*, 126.

[121] Sapir, "Genuine, Culture and Spurious," 314–316, 321. To William F. Ogburn, Sapir seemed "to be struggling to articulate something that [he felt] emotionally rather than coldly and scientifically." William F. Ogburn to Edward Sapir, 31 August 1922, quoted in Darnell, *Edward Sapir*, 149.

[122] Sapir, "Culture, Genuine and Spurious," 316.

[123] Sapir, "Culture, Genuine and Spurious," 316.

like those of Periclean Athens and Elizabethan England, were "perfectly conceivable in any type or stage of civilization," Sapir thought that they were more likely to appear where the machine had made few inroads and where there was, as a result, less danger of reducing "the individual to an unintelligible fragment of the social organism." He went on to dismiss the "curious notion" that a "new" country, such as the United States, was "especially favorable soil for the formation of a virile culture." People in new countries, he pointed out, were preoccupied with obtaining "the immediate ends of existence." Eventually, perhaps, Americans' "geographically widespread culture, of little depth or individuality," might give way to a genuine culture. Until then, Sapir recommended that Americans draw sustenance from the "localized," "autonomous cultures" that already existed in places like Greenwich Village and Taos.[124]

Ironically, in *Language* (1921), the only book he ever wrote for a popular audience, Sapir observed that the "drift" of the American language and, by extension, American culture, was away from England toward "autonomous and distinctive developments" and "immersion in the larger European culture." By drift, Sapir had in mind unconscious sound patterns that moved a language in a definite direction in accordance with its "genius." To illustrate what he admitted was a "somewhat mystical" concept, Sapir cited the tendency of Americans English-speakers to replace "whom" with "who" in the question "who do you see?" Insofar as America was "still specifically 'English'" in the early 1920s, it seemed to Sapir to be so "only colonially or vestigially." In both language and culture, America was drifting away from England.[125]

LESSONS FROM THE SOUTH SEAS

As an "artist" gifted with what Alfred Kroeber described as "intellectualized but strong sensationalism" and "a higher order of intuitiveness," Margaret Mead brought home to educated Americans, better than any other American

[124] Sapir, "Culture, Genuine and Spurious," 318, 321, 328, 330. Sapir admired Randolph Bourne's "exquisite sensibility to the esthetic in literature, to the nuances of thought and feeling and expression," and Brooks's "critical writing." Edward Sapir, "Randolph Bourne," *Dial*, 11 January 1919, 45; Edward Sapir to Robert H. Lowie, 14 March 1922, in *Letters from Edward Sapir to Robert H. Lowie*, ed. Luella Cole (Berkeley: privately published, 1965), 52.
[125] Edward Sapir to Robert H. Lowie, 8 April, 19 April, 23 May 1921, in *Letters from Edward Sapir to Robert H. Lowie*, 46–48; Edward Sapir, *Language* (1921; repr., New York: Harcourt, 1955), iii, 149–154, 159–160, 183. On drift, see Kroeber and Kluckhohn, *Culture*, 183; Richard J. Preston, "Sapir's Conception of Drift as a Cultural Process," in *Papers from the Sixth Annual Congress, Canadian Ethnological Society, 1979* (Ottawa: National Museums of Canada, 1981), 213–219; Yakov Malkiel, "Drift, Slope, and Slant: Background of, and Variations upon, a Sapirian Theme," *Language* 57 (1981): 535–570; Michael Silverstein, "The Diachrony of Sapir's Linguistic Description; or, Sapir's 'Cosmographical' Linguistics," in *New Perspectives in Language, Culture, and Personality*, ed. William Cowan, Michael K. Foster, and Konrad Koerner (Amsterdam: John Benjamins, 1986), 67–110.

anthropologist of her generation, the lessons anthropology had to teach. By eschewing jargon and describing what she saw as vividly as possible, she mediated between "high erudition and the middle-brow mind" while instructing her readers on adolescence, sex, education, and other current concerns. Indeed, as a "genetic-brand" intellectual who thought "what everyone else was thinking," Mead became, arguably, "America's self-consciousness."[126] The eldest of the four surviving children of an economist who taught at the University of Pennsylvania and a feminist who took her along on fieldwork in sociology, Mead was born in 1901. Educated at DePauw University and Barnard College, where she majored in psychology, Mead became convinced of the urgency of salvage ethnology and decided to become an anthropologist.[127]

Mead's primary goal, in the first two decades of a long career that extended until her death in 1978, was to combat all absolutist explanations of human nature by documenting the "malleability" of human nature. Far from being rigid and unyielding, human nature, she maintained, was "extraordinarily adaptable." By the late 1930s, Mead had largely accomplished her goal, thanks in large part to the popular success of three books published between 1928 and 1935. All three grappled with "the problem of how the human character is moulded by the diverse cultural settings into which human beings, cultureless and flexible, are born." All three also testified to "the dominance of culture forms over 'innate character.'"[128]

In 1928, Mead published *Coming of Age in Samoa*, an account of her nine months of fieldwork on the island of Ta'u in American Samoa in 1925–26. Dispatched by Boas to see whether "the difficulties of puberty" would be found in a culture without American "inhibitions," Mead discovered that the Samoan girls' easygoing relations with parents and freedom to experiment sexually

[126] Alfred Kroeber, review of *Growing Up in New Guinea*, *American Anthropologist* 33 (1931): 248; Winthrop Sargeant, "It's All Anthropology," *New Yorker*, 30 December 1961, 31–32, 36; David Dempsey, "The Mead and Her Message: Some Field Notes on an Anthropological Phenomenon," *New York Times Magazine*, 26 April 1970, 23, 74, 79; Nancy C. Lutkehaus, "Margaret Mead and the 'Rustling-of-the-Wind-in-the-Palm-Trees School' of Ethnographic Writing," in *Women Writing Culture*, ed. Ruth Behar and Deborah A. Gordon (Berkeley: University of California Press, 1995), 185–206; Peter M. Worsley, "Margaret Mead: Science or Science Fiction? Reflections of a British Anthropologist," *Science and Society* 21 (1957): 122–134; Clifford Geertz, "Margaret Mead, December 16, 1901–November 15, 1978," *Biographical Memoirs of the National Academy of Sciences* 58 (1989): 329–341; Marshall Sahlins, "Views of a Culture Heroine," *New York Times Book Review*, 26 August 1984. For biographical information, see Jane Howard, *Margaret Mead: A Life* (1984; repr., New York: Random House, 1985); Mary Catherine Bateson, *With A Daughter's Eye* (1984; repr., New York: Simon and Schuster, 1985); Lois W. Banner, *Intertwined Lives: Margaret Mead, Ruth Benedict, and Their Circle* (New York: Knopf, 2003); Nancy C. Lutkehaus, *Margaret Mead: The Making of an American Icon* (Princeton, N.J.: Princeton University Press, 2008).

[127] Margaret Mead, "Margaret Mead," in *A History of Psychology in Autobiography*, vol. 6, ed. Gardner Lindzey (New York: Prentice-Hall, 1974), 310–311; Margaret Mead, *Blackberry Winter: My Earlier Years* (New York: Simon and Schuster, 1972).

[128] Margaret Mead, preface to *From The South Seas: Studies of Adolescence and Sex in Primitive Societies* (New York: William Morrow, 1939), x.

allowed them to come of age without the anxiety and guilt "so frequently a cause of maladjustment among [American adolescents]." Relegating most of her technical information to appendices, Mead devoted the bulk of *Coming of Age in Samoa* to recapitulating the life cycle of the typical Samoan adolescent girl. But in the last two chapters, added at the prompting of her publisher, William Morrow, she examined American adolescence "in the light of Samoan contrasts." On the basis of this cross-cultural comparison, Mead reached two conclusions. First, if adolescence was "a time of stress and strain" in America, it was not because of anything inherent in adolescence but because American "cultural conditions" made it so. And second, in growing up amid "a double sex standard for men and women," American adolescents paid high, although unavoidable, prices for "the possibility of choice." Unfortunately, neither parents nor teachers taught American adolescents how to "choose wisely."[129]

Although *Coming of Age in Samoa* reminded Freda Kirchwey of the proverbial South Seas island to which "we run to escape conflicting standards, the difficulties of an age without faith, to find love which is free, easy, and satisfying," she wondered whether Americans would "exchange" their "unsatisfied desires and complicated choices for [the Samoan girl's] more even progress in the world." The *American Mercury*'s H. L. Mencken praised *Coming of Age in Samoa* as a "sweet story," but wished that Mead had "confined herself to an objective account of life in Samoa." Too much of what she said about "the woes of American high-school girls" had already been said before. Still, Mencken hoped that Mead's "methodology might be applied to an investigation of human existence nearer home."[130] (As we shall see in Chapter 2, Mencken was to welcome Robert and Helen Lynd's *Middletown* for turning the anthropological spotlight on Americans.)

Although nonspecialists hailed *Coming of Age in Samoa*, Mead's fellow anthropologists were more ambivalent. Franz Boas thought that Mead's "observations" were "very good," even though she had written her concluding chapters "for popular presentation." Elsie Clews Parsons conceded that Mead "did not have to go to Samoa" to analyze "what is lacking in our culture," but predicted that Mead's "Samoan comparisons" would give her book "great authenticity as a best seller." George Dorsey hailed *Coming of Age in Samoa* for the light it threw on "love's coming of age in Vienna and all points west in civilization." Robert Lowie welcomed *Coming of Age in Samoa* as a notable departure from "the conventional descriptive pattern" of ethnographies: instead of depicting the round of Samoan life, Mead concentrated on the "adjustment" of adolescent girls to Samoan culture. Although he found Mead's

[129] Franz Boas to Margaret Mead, 14 July 1925, Boas Papers; Franz Boas to Elsie Clews Parsons, 28 March 1926, quoted in Deacon, *Elsie Clews Parsons*, 254; Franz Boas to William F. Ogburn, 15 October 1935, Boas Papers; Margaret Mead, *Coming of Age in Samoa: A Psychological Study of Primitive Youth for Western Civilization* (1928; repr., New York: William Morrow, 1971), 201, 234, 244, 246–247.

[130] Freda Kirchwey, "Sex in the South Seas," *Nation*, 24 October 1928, 42; H. L. Mencken, "Adolescence," *American Mercury*, November 1928, 379–380.

"pedagogical sermonizing" distasteful, Lowie was convinced by her "graphic picture[s]" of "Polynesian free love" and "child life." To Robert Redfield, however, *Coming of Age in Samoa* seemed more of a "laboratory exercise" than an "anthropological monograph." Mead, he said, "hardly sketched" the "cultural milieu" and described only "as much of Samoan culture" as was "necessary to solve the problem," adolescent adjustment, she had set herself.[131]

In 1930, Mead published *Growing Up in New Guinea*, an account of her eight months of fieldwork among the Manus of the Admiralty Islands in 1928–29. The Manus, as Mead depicted them, bore an uncanny resemblance to middle-class Americans: they were hard-working and extremely competitive, worshiped property and material success, deferred gratification, possessed a strong sense of sin, and lacked imagination. But in an inversion of customary American parental roles, Manus fathers nurtured children while Manus mothers enforced their obedience. Just as "heartily spoiled" as American children, Manus children grew up "without responsibility in, or even familiarity with the adult work," to become "grasping, competitive" adults. In the book's concluding chapters, Mead examined American education from a cross-cultural perspective. Like Manus children, American children grew up to become unhappy adults because their parents failed to "equip them to grow up graciously."[132]

[131] Franz Boas to Elsie Clews Parsons, 26 October 1928; Elsie Clews Parsons to Franz Boas, 23 October 1928, Boas Papers; George Dorsey, "Natural or Savage?" *New York Herald Tribune Books*, 2 September 1928; Robert H. Lowie, review of *Coming of Age in Samoa*, *American Anthropologist* 31 (1929): 532–34; Robert Redfield, review of *Coming of Age in Samoa*, *American Journal of Sociology* 34 (1929): 728–730. In 1983, fifty-five years after the publication of *Coming of Age in Samoa* and five years after Mead's death, the New Zealand anthropologist Derek Freeman published an exposé of her Samoan fieldwork in which he accused her of having gone to Samoa without preparation but with an agenda: to wit, to find a "negative case" on the basis of which the Boasians could deny that human behavior had any biological dimension. Spending too little time in the field, never mastering the native language, and allowing herself to be "duped" by her adolescent informants, Mead misrepresented Samoan life as a tropical paradise. Drawing on his own extensive fieldwork in Samoa, Freeman depicted the Samoans as competitive, violent, and puritanical. Widely promoted by Harvard University Press, Freeman's book, *Margaret Mead and Samoa*, provoked a spirited response from numerous anthropologists. While admitting that Mead might have romanticized the Samoans, they denied that she had been deceived by her informants or that she had somehow been "unscientific." Mead, they said, was a "smart and penetrating observer" whose fieldwork was sound. If Freeman found more stress and conflict among the Samoans than Mead did, his findings reflected the "personal equation" in fieldwork, not any errors by Mead. Derek Freeman, *Margaret Mead and Samoa: The Making and Unmaking of an Anthropological Myth* (1983; repr., New York: Penguin Books, 1984); Lowell Holmes, "A Tale of Two Studies," *American Anthropologist* 85 (1983): 929–935; Bradd Shore, "Paradox Regained: Freeman's *Margaret Mead and Samoa*," *American Anthropologist* 85 (1983): 935–944. See also Annette B. Weiner, "Ethnographic Determinism: Samoa and the Margaret Mead Controversy," *American Anthropologist* 85 (1983): 909–919; David M. Schneider, "The Coming of a Sage to Samoa," *Natural History*, June 1983, 4–10; Colin M. Turnbull, "Trouble in Paradise," *New Republic*, 28 March 1983, 32–34.

[132] Margaret Mead, *Growing Up in New Guinea: A Comparative Study of Primitive Education* (1930; repr., New York: William Morrow, 1975).

Mead's cross-cultural comparison elicited a lot of comment from reviewers. As an anonymous reviewer pointed out in the *New York Times Book Review*, "Manus civilization and our own" both respected "wealth" and the "man of property," lacked "a native culture," and failed to teach their children the "discipline and adjustment" that adulthood demanded. To Isidor Schneider, writing in the *New Republic*, Mead's description of Manus society "sounded like a bitter satire of American life": trade "obsesse[d]" the Manus, "concern over property" made them "peevish and quarrelsome," and they appeared to be "the Puritans of Oceania." "Why should a highly complex civilization be compared with a relatively simple one?" asked Alan Burton Clarke in the *Bookman*. Clarke thought that Mead's comparison of Manus civilization and American civilization was "rather exaggerated."[133] While defending Mead's cross-cultural comparison as "not mere filler, but an integral result of her method and legitimate part of her scheme," Alfred Kroeber criticized her failure to marshal more ethnographic and historical "documentation" in support of some of her generalizations. Had Mead's "artistic inspiration," Kroeber wondered, run out after her "main work," ethnographic description, was done? Kroeber's criticism was echoed by the sociologist Nels Anderson and by Melville Herskovits, both of whom expressed skepticism about the "lessons" Mead drew from Manus for "our civilization."[134]

In 1935, Mead published *Sex and Temperament in Three Primitive Societies*. In eighteen months of fieldwork among the Arapesh, Mundugumor, and Tchambuli peoples of New Guinea in 1931–33, she investigated the extent to which temperamental differences between the sexes were innate and the extent to which they were culturally determined. Neither the Arapesh nor the Mundugumor, Mead reported, drew a sharp distinction between the temperaments of men and women. Where the Arapesh idealized "the mild, responsive man married to the mild, responsive woman," the Mundugumor idealized "the violent aggressive man married to the violent aggressive woman." The Tchambuli, by contrast, resembled Americans in the sharp distinction they drew between the temperaments of men and women. But in an inversion of Americans' customary "sex-attitudes," the Tchambuli woman was "the dominant, impersonal, managing partner," the man "the less responsible and the emotionally dependent person." Mead's findings suggested that "if those temperamental attitudes which we [Americans] have traditionally regarded as feminine" ("passivity, responsiveness, and a willingness to cherish children") could, in one tribe standardized "as the masculine pattern," yet in another

[133] [Anonymous], "Primitive Life in New Guinea," *New York Times Book Review*, 16 November 1930; Isidor Schneider, "Manus and Americans," *New Republic*, 5 November 1930, 329–330; Alan Burton Clarke, review of *Growing Up in New Guinea, Bookman* 72 (1930): 196–197.

[134] A. L. Kroeber, review of *Growing Up in New Guinea*, 249–250; Nels Anderson, review of *Growing Up in New Guinea, Survey*, 15 November 1930, 228; Melville J. Herskovits, "Primitive Childhood," *Nation*, 4 February 1931, 131–132.

tribe "be outlawed for the majority of women as well as for the majority of men," there was no longer "any basis for regarding such aspects of behavior as sex-linked." Rather, they were "socially produced." The lesson that Mead drew from her fieldwork was that instead of forcing children to conform to a single pattern of behavior, American parents should allow them to find 'congenial' patterns in which their individual temperaments could find expression.[135]

Mead's point in *Sex and Temperament* that human nature was "almost unbelievably malleable" convinced nonspecialists such as John Chamberlain that "the human organism is infinitely pliable, infinitely malleable, infinitely elastic," and Jeanette Mirsky that the "misfits" of American society resulted from "assigning definite and different traits to the sexes" and from "setting a single pattern for men and women." Florence Finch Kelley hailed Mead as "a dangerous person" who shattered "the complacent, fundamental conviction of the Occidental world, both scientific and social, that the sexes are innately different in their psychological attributes and that the male is dominant by the right of brain and brawn." Malcolm Cowley welcomed *Sex and Temperament* as a sign that anthropologists were "coming home" to apply "their desert and jungle lore to the tribal cultures of the German blond Nordics and the white Protestant 100-percent American he-men." So convincing did Cowley find Mead's demonstration of the lack of any "real connection" between sex and temperament and "her emphasis on the infinite adaptability of human nature" that he concluded that "nothing is humanly impossible."[136] Although Joseph Wood Krutch suspected that Mead went into the field with "a thesis to prove," he praised the "entertainment value" of *Sex and Temperament*, which combined "the charm of 'Gulliver's Travels' and 'Erewhon' with that of 'Alice in Wonderland.'"[137]

Specialists, though, remarked on the serendipity of Mead's findings. Indeed, her findings seemed to William F. Ogburn "almost too good to be true." Hortense Powdermaker pointed out that neither "cultural relativity" nor the idea that men and women follow "culturally assigned" roles was a new idea. While praising Mead for the light she threw on "how an individual takes on his cultural role," Powdermaker criticized her elision of "genital differences." Richard Thurnwald warned that Mead's "attempt to mingle anthropological research with educational planning" risked leading "the student in anthropology astray."

[135] Margaret Mead, *Sex and Temperament in Three Primitive Societies* (1935; repr., New York: William Morrow, 1980), ix, xiv, 164, 279–280, 310, 321; Margaret Mead, "A Reply to a Review of 'Sex and Temperament in Three Primitive Societies,'" *American Anthropologist* 39 (1937): 558–561.
[136] John Chamberlain, "The World in Books," *Current History* 42 (1935): v; Jeanette Mirsky, "Patterns and Misfits," *Survey*, October 1935, 315; Florence Finch Kelley, "A Challenging View of the Sexes," *New York Times Book Review*, 26 May 1935; Malcolm Cowley, "News from New Guinea," *New Republic*, 5 June 1937, 107.
[137] Joseph Wood Krutch, "Men and Women," *Nation*, 39 May 1935, 634.

Outraged by Mead's failure to document her "statement[s] on subjective attitudes," Robert Lowie "alternate[d] between depression and towering rage."[138]

PATTERNS OF AMERICAN CULTURE

Where Mead used cross-cultural comparison to diagnose problems in contemporary American life, Ruth Fulton Benedict domesticated the connotation of "patterning" long integral to the German conception of *Kultur*.[139] Left fatherless at the age of two in 1889, Benedict escaped from an unhappy childhood into an imaginary world, her sense of alienation heightened by an attack of the measles that left her partially deaf. After studying English literature and writing poetry at Vassar College, she underwent a crisis of vocation before marrying Stanley Benedict, a research chemist at Cornell Medical College. In 1919, Benedict escaped from an unhappy, childless marriage by taking courses from Alexander Goldenweiser at the New School for Social Research.[140]

Benedict discovered patterning while working on a library-based dissertation on the "Guardian Spirit" among Southwestern tribes. "Man," she concluded in 1923, "builds up his culture out of disparate elements, combining and recombining them."[141] While collecting myths and folktales among the Pueblo peoples in 1925, Benedict acquired "a great fondness" for the American Southwest. For her, the wholeness of Pueblo culture stood in dramatic contrast to a fragmented American civilization.[142]

Forced by her partial deafness to work through interpreters, Benedict dealt more authoritatively with literary texts than with informants. From German texts in particular, Benedict derived a number of concepts that were to figure

[138] William F. Ogburn to Margaret Mead, 29 April 1935, Margaret Mead Papers, Manuscripts Division, Library of Congress, Courtesy of the Institute for Intercultural Studies, Inc. (hereafter Mead Papers), box 18; Hortense Powdermaker, "Primitive Ideals for Men and Women," *Saturday Review of Literature*, 29 June 1935, 16; Richard C. Thurnwald, review of *Sex and Temperament in Three Primitive Societies*, *American Anthropologist* 38 (1936): 666–667; Robert H. Lowie to William F. Ogburn, 3 October 1935, Lowie Papers, box 2.

[139] Robert F. Berkhofer, Jr., "Clio and the Culture Concept: Some Impressions of a Changing Relationship in American Historiography," in *The Idea of Culture in the Social Sciences*, ed. Louis Schneider and Charles Bonjean (Cambridge: Cambridge University Press, 1973), 79.

[140] Judith Schacter Modell, *Ruth Benedict: Patterns of a Life* (Philadelphia: University of Pennsylvania Press, 1983); Margaret M. Caffrey, *Ruth Benedict: Stranger in This Land* (Austin: University of Texas Press, 1989); Banner, *Intertwined Lives*; Virginia Heyer Young, *Ruth Benedict: Beyond Relativity, Beyond Pattern* (Lincoln: University of Nebraska Press, 2005).

[141] Ruth Benedict, "The Concept of Guardian Spirit in North America," *Memoirs of the American Anthropological Association* 29 (1923): 84–85.

[142] Ruth Benedict, *Patterns of Culture* (1934; repr., Boston: Houghton, 1959), 260–261; Ruth Benedict, *Zuñi Mythology* (New York: Columbia University Press, 1935), xxxix; Ruth Benedict to Margaret Mead, 6 August 1925, quoted in Mead, *An Anthropologist at Work*, 291; Barbara A. Babcock, "'A New Mexican Rebecca': Imagining Pueblo Women," *Journal of the Southwest* 32 (1990): 401*n*.

prominently in her work. From Friedrich Nietzsche's *The Birth of Tragedy*, she took the terms "Apollonian" and "Dionysian," which she applied to "personality types" in the Southwest; from Wilhelm Dilthey's philosophy of history, the concept of *Lebensstimmungen* (life moods), which reinforced her belief in the incommensurability of cultures; from Wilhelm Worringer's *Formprobleme der Gotik* (*Form Problems of the Gothic*), the analogy between the unconscious development of an art style and the unconscious development of a cultural pattern; and from Oswald Spengler's *The Decline of the West*, the notion of "destiny ideas," which she eventually converted into, first, "configurations," then "patterns."[143]

In 1929, Benedict described the project that was to engage her until her death in 1948: she would make Americans "culture-conscious." Anthropologists, she told the readers of the *Century* magazine, had learned two lessons from fieldwork, their "laboratory of custom": first, that man was "the culture-building animal," and second, that cultures "grow up blindly, the useful and the cumbersome together." Even though men and women could not do without culture because it invested them with "a common symbolism, a common religion, and a common set of values to pursue," every culture was burdened by "compulsions." Among the compulsions that burdened American culture were "warfare," wage-earners' "dissatisfaction and frustration," and the "overdevelopment of acquisitiveness." Benedict, however, held out the hope that in becoming culture-conscious, Americans would come to use their intelligence to guide culture change and, in the process, acquire "respect" for the "epic" of American culture.[144]

By August 1932, Benedict had begun work on a popular book in which she would evoke "the contrasting configurations of culture in different societies" along the lines of Spengler's destiny ideas. Much easier to discern in primitive cultures than in more complex ones, these configurations illuminated the "workings of culture." Because anthropologists had been so slow to provide "more than a perfunctory outline of [any] particular culture," Benedict decided to bring out in relief the distinctive features of three contrasting cultures. By September 1933, she had chosen a title for her book. For "configurations," which was "clumsy" and "Latinized," Benedict substituted "patterns" – a word

[143] Ruth Benedict, "Psychological Types in the Cultures of the Southwest," *Proceedings. Twenty-third International Congress of Americanists, 1928* (1930), 527–581; reprinted in *An Anthropologist at Work*, 248–261; Benedict, *Patterns of Culture*, 50–54, 78–79; Virginia Wolf Briscoe, "Ruth Benedict, Anthropological Folklorist," *Journal of American Folklore* 92 (1979): 461; Judith Schacter, "'It is besides a pleasant English word': Ruth Benedict's Concept of Patterns Revisited," in *Reading Benedict/Reading Mead: Feminism, Race, and Imperial Visions*, ed. Dolores Janiewski and Lois W. Banner (Baltimore: Johns Hopkins University Press, 2004), 205–228.
[144] Ruth Fulton Benedict, "The Science of Custom: The Bearing of Anthropology on Contemporary Thought," *Century*, April 1929, 641–649.

that not only had already been "used in the sense" she intended, but was "a pleasant English word" besides.[145]

Published in 1934, *Patterns of Culture* began with the story of the Digger Indian Ramon. "In the beginning," Ramon said, "God gave to every people a cup, a cup of clay, and from this cup they drank their life. They all dipped in the water, but the cups were different. Our cup is broken now. It has passed away." In telling Ramon's story, Benedict implied that cultures varied in coherence.[146]

Although varying in coherence, all cultures, Benedict suggested, were necessarily selective. From an "arc of cultural possibilities" on which were "ranged the possible interests provided either by the human age-cycle or by the environment or by man's various activities," certain characteristics were selected for recognition, standardization, and elaboration. For in culture, as in language, selection was "the prime necessity." Any culture that "capitalized" on more than a few segments of the arc of cultural possibilities would prove to be as "unintelligible" as a language that made use of all possible sounds.[147] In accordance with their "unconscious canons of choice," cultures "made over" the traits they had selected into "consistent patterns." Because cultures amounted to "more than the sum of [their] traits," they must be studied not as "aggregates" or as "thing[s] of shreds and patches," but rather as "articulated wholes."[148]

Asserting that Americans could "most economically" understand their "own cultural processes" only "by a detour," Benedict delineated the contrasting patterns of the Zuñi of New Mexico, the Dobu of the South Pacific, and the Kwakiutl of Vancouver Island. In Benedict's eyes, the Zuñi, as an "Apollonian" people living within self-imposed bounds, stood out for their sobriety, moderation, and condemnation of individual assertiveness. The "Dionysian" Plains Indians, by contrast, glorified individuals who attempted "to break through" their five senses "into another order of experience" and valued the "illuminations of frenzy."[149] Benedict saw a remarkable resemblance between

[145] Ruth Benedict to Alfred A. Knopf, 25 August 1932, Ruth Fulton Benedict Papers, Special Collections, Vassar College Libraries (hereafter Benedict Papers), box 2, folder 14; Ruth Benedict to Ferris Greenslet, 16 September 1933, Benedict Papers, box 101, folder 1123. "Configurations" also carried a psychological connotation; "patterns" did not. Alfred Kroeber, review of *Patterns of Culture*, *American Anthropologist* 37 (1935): 689.
[146] Benedict, *Patterns of Culture*, 19; Sidney W. Mintz, "Enduring Substances, Trying Theories: The Caribbean Region as *Oikoumene*," *Journal of the Royal Anthropological Institute* 2 (1996): 304; Matthews, "Social Scientists and the Culture Concept," 93–94.
[147] Benedict, *Patterns of Culture*, 23, 34–36, 40; David F. Aberle, "The Influence of Linguistics on the Development of Early Culture and Personality Theory," in *Essays in the Science of Culture*, ed. Gertrude Dole and Robert Carneiro (New York: Crowell, 1960), 1–29; Regna Darnell, *Invisible Genealogies: A History of Americanist Anthropology* (Lincoln: University of Nebraska Press, 2001), 193; Fred H. Matthews, "The Revolt against Americanism: Cultural Pluralism and Cultural Relativism as an Ideology of Liberation," *Canadian Review of American Studies* 1 (1970): 19.
[148] Benedict, *Patterns of Culture*, 42, 46–48; Franz Boas, introduction to *Patterns of Culture*, xvii.
[149] Benedict, *Patterns of Culture*, 73, 91, 95.

the Dobu and Americans' Puritan ancestors: both groups were dour, prudish, jealous, and fiercely exclusive "in ownership." Yet, unlike the Puritans, the Dobu engaged in prenuptial promiscuity and esteemed "sex passion and technique." The Dobu, moreover, were "paranoid": fearing "treachery," they resorted to "powerful magic" and even "potent poisons" in a "cut-throat struggle" with their neighbors.[150] To Benedict's mind, the "wasteful" rivalry of potlatches in which the "megalomaniac" Kwakiutl competed for status by seeing who could give the most goods away parodied conspicuous consumption among Americans.[151]

Patterns of Culture ended with a plea for tolerance for difference. Benedict contrasted the situation of individuals whose "congenital responses" fell in that arc of behavior capitalized by their culture, who thus felt "favored" and "at home" in their culture, with that of individuals who were marginalized, if not deemed "abnormal," because their congenital responses were "not supported." Normality and abnormality, she suggested, were thus relative. In some Native American cultures, the same homosexuals who were stigmatized in mainstream American culture played honored roles as *berdache* ("men-women"). Looking on the anthropological axiom of cultural relativism as "a doctrine of hope," Benedict declared "social thinking at the present time" had "no more important task before it than that of taking account of cultural relativity."[152]

Patterns of Culture proved to be the best received of all anthropological works published between the wars. In the words of an anonymous reviewer in the *New York Times Book Review*, Benedict's book revealed how "the sciences no longer work alone." For a "quartet of sciences, anthropology, sociology, psychology, and philosophy" was "responsible for" *Patterns of Culture*. In the *Springfield Republican*, Dorothy Hopkins placed *Patterns of Culture* on the "list of writings which suggest intelligent means toward desired social and political changes."[153] Melville Herskovits praised Benedict's "incisive style" and "great felicity of phrasing." Alfred Kroeber commended the "insight, dignity, and charged style" with which Benedict reached out to "the audience of cultivated intelligence generally." Although critical of Benedict's "tabloid description[s]" of the Zuñi, Dobu, and Kwakiutl, Raymond Firth thought that her cross-cultural comparisons gave "precision and a greater validation to generalizations formed initially on the basis of a study of a single community."[154]

---

[150] Benedict, *Patterns of Culture*, 155, 158.
[151] Benedict, *Patterns of Culture*, 182, 188–189, 197, 217.
[152] Benedict, *Patterns of Culture*, 249, 258, 263–264.
[153] [Anonymous], review of *Patterns of Culture*, *New York Times Book Review*, 21 October 1934; Dorothy Hopkins, review of *Patterns of Culture*, *Springfield Republican*, 11 November 1934.
[154] Melville J. Herskovits, "Three Types of Civilization," *New York Herald Tribune Books*, 28 October 1936; Kroeber, review of *Patterns of Culture*, 689–690; Raymond Firth, review of *Patterns of Culture*, *Man* 36 (1936): 31–32.

As what Alfred Kroeber hailed as "propaganda for anthropology," but a later critic disparaged as "anthropology for the common man," *Patterns of Culture* eloquently conveyed what had by 1934 become conventional wisdom among American anthropologists: as Marshall Sahlins put it, "cultures are generally foreign in origin and local in pattern." In addition, *Patterns of Culture* signaled the profound change wrought in American thought by the Great Depression. No longer deploring the "maladjustments" produced by intangible culture lagging behind material culture, educated Americans increasingly viewed intangible culture as an envelope protecting them from the demoralizing loss of meaning that had befallen the Diggers.[155]

DOMESTICATING THE CULTURE CONCEPT

The Boasian campaign to make Americans culture-conscious benefited from the heightened cultural nationalism of the Great Depression. In the aftermath of the stock market crash of the fall of 1929, criticism of the standardization, materialism, and spuriousness of American culture gave way to curiosity about how it hung together amid unprecedented economic, social, and political strain at a time when industrial societies elsewhere were becoming polarized.[156] Indeed, the Depression spawned an enormous body of writing devoted to the American scene – art, reportage, social science, and history – that sought to document the American way of life. This national stock-taking, moreover, coincided with what Warren Susman termed the domestication of "the idea of culture," as educated Americans increasingly began to think of culture along anthropological lines.[157]

As the culture concept was domesticated, commentators viewed America in cultural terms, called attention to clashes between indigenous cultures, and adopted cultural approaches to their subjects. In their 1930 manifesto *I'll Take My Stand*, twelve Southern intellectuals defended the Southern "agrarian" way of life, rooted in "the soil," against the rootless "industrial" way of life

[155] Kroeber, review of *Patterns of Culture*, 689; Elgin Williams, "Anthropology for the Common Man," *American Anthropologist* 49 (1947): 84–90; Matthews, "Social Scientists and the Culture Concept," 90, 93–94; Berkhofer, "Clio and the Culture Concept," 79–82; Marshall Sahlins, "What Is Anthropological Enlightenment? Some Lessons of the Twentieth Century," in *Culture in Practice: Selected Essays* (New York: Zone Books, 2000), 515. Although *Patterns of Culture* sold fewer than 4,000 copies in its first five years in print, its sales benefited from the postwar paperback revolution, exceeding a million copies by 1964. David Dempsey, "What's in It for Authors?", *New York Times Book Review*, 5 January 1964.

[156] John Higham, "Having Together: Divergent Unities in American History," in *Hanging Together*, 3–21.

[157] William Stott, *Documentary Expression and Thirties America* (1973; repr., Chicago: University of Chicago Press, 1986); Alfred Kazin, *On Native Grounds: An Interpretation of Modern American Prose Literature* (1942; repr., San Diego: Harcourt, 1982), 485–518; Warren I. Susman, "The Culture of the Thirties," in *Culture as History: The Transformation of American Society in the Twentieth Century* (New York: Pantheon, 1984), 157, 154.

that prevailed elsewhere in America. The South, they asserted, was a "culture" in the European sense of the word. It was organic and homogeneous.[158] For yet another Southern intellectual, W. J. Cash, "the mind of the South" constituted "a very definite culture" that had been shaped over more than three centuries "by conscious and unconscious efforts" to protect the South from the encroachments of "the Yankee Mind, the Modern Mind, and the Negro." In *The Mind of the South* (1941), he traced the southern "mental pattern" to "a complex of established relationships and habits of thought, sentiments, prejudices, standards of values, and associations of ideas." In so doing, Cash distinguished "culture in its wide sense," his subject matter, from culture "in the narrow sense," the "intellectual and aesthetic attainments" on which rested the vaunted Southern claim to possessing a superior culture.[159]

Where Southern writers were preoccupied with the contemporaneous clash between agrarian and industrial ways of life, the historian Arthur Meier Schlesinger, Sr., reached back into the late nineteenth century to evoke a clash between "two cultures – one static, individualistic, agricultural, the other dynamic, collectivistic, urban." In *The Rise of the City, 1878–1898* (1933), he showed how America's "traditional rural culture" had disintegrated in the face of a dynamic urban culture in "close correlation" with the social, economic, and intellectual forces that brought about "new horizons, new attachments of interest, new views and new men."[160]

Inspired by the cultural relativism of both Johann Gottfried von Herder and Ruth Benedict, the folklorist Constance Rourke excavated a usable American past from sometimes obscure folkways. In *American Humor: A Study of National Character* (1931), she canvassed comic almanacs, joke books, song sheets, melodrama, vaudeville, and tall tales in an effort to show that "American vagaries" had "woven together a tradition which is various, subtle, sinewy, scant at times but not poor." In 1933, Rourke observed that it was unrealistic to expect "to achieve a mature, full-blown and aristocratic [American] literature at a stroke." A national literature depended, instead, on the "slow accretions of folk elements." Convinced of the existence of such "a deeply rooted, widespread folk expression," Rourke embarked on an ambitious cultural history of America that was cut short by her death in 1941. In a fragment from her unfinished manuscript, *The Roots of American Culture*, Rourke quoted Ruth

---

[158] Twelve Southerners, *I'll Take My Stand: The South and Agrarian Tradition* (1930; repr., Baton Rouge: Louisiana State University Press, 1977), xliv, xlvii, 3; Fred H. Matthews, "Role Models? The Continuing Relevance of the 'New York Intellectuals,'" *Canadian Review of American Studies* 19 (1988): 73.

[159] W. J. Cash to Blanche Knopf, 3 March 1930, quoted in Bruce Clayton, *W. J. Cash: A Life* (Baton Rouge, Louisiana State University Press, 1991), 93; W. J. Cash, *The Mind of the South* (1941; repr., New York: Vintage, 1960), viii, 94; Clayton, *W. J. Cash: A Life*, 127.

[160] Arthur Meier Schlesinger, Sr., *The Rise of the City, 1878–1898* (New York: Macmillan, 1933), 53, 57, 415. In a review of *The Rise of the City*, Henry Steele Commager praised Schlesinger's use of the term "culture" as "a corrective to the more conventional [belletristic] interpretation of 'culture.'" Henry Steele Commager, "Transition," *New Republic*, 6 July 1933, 215.

Benedict in support of her contention that "it is the whole configuration in the
particular period which is important." If Americans were truly "to appraise the
special qualities of [their] nascent culture," Rourke insisted that they pay at
least as much attention to "minor figures" and to "the culture of a group, a
town, a region" as they did to masterpieces.[161]

Americans became even more culture-conscious with the onset of what
Philip Gleason has called the "democratic revival" of the late 1930s and early
1940s. Responding to the rise of totalitarianism abroad, they celebrated the
American democratic way of life. This affirmation of America's democratic
heritage culminated in 1944 in the publication of *An American Dilemma*, a
monumental study of race relations in the United States commissioned by the
Carnegie Corporation and overseen by the Swedish economist Gunnar Myrdal.
In *An American Dilemma*, Myrdal depicted the contradiction between "the
American Creed," with its ringing endorsement of equality of opportunity,
and Americans' invidious racial practices.[162]

During the democratic revival, John Dewey appropriated the culture concept to ground democracy in a "culture of science." In *Freedom and Culture*
(1939), he argued that the culture concept not only ruled out of court the
existence of any inherent desire for freedom, but implied that the promotion
of freedom depended on the possession of the right kind of culture. What kind
of culture, then, was "so free in itself that it conceives and begets political
freedom as its accompaniment and consequence"? Could American culture,
Dewey asked, be engineered in such a way that it would become "a servant
and an evolving manifestation of democratic ideals"?[163]

M. L. Wilson, an agricultural economist who served as undersecretary of
agriculture during the New Deal, was "a rip-snorting pragmatist" who considered Dewey's *Freedom and Culture* "the best statement" of understanding of
democracy as a "cultural pattern." From his reading of anthropology, Wilson
derived skepticism toward the assertion that "'human nature' is unalterable," a
cultural approach that he applied to agriculture, and the notion of pattern. New
economic factors and technological devices had "thrown out of balance" the

[161] Constance Rourke, *American Humor: A Study of National Character* (1931; repr., Tallahassee:
Florida State University Press, 1986), xi; Constance Rourke, "The Significance of Sections,"
New Republic, 20 September 1933, 149; Constance Rourke, *The Roots of American Culture
and Other Essays*, ed. Van Wyck Brooks (New York: Harcourt, 1942), 49–51; Joan Shelley
Rubin, *Constance Rourke and American Culture* (Chapel Hill: University of North Carolina
Press, 1980).
[162] Philip Gleason, "Americans All" and "The Study of American Culture," in *Speaking of Diver-
sity: Language and Ethnicity in Twentieth-Century America* (Baltimore: Johns Hopkins Uni-
versity Press, 1992), 153–206; Purcell, *The Crisis of Democratic Theory*, 117–138, 179–231;
Walter A. Jackson, *Gunnar Myrdal and America's Conscience: Social Engineering and Racial
Liberalism, 1938–1987* (Chapel Hill: University of North Carolina Press, 1990).
[163] John Dewey, *Freedom and Culture* (New York: Putnam, 1939), 102, 124, 151, 153; David A.
Hollinger, "The Defense of Democracy and Robert K. Merton's Formulation of the Scientific
Ethos," in *Science, Jews, and Secular Culture: Studies in Mid-Twentieth-Century American
Intellectual History* (Princeton, N.J.: Princeton University Press, 1996), 80–96.

"essential unity and balance" of the American "agricultural pattern." Could America's "rural culture and the modern world of science and technology," he wondered, be brought back "into harmony"? Wilson turned to anthropology as "an integrated science of mankind that can tell us with scientific validity what man's fundamental nature is, and what his best environment should be." Wilson's contacts with anthropologists made him not only a proponent of the cultural approach but also a "missionary" for cultural anthropology. As an advocate of adult education, Wilson organized "Schools of Philosophy," four-to-five-day statewide conferences for Agricultural Extension Service workers and other local leaders, and, in the spring of 1938, sponsored a series of lectures on democracy within the U.S. Department of Agriculture in which Ruth Benedict gave one of the lectures. Indeed, Wilson told Benedict that the "first three or four chapters" of *Patterns of Culture* "state my fundamental social philosophy better than anything I know."[164]

In *Knowledge for What? The Place of Social Science in American Culture* (1939), Robert Lynd invoked the culture concept as a warrant for bringing all of American life within the domain of social science, asserting social scientists' prerogative to set their own research agendas, and ministering to the acute problems then facing Americans. Attracted by the "wholeness" and "interrelatedness" of culture "in the anthropologist's sense," Lynd explicitly rejected "culture in the refined sense of *belles letters* and sophisticated learning" in favor of a broad conception of culture as "all the things that a group of people inhabiting a common geographical area do, the ways they do things and the ways they think and feel about things, their material tools and their values and symbols." If social scientists conceived of culture as a whole, they would discover that nothing in American life escaped them, that "all the jumbled details of living" in the United States – "automotive assembly lines, Wall Street, sharecroppers, Supreme Court, Hollywood, and the Holy Rollers" – were "interacting parts in a single whole." And because its frame of reference was so "inclusive," the culture concept could serve as an integrating concept that would promote cross-fertilization among the social sciences.[165]

By 1939, a few American historians were beginning to appropriate the culture concept to fashion a new cultural history. In her introduction to *The Cultural Approach to History* (1940), a collection of papers from the preceding year's meetings of the American Historical Association, Caroline F. Ware

[164] M. L. Wilson, in *American Spiritual Biographies: Fifteen Self-Portraits*, ed. Louis Finkelstein (New York: Harper, 1948), 23n; M. L. Wilson, "Applied Science and Applied Folkways," in *Democracy Has Roots* (New York: Carrick and Evans, 1939), 49–50; M. L. Wilson, "Patterns of Rural Culture," in O. E. Baker, Ralph Borsodi, and M. L. Wilson, *Agriculture in Modern Life* (New York: Harper, 1939), 217–219, 227, 240; M. L. Wilson, *A Theory of Agricultural Democracy* (Washington: United States Department of Agriculture, 1941), 12; M. L. Wilson to Ruth Benedict, 6 November 1940, Mead Papers, box F6.

[165] Robert S. Lynd, *Knowledge for What? The Place of Social Science in American Culture* (1939; repr., Princeton, N.J.: Princeton University Press, 1970), 19–20, 50.

asserted that anthropology was the one discipline that had "necessarily freed itself from the frame of reference of western culture." She went on to note a number of potential uses to which historians could put the culture concept. By implying that any given society had to be seen as "an integral – though not necessarily a completely integrated – whole" characterized by a distinctive "pattern of behavior," the concept provided a warrant for holism. By giving historians "a basis for selection, organization, and interpretation" of their material, it solved the problem of selection that had bedeviled the New Historians. And by giving voice to the "inarticulate masses" and "nondominant cultural groups" of America, the culture concept sanctioned attempts to write history "from the bottom up."[166] Among the contributors to *The Cultural Approach to History* were Thomas C. Cochran, who cited *Patterns of Culture* as essential reading for any historian who wished to write "a comprehensive social history of the corporation"; Ralph E. Turner, who quoted Alexander Goldenweiser and Robert Lowie in support of his contention that the industrial city had traditionally functioned as "a center of culture change" in world history; and Ralph H. Gabriel and Merle Curti, who participated in a round-table on "The Flowering of New England."[167]

Although Ruth Benedict predicted that *The Cultural Approach to History* would "stimulate much valuable historical work," Crane Brinton thought that there was then little more to cultural history than "the history of wholes," which he thought "too vague, too fuzzy, to be of much use." Even though he was more sympathetic to Ware's conception of cultural history than was Brinton, Charles Beard could not imagine how historians could escape from their frame of reference. Beard, however, was prescient when he observed that "at this stage in the development of American thought about historiography" it was Ware's "controlling conception," more than any "specific fulfillments," that distinguished *The Cultural Approach to History*. As we shall see, the culture concept would inform both consensus history and the work of the myth–symbol school of American studies after 1945.[168]

---

[166] Caroline F. Ware, introduction to *The Cultural Approach to History*, ed. Caroline F. Ware (New York: Columbia University Press, 1940), 3–16; [The Editors], "Educating Clio," *American Historical Review* 45 (1940): 505–532; Ellen Fitzpatrick, "Caroline F. Ware and the Cultural Approach to History," *American Quarterly* 43 (1989): 173–198; Ellen Fitzpatrick, *History's Memory: Writing America's Past, 1880–1980* (Cambridge, Mass.: Harvard University Press, 2002), 147–154, 185–186.

[167] Thomas C. Cochran, "The Social History of the Corporation in the United States," in *The Cultural Approach to History*, 168–181; Ralph E. Turner, "The Industrial City: Center of Cultural Change," ibid., 228–242; "The Flowering of New England," ed. Ralph H. Gabriel, ibid., esp. 252, 259–264.

[168] Ruth Benedict to Caroline Ware, 23 April 1941, quoted in Fitzpatrick, "Caroline F. Ware and the Cultural Approach to History," 192; Crane Brinton, review of *The Cultural Approach to History, Journal of the History of Ideas* 3 (1942): 229–231; Charles A. Beard, review of *The Cultural Approach to History, American Historical Review* 46 (1941): 844–845.

TOWARD AN INDIGENOUS AMERICAN CONCEPT OF CULTURE

In the eighteen years that elapsed between Benedict's *Patterns of Culture* and Kroeber and Kluckhohn's inventory of the meanings of culture, anthropologists made a number of important conceptual refinements to the concept. Ralph Linton initiated the process in his influential textbook, *The Study of Man*, published in 1936, where he not only "introduce[d] new and needed concepts," but also attempted to establish exact references for them.[169] First, Linton distinguished generic culture ("the total social heredity of mankind") from a particular culture (the way of life characteristic of a particular group). Next, he distinguished culture from "society" ("any group of people who have lived and worked together long enough to get themselves organized and to think of themselves as a social unit with well-defined limits"). Finally, Linton distinguished "status" (a position prescribing "rights and duties") from "role" (putting "into effect" those rights and duties). Status could be either "ascribed" at birth or "achieved."[170] According to the sociologist Robert K. Merton, it was only after the publication of Linton's textbook that the concepts of status and role "became systematically incorporated into a developing study of social structure."[171] Linton's conceptual distinctions, moreover, helped to lay the basis for the postwar integration of anthropology, sociology, and psychology in the Harvard Department of Social Relations.[172]

Linton's definition of culture included behavior, much as had Tylor's omnibus definition of 1871. By 1952, however, the prevailing approach among American anthropologists was to view culture as an abstraction detached from behavior. Linton himself initiated this process in *The Study of Man* when he distinguished "ideal" cultural patterns (prescriptions of how persons ought to behave) from "real" patterns (descriptions of how they actually did behave), and warned against confusing actual behavior with the "culture construct" that fieldworkers abstracted from their informants' statements and their own observations of actual behavior. As we shall see in Chapter 4, Clyde Kluckhohn would build on Linton's distinction to distinguish the "patterns" of "overt culture" (those parts of culture amenable to observation by the fieldworker) from the "configurations" of "covert culture" (those parts of a culture that the fieldworker had to infer). By 1947, when Kluckhohn and Alfred Kroeber began work on their inventory of the concepts and definitions of culture, they placed

---

[169] Clyde Kluckhohn, "The Place of Theory in Anthropological Studies," *Philosophy of Science* 6 (1939): 339. *The Study of Man* was "the most influential" anthropological textbook published between the world wars. George W. Stocking, Jr., "Ideas and Institutions in American Anthropology: Thoughts toward a History of the Interwar Years," in *The Ethnographer's Magic*, 141.

[170] Ralph Linton, *The Study of Man* (1936; repr., New York: Appleton-Century, 1964), 78, 91, 114–115.

[171] Robert K. Merton, "Continuities in the Theory of Reference Groups and Social Structure," in *Social Theory and Social Structure*, enlarged ed. (New York: Free Press, 1968), 422n.

[172] Clyde Kluckhohn, "Ralph Linton, February 27, 1893–December 24, 1953," in *Biographical Memoirs of the National Academy of Sciences* 31 (1958): 241.

"values," the "structuralizing principles" of what Kuckhohn called "implicit culture," at the core of culture.[173]

When Stuart Chase surveyed the "landmarks and achievements" of American social science for the Social Science Research Council and the Carnegie Corporation in his 1948 book *The Proper Study of Mankind*, no achievement ranked higher in his estimation than "the culture concept," which was even then "coming to be regarded as the foundation stone of the social sciences." According to Chase, the culture concept took social scientists "clean out of Western civilization and its values," centered attention on the group rather than the individual and on "society" rather than on "great men," emphasized "common denominators" and "universals," and held out hope that many of the problems then facing mankind could be "solved" because they were rooted in "cultural patterns" that "change, and [could] be changed" rather than in unchanging human nature.[174]

Although he was delighted by the pride of place Chase accorded the culture concept, Clyde Kluckhohn regretted that Chase had not paid more attention to "patterning" – the "organization" of culture and the "interdependence of [its] various aspects" – and to the "problems of meanings and of values."[175] Accordingly, when Kluckhohn and Alfred Kroeber took stock of the culture concept in their 1952 inventory, they depicted culture as a "form" or "pattern" abstracted from behavior. They also emphasized the fact that cultures not only had content – that is, "artifacts, linguistic texts, and lists of atomized traits" – but "organization" or "structure" as well. Finally, they identified "values" as the "structural essence" of any culture.[176] Unlike Tylor, who gave equal weight to "ideation," "behavior," and "artifacts," Kroeber and Kluckhohn emphasized "ideation." Indeed, as we shall see in the Epilogue, anthropologists' emphasis on patterning and values helped pave the way for a convergence between the anthropological and humanistic conceptions of culture.[177]

In 1953, Merle Curti deemed culture, which he defined holistically as the "totality of institutions, adjustments, and values binding a distinctive social

[173] Linton, *The Study of Man*, 100–101; Clyde Kluckhohn, "Patterning as Exemplified in Navaho Culture," in *Language, Culture and Personality*, ed. Leslie Spier, A. I. Hallowell, and Stanley S. Newman (Menasha, Wisc.: Sapir Memorial Publication Fund, 1941), 109–130; Clyde Kluckhohn and William H. Kelly, "The Concept of Culture," in *The Science of Man in the World Crisis*, ed. Ralph Linton (New York: Columbia University Press, 1945), 78–105, esp. 100–102; Kroeber and Kluckhohn, *Culture*, 167.

[174] Stuart Chase, "The Culture Concept," in *The Proper Study of Mankind: An Inquiry into the Science of Human Relations* (New York: Harper, 1948), 59–68. According to Charles Dollard, president of the Carnegie Corporation, the purpose of Chase's book was to disabuse congressmen of their "appalling ignorance" when it came to the social sciences, which, in the eyes of one senator, amounted to nothing more than "various kinds of ideology." Charles Dollard to Clyde Kluckhohn, 8 January 1947, HUG 4490.3, Kluckhohn Papers.

[175] Clyde Kluckhohn, "Taking Stock of Social Science," *New York Herald Tribune Book Review*, 3 October 1948.

[176] Kroeber and Kluckhohn, *Culture*, 36, 155–157, 172–173, 178, 181, 185.

[177] Berkhofer, "Clio and the Culture Concept," 81–82.

group together," "one of the most important and emancipating of all twentieth-century contributions to knowledge in the social field." When viewed through the lens of culture, human nature came to be seen "to develop only in relation to a particular culture, and to be susceptible to change as the culture changed." If "the relativistic and pragmatic aspects of the culture concept" were "fully and widely appreciated," Curti predicted, man would be "emancipate[d]" from "many age-old superstitions" and acquire "a realistic basis for improved social relations."[178]

As Curti's definition indicates, non-anthropologists in the early 1950s conceived of culture holistically. Indeed, in 1954, John R. Everett, president of Hollins College, identified Tylor's "complex whole" as "the indigenous American concept of culture." Reporting in the *American Quarterly* on a UNESCO conference that he attended in Paris, Everett contrasted the "sociological" [*sic*] American understanding of culture with the "hierarchical" European view. For Europeans, culture denoted the masterpieces produced by a "creative minority" for an "appreciative minority." Americans, by contrast, insisted that culture be "accessible," and that it be judged not by its masterpieces, but rather by the "opportunities it affords people to rise above the necessary business of getting and spending." This broad conception of culture not only answered the taunts of skeptics about the rarity of American masterpieces, it also lifted the heads of American males above the "catchpenny opportunism" that Van Wyck Brooks had complained about in 1915. In addition, it helped to explain the paradoxical situation in which Americans poured millions of dollars into cultural institutions such as universities, museums, and libraries while considering culture "an obnoxious word designating activities . . . primarily for women."[179] As we shall see in Chapter 5, the culture that American cultural diplomats were then attempting to export to Europe was not Matthew Arnold's narrow conception, but Ruth Benedict's broad conception.[180]

By the early 1950s, the culture concept had recast a number of long-standing American concerns. First and foremost, it served as a foil of race and racial thinking, withholding any scientific standing from invidious racial notions. Indeed, what had become conventional wisdom among social scientists, the equipotentiality of all races, was distilled in a statement drawn up by a commission of international experts in 1949 and circulated worldwide by UNESCO in 1950. The experts agreed that neither national groups (Americans, Englishmen, Frenchmen), nor religious groups (Catholics, Moslems, Jews), nor linguistic groups ("groups who speak English or any other language"), nor geographical groups ("people who live in Iceland or England or India"), nor

[178] Merle Curti, "The Setting and the Problems," in *American Scholarship in the Twentieth Century*, ed. Merle Curti (Cambridge, Mass.: Harvard University Press, 1953), 3–5.
[179] John R. Everett, "American Culture in the World To-Day: Reflections on a UNESCO Meeting," *American Quarterly* 6 (1994): 245–252.
[180] Harry Levin, "Some European Views of Contemporary American Literature," *American Quarterly* 1 (1949): 264.

cultural groups ("people who are culturally Turkish or Chinese or the like") "necessarily coincide with racial groups." Neither did the "cultural traits of such groups" have any "demonstrable connection with racial traits." Indeed, "for all practical purposes 'race' [was] not so much a biological phenomenon as a social myth." Regrettably, the "myth of 'race' [had] created an enormous amount of human and social damage."[181]

As we have seen, the culture concept served as a tool for anthropologists and social scientists in cognate fields in achieving autonomy; as a counter to Western ethnocentrism; as the antithesis of civilization in making manners and morals relative to time and place; as a warrant for cultural critique and weapon in the American liberal intelligentsia's culture war against provincialism; and as an invitation to engage in social engineering (to correct cultural lag, to build or rebuild American culture). Last but certainly not least, it underwrote the rediscovery of America.

By the early 1950s, anthropologists spoke of generic and "partitive" (or particular) culture. Although Kroeber and Kluckhohn considered distinguishing between these two "levels" of culture to be more of a practical than a theoretical problem, the archaeologist Walter W. Taylor, who had earned his Ph.D. at Harvard under Kluckhohn, accused the two men of sliding in their inventory between conceiving of culture "holistically" and conceiving of it "partitively." According to Taylor, only particular cultures were "anthropological" because only they had "specific structures." "Total human culture," by contrast, was "additive or summative of many varieties."[182] As we shall see in the next chapter, ethnographies of the American scene, based on long-term fieldwork in purportedly representative American microcosms, raised questions about the relation of particular cultures to American culture in general by delineating the distinctive subcultures of social classes and of ethnic and racial groups.

[181] A. Métraux, "UNESCO and Anthropology," *American Anthropologist* 53 (1951): 298; A. Métraux, "United Nations Economic and Security Council, Statement by Experts on Problems of Race," *American Anthropologist* 53 (1951): 142, 144.
[182] Walter W. Taylor to Clyde Kluckhohn, 2 January 1952; A. L. Kroeber to Clyde Kluckhohn [January] 1952, HUG 4490.9, Kluckhohn Papers; Kroeber and Kluckhohn, *Culture*, 185n. See also Berkhofer, "Clio and the Culture Concept," 90–91.

2

Social Class in the Ethnography of the American Scene

When Robert and Helen Lynd published *Middletown: A Study in Contemporary American Culture* in 1929, their book received great critical and popular acclaim. Vigorously promoted by publisher Alfred Harcourt, warmly praised in book reviews, and prominently featured in bookstore windows, *Middletown* went through six printings in 1929 alone. Selling more than 30,000 copies over the next eight years, the Lynds' book became the first best seller in American social science. In the process, *Middletown* did more than any other work published before Ruth Benedict's *Patterns of Culture* to popularize the anthropological concept of culture.[1]

Middletown also inaugurated "the 'ethnography' of the American scene." Inspired by the Lynds' success, social scientists fanned out across the United States to subject other American communities to even more intense anthropological scrutiny. Like *Middletown*, many of these community studies documented the salience of class distinctions, thereby challenging a fundamental tenet of American exceptionalism: that the United States, unlike Europe, did not have a class system. These community studies also wove the dense social fabric that many American intellectuals felt lacking. By the 1950s, thanks to the success of ethnographies of the American scene, social scientists rivaled novelists and foreign travelers as authoritative commentators on the American scene.[2]

Yet the effect of *Middletown* and its 1937 sequel, *Middletown in Transition*, on the ways in which Americans viewed class distinctions on the American

---

[1] Robert B. Downs, *Books That Changed America* (New York: Macmillan, 1970), 216–228. Sales figures come from Richard Wightman Fox, "Epitaph for Middletown: Robert S. Lynd and the Analysis of Consumer Culture," in *The Culture of Consumption: Critical Essays in American History, 1880–1980,* ed. Richard Wightman Fox and T. J. Jackson Lears (New York: Pantheon, 1983), 101–141, on 122.

[2] Walter R. Goldschmidt, "Social Class and the Dynamics of Status in America," *American Anthropologist* 57 (1955): 1209–1217.

scene paled in comparison with that of W. Lloyd Warner and his students and colleagues, who shifted the focus away from classes as economic entities determined by occupation and income to "social classes," construed as little worlds or subcultures distinguished by their cultural attributes or symbols of status. In so doing, they focused attention on consumption and leisure rather than on production. By incorporating class into an elaborate analytic framework that included ethnicity and race, Warner and his associates provided the lens through which social scientists and educated Americans viewed inequality.

After 1950, however, social scientists began to play down the salience of class distinctions on the American scene. Turning away from the ethnography of the American scene toward survey research, they substituted a status continuum for Warner's layer-cake conception of American stratification patterns. Playing down the divisive connotations of social class, they viewed social mobility in America as an escalator on which Americans were in continuous movement up (and down) rather than as a ladder with widely spaced rungs. By the late 1950s, some social scientists were even disputing the validity of social class as an analytic category.

CLASS WITHOUT CLASS CONFLICT

American notions of class have had a long and checkered history. Colonial Americans lived in a rank-ordered society in which birth, breeding, gentility, and education were the markers of a leisured aristocratic gentry who aped the latest English fashions. This venerable system of fixed status, however, foundered after the American Revolution accelerated egalitarian impulses undermining inherited privilege and opened up opportunities for self-made men. Although wealth grew more maldistributed after the Revolution, most Americans subscribed to a belief in social harmony. While recognizing invidious distinctions of occupation and income, they insisted that "classes" on the American scene were not "fixed" (that is, legally mandated) as in Europe, but were rather natural products of a market economy and of differences in individual talent, achievement, and luck. Even when the workingmen's movements of the 1830s arrayed "producers" against "nonproducers," class distinctions seemed reconcilable to most Americans. The situation, then, was what Martin Burke has termed "class without class conflict": Americans recognized the existence of classes based on invidious differences in occupation and income, but denied that their existence implied class conflict. Class distinctions in the United States, moreover, paled in comparison with ethnic distinctions sharpened by substantial Irish and German immigration before the Civil War, the color line between white Americans and nonwhites, and the sectional divisions exacerbated by the conflict over slavery. Outside the South, where wealthy planters cultivated European ideals of leisure and exemption from labor,

Americans celebrated the work ethic and discouraged displays of rank and privilege.[3]

After the Civil War, many Americans continued to subscribe to the axiom of social harmony despite the growing concentration of wealth and power and the labor strife of the 1870s and 1880. Until his death in 1881, Lewis Henry Morgan looked forward to the day when the rest of the industrial world would follow the American example of evolving beyond class distinctions based on hereditary privilege. Although political economists tried to explain away popular sentiment that capital and labor were antagonistic, fears of potential class conflict overrode all talk of a "natural" social hierarchy. In 1883, the sociologist William Graham Sumner dramatically broke with the axiom of social harmony when, in *What Social Classes Owe to Each Other*, he acknowledged that the economic interests of capitalists and laborers were fundamentally antagonistic. Yet, at the same time, Sumner pointed to the "social and industrial forces" that were drawing Americans together. Indeed, Sumner concluded, "we cannot separate ourselves even if we wanted to."[4]

Sumner's colleagues and successors did not ignore "class phenomena," but, impressed by the relatively large size of the American middle class ("the imperial middle," in Benjamin DeMott's words), they viewed American society as fluid. So long as classes remained open, and not fixed, Charles Horton Cooley allowed as how there might be class struggle in America, but not class war. Arthur Bentley considered class a viable category of social analysis only "in a rigorous caste organization of society," which definitely did not obtain in the United States.[5]

Thorstein Veblen, however, stood out as a conspicuous exception to the tendency of American social scientists to play down the importance of class distinctions on the American scene. He was also the first American social scientist to develop the cultural dimensions of class. Beginning with *The Theory*

---

[3] Gordon S. Wood, introduction to *The Rising Glory of America, 1760–1820* (New York: George Braziller, 1971), 1–22; Gordon S. Wood, *The American Revolution* (New York: Modern Library, 2002); Jon Butler, *Becoming America: The Revolution before 1776* (Cambridge, Mass.: Harvard University Press, 2000); Joyce Appleby, *Inheriting the Revolution: The First Generation of Americans* (Cambridge, Mass.: Harvard University Press, 2000); Martin J. Burke, *The Conundrum of Class: Public Discourse on the Social Order in America* (Chicago: University of Chicago Press, 1995).

[4] Lewis Henry Morgan, quoted in Donald Worster, *A River Running West: The Life of John Wesley Powell* (New York: Oxford University Press, 2001), 444; William Graham Sumner, *What Social Classes Owe to Each Other* (1883; repr., Caldwell, Idaho: Caxton, 1954); Burke, *The Conundrum of Class*, ix–x, 159–162.

[5] Charles H. Page, *Class and American Sociology: From Ward to Ross* (1940; repr., New York: Schocken, 1969), 3–25, 249–254; Milton M. Gordon, *Social Class in American Sociology* (1958; repr., New York: McGraw-Hill, 1963); Dorothy Ross, *The Origins of American Sociology* (Cambridge: Cambridge University Press, 1991), 246, 335, 387; Benjamin DeMott, *The Imperial Middle: Why Americans Can't Think Straight about Class* (1990; repr., New Haven, Conn.: Yale University Press, 1992).

of the Leisure Class in 1899 and culminating in *Absentee Ownership and Business Enterprise in Recent Times: The Case of America* in 1923, Veblen developed a formidable critique of American civilization. Central to Veblen's critique was the distinction between "industry," maximum production for the common good, and "business enterprise," sabotage of production for private gain. Drawing on evolutionary anthropology and instinct psychology (both out of fashion by the time of his death in 1929), Veblen argued that a "pecuniary economy" diverted mankind's "instinct for workmanship" into "conspicuous consumption." However wasteful these pursuits might appear from the point of view of the rational, self-interested economic man postulated in classical economics, they nonetheless established Americans' social status. Veblen, however, never gave up hope that the "matter-of-fact approach" to reality instilled by the "machine-process" would eventually free Americans from the prevalent "habits of thought" of "business civilization." Although Veblen's polysyllabic language, caustic style, and dead-pan irony made him, arguably, the most influential American social scientist of his generation, he did not establish a school of class analysis.[6]

Class analysis receded further as American social scientists rejected evolutionary theory and shifted from broad generalization to detailed empirical research.[7] Sociologists at the University of Chicago are a case in point. They gave more emphasis to ethnicity and race than to class. Although he recognized the propensity of Americans to organize themselves around their "vocational interests," Robert Park did not think that class was a viable "category of analysis" in analyzing American society. "Do classes assume the character or acquire the exclusiveness of caste or nationality?" he asked rhetorically in his programmatic 1915 essay "The City." No, he answered, not on the American scene. Defining sociology as social process in *Introduction to the Science of Sociology* (1921), the Chicago school's "green bible," Park and coauthor Ernest Burgess ignored not only class and power but even social structure. The city and urbanism were what mattered to Park and Burgess. "Competition," they insisted, was the characteristic form of interaction among Americans, and it precluded the emergence of classes. Moreover, the Chicago sociologists' processual framework, which stressed "movement, change, and constant flow," "openness in direction," and "uncertainty in outcome," militated against their recognition of classes as structural constraints on

---

[6] Donald G. McRae, "Social Stratification: A Trend Report," *Current Sociology* 2 (1953): 11; Page, *Class and American Sociology*, 250, xiii; Hugh J. Dawson, "E. B. Tylor's Theory of Survivals and Veblen's Social Criticism," *Journal of the History of Ideas* 54 (1993): 489–504; Max Lerner, "Editor's Introduction," in *The Portable Veblen* (New York: Viking, 1948), 3, 8, 46; David Riesman, *Thorstein Veblen: A Critical Interpretation* (1953; repr., New York: Scribner, 1960), 78, 113, 127.

[7] Ely Chinoy, review of *Social Class in America*, by Milton M. Gordon, *American Sociological Review* 24 (1959): 116.

individual agency.[8] It is hardly surprising, then, that class distinctions did not bulk large in ethnographies of Chicago's colorful "natural areas" and distinctive "social types" such as Harvey Warren Zorbaugh's 1929 *The Gold Coast and the Slum*.[9]

The late 1920s did, however, see some stirrings of interest in class analysis. In *Social Mobility* (1927), the Russian émigré sociologist Pitirim Sorokin explored "social stratification, class characteristics, and social mobility," and, in 1928, F. Stuart Chapin developed a "living room scale" that measured the socioeconomic status of would-be foster parents on the basis of their living-room furniture. Yet, when the Lynds' *Middletown* was published in January 1929, class was still not a central category in the discourse of American social scientists. The concept thus did not figure in George Lundberg, Read Bain, and Nels Anderson's textbook, *Trends in American Sociology*, published in 1929.[10] As late as 1944, Gunnar Myrdal complained that while American sociology "must be given the highest ranking in the world," it remained "weak and undeveloped in general" when it dealt with "the problems of social stratification."[11]

Yet, even as Myrdal wrote, class distinctions were becoming far more salient in American social science. One reason was the way in which labor militancy and radical political movements on both the left and the right during the Depression raised the specter of class struggle. Yet, at the same time, the growing influence of anthropology following the publication of the Lynds'

---

[8] Robert E. Park, "The City: Suggestions for the Investigation of Human Behavior in the Urban Environment," in Robert E. Park, Ernest W. Burgess, and Roderick D. McKenzie, *The City* (1925; repr., Chicago: University of Chicago Press, 1967), 1–46; Fred H. Matthews, *Quest for an American Sociology: Robert E. Park and the Chicago School* (Montreal: McGill-Queens University Press, 1977), 124; Fred H. Matthews, "Social Scientists and the Culture Concept, 1930–1950: The Conflict between Processual and Structural Approaches," *Sociological Theory* 7 (1989): 87–101. For Park's lack of interest in class, see Lester R. Kurtz, *Evaluating Chicago Sociology: A Guide to the Literature, with an Annotated Bibliography* (Chicago: University of Chicago Press, 1984), 5, 106n; Norbert Wiley, "The Rise and Fall of Dominating Theories in American Sociology," in *Contemporary Issues in Theory and Research: A Metasociological Perspective*, ed. William E. Snizek et al. (Westport, Conn.: Greenwood, 1979), 60.

[9] Harvey Warren Zorbaugh, *The Gold Coast and the Slum: A Sociological Study of Chicago's Near North Side* (1929; repr., Chicago: University of Chicago Press, 1976); Andrew Abbott, *Department and Discipline: Chicago Sociology at One Hundred* (Chicago: University of Chicago Press, 1999), 199–200, 202.

[10] Pitirim A. Sorokin, *Social Mobility* (New York: Harper, 1927); F. Stuart Chapin, "A Quantitative Scale for Rating the Home and Social Environment of Middle Class Families in an Urban Community," *Journal of Educational Psychology* 19 (1928): 99–111; Gordon, *Social Class in American Sociology*, 52–62; Olivier Zunz, *Why the American Century?* (Chicago: University of Chicago Press, 1998), 98–99; Milton M. Gordon, "Social Class in American Sociology," *American Journal of Sociology* 55 (1949): 263–264; George A. Lundberg, Read Bain, and Nels Anderson, eds., *Trends in American Sociology* (New York: Harper, 1929).

[11] Gunnar Myrdal, with the assistance of Richard Sterner and Arnold Rose, *An American Dilemma: The Negro Problem and Modern Diplomacy* (1944; repr., New York: Pantheon, 1962), 670; Chinoy, review of *Social Class in American Sociology*, 116.

Middletown ignited "a great social stratification boom" in American social science. Many of the community studies produced by the late 1940s were undertaken from an anthropological perspective, and they, too, documented the salience of class distinctions in representative American communities. By then, "class structure" had become "a focus of research interest" among American social scientists. In 1953, the first book of readings on stratification was published. It was followed in 1954 by the publication of the first textbook on "social class" or "social stratification." By 1955, social class or social stratification had definitely "arrived" as "a major subdiscipline within the field of American sociology." In 1957, the Polish sociologist Stanislaw Ossowski observed that "studies of the class structure of American society have attained a leading place in the set of problems with which American sociology is concerned."[12]

THE SOCIAL ANTHROPOLOGY OF CONTEMPORARY LIFE

Far from being trained social scientists, Robert and Helen Lynd were Protestant moralists schooled in the Social Gospel movement. They were also disaffected Midwesterners. Born in LaGrange, Illinois, in 1896, Helen Merrell had grown up in a strict Congregationalist family. After studying English, history, and philosophy at Wellesley College, she taught school for two years before earning an M.A. in history from Columbia.[13] Born in New Albany, Indiana, in 1892, Robert Lynd had grown up across the Ohio River in Louisville, Kentucky, where his father, a self-made banker and devout Presbyterian, was "one of the straightest men [he] ever knew." After studying English literature at Princeton, he worked as managing editor of *Publisher's Weekly* and head of advertising for the publisher Charles Scribner before deciding to enter the ministry. During the summer of 1921, as a student at Union Theological Seminary, Lynd preached to roustabouts in the oil fields of Elk Basin, Wyoming. The exposé of the harsh working conditions condoned by a subsidiary of Standard Oil Company that he published in *Survey* magazine in

---

[12] Milton R. Gordon, "Social Class and American Intellectuals," *American Association of University Professors Bulletin* 40 (1954–55): 517; Ely Chinoy, "Research in Class Structure," *Canadian Journal of Economics and Political Science* 16 (1950): 255; Harold W. Pfautz, "The Current Literature on Social Stratification: Critique and Bibliography," *American Journal of Sociology* 58 (1953): 391–418; Reinhard Bendix and Seymour Martin Lipset, eds., *Class, Status, and Power: A Reader in Social Stratification* (Glencoe, Ill.: Free Press, 1953); Gordon, *Social Class in American Sociology*, 10–11; Stanislaw Ossowski, *Class Structure in the Social Consciousness*, trans. Sheila Patterson (New York: Free Press, 1963), 102. The Polish edition of Ossowski's book was published in 1957.

[13] Helen Merrell Lynd, with the collaboration of Staughton Lynd, *Possibilities*, rev. ed. (Bronxville, N.Y.: Sarah Lawrence College, 1983), 18–29; "The Reminiscences of Helen Lynd," ed. Mrs. Walter Gellhorn (Oral History Research Office, Columbia University, 1973), 1–35.

1922 brought him to the attention of the Institute of Social and Religious Research.[14]

The Institute of Social and Religious Research was an ecumenical Protestant agency funded by the Baptist layman John D. Rockefeller, Jr. It had been established in 1921 after the Interchurch World Movement fell short of its ambitious goal of consolidating and modernizing American Protestantism. By sponsoring "scientific" surveys of churches and other religious agencies, the Institute's staff hoped to promote greater cooperation among Protestant denominations while allaying class antagonism. In 1923, the staff commissioned Robert Lynd to survey the "spiritual life" of a representative Midwestern community, ascertain its inhabitants' "religious and ethical attitudes and capacities," and measure "the adjustment or maladjustment of [Protestant] agencies to them." The staff hoped that Lynd would develop "a method by which smaller cities may be helped to appraise their own life."[15]

By 1923, surveys were familiar tools in the repertory of social reformers. After having been developed in France and England around the middle of the nineteenth century, they had proliferated in America since the 1890s and represented the application of scientific method to social problems and conditions. Their primary aim was publicity: if their findings and recommendations became "common knowledge," it was believed, surveys would serve as "force[s] for intelligent coordinated action." The first American surveys, like the monumental Pittsburgh Survey, focused on entire communities; later surveys, like the Lynds' survey of spiritual life in Muncie, were more specialized.[16]

The Lynds chose Muncie as the site of their survey because they considered the city "as representative as possible of contemporary American life." It was, after all, located in the American heartland, the Midwest. Thanks to the resounding success of postwar American literature, itself largely the creation of disaffected Midwesterners, the Midwest had not only become the archetypal

[14] "Miscellaneous Ideas about Robert S. Lynd," 9 March 1954, Robert S. and Helen Merrell Lynd Papers, Manuscripts Division, Library of Congress (hereafter Lynd Papers), R2:C2; [Robert S. Lynd], " – But Why Preach?" *Harper's*, June 1921, 82–83; Robert S. Lynd, "Addenda," March 1963, Lynd Papers, R1:C2; Robert S. Lynd, "Done in Oil," *Survey*, 1 November 1922, 137–146; Charles E. Harvey, "Robert S. Lynd, John D. Rockefeller, Jr., and *Middletown*," *Indiana Magazine of History* 79 (1983): 330–354. For biographical information on Robert Lynd, see Fox, "Epitaph for Middletown"; Mark C. Smith, *Social Science in the Crucible: The American Debate over Objectivity and Purpose, 1918–1941* (Durham: Duke University Press, 1994), 120–158; Dwight Hoover, *Middletown Revisited* (Muncie: Ball State University, 1990); Sarah E. Igo, *The Averaged American: Surveys, Citizens, and the Making of a Mass Public* (Cambridge, Mass.: Harvard University Press, 2007), 23–102.

[15] Harvey, "Robert S. Lynd, John D. Rockefeller, Jr., and *Middletown*"; Galen M. Fisher, "History of the Small City Study," 20 March 1924, 9, folder 15, box 2, Record Group (hereafter RG) IV 3 A 5, Raymond B. Fosdick Papers, Rockefeller Archive Center, Sleepy Hollow, New York (hereafter RAC).

[16] Shelby M. Harrison, *The Social Survey: The Idea Defined and Its Development Traced* (New York: Russell Sage Foundation, 1931), 20; Niles Carpenter, "Social Surveys," *Encyclopedia of the Social Sciences*, ed. Edwin R. A. Seligman (New York: Macmillan, 1934), 14:164.

region of America but also, in Frederick Hoffman's words, a "metaphor of abuse."[17]

Yet Muncie was unusually homogeneous for a Midwestern industrial city in the 1920s. Only 2 percent of the city's population of 38,000 were foreign-born; another 6 percent were African-Americans. Muncie's homogeneity warranted the Lynds' concentration on "cultural change" to the neglect of the ethnic and racial competition emphasized by Chicago sociologists.[18]

Once their fieldwork got under way, the Lynds found it difficult to navigate between the conflicting advice they were receiving from members of the Institute's staff. Some of the staff, responding to entreaties from participating denominational boards, pressed the Lynds to work closely with local religious leaders in devising "practical programs" for Muncie's Protestant churches. Other members of the staff insisted that the Lynds confine themselves to "fact-finding." Torn between the contradictory goals of promoting moral reform and promoting science, the Lynds adopted a "cultural approach" to Muncie. They decided to approach the city as if they were anthropologists who had come upon an exotic community in the South Pacific.[19]

Exactly where the Lynds got this inspired notion is unclear. Helen Lynd credited her husband. Robert Lynd noted the influence of two works by English anthropologists: A. R. Radcliffe-Brown's *The Andaman Islanders* (1922) and W. H. R. Rivers's *Social Organization* (1924). A more likely source, though, was the Lynds' close friend, the psychologist and Rockefeller Foundation officer Lawrence K. Frank, who was then urging that anthropology departments be established in universities across the country.[20]

In any event, the Lynds' adoption of a cultural approach served a number of purposes. First of all, it provided the Lynds with the categories they used to organize the copious data that they and their staff (consisting of an interviewer, a statistician, and a stenographer) were collecting. From Rivers's *Social Organization*, they derived six "main-trunk activities": "getting a living," "making a home," "training the young," "using leisure," "engaging in religious activities," and "engaging in community activities." Second, adoption of a cultural approach sanctioned the Lynds' conversion of what had been commissioned as a survey of spiritual life into a "total-situation study." Third, the cultural approach buttressed the Lynds' claims to being disinterested outsiders who were capable of regarding Midwestern life objectively. "Nothing can be more enlightening," they wrote, "than to gain precisely the degree of objectivity and

---

[17] Frederick J. Hoffman, *The Twenties: American Writing in the Postwar Decade*, rev. ed. (1962; repr., New York: Free Press, 1965), 369.

[18] Robert S. Lynd and Helen Merrell Lynd, *Middletown: A Study in Contemporary American Culture* (1929; repr., New York: Harcourt, 1959), 3.

[19] Fox, "Epitaph for Middletown," 117–118, 121; Robert S. Lynd, "Problem of Being Objective in Studying One's Own Culture," outline for 9 December 1938 talk at Princeton University, Lynd Papers, R2:C2.

[20] On Lawrence Frank, see Stephen J. Cross, "Designs for Living: Lawrence K. Frank and the Progressive Legacy in American Social Science" (Ph.D. diss., Johns Hopkins University, 1994).

perspective with which we view 'savage' peoples."[21] Finally, the cultural approach provided the Lynds with "a scheme for throwing familiar things into less immediate, more universal categories." Veblen had already demonstrated how the juxtaposition of exotic customs from primitive societies with familiar American customs could render the commonplace at once strange and arbitrary. Unlike Veblen, who felt compelled to issue frequent disclaimers that his use of such loaded terms as "conspicuous consumption" did not imply value judgments, the Lynds were able to engage in irony and criticize what they purported to describe objectively.[22]

Although the Lynds recommended Radcliffe-Brown's *Andaman Islanders* to their research assistants as a model of the wholeness and interrelatedness they were aiming at in their own work, they owed their primary intellectual debts to the homegrown theorists Thorstein Veblen, William Ogburn, and Clark Wissler.[23] Veblen's influence can be seen in the Lynds' focus on the impact of "high-speed machine production" on city life, emphasis on the main-trunk activity of "getting a living," characterization of American culture as a "pecuniary" one in which "living in all its aspects leans more on money than ever before," and, above all, interest in class distinctions.[24] From Ogburn, the Lynds borrowed the concept of "cultural lag" between material and non-material culture to trace the many strains and anxieties that beset American machine civilization. Like Ogburn, they viewed new "tools" and "inventions" as "the most prolific breeder[s] of change" and attributed many of the instances of cultural lag they documented to "unevenness in the diffusion of material culture." The "pressure of maladjustment," in turn, "bewildered" Munsonians, who had "one foot on the relatively solid ground of established institutional habits and the other fast to an escalator erratically moving in several directions at a bewildering variety of speeds."[25] Finally, the Lynds adapted a version of Wissler's culture-area concept to picture "increasingly frequent and strong culture waves" sweeping over Muncie from "centers of cultural diffusion," "drenching" Munsonians with new "material and non-material habits" and new conceptions of "what things are essential to living." Like Wissler, the Lynds analyzed American culture in terms of such component complexes as "the cluster of habits that [had]

[21] Lynd and Lynd, *Middletown*, 3–5.
[22] Lynd, "Problem of Being Objective in Studying One's Own Culture," 5; Fox, "Epitaph for 'Middletown,'" 120–121.
[23] Lynd, "Problem of Being Objective in Studying One's Own Culture," 6.
[24] Lynd and Lynd, *Middletown*, 7, 21, 49. On the esteem in which the Lynds held Veblen, see Helen Lynd, *Possibilities*, 29–30; Robert S. Lynd, quoted in Malcolm Cowley, "Books That Changed Our Minds," *New Republic*, 21 December 1938, 206; Staughton Lynd, "Robert S. Lynd: The Elk Basin Experience," *Journal of the History of Sociology* 2 (1979–80): 14; Charles H. Page, *Fifty Years in the Sociological Enterprise: A Lucky Journal* (Amherst: University of Massachusetts Press, 1982), 45; Daniel Horowitz, *The Morality of Spending: Attitudes toward the Consumer Society in America, 1875–1940* (1985; repr., Chicago: Ivan Dee, 1992), 151.
[25] Lynd and Lynd, *Middletown*, 222, 97–98, 498–499.

grown up overnight around the automobile" and had, in the process, displaced "horse culture."[26]

By establishing 1890 as a "base-line" against which to measure the changes that had taken place in Muncie over the course of a generation, and by delineating a "rough hierarchy of rates of change" among the six major lines of activity, the Lynds refined Ogburn's notion of cultural lag. Getting a living, the activity most affected by new tools and technology, had changed the most since 1890; engaging in religious activities, the most sheltered main-trunk activity, had changed the least. But even in "the performance of the same function," the Lynds discerned "differential rates of adjustment." The elderly tended to be slower in adopting new tools and habits than the young, and women were slower than men. But the differential impact of social change was most striking in the difference between the ways of life of the "working class" and the "business class." Generally speaking, "the working class today [employed] the habits of the business class of roughly a generation ago."[27]

The concepts of pecuniary culture, cultural lag, and culture area, in turn, informed the Lynds' conception of Muncie's social organization. "The division into working class and business class," they declared, constituted "the outstanding cleavage" in Muncie. By working class, the Lynds had in mind the 71 percent of Muncie's work force who "address[ed] their activities in getting their living primarily to *things*, utilizing material tools in the making of things and the performance of services." By business class, they meant the remaining 29 percent of Muncie's work force who "address[ed] their activities predominantly to *people* in the selling or promotion of things, services, and ideas."[28]

Unlike Veblen, who satirized the leisure class's reverence for "archaic traits," the Lynds depicted members of the working class as lagging a generation or so behind members of the business class in the adoption of new tools and habits. Although this lag could be attributed in part to cultural inertia, it also stemmed from the economic consequences of class division in Muncie. Indeed, "irregularity of employment" was perhaps the principal difference between the working class and the business class. In getting a living, workingmen had to get up earlier in the morning and work longer hours than members of the business class; subject to periodic lay-offs and shut-downs that depleted savings, they enjoyed far less economic security. Many working-class families, moreover, could afford such big-ticket items as automobiles only by skimping on

---

[26] Lynd and Lynd, *Middletown*, 5, 251; Maurice R. Stein, "The Eclipse of Community: Some Glances at the Education of a Sociologist," in *Reflections on Community Studies*, ed. Arthur J. Vidich, Joseph Bensman, and Maurice R. Stein (New York: Wiley, 1964), 223. In 1930, Robert Lynd told William F. Ogburn how he had been "interested for a couple of years in taking the whole process of diffusion . . . and attempting a restatement in terms of our own nonprimitive culture's concrete phenomena." Robert S. Lynd to William F. Ogburn, 4 July 1930, William F. Ogburn Papers, Special Collections Research Center, University of Chicago, box 13, folder 13.

[27] Lynd and Lynd, *Middletown*, 5–6, 497.

[28] Lynd and Lynd, *Middletown*, 21–24 (emphasis in original).

necessities and buying on credit. Even worse, high-speed machine production was eroding workingmen's skills, lessening their chances for promotion, and rendering them vulnerable to superannuation by their mid-forties. Workingmen coped with blocked mobility by sending their wives into the paid labor force outside the home, keeping their children in school long enough to earn the credentials required for white-collar employment, and acquiring consumer goods that they could flaunt as badges of status.[29]

The Lynds' two-class scheme had a number of advantages over the more familiar tripartite model of upper class, middle class, and lower class. It "brought vocational cleavage to the fore," corresponded to the long-standing line between white-collar and blue-collar work, expressed the Lynds' sympathy for manual workers, and echoed the invidious nineteenth-century distinction between producers and nonproducers. But the Lynds' simple distinction between business class and working class did not acknowledge the existence of either a white-collar group or an upper class in Muncie. Instead, the Lynds lumped all nonmanual workers – from the lowly clerk to the wealthy glass manufacturer – into an undifferentiated business class.[30]

The Lynds had settled on the terms working class and business class in response to criticism from the Institute staff and outside experts who read drafts of their manuscript. Critics objected to the Lynds' frequent references to "culture," anthropological scaffolding, and "semi-scientific jargon," in particular their use of the terms "tools users" and "users of institutional devices" to refer to members of the working class and of the business class, respectively. Critics also wondered why the Lynds did not acknowledge the existence of a discrete middle class or an upper class in Muncie. Above all, critics objected to the Lynds' injection of their own opinions into what purported to be a fact-finding study.[31]

When these criticisms delayed the publication of their manuscript, the Lynds enlisted Clark Wissler's assistance. As someone who had long urged the application of anthropologists' "objective" and "analytic" techniques to a "civilized community," Wissler had a vested interest in seeing the Lynds' manuscript published. Moreover, as an Indiana native who had grown up less than thirty-five miles away from Muncie, Wissler could vouch for the accuracy of their portrait of the city. Wissler excused the Lynds' failure to acknowledge the existence of a discrete middle class in Muncie by pointing to the city's small size and the orientation of its work force around production rather than consumption. He attributed the Lynds' omission of the Ball brothers, wealthy glass

---

[29] Lynd and Lynd, *Middletown*, 264, chaps. 5–8 passim.

[30] Lynd and Lynd, *Middletown*, 23n.

[31] Stanley Went, "General Comments on Section I of the Small City Study," 5 May 1927; Luther Fry, "Notes on 'The Making of a Home' Section of the Small City Study," 24 May 1927; Galen M. Fisher to Robert S. Lynd, 30 November 1926; Galen M. Fisher, "Notes on Small City Manuscript," 6 May 1927; "Minutes of the Conference Held March 19 [1926]"; Trevor M. Bowen to Robert S. Lynd, 27 May 1927; Trevor M. Bowen, "Notes on First Section, Chapters I to IX, of Lynd's Manuscript," 6 May 1927, Lynd Papers, R4:C7.

manufacturers who stood "somewhat apart from the general level" of Muncie's population, to their desire to conceal the city's identity. And though he admitted that some of the Lynds' terminology was clumsy, and would not be used by anthropologists, Wissler explained that the Lynds used these terms "for the sake of making very sharp contrasts in the picture." The Lynds, in short, aimed less at "scientific analysis" than at "impressing the reader."[32]

Authorized to publish their manuscript, the Lynds got rid of much of the "verbiage" to which their critics objected and found a publisher, Alfred Harcourt. They also persuaded Wissler to vouch for their scientific standing. In his foreword to *Middletown*, Wissler assured their readers of the Lynds' objectivity. In the process of training the "eye of an outsider on American life," the Lynds had developed "an objective method of [studying] ourselves" and pioneered "the social anthropology of contemporary life."[33]

THE LYND ANTHROPOLOGICAL EXPEDITION TO THE WILD JUNGLE OF BABBITT-LAND

Judging by reviews of *Middletown*, American readers were slow to recognize the challenge that the Lynds' evidence posed to the popular view of America as a classless society. In fact, English reviewers were more likely to remark on class distinctions on the American scene than were their American counterparts. To English reviewers, class differences seemed "less varied" in America because of the absence of an "idle" leisure class and because of Americans' disinclination to display private wealth. American reviewers, by contrast, were more impressed by the many instances of "social illiteracy" the Lynds documented. John Dewey, for example, was "struck by the number of connections in which some large part of the population of that town finds itself 'bewildered' or 'confused.'" Stuart Chase remarked on "the number of times that the word 'bewilderment' creeps into the text." The few American reviewers who did comment on the Lynds' distinction between working class and business class agreed that "class lines" had "tended to deepen under the impact of industrialism." One, who taught social work at Indiana University, called attention to the "social bifurcation" that, "somewhat to the dismay of those Americans who stoutly deny social classes exist in America," came "out plainly throughout the study of Middletown."[34]

---

[32] Clark Wissler, quoted in "Conference on Mr. Lynd's Manuscript on 'The Study of a Small Industrial City' at Town Hall Club," 16 November 1926, Lynd Papers, R4:C7.

[33] Robert S. Lynd, memo, 2 March 1928, Lynd Papers, R4:C7; Clark Wissler, foreword to *Middletown*, v–vi.

[34] Raymond Mortimer, "A Tribe in the Middle West," *Nation & Athenaeum*, 10 August 1929, 627; "An American City," *New Statesman*, 15 June 1929, 300; John Dewey, "The House Divided against Itself," *New Republic*, 24 April 1929, 270; Stuart Chase, "The Bewildered Western World," *New York Herald Tribune Books*, 3 February 1929; Allan Nevins, "Fascinating Spectacle of an American Town Under the Microscope," *New York World*, 17 February 1929; R. Clyde White, "Middletown," *Indianapolis News*, 17 February 1929.

Almost invariably, both English and American reviewers compared *Middletown* with the novelist Sinclair Lewis's portraits of Midwestern life in *Main Street* (1920) and *Babbitt* (1922). Most who did so considered *Middletown* superior because it was "scientific." In John Frederick Lewis's opinion, "the Lynd Anthropological Expedition" to "the wild jungle of Babbitt-land" had produced "a work of true science" that superseded "the myriad realistic novels of small-town life." The historian Allan Nevins praised *Middletown* for substituting "the exact facts of 'social anthropology' for guesswork." To the literary critic F. R. Leavis, the Lynds' "remarkable work of anthropology" anatomized the "standardized civilization" that accompanied machine production. "Rapidly enveloping the world," standardization made the "plight of culture" seem "much more desperate" to Leavis than it had seemed to Matthew Arnold. Defending the Lynds against the charge that they nursed grievances against the Midwest, R. L. Duffus characterized their approach as "scientific and sociological almost to a fault." Harvey Warren Zorbaugh considered *Middletown* "the most significant document in the sociological literature of the community" because it exemplified "perhaps the most important intellectual achievement of our generation" – "our ability to detach ourselves from our culture – to stand it off and regard it objectively."[35]

Yet, despite their disclaimer that they were not trying "to prove any thesis with the data presented," the Lynds certainly had an ax to grind. By engaging in ethnographic defamiliarization, they debunked American provincialism and convinced C. Hartley Grattan that "a man with stone-age ideas can drive around in a high-priced automobile." In H. L. Mencken's irreverent opinion, the Lynds revealed just "how far short of libel Sinclair Lewis fell in 'Main Street' and 'Babbitt'" by documenting, "in cold-blooded, scientific terms," the "almost unbelievable stupidities" of "the normal Americano." Indeed, Mencken found *Middletown* "as exhilarating as even the dirtiest of the new novels."[36]

Middletown, then, arrayed the cultural authority of American social science behind literary critiques of American machine civilization. The journalist Max Lerner was virtually alone among reviewers in questioning whether the Lynds had, in fact, set aside their prepossessions and gone to Muncie as disinterested observers. "Is it accident or the authors' intention," he asked, "that when I am reading about Middletown I seem to be revisiting Zenith, where I first met Babbitt?" Although the Lynds "tried honestly to verify or reject" the

[35] John Frederick Lewis, Jr., "Revenge for the Ancients in Impartial Survey of American Town, Revealing Low Culture," *Philadelphia Record*, 2 February 1929; Nevins, "Fascinating Spectacle of an American Town Under the Microscope"; F. R. Leavis, *Mass Civilization and Minority Culture* (Cambridge: Gordon Fraser, 1930), 3–6; R. L. Duffus, "Getting at the Truth about an Average American Town," *New York Times Book Review*, 20 January 1929; Harvey W. Zorbaugh, review of *Middletown, Journal of Educational Sociology* 2 (1929): 549.

[36] Lynd and Lynd, *Middletown*, 6, 249n; C. Hartley Grattan, "A Typical American City," *New Republic*, 27 February 1929, 48; H. L. Mencken, "A City in Moronia," *American Mercury*, March 1929, 379–381; H. L. Mencken, "A Treatise on the Americano," *Baltimore Evening Sun*, 14 January 1929.

impressions they had derived from the "literature of national introspection and the voluminous protest against the barrenness of American life," they actually performed what, in Lerner's opinion, was "primarily a novelist's task under the pretensions of social science."[37]

No reviewer, however, questioned Middletown's representativeness, primarily because it was located in the Midwest. Characteristic of the literature of national introspection that followed the First World War was interest in, if not sordid fascination with, the small town. Commentary on American civilization in the 1920s, much of it critical, traced American civilization to the small town. In *Civilization in the United States*, Louis Raymond Reid declared that "the civilization of America is predominantly the civilization of the small town." In *Absentee Ownership and Business Enterprise in Recent Times: The Case of America*, Veblen saw in "the country town" "one of the great American institutions; perhaps the greatest" in terms of its "shaping public sentiment and giving character to American culture." And thanks largely to the resounding success of novels by Sinclair Lewis and other disaffected Midwesterners, the Midwest had become the archetypal region of America.[38]

CONTRASTING AMERICAN MICROCOSMS

Clark Wissler was far from the only anthropologist who welcomed the Lynds' treatment of an American community as though it were "a primitive tribe." Roland Dixon hailed *Middletown* as "a corking piece of work" that "ought to set a new standard for future investigations." Edward Sapir deemed the Lynds' book "a work of first class importance" and considered undertaking a study of New Haven, Connecticut, along the lines of *Middletown*. Melville Herskovits pronounced *Middletown* "a stunning piece of work – much more effective than 'Main Street,'" and promised Alfred Harcourt that he would "certainly require every one of [his] students" at Northwestern University "to read it." Erna Gunther, however, thought that *Middletown* bore "little resemblance of being anthropological literature." The Lynds did not seem to her "emotionally concerned": they neither participated "at least in some phases of [their] problem culture" nor studied these phases from the "native point of view."[39]

[37] Maxwell A. Lerner, "Middletown Has an Air of Mr. Babbitt's Zenith, Ohio," *New York Evening Post*, 9 February 1929; Gary Gerstle, "The Protean Character of American Liberalism," *American Historical Review* 99 (1994): 1061–1063.
[38] Louis Raymond Reid, "The Small Town," in *Civilization in the United States*, ed. Harold E. Stearns (New York: Harcourt, 1922), 286; Thorstein Veblen, "The Country Town," in *The Portable Veblen*, 407; Thomas L. Hartshorne, *The Distorted Image: Changing Conceptions of the American Character since Turner* (Cleveland: Case Western Reserve University Press, 1968), 95–97; Hoffman, *The Twenties*, 369; Andrew R. L. Cayton and Susan E. Gray, "The Story of the Midwest: An Introduction," in *The American Midwest: Essays on Regional History*, ed. Andrew R. L. Cayton and Susan E. Gray (Bloomington: Indiana University Press, 2001), 1–26.
[39] Roland B. Dixon to Robert S. Lynd, 1 February 1929; Edward Sapir to Robert S. Lynd, 1 March 1929, Lynd Papers, R4:C7; Melville Herskovits to Harcourt Brace, n.d., Lynd Papers, R7:C12.

Thanks in part to Alfred Harcourt's vigorous promotion of *Middletown* as the last word on machine-age Americans, the word "Middletown" became synonymous with a representative microcosm of modern American civilization, and the Lynds' book the standard against which subsequent ethnographies of the American scene were measured.[40] Thus, when Robert Redfield published his ethnography of the Mexican village of Tepoztlán, Morelos, in 1930, reviewers likened his book to "a miniature Middletown." Some went further, drawing an invidious comparison between Tepoztlán and Middletown as contrasting American microcosms. Carleton Beals emphasized Tepoztlán's deeper "cultural roots." Although not as "adaptable," "practical," or "mechanical" as life in Middletown, life in Tepoztlán was far "more beautiful." Perhaps even more important, it did not deny "the inner man."[41] The invidious distinction between "folk culture" and "machine civilization" became grist for Stuart Chase's mill in his 1931 best seller, *Mexico: A Study of Two Americas.* Supplementing his own impressions of Tepoztlán as a tourist with authoritative material gleaned from Redfield's book, Chase vividly evoked the stability and self-sufficiency of Mexican folk culture, the inability of its "machineless men" to "produce the humblest thing without form and design," and an agricultural calendar in which every third day was a holiday. Tepoztlán thus stood in dramatic contrast with Middletown. Far from being self-sufficient, Middletown existed "only as a cell in a vast interdependent industrial structure," its citizens haunted by unemployment, their lives lacking both "dignity" and "unity," and relentlessly driven by the clock. Mexican villagers, Chase concluded, possessed "several qualities the average American would give his eyeteeth to get." As a "parvenu cousin," Chase exhorted them to hold on to their "handicraft culture" and "analyze the Yankee invasion," taking "what is genuinely helpful" (such as electric power and improved sanitation) while "boycott[ing] the rest."[42]

But it was Ruth Benedict who immortalized "Middletown" as an American microcosm. In *Patterns of Culture*, she deplored "the obsessive rivalry of *Middletown* where houses are built and clothing bought and entertainments attended that each family may prove that it has not been left out of the game." Likening conspicuous consumption to the potlatch among the Kwakiutl, Benedict charged that Americans "sought and valued" wealth not "for its direct satisfaction of human needs but as a series of counters in the game of rivalry." Among the Kwakiutl, social rivalry was carried out "in a way that all success must be built upon the ruin of rivals"; among Americans, "in such a way that

[40] Roland Marchand, *Advertising the American Dream: Making Way for Modernity, 1920–1940* (Berkeley: University of California Press, 1985), 75.
[41] Robert Redfield, *Tepoztlán: A Mexican Village. A Study of Folk Life* (1930; repr., Chicago: University of Chicago Press, 1973); A. L. Kroeber, review of *Tepoztlán, American Anthropologist* 33 (1931): 236–237; Carleton Beals, "Mexico's Middletown," *Saturday Review of Literature*, 19 July 1930, 1202.
[42] Stuart Chase, with Marian Tyler, *Mexico: A Study of Two Americas* (New York: Macmillan, 1931), 130, 154, 170, 208, 310–311, 324–325.

individual choices and direct satisfactions are reduced to a minimum and conformity is sought beyond all other human gratifications." Indeed, it seemed to Benedict that "the fear of being different" was the "dominating motivation" that the Lynds documented in *Middletown*.[43]

CLASS LINES HARDEN

In 1931, on the strength of Robert MacIver's accolade that *Middletown* was "perhaps the most noteworthy single volume in the field of American sociology which has appeared in the last decade," Robert Lynd was appointed to a chair in sociology at Columbia University after having turned down a similar position at the University of Michigan. As his Ph.D. dissertation, Lynd presented a version of *Middletown* from which his wife's contributions had been cut. Two years earlier, Helen Lynd had been one of the charter faculty at Sarah Lawrence College. At Columbia, it was hoped that the "down-to-earth" Lynd would balance a department "overweighted on the side of abstract theory" by developing a "program on the sociology of the metropolis." Soon after joining Columbia's faculty, Lynd embarked on a study of the "adjustment patterns" since the onset of the Depression in suburban Montclair, New Jersey, and, in collaboration with a psychiatrist, studied the impact of prolonged unemployment on the "organization and function" of white-collar families in Manhattan.[44]

But Lynd laid these projects aside in the summer of 1935 to return to Muncie to collect material for what Alfred Harcourt envisaged as an appendix to a new edition of *Middletown*, one that would trace "the main lines of social change since 1925, in particular the major readjustments stemming from the Depression." Accompanied by five graduate students while his wife remained behind in New York, Lynd went to Muncie expecting "to find sharp differences in group alignments." What he found instead was that Munsonians were continuing to live "by the values by which [they had] lived in 1925," the chief additions

[43] Ruth Benedict, *Patterns of Culture* (1934; repr., Boston: Houghton Mifflin, 1959), 247–248, 273; Richard H. Pells, *Radical Visions and American Dreams: Culture and Social Thought in the Depression Years* (1973; repr., Middletown: Wesleyan University Press, 1984), 101–102; Helen Delpar, *The Enormous Vogue of Things Mexican: Cultural Relations between the United States and Mexico, 1920–1935* (Tuscaloosa: University of Alabama Press, 1992), 69–70.

[44] Robert MacIver, quoted in "Robert Staughton Lynd," *Political Science Quarterly* 86 (1971): 556; Page, *Fifty Years in the Sociological Enterprise*, 43; Robert MacIver, *As a Tale is Told: The Autobiography of R. M. MacIver* (Chicago: University of Chicago Press, 1968), 115; Seymour Martin Lipset, "The Department of Sociology," in *A History of the Faculty of Political Science, Columbia University* (New York: Columbia University Press, 1955), 294–295; Robert S. Lynd, "A Study of the Impact of the Depression on Family Organization and Function," n.d.; Robert S. Lynd, "Memorandum on the Study of Changing Family Patterns in the Depression," 14 March 1933, Lynd Papers, R2:C3; Fox, "Epitaph for Middletown," 131–134; Lizabeth Cohen, *A Consumers' Republic: The Politics of Mass Consumption in Postwar America* (New York: Knopf, 2003), 19, 29.

to which were "defensive, negative elaborations of already existing values." After returning to New York, a disillusioned Lynd, with help from his wife, penned a critical sequel to *Middletown*.[45]

Published in 1937 under the title *Middletown in Transition*, the Lynds' sequel documented the hardening of class lines in Muncie since 1925 and, striking a new note, exposed the pervasiveness of "business-class control." By 1935, the working class was slightly smaller than it had been ten years earlier – 65 percent of Muncie's workforce – and working-class neighborhoods had grown more separate from business-class neighborhoods. In the meantime, the Depression had dealt a near-fatal blow to the "exuberant boast of a classless society." In 1925, upward mobility for workingmen generally took the form of climbing the "American ladder of opportunity" to the foreman's or supervisory rung. Ten years later, the management had become even more specialized as "technically trained personnel" replaced "men who have come up from operating machines and punching the time clock" in supervisory positions. Yet, despite overwhelming evidence of blocked mobility, most workingmen in Muncie continued to subscribe to "the coveted American dream" of "bossing oneself." Few were any more class-conscious in 1935 than they had been ten years earlier. Given the choice between jobs or working-class solidarity, workingmen opted for jobs. As a result, "fear, resentment, insecurity, and disillusionment" had been "largely an *individual* experience for each worker, and not a thing generalized by him into a '*class*' experience."[46]

Toward the end of *Middletown in Transition*, too late to inform their analysis, the Lynds sketched a "nascent 'class' system," composed of six classes, that replaced their earlier distinction between the business class and the working class. At the top of Middletown's social hierarchy stood a "small, self-conscious upper class" that had coalesced around the second generation of the "X family" – the Ball brothers. Unlike ten years earlier, when Muncie's "few wealthy families" had "tended to avoid ostentation and to merge themselves in the general business class," they now lived apart from the rest of the community in an exclusive neighborhood, packed their children off to Eastern boarding schools, and engaged in such conspicuous leisure activities as riding to hounds and piloting private planes. By 1935, a discrete "middle class" comprising "'small' white collar folk" – "struggling manufacturers with no particular future," "smaller retailers and tradespeople, salesmen, officeholders, schoolteachers," and "hired professional assistants" – had fallen out of the business class.

---

[45] Robert S. Lynd and Helen Merrell Lynd, *Middletown in Transition: A Study in Cultural Conflicts* (1937; repr., San Diego: Harcourt, 1982), x–xi, 489; "Lynd, Author of Middletown Back in City After 10 Years," *Muncie Evening Press*, 12 June 1935; Paul Kelso, "'Middletown' Authors [*sic*] Leaving Today after Two Weeks' Visit," *Muncie Morning Star*, 26 June 1935.

[46] Lynd and Lynd, *Middletown in Transition*, 72, 67, 70–71, 41 (emphasis in original). As late as 1955, workingmen continued to dream of self-employment. See, for example, Ely Chinoy, *Automobile Workers and the American Dream* (1955; repr., Urbana: University of Illinois Press, 1992), 4–5, 88–89.

Similarly, what had been an undifferentiated working class had fragmented into a small "aristocracy of local labor," a much larger group of semiskilled and unskilled workers, and, at the bottom, irregularly employed "poor whites" then migrating to Muncie from Appalachia. Although this migration was under way in 1924, it had not been mentioned in *Middletown*.[47]

In elaborating Muncie's class system, the Lynds may have been responding to calls for "greater refinement of analysis" urged on them by Malcolm Willey and Ernest Burgess, both of whom considered their two-class scheme "simple and too simplifying."[48] More likely, though, the Lynds elaborated their class scheme because their argument demanded it. Working-class fragmentation, stemming in part from the influx into Middletown of "green peas," Appalachian migrants, helped to account for workingmen's lack of "any driving sense of class consciousness" and their acceptance of "watered [down] versions of the official business-class symbols."[49]

Recognition of the existence of a discrete middle class in *Middletown in Transition* may have testified to Robert Lynd's greater familiarity with the work of Karl Marx. More likely, though, it reflected his response to Lewis Corey's *The Crisis of the Middle Class* (1935). According to Corey, the rise of big business had fragmented the middle class into an "old" middle class of small, self-employed businessmen who owned property and a much larger "new" middle class of salaried employees who possessed marketable skills but little or no capital. If sufficiently radicalized by unemployment and economic insecurity, members of this new middle class might ignore the invidious distinction between nonmanual and manual work, make common cause with workingmen, and even band together with them in unions. The Lynds, however, were much less hopeful that class lines would blur. Alarmed by the appeal to beleaguered lower middle-class Americans of demagogues such as the late Senator Huey Long and the "Radio Priest" Father Charles Coughlin, they evoked the prospect of an indigenous fascism coalescing around just the "right strong man."[50]

It would have been hard for the Lynds to overlook the Ball brothers, who made national news in 1935 when they purchased a bankrupt holding company for a bargain-basement price of $3 million. The Balls' glass factories had

[47] Lynd and Lynd, *Middletown in Transition*, 455–461.

[48] Ernest W. Burgess, review of *Middletown in Transition*, *American Journal of Sociology* 43 (1937): 487; Malcolm M. Willey, review of *Middletown in Transition*, *Annals of the American Academy of Political and Social Science* 195 (1938): 239.

[49] Lynd and Lynd, *Middletown in Transition*, 454–455. On the migration of Appalachians to the industrial Midwest, see James N. Gregory, *The Southern Diaspora: How the Great Migrations of Black and White Southerners Transformed America* (Chapel Hill: University of North Carolina Press, 2005).

[50] Lynd and Lynd, *Middletown in Transition*, 457–458, 509; Lewis Corey, *The Crisis of the Middle Class* (New York: Covici-Friede, 1935); Michael Denning, *The Cultural Front: The Laboring of American Culture in the Twentieth Century* (London: Verso, 1997), 99–102; Alan Brinkley, *Voices of Protest: Huey Long, Father Coughlin, and the Great Depression* (New York: Knopf, 1982).

flourished during the Depression as American housewives economized by canning fruit and vegetables from their gardens. But the attention paid to the "X family" in *Middletown in Transition* also reflected Robert Lynd's growing fear that the monopoly power of big business was undermining American democracy – a fear that was to haunt him for the rest of his life.[51]

Some reviewers found *Middletown in Transition* "less convincing" than *Middletown*. Caroline Ware criticized the "all too brief" fieldwork in Muncie, which led the Lynds to rely too much on "the judgments of leaders in various parts of life" and "the columns of the [local] press" and neglect the opinion of "the rank and file of industrial workers." Other reviewers, however, judged *Middletown in Transition* superior to *Middletown*. Melville Herskovits praised the "sureness of approach," omission of "irrelevant statistical data," and "much finer treatment of the subtleties of culture." Stuart Chase thought the literary style much improved. He cited the Lynds' phrase "the thick blubber of custom," which "haunts the mind." To Alvin Johnson, the subject matter of *Middletown in Transition* – how Munsonians coped with the "devastating scourge" of the Depression – was even more compelling than Muncie caught in the throes of rapid change. No reviewer expressed any doubts about Muncie's representativeness. "This is not really Middletown," declared R. L. Duffus. "It is America."[52]

A number of reviewers also recognized the challenge that *Middletown in Transition* posed to the long-standing American axiom of class without class conflict. "Middletown still ducks all the economic and social implications of class stratification," as Douglas Aikman put it. R. L. Duffus noted the "growing tension among the different economic levels in Middletown," although this was without a commensurate "growth of class feeling." E. Wight Bakke found "much food for thought in the [Lynds'] analysis of the hardening of class lines in Middletown," especially considering how the Depression had sounded "the death knell of the buoyant confidence in the traditional up-the-ladder journey of all Americans." To Geoffrey Gorer, "the factual, if not the psychological hardening of the class situation" made "more palpable" the "contradiction" between "individual competition" and "group co-operation."[53]

[51] Charles Wertenbaker, "Mr. Ball Takes the Trains," *Saturday Evening Post*, 6 February 1937, 5–6, 71–74; "Mr. X Goes to Town," *Time*, 19 April 1937, 80–86.

[52] Norman J. Ware, review of *Middletown in Transition*, *American Economic Review* 27 (1937): 842; Caroline F. Ware, review of *Middletown in Transition*, *American Historical Review* 43 (1938): 427; Melville J. Herskovits, "American Microcosm," *Nation*, 24 April 1937, 474; Stuart Chase, "Middletown, as American as a Baked Apple," *New York Herald Tribune Books*, 25 April 1937; Alvin Johnson, review of *Middletown in Transition*, *Yale Review* 26 (1937): 815; R. L. Duffus, "Middletown Ten Years After," *New York Times Book Review*, 25 April 1937; Geoffrey Gorer, "Erewhon Revisited," *New Stalesman and Nation*, 11 September 1937, 380.

[53] Duncan Aikman, "Mr. Babbitt Still Runs Middletown," *Saturday Review of Literature*, 24 April 1937, 14; Duffus, "Middletown Ten Years After"; E. Wight Bakke, review of *Middletown in Transition*, *Yale Law Journal* 47 (1937): 153–154.

Salient class distinctions figured even more prominently in a "picture essay" on Muncie that appeared in *Life* magazine in May 1937. Dispatched to Muncie to capture "the average 1937 American as he really is," the photographer Margaret Bourke-White returned with photos documenting the gulf between the rich and the poor in the city: one photo showed members of Muncie's "most exclusive young set," attired in pink coats, riding to hounds on the farm of one of the Ball brothers; another, the family of a former worker for Ball brothers who, having exhausted his indemnity from the loss of a leg in an industrial accident, was scraping by on welfare in a "slum and Negro section." Still another photo showed destitute Appalachian migrants raising chickens "fer eatin'" in their one-room shack in "Shedtown."[54]

Although several Munsonians complained that the Lynds had been "cold" and "mechanical" in their treatment of Muncie, they did not dispute the accuracy of the Lynds' representations of life in Muncie.[55] Many Munsonians, however, heartily resented Bourke-White's photos for focusing exclusively on "the upper crust and the lower (soaked) crust" while leaving out "the middle filling" – "the most important part of any community-pie." To counter Bourke-White's unflattering portrait of Muncie, the *Muncie Evening Press* held a contest in which the editors selected a pipe fitter, his wife, and their two children as a "typical family" in America's "typical city," and then treated these "solid, likeable, hospitable folk" to an all-expense-paid weekend in Chicago. Long years of economic uncertainty and hardship notwithstanding, Munsonians (like the "Okies" then fleeing the Dust Bowl for California) were reluctant to place themselves on rungs in a nascent American class system; they preferred to see themselves as "plain folk." When the Associated Press reporter John Selby visited Muncie in the summer of 1938, "nobody mentioned the word 'class' excepting the writer." Whenever Selby himself mentioned the word "class," "it always brought a raised eyebrow."[56]

CLASS AND POWER

Robert Lynd liked to tell his students that "I'm one of them urgent boys." In *Middletown*, he and his wife had called attention to the widening gulf between the business class and the working class. In *Middletown in Transition*, they had depicted this gulf as far wider than it had been ten years earlier. By 1939, Lynd thought it urgent for social scientists to investigate such topics as the emergence

[54] "Muncie, Ind. Is the Great U.S. 'Middletown,'" *Life Magazine*, 10 May 1937, 15–26.
[55] Robert S. Lynd, Notes for a talk to the Muncie Rotary Club, June 1935, Lynd Papers, R8:C13; Lynd and Lynd, *Middletown in Transition*, xii; Wilbur E. Sutton to Robert S. Lynd, 6 May 1937; John B. Lewellen to Robert S. Lynd, 26 May 1937, Lynd Papers, R8:C13; Raymond G. Fuller, "Muncie Looks at Middletown," *New Republic*, 8 September 1937, 127–128.
[56] Robert H. Myers to Robert S. Lynd, 6 June 1937, Lynd Papers, R1:C1; Lola Goelet Yoakem to Robert S. Lynd, 24 May 1937, Lynd Papers, R8:C13, "Meet the 'Typical Family' of America's 'Typical City,'" *Muncie Evening Press*, 5 June 1937; "Mr. Selby Takes a Look at 'Middletown' and Finds He Disagrees with the Lynds," *Muncie Sunday Star*, 7 August 1938.

of "an American proletariat," class consciousness, and class conflict. "The gilt is wearing thin," Lynd declared, "on the old formula that 'The sky is the limit for any man who works hard, saves his money, and watches his chances.'" Yet, even though no aspect of American culture demanded "more imperatively the best analysis of our social sciences," social scientists played down "the omnipresent fact of class antagonisms and conflicts" in American society and eschewed the terms "class" and "class struggle."[57]

From 1939 until his retirement from Columbia in 1960, Lynd became ever more outspoken in his denunciations of "class stratification." He traced class stratification to monopoly, the concentration of political power in the hands of "big business," and "arbitrary maintenance of privilege," all of which, he believed, rendered real democracy impossible. Although he never joined the Communist Party nor subscribed to "an exclusive economic determinism," Lynd did equate class standing with "occupation and resulting wealth." Convinced that the incompatibility between "economic un-democracy" and "political democracy" would doom "the old liberal middle way," he insisted that Americans choose between socializing the economy and running it "for the purposes of democracy" or letting big business run the "democratic state" for its own profit. After the Second World War, a dispirited Lynd, renouncing any hope that middle-class Americans would effect "fundamental changes" in American life, threw his lot in with organized labor.[58]

In the meantime, Lynd's standing fell among social scientists. He never completed either of the two studies of the unemployed that he had laid aside to work on *Middletown in Transition*, nor did he get very far on an ambitious study of power on which he worked desultorily in the 1940s and 1950s. At Columbia, his relations with his colleague Robert MacIver became increasingly strained until they reached a "breaking point" when MacIver wrote a review critical of *Knowledge for What?*. Intimidated by the survey research pioneered by the Austrian émigré Paul Lazarsfeld, whom he helped to bring to Columbia, and by the middle-range theorizing of Robert K. Merton, Lynd developed a writer's block, suffered a series of heart attacks, and sank into despondency.

---

[57] Robert S. Lynd, quoted in Daniel Bell, review of *Knowledge for What?*, *Modern Quarterly* 11 (1939): 90; Robert S. Lynd, *Knowledge for What? The Place of Social Science in American Culture* (1939; repr., Princeton, N.J.: Princeton University Press, 1970), 92, 25, 227–228.

[58] Robert S. Lynd, foreword to *Business as a System of Power*, by Robert A. Brady (New York: Columbia University Press, 1943), vii–xviii; Robert S. Lynd, "Role of the Middle Class in Contemporary Social Change," notes for talk to the John Reed Society, Harvard University, 3 November 1947, Lynd Papers, R1:C2; Robert S. Lynd, "Who Calls the Tune?" *Journal of Higher Education* 19 (1948): 170; Robert S. Lynd, "Tiptoeing around Class," review of *The Psychology of Social Classes*, by Richard Centers, *New Republic*, 25 July 1949, 17–18; Robert S. Lynd, *You Can Do It Better Democratically* (Detroit: UAW-CIO Education Department, 1949), 6, 8, 10, 12, 25; Robert S. Lynd, "Power in American Society as Resource and Problem," in *Problems of Power in American Democracy*, ed. Arthur Kornhauser (Detroit: Wayne State University Press, 1957), 1–45; John H. Bunzel, "Liberal Ideology and the Problem of Power," *Western Political Quarterly* 13 (1960): 374–388; John H. Bunzel, "The Commitment to Power of Robert S. Lynd," *Ethics* 71 (1961): 90–103.

Although Lynd's "homegrown leftism" continued to attract students, his "hortatory" lectures reminded one of them of the preaching of "Midwestern evangelists."[59]

Robert Lynd was a transitional figure whose career recapitulated the trajectory of many early American social scientists from the ministry to the academy. Not particularly well-versed in European theory, Lynd drew eclectically on the homegrown theorists Thorstein Veblen, William Ogburn, and Clark Wissler. As a generalist who chafed at disciplinary boundaries, Lynd owed his biggest intellectual debts to anthropology, which sanctioned his holistic approach to American culture, underwrote his claims to "objectivity" as a researcher, and shaped his understanding of social change in twentieth-century America. Although Lynd and his wife pioneered the social anthropology of contemporary life, their influence in shaping the ways social scientists and educated Americans conceived of the American scene paled in comparison with that of W. Lloyd Warner.

THE MIDDLETOWN TO END ALL MIDDLETOWNS

An ebullient man of vaulting ambition and a consummate academic entrepreneur, William Lloyd Warner was born near Redlands, California, in 1898. In 1917, several months shy of graduating from high school in San Bernardino, Warner joined the army but was discharged for medical reasons before he saw any service. While recuperating from tuberculosis, he attended the University of Southern California for a year, then transferred to the University of California at Berkeley. Suspended for Socialist activities, Warner briefly tried his luck in New York. Returning to Berkeley, he was reinstated as a student thanks to the intercession of Robert Lowie, who "gave him some moral support and a little financial aid during a period of emotional stress." Switching his major from English to anthropology, Warner imbibed the Boasian historical approach from Lowie and Alfred Kroeber, both of whom emphasized the importance of "tribal contacts" (diffusion) and "chronological relations" (culture history). After earning a B.A. in 1925, Warner began work toward a Ph.D. in anthropology.[60]

---

[59] Robert M. MacIver, "Enduring Systems of Thought," and Robert S. Lynd, "Intelligence Must Fight," *Survey Graphic*, August 1939, 496–499; MacIver, *As a Tale That Is Told*, 137; Lipset, "The Department of Sociology," 296–297; S. M. Miller, "Struggles for Relevance: The Lynd Legacy," *Journal of the History of Sociology* 2 (1979–80): 58–63; Helen Lynd, "Oral History," 107–108, 247; Staughton Lynd, "Father and Son: Intellectual Work Outside the University," *Social Policy* 23 (1993): 4–5; James S. Coleman, "Columbia in the 1950s," in *Authors of Their Own Lives: Intellectual Biographies by Twenty American Sociologists*, ed. Bennett M. Berger (Berkeley: University of California Press, 1990), 78.

[60] Robert H. Lowie to Franz Boas, 31 January 1936, Boas Papers; Robert H. Lowie, introduction to *A Black Civilization: A Social Study of an Australian Tribe*, by W. Lloyd Warner, rev. ed. (New York: Harper, 1958), xiv–xv; George W. Stocking, Jr., *Victorian Anthropology* (New York: Free Press, 1987), 287–288. For biographical information on Warner, see Mildred Hall Warner, *W. Lloyd Warner: Social Anthropologist* (New York: Publishing Center for Cultural Resources, 1988).

Warner's career, however, veered off in a radically new direction in 1926. In the spring, Bronislaw Malinowski paid a brief visit to Berkeley, leaving "a meteoric trail behind," then returned to teach summer school. Touring American universities at the behest of officers of the Rockefeller Foundation, Malinowski urged American anthropologists to shift their attention from the "purely retrospective interests" of culture history to the synchronic study of "social process" and "interrelation of the various aspects of culture."[61] Later that spring, A. R. Radcliffe-Brown passed through Berkeley on his way from Cape Town, South Africa, to a new chair in Sydney, Australia. Critical of what he regarded as the Boasians' "conjectural" historical reconstruction, Radcliffe-Brown espoused "social anthropology" as a "science of man" aimed at formulating the natural laws of social change. Thinking that Warner had "the making of a first-class anthropologist," Radcliffe-Brown invited him to undertake fieldwork among the Australian aborigines. "Eager to visit a tribe with a living culture," Warner accepted.[62]

Before setting sail for Australia, Warner went to Harvard, where he learned how to take anthropometric measurements from Earnest Hooton.[63] Then, after working with Radcliffe-Brown in Sydney on Australian kinship and social organization (interests Lowie had kindled), Warner plunged into seven months of fieldwork among the Murngin, the name he gave to a group of about 3,000 aborigines who lived in northeast Arnhem Land. (Today they are known as the Yolngu.) After collecting voluminous material on their genealogies, social organization, ritual, and myths, Warner returned to Sydney, where he roomed with Radcliffe-Brown, a bon vivant who opened doors for him in society, plied him with good food and wine, and deepened his "nascent devotion" to Émile Durkheim (whose book *Suicide* Warner proclaimed "the greatest book ever written"). In 1928, a fellowship from the Australian National Research Council allowed him to return for a second season of fieldwork among the Murngin.[64]

---

[61] A. L. Kroeber to Leonard Outhwaite, 29 March 1926; "Report by Dr. B. Malinowski to the Laura Spelman Rockefeller Memorial, Concerning his Travels in America in 1926 as Visiting Professor, March 1926," 8, folder 559, box 56, series 6, RG 3, Laura Spelman Rockefeller Memorial, RAC; Bronislaw Malinowski, "Anthropology as Social Science," minutes of the Hanover Conference, August 1926, 52, folder 564, box 52, series 6, RG 3, Laura Spelman Rockefeller Memorial, RAC. See also George W. Stocking, Jr., "Philanthropoids and Vanishing Cultures: Rockefeller Funding and the End of the Museum Era in Anglo-American Anthropology," in *Objects and Others: Essays on Museums and Material Culture*, ed. George W. Stocking, Jr. (Madison: University of Wisconsin Press, 1985), 112–145.

[62] A. R. Radcliffe-Brown, quoted in Mildred Hall Warner, *W. Lloyd Warner*, 3; Lowie was amused by the "sort of spiritual paternity towards Warner" he shared with Radcliffe-Brown, though he "never had been able to adapt [him]self . . . to a master-disciple relationship." Lowie to Boas, 31 January 1936.

[63] Warner's work with Earnest Hooton, who taught him how to measure bones, inspired him to imagine doing "something in the way of clearing up the boundaries between the sociological and physiological branches of the science." W. Lloyd Warner to Robert H. Lowie, Sept. [1926], Lowie Papers, box 14.

[64] Mildred Warner, *W. Lloyd Warner*, 32–42; W. Lloyd Warner to Robert H. Lowie, n.d., 9 November 1927, Lowie Papers, box 14; Ralph Beals, "Julian Steward: The Berkeley Days," *Journal of the Steward Anthropological Society* 161 (1979): 6.

In his fieldwork, Warner fused the two approaches in which he had been schooled.[65] Drawing on the genealogies and kinship charts he had collected, Warner explicated Murngin social organization in terms of an elaborate kinship system comprising some seventy-one different statuses. He then showed how Murngin rituals and myths helped to maintain "social solidarity." Finally, drawing on archaeological excavations, the distribution of cultural traits, and accounts of European explorers, Warner reconstructed the unwritten history of the Murngin and traced their contacts with Malay traders.[66]

Not published until 1937, Warner's ethnography of the Murngin, *A Black Civilization*, was distinguished by "excellent field observations" and "descriptive material" and by his acute ability, as Lowie put it, to "sense the atmosphere of a culture." Although marred by "careless writing" and "loose phraseology," which Lowie blamed on Warner's "abominable practice of dictating whole chapters," *A Black Civilization* was hailed as "the best study of an Australian tribe" yet published. Its "French – and, at that . . . sociological – flavor," Lowie commented, was "not without piquancy."[67]

In 1929, Warner returned to the United States to resume work toward a Ph.D. at Harvard. He brought with him the ambitious project of applying the same techniques he had used among the Murngin to the natives of an American community. Reading *Middletown* only whetted his interest because he, like Erna Gunther, did not think that the Lynds had captured the native point of view.[68]

Soon after he settled down in Cambridge, Warner attracted the notice of the Australian-born social psychologist Elton Mayo, a researcher at the Graduate School of Business Administration and a member of the Committee of Industrial Physiology. With lavish support from the Rockefeller Foundation, the Committee of Industrial Physiology was then investigating worker fatigue and morale at the Western Electric Company's Hawthorne plant in Cicero, Illinois. As an admirer of Sigmund Freud, Carl Jung, and Pierre Janet, Mayo proposed that the interview methods of clinical psychology be applied to the treatment of the psychoneuroses that he dubbed the "psychopathologies of industrial life." Drawing on the work of his friend Bronislaw Malinowski, Mayo urged that social scientists who wanted to study "a functional society"

[65] Warner contended that the historical approach to the study of culture had to be supplemented by the sociological approach. W. Lloyd Warner, "Methodology and Field Research in Africa," *Africa* 6 (1933): 53–54. Lowie often heard Warner "justifying a historical approach and insisting that he had combined it with a sociological one at Newburyport." Lowie to Boas, 31 January 1936.

[66] Warner, *A Black Civilization*, 4, 7, 10–11, 443–463.

[67] Lowie to Boas, 31 January 1936; Lowie, introduction to *A Black Civilization*, xv; A. P. Elkin, review of *A Black Civilization*, *Oceania* 8 (1937): 119. Elkin's opinion was seconded by Ralph Linton in the *Annals of the American Academy of Political and Social Science* 193 (1937): 207, and by Lauriston Sharp in the *American Anthropologist* 41 (1939): 150. For a retrospective assessment, see J. A. Barnes, *Inquest on the Murngin* (London: Royal Anthropological Institute of Great Britain and Northern Ireland, 1967).

[68] Mildred Warner, *W. Lloyd Warner*, 42.

familiarize themselves with "the investigations of the anthropologists." On the basis of his own reading in the anthropological literature, Mayo postulated the existence in "primitive" societies of a "non-logical social code" that bound men and women together by regulating their interpersonal relations. Following Durkheim, Mayo rooted what he perceived as the pervasive "anomie" of industrial civilization in the "relative annihilation of the cultural traditions of work and craftsmanship" by "highly systematized industrial procedures."[69] Perhaps reflecting his participation in the seminar on Vilfredo Pareto that the physiologist Lawrence J. Henderson had organized at Harvard, Mayo warned businessmen of the dangers of ignoring the "human factor" in their relations with their employees.[70]

In 1930, Mayo, who had long toyed with the notion of sponsoring the fieldwork of an anthropologist in a modern community, recruited Warner to serve as a consultant for the Hawthorne study. Unlike Mayo, whose interest lay in how well the individual worker was, or was not, adjusting to factory life, Warner viewed social relations among the workers as the key to unlocking the social organization of the factory. Accordingly, he advised Hawthorne researchers to treat each interview as a "social situation," to attend to the "attitudes" of their informants, and to be on the look out for "solidarities" and "antagonisms" among the workers. Warner's advice helped to lead to the discovery of informal sanctions regulating workers' output.[71]

After the Committee of Industrial Physiology agreed to sponsor the study of a modern community, Warner chose Newburyport, a static industrial city of some 17,000 residents located forty miles from Cambridge. Despite the

[69] Elton Mayo to Charles E. Merriam, 21 July 1925, folder 572, box 53, series 3.6, Laura Spelman Rockefeller Memorial, RAC; David L. Edsall to Edmund E. Day, 25 April 1930, folder 4069, box 342, series 200, RG 1.1, Rockefeller Foundation Archives, RAC; Elton Mayo, *The Human Problems of an Industrial Civilization* (New York: Macmillan, 1933), 107–113, 120, 165–166, 188. For contrasting views of Mayo, see George Caspar Homans, *Coming to My Senses: The Autobiography of a Sociologist* (New Brunswick, N.J.: Transaction Publishers, 1984), chaps. 9–10; Richard C. S. Trahair, *The Humanist Temper: The Life and Work of Elton Mayo* (New Brunswick, N.J.: Transaction Publishers, 1984); Richard Gillespie, *Manufacturing Knowledge: A History of the Hawthorne Experiments* (Cambridge: Cambridge University Press, 1991).

[70] Barbara S. Heyl, "The Harvard Pareto Circle," *Journal of the History of the Behavioral Sciences* 4 (1968): 317; William Foote Whyte, *Participant Observer: An Autobiography* (Ithaca: ILR Press, 1994), 55–57; Stephen J. Cross and William R. Albury, "Walter B. Cannon, L. J. Henderson, and the Organic Analogy," *Osiris* 3 (1987): 165–192.

[71] Elton Mayo to Charles E. Merriam, 16 March 1925, quoted in Gillespie, *Manufacturing Knowledge*, 155; W. Lloyd Warner to W. J. Dickson, 27 February 1931, Western Electric Company Hawthorne Studies Collection, Baker Library Historical Collections, Harvard Business School (hereafter Hawthorne Studies Collection); F. J. Roethlisberger and William J. Dickson, *Management and the Worker* (1939; repr., Cambridge, Mass.: Harvard University Press, 1949), 389–391; F. J. Roethlisberger, *The Elusive Phenomena: An Autobiographical Account of My Work in the Field of Organizational Behavior* (Boston: Harvard Business School Press, 1977), 48–49, 54–56; Gillespie, *Manufacturing Knowledge*, 85, 154–157, 163, 167.

presence of eight European ethnic groups and a small number of African-Americans who together made up nearly half of its population, Newburyport's social organization was "stable" and "historic." It was dominated by Yankees who bore a "coherent tradition" that not only remained "unadulterated" but was vital enough to cope with "the crises of modern life." As a "well integrated" and "adjusted" city, Newburyport stood in dramatic contrast with Cicero, the "disorganized" Chicago suburb that Warner considered studying until the Western Electric Company withdrew its promised financial support. Unlike the Lynds, who went to Muncie to study the impact of social change, Warner went to Newburyport to study social persistence – a topic very much on the minds of American intellectuals as they worried about how American society hung together amid the unprecedented economic and social strain of the Depression.[72]

To help him put "Yankee City," or Newburyport, under the microscope, Warner recruited a group of promising Harvard students – among them Conrad Arensberg, Eliot Chapple, Allison Davis, Burleigh Gardner, Buford Junker, Solon Kimball, and Leo Srole. They were joined by Paul S. Lunt, descendant of an "old" Newburyport family, and Josiah Orme Low, a retired securities broker. From 1930 until 1935, this team of researchers collected "millions of social facts." They interviewed hundreds of informants, observed both sacred and secular community rituals, distributed detailed questionnaires, reconstructed the genealogies of both historic families and historic houses, linked the membership lists of more than 200 voluntary associations, and compiled "social personality cards" on virtually all of the city's 17,000-plus residents. It was research on a monumental scale – "the Middletown to end all Middletowns" in Stuart Chase's apt words.[73]

Warner's ambitions, however, reached far beyond Newburyport. The logic of "comparative sociology," Radcliffe-Brown's program for applying "the generalizing method of the natural sciences to the phenomena of the social life of man," required that Newburyport be studied, not in isolation, but rather as a "type" in comparison with other communities, both "primitive" and modern.[74]

---

[72] W. Lloyd Warner and Paul S. Lunt, *The Social Life of a Modern Community* (New Haven, Conn.: Yale University Press, 1941), 4–5; W. Lloyd Warner, "Social Anthropology and the Modern Community," *American Journal of Sociology* 46 (1941): 787; W. Lloyd Warner to M. L. Putnam, 26 November 1930, Hawthorne Studies Collection; Elton Mayo to David L. Edsall, 19 January 1931, folder 4070, box 342, series 200, RG 1.1, Rockefeller Foundation Archives, RAC; Trahair, *The Humanist Temper*, 246; Gillespie, *Manufacturing Knowledge*, 88–89, 155–156; Murray G. Murphey, "On the Scientific Study of Religion in the United States, 1870–1980," in *Religion and Twentieth-Century American Intellectual Life*, ed. Michael J. Lacey (New York: Cambridge University Press, 1991), 148.

[73] Mildred Warner, *W. Lloyd Warner*, 50–51, 79–92; Warner and Lunt, *The Social Life of a Modern Community*, 38–75; Stuart Chase, *The Proper Study of Mankind: An Inquiry into the Science of Human Relations* (New York: Harper, 1948), 132.

[74] Warner, "Social Anthropology and the Modern Community," 786: George W. Stocking, Jr., *After Tylor: British Social Anthropology, 1888–1951* (Madison: University of Wisconsin Press, 1995), 354, 431.

The first opportunity for extending the Newburyport research came in 1931, when the Harvard Department of Anthropology, having received a five-year grant of $75,000 from the Rockefeller Foundation to train graduate students, embarked on a survey of Ireland. Running from 1931 until 1936 and directed by Earnest Hooton, the Harvard Irish Survey comprised archaeological work at a number of sites, a racial survey to "obtain a clear picture of the racial composition of the Irish people," and a social anthropological study. After being appointed the director of the social anthropological study, Warner chose County Clare, with its mixture of "older Gaelic and modern British influences" and the Irish and English languages, as the site of "the first up-to-date functional study of rural and town life in Ireland." In 1932, Conrad Arensberg, who had studied ethnic groups in Newburyport, began to investigate rural markets and inheritance patterns in County Clare. He was joined, the following year, by Solon Kimball, another Newburyport veteran, who studied merchants in the market town of Ennis. Arensberg and Kimball hoped to compare Ennis and its environs, but they scaled back their ambitious plans after war broke out in Europe in September 1939. In 1940, they published *Family and Community in Ireland* in the attempt "to place rural southern Ireland on the roster" of "a contemporary sociology . . . of all the world's peoples, both modern and 'primitive.'" Testing the hypothesis that "it is useful to regard society as an integrated system of mutually interrelated and functionally interdependent parts," Arensberg and Kimball traced such Irish characteristics as delayed marriage, high rates of bachelorhood and emigration, and declining population to a "familistic" social system.[75]

A second opportunity for extending the Newburyport research arose in 1933 when Warner persuaded the Committee of Industrial Physiology to sponsor fieldwork in a southern city "directly comparable" to Newburyport.[76] In a novel experiment, he dispatched a white couple, Burleigh and Mary Gardner, and a black couple, Allison and Elizabeth Davis, to Natchez, Mississippi. All four fieldworkers were Newburyport veterans. The Davises were also veterans

[75] "Proposed Plan for Graduate Research in Anthropology at Harvard" (1930); "Report upon Utilization of RF Grant," 1933, folder 4044, box 339, series 200, RG 1.1, Rockefeller Foundation Archives, RAC; W. Lloyd Warner to Robert H. Lowie, 23 September 1932, Lowie Papers, box 14; Conrad M. Arensberg and Solon T. Kimball, *Family and Community in Ireland*, 2nd ed. (Harvard: Cambridge University Press, 1968), xxx.
[76] Warner told St. Clair Drake that "he sold the research plan to the Harvard Graduate School of Business Administration on a point of business practicality. There was a box factory in Natchez, and Warner suggested to Harvard that 'if there is a caste system and Northern capital starts to invest, it looks as if you are going to have two toilets, two lunchrooms, two of everything, and that's going to increase the cost of investment. Therefore, you ought to know something about the South.' They bought the idea that you couldn't understand the box factory if you didn't understand the town, and that you couldn't understand the town if you didn't understand the surrounding county!" St. Clair Drake, "In the Mirror of Black Scholarship: W. Allison Davis and *Deep South*," *Harvard Educational Review* 2 (1974): 46–47.

of Bronislaw Malinowski's seminar at the London School of Economics. The "whole Negro-white research," however, was "delicate and filled with dynamite." To circumvent southern mores, which prevented whites from associating with blacks as social equals, Burleigh Gardner and Allison Davis shared field notes while motoring in Gardner's car. Just to be safe, though, the fieldworkers sent copies of their field notes to Warner in Cambridge.[77] In *Deep South* (1941), Allison Davis and the Gardners fleshed out Warner's conception of a "caste-class order," depicting a superior white caste and an inferior black caste, each in turn stratified into social classes. Marriage between members of the castes was prohibited, and social mobility for blacks was limited. Although upper-class African-Americans ranked above lower-class whites in the class system, they nonetheless suffered the strictures of caste. This put them under enormous psychological strain.[78]

FROM HARVARD TO CHICAGO (AND BEYOND)

Collating the millions of social facts collected in Newburyport, and incorporating them into a comparative framework that included material from Natchez, would have been difficult under the best of circumstances, but the difficulty was compounded by Warner's move to the University of Chicago in 1935. Warner's failure to learn enough German to pass his qualifying examinations, slowness in writing up his Australian fieldwork, indifferent undergraduate teaching, and pessimism about the prospects for interdisciplinary social science at Harvard, combined with Alfred Tozzer's animosity, all contributed to his move. Then, too, Robert Redfield, who in 1934 had been appointed Dean of the Social Sciences Division at the University of Chicago, made Warner an offer that he could not refuse: a joint appointment, as tenured associate professor, in the departments of Anthropology and Sociology with half-time off for research. A. R. Radcliffe-Brown, who had joined the Chicago faculty since 1931, looked forward to Warner's coming to Chicago, as did Robert Park, by then professor

[77] "Minutes of the Committee Meeting Held December 16, 1932," Elton Mayo Papers, HBS Archives, Baker Library Historical Collections, Harvard Business School (hereafter Mayo Papers), box 11, folder 3.036; David L. Edsall to Max Mason, 5 January 1933, folder 4070, box 342, series 200, RG 1.1, Rockefeller Foundation Archives, RAC; W. Lloyd Warner to Edmund E. Day, 11 September 1933, folder 4045, box 339, series 200, RG 1.1, Rockefeller Foundation Archives, RAC; Elton Mayo to W. Lloyd Warner, 18 November 1933, Mayo Papers, box 4, folder 1.081; "Report upon Utilization of RF Grant," 1933, 15, folder 4045, box 339, series 200, RG 1.1, Rockefeller Foundation Archives, RAC.
[78] Mildred Hall Warner, *W. Lloyd Warner*, 94–99; W. Lloyd Warner, "American Caste and Class," *American Journal of Sociology* 42 (1936): 234–237; Allison Davis, Burleigh B. Gardner, and Mary R. Gardner, *Deep South: A Social Anthropological Study of Caste and Class* (Chicago: University of Chicago Press, 1941); Alice O'Connor, *Poverty Knowledge: Social Science, Social Policy, and the Poor in Twentieth-Century U.S. History* (Princeton, N.J.: Princeton University Press, 2001), 84–85.

emeritus, who hoped that Warner would revive the Chicago school's rich ethnographic tradition.[79]

Warner's move led to extended negotiations between Chicago and Harvard over custody of the Newburyport materials, accommodation of Warner's research assistants, and subventions for the publications then envisaged.[80] At Chicago, Warner used cumbersome Hollerith calculators, wielded by scores of W.P.A. workers, to sort the thousands of "personality cards" compiled in Newburyport. At Harvard, Eliot Chapple analyzed the hundreds of interviews collected in Newburyport until he began to have second thoughts about Warner's approach and left the team. Looking for ways in which the study of social organization might be made more "objective," Chapple collaborated with Conrad Arensberg on developing an "Interaction Chronometer," an instrument with which to measure interaction, and formulated his own "theory of social interaction."[81]

In an expansive moment, Warner predicted that if the material from Newburyport and Natchez were published in the detail he intended, it would eventually result in the publication of fourteen volumes of some six hundred pages each. But Warner soon scaled back his ambitions. When he submitted drafts of four volumes to Harvard University Press in 1938, the sociologist Talcott Parsons, who read the manuscripts for the press, found their literary style "very trying at many points" and recommended that they not be published "without being thoroughly gone over." Parsons also poured cold water on Warner's plans

[79] Alfred Tozzer to Franz Boas, 26 February 1935, 27 February 1936, Boas Papers; Lowie to Boas, 31 January 1936; George W. Stocking, Jr., *Anthropology at Chicago: Tradition, Discipline, Department* (Chicago: Joseph Regenstein Library, University of Chicago, 1979), 25; W. Lloyd Warner to Edmund E. Day, 25 October 1934, folder 4046, box 339, series 200, RG 1.1, Rockefeller Foundation Archives, RAC; Robert Redfield to W. Lloyd Warner, 28 February, 23 May 1935, Robert Redfield Papers, Special Collections Research Center, University of Chicago (hereafter Redfield Papers), box 40, folder 4; Robert E. Park to Lawrence J. Henderson, 8 April 1935, Lawrence Joseph Henderson Papers, HBS Archives, Baker Library Historical Collections, Harvard Business School, box 14, folder 9; Robert E. Park to Robert Redfield, 10 April 1935, Robert Ezra Park Papers Addenda, Special Collections Research Center, University of Chicago (hereafter Park Papers), box 2, folder 5.

[80] Wallace B. Donham to Elton Mayo, 4 June 1935; W. Lloyd Warner to Elton Mayo, 17 December 1936; Wallace B. Donham to W. Lloyd Warner, 22 May 1937, Mayo Papers, box 4, folder 1.081; W. Lloyd Warner to Stacy May, 29 June 1937; Stacy May to W. Lloyd Warner, 6 July 1937, folder 4048, box 339, series 200, RG 1.1, Rockefeller Foundation Archives, RAC; Wallace B. Donham to W. Lloyd Warner, 3 June 1935; W. Lloyd Warner to Donald Slesinger, 26 June 1935, Redfield Papers, box 40, folder 4; W. Lloyd Warner to Elton Mayo, 28 December 1939, 26 February 1940; Elton Mayo to W. Lloyd Warner, 9 April 1940; W. Lloyd Warner to Elton Mayo, 29 May 1940, Mayo Papers, box 4, folder 1.083.

[81] Eliot D. Chapple to W. Lloyd Warner, 23 March 1938; W. Lloyd Warner to Eliot Chapple, 5 May 1938; W. Lloyd Warner to Elton Mayo, 5 May 1938; Wallace B. Donham to W. Lloyd Warner, 21 May 1938, Mayo Papers, box 4, folder 1.083; Eliot D. Chapple, "Measuring Human Relations: An Introduction to the Study of the Interaction of Individuals," *Genetic Psychology Monographs* 22 (1940): 129; William Foote Whyte, "The Slum: On the Evolution of *Street Corner Society*," in *Reflections on Community Study*, 9–10.

for an introductory volume that would tell how the fieldworkers framed a conceptual scheme, only to revise it in the light of their fieldwork in Newburyport, all to the end of persuading anthropologists and sociologists to set aside "departmentalizations of knowledge," renounce the "ruinous dichotomy" between "primitive" and "modern" social behavior, and add modern society to the "comparative sociology of man."[82]

In his search for a subvention, Warner sounded out the Committee of Industrial Physiology, only to learn that their grant from the Rockefeller Foundation had expired. He then vowed to pay all the editing expenses "out of [his] own pocket" until he met the heir of the Crane Plumbing Corporation, whose family had endowed a memorial fund at Yale. The Richard Teller Crane, Jr., Memorial Fund subsequently provided nearly $20,000 to subsidize publication by the Yale University Press of what came to be known as the Yankee City series, the first four volumes of which were published between 1941 and 1947, with the fifth and final volume not appearing until 1959. A projected sixth volume, which was to have been a data book, was never published.[83]

THE YANKEE CITY SERIES

In the first volume of the Yankee City series, *The Social Life of a Modern Community*, published in 1941, Warner and coauthor Paul Lunt explained how the fieldworkers "discovered" the existence of six social classes in Newburyport. By "class," Warner and Lunt did not mean "occupation and resulting wealth," but rather "status," a more subjective entity determined by the consumer goods one flaunted and whom one associated with. When the fieldworkers first went to Newburyport, Warner and Lunt explained, they expected to find the rich at the top of the city's social hierarchy and the poor at the bottom. But interviews quickly revealed that informants assigned members of the same occupational group to more than one class. The researchers discovered "similar inequalities of status" among other professional and business groups. It thus appeared that something more than occupation and income was necessary to attain high rank. Source of income – whether inherited money, or investments, or salary, or wages – was important. So, too, were the neighborhood and the type of house in which one lived, family reputation, and participation in cliques and voluntary associations. Education, speech, and manners also came into play. Above all, one had to "act right." For informants

---

[82] "An Agreement for the Completion and Publication of the Newburyport Research," n.d., W. Lloyd Warner, Biography and Addenda, Special Collections Research Center, University of Chicago, box 3; Talcott Parsons to Elton Mayo, 11 July 1938; Elton Mayo to W. Lloyd Warner, 23 December 1938; W. Lloyd Warner to Elton Mayo, 3, 17 January 1939, Mayo Papers, box 4, folder 1.083.

[83] W. Lloyd Warner to Elton Mayo, 21 December 1938, 30 November 1939, Mayo Papers, box 4, folder 1.083; Mildred Warner, *W. Lloyd Warner*, 123–124.

to be certain of one's status, one had to possess the appropriate symbols required for association with "the 'right kind' of people."[84]

As the "fundamental" social structure of Newburyport, the class system took the place of the kinship system among the Murngin, the familistic system in County Clare, and the caste-class order in Natchez. Newburyport's class system consisted of six classes. At the top of the city's social hierarchy was the "upper-upper class." Constituting just 1.4 percent of the city's population, it was composed of residents who worshiped the lineages of both their families and their houses. Just below them was the "lower-upper class." Slightly larger than the upper-upper class (1.6 percent of the city's population), it comprised "new families" scrambling to convert their wealth, which often exceeded that of upper-upper-class families, into the "acceptable behavior" required for their admission into Newburyport's most exclusive cliques and associations. Next came the "upper-middle class," 10 percent of the city's population. As upwardly mobile men and women anxious to instill self-discipline and ambition in their children, upper-middle-class Newburyporters took responsibility for seeing "that things are done." Together, these three classes comprised the "big people" – approximately 13 percent of the city's population. Below them, at the "level of the common man," were the small businessmen, white-collar workers, and highly skilled workers who made up the "lower-middle class" (28 percent of the population), and the "highly respectable" semi-skilled workers and small tradesmen, 33 percent of the city's population, who belonged to the "upper-lower class." At the bottom of the Newburyport's class system were found the "pitied unfortunates," "greenhorns," and "ethnic peoples" of the "lower-lower class" (26 percent of the population).[85]

Unlike the Lynds, who had been dismayed by the salience of invidious class distinctions in what purported to be a classless society, Warner considered social classes the inevitable byproducts of a complex division of labor. Indeed, a class system differed from a caste–class order in allowing both cross-class marriage and social mobility. Yet, because it took time to overcome the "principles of exclusion" erected by the superior classes, upward mobility in Newburyport was necessarily a slow process. Rags-to-riches stories were rare; mobility generally took the form of movement into an adjacent class; and three generations normally elapsed before a lower-upper-class family managed to climb into the upper-upper class. Since "basic acceptance" by one's social superiors was the "minimum" requirement for mobility, gains in occupation or income alone were not sufficient. Instead, the upwardly mobile person had to manipulate "every possible device" of self-advancement "with consummate skill" – from gaining admission into exclusive cliques and associations, to moving to a new neighborhood, refining one's speech, and even altering one's reading. "Profiles,"

[84] Warner and Lunt, *The Social Life of a Modern Community*, 81–83.
[85] W. Lloyd Warner and Leo Srole, *The Social Systems of American Ethnic Groups* (New Haven, Conn.: Yale University Press, 1945), 2; Warner and Lunt, *The Social Life of a Modern Community*, 127–201 passim.

composite fictional portraits of the city's "human types" designed to convey a sense of "how it feels to live in the class system of Yankee City," indicated that lower-upper-class women tended to be more mobile than lower-upper-class men because they found it easier to marry into the "highly endogamous" upper-upper class; that outsiders were more mobile than Newburyport natives because less was known about their pasts; and that there was greater mobility among the dead than among the living since their bones could be exhumed and buried next to the graves of the illustrious ancestors of the city's old families.[86]

In the second volume of the Yankee City series, *The Status System of a Modern Community*, published in 1942, Warner and Lunt mapped "total interaction" in Newburyport. To account for variations in behavior found in each of the city's six classes, they correlated class standing with family, membership in cliques and associations, education, church affiliation, and economic and political activity. An enormous table some eighty-seven pages long summed up the "interconnections" of the eighty-nine social statuses that were the functional equivalents in Newburyport of the seventy-one kinship statuses Warner had found among the Murngin. This "positional system" reflected Warner's conception of Newburyport not as an "atomic sand pile of separated individuals," but rather as "a set of interconnected human beings" bound together "in a vast web of relations." Thus social relations, and not individuals, were Warner's "basic unit[s] of analysis."[87]

Ethnicity and race bulked far larger in Newburyport than in Muncie. In the third volume of the Yankee City series, *The Social Systems of American Ethnic Groups* (1945), Warner and coauthor Leo Srole examined how well Yankee City's eight ethnic groups – Irish, French Canadians, Jews, Italians, Armenians, Greeks, Poles, and Russians – had assimilated the Yankee tradition. Defining an "ethnic" as any person who considered himself or was considered by neighbors to be "a member of a group with a foreign culture," Warner and Srole distinguished ethnics in Newburyport by their possession of "divergent set[s] cultural traits" that the Yankees considered "inferior." Thus Newburyport's Jews constituted a "cultural colony," and not a "racial" or even "religious" one. Like many American social scientists in the 1940s, Warner and Srole fully expected ethnic Americans eventually to be absorbed into the American mainstream as upwardly mobile individuals exchanged their "foreign" cultural traits for "American" ones. But Warner and Srole did not foresee the same trajectory for African-Americans, who, as a "racial group," were set apart from the American mainstream by permanent biological traits that could not be exchanged for cultural traits. Unless

---

[86] Warner and Lunt, *The Social Life of a Modern Community*, 223, 101. See, in particular, the profiles "New Family" (141–152), "Niece Delgracia" (161–168), and "These Bones Shall Rise Again" (155–158).

[87] W. Lloyd Warner, "A Methodological Note," in St. Clair Drake and Horace R. Cayton, *Black Metropolis: A Study of Negro Life in a Northern City* (1945; repr., Chicago: University of Chicago Press, 1993), 772; Warner, "Social Anthropology and the Modern Community," 791; W. Lloyd Warner and Paul S. Lunt, *The Status System of a Modern Community* (New Haven; Yale University Press, 1942), 3–24, 113–199.

white Americans adopted new "methods of evaluation," Warner and Srole feared that racial minorities were "doomed to a permanent inferior ranking."[88]

Where the first three volumes of the Yankee City series were concerned with social persistence, the fourth dealt with social change. In *The Social System of the Modern Factory* (1947), Warner and coauthor Josiah Low analyzed a successful strike staged by shoemakers in Yankee City in 1933 – a strike that caught field-workers by surprise because, until then, the shoemakers had shown few signs of militancy. Although the shoemakers claimed that wage reductions triggered their walkout, Warner and Low attributed the strike to the vertical and horizontal extension of the shoe industry in Newburyport. Technological change, they argued, had widened the social distance between factory owners and shoemakers by eroding the "skill hierarchy" that had earlier made it possible for a worker to rise from the shop floor into supervisory ranks. De-skilled shoemakers were now joining industrial unions that put their collective mobility as workers ahead of their own individual mobility. By this time as well, the city's factories were owned, and frequently managed, by nonresidents. Hence a combination of the blocked mobility to which the Lynds had called attention and absentee ownership, which had figured prominently in Veblen's critique of business enterprise, accounted for the shoemakers' strike. Echoing Elton Mayo, Warner and Low warned managers against ignoring the "human factor" in "highly rationalized systems."[89]

JONESVILLE AS A LABORATORY

Warner did not get around to spelling out his techniques for assigning the inhabitants of a community into their respective classes until 1949, when, in *Social Class in America*, he explicated two methods for "measuring" social status. In so doing, he was aided by Marchia Meeker and Kenneth Eells, two associates from Social Research, Inc. (SRI), a consulting firm that Burleigh Gardner had founded in 1946. SRI used focus groups, in-depth interviews, and projective tests to "sell the U.S. by class" to clients like Macfadden Publications and the *Chicago Tribune*.[90] The first method, Evaluated Participation (EP), systematized informal procedures that had been used to stratify

[88] Warner and Srole, *The Social Systems of American Ethnic Groups*, 28, 285–286, 295–296; Harold Orlansky, "The Jews of Yankee City," *Commentary*, January 1946, 78–79. After Warner and Lunt coined the term "ethnicity" in *The Social Life of a Modern Community*, the term gained currency, edging out, for the time being, "minority." Philip Gleason, "Minorities (Almost) All," in *Speaking of Diversity: Language and Ethnicity in Twentieth-Century America* (Baltimore: Johns Hopkins University Press, 1992), 91–97; Werner Sollors, *Beyond Ethnicity: Consent and Descent in American Culture* (Oxford: Oxford University Press, 1986), 23.

[89] W. Lloyd Warner and J. O. Low, *The Social System of the Modern Factory* (New Haven, Conn.: Yale University Press, 1947), 6–7, 179, 73, 157–160, 192.

[90] Burleigh Gardner, introduction to Lee Rainwater, Richard P. Coleman, and Gerald Handel, *Workingman's Wife: Her Personality, World and Life Styles* (New York: Oceana, 1959), ix–xiii; Zunz, *Why the American Century?*, 103–105; John Easton, "Consuming Interests," *University of Chicago Magazine*, August 2001, http://magazine.uchicago.edu/0108/features; Cohen, *A Consumer's Republic*, 311–313.

Newburyport. A cumbersome method in which fieldworkers compared informants' evaluations with their own observations, EP was expensive, required
skilled interviewers, and was difficult to use in cities larger than Newburyport.
The second method, the Index of Status Characteristics (ISC), was much simpler to use. It determined an individual's social standing on the basis of four
weighted indices: occupation (given the most weight), source of income, and
house type (given lesser weight), and neighborhood of residence (given the least
weight). To demonstrate just how easy the ISC was to use, as a formula for
translating the possession of badges of status into "socially approved behavior,"
Warner and his coauthors assigned characters from Sinclair Lewis's *Babbitt*
to their respective social classes. George F. Babbitt thus ranked in the upper-
middle class on the basis of his occupation as a realtor, income derived from
sales commissions and real-estate investments, ownership of a Dutch colonial
bungalow, and residence in the Floral Heights neighborhood.[91]

The ISC had been developed in fieldwork by fieldworkers from the University of Chicago Committee on Human Development, which in 1941 had
embarked on long-term studies of social stratification, educational achievement, and character formation in Morris, Illinois, a small farming community
sixty miles west of Chicago.[92] Morris differed from Newburyport in three
important respects: first, there were only two ethnic groups of any size, Nor-
wegians and Poles; second, no upper-upper class existed, which suggested that
in the newer regions of America (like the Midwest), occupation and resulting
income counted for more than lineage in determining social standing; and third,
Morris had boomed as the Second World War brought defense factories paying
"undreamed-of" wages, substantial in-migration, and the induction of several
hundred of the town's young men into the armed forces.[93]

The Morris researches led to the publication of a number of monographs,
including *Democracy in Jonesville*, published in 1949. Depicting Morris as "a
laboratory for studying Americans," Warner and his coauthors inquired into
how Americans reconciled the discrepancy between the "secular realities of
social class" and their "equalitarian principle[s]." Reconciliation of these conflicting impulses, they suggested, depended on keeping American society open,
lest "the channels of mobility [come] to be blocked." Thus the American democratic system would survive, and "social and political catastrophe" be averted,
only so long as "the principles of rank" were "tempered by those of equality."[94]

[91] W. Lloyd Warner, Marchia Meeker, and Kenneth Eells, *Social Class in America: A Manual of Procedure* (1949; repr., New York: Harper, 1960), 232–242.

[92] "History of the Morris Study" (draft), n.d., Robert J. Havighurst Papers, Special Collections Research Center, University of Chicago (hereafter Havighurst Papers), box 14. The Committee on Human Development eventually became Warner's "home" and "major interest." Robert J. Havighurst to Robert McMillan, 2 October 1974, Havighurst Papers, box 8; Abbott, *Department and Discipline*, 39.

[93] "History of the Morris Study."

[94] W. Lloyd Warner et al., *Democracy in Jonesville: A Study in Quality and Inequality* (1949; repr., New York: Harper, 1964), ix, xiv, 22–28, 266–286, 296–298.

August B. Hollingshead's *Elmtown's Youth: The Impact of Social Classes on Adolescents* (1949) also issued from Committee on Human Development's fieldwork in Morris. Studying "character" development in Morris from May 1941 until December 1942, then again in 1945 after he was demobilized from the Air Force, Hollingshead tested the hypothesis that "the class position of an adolescent's family was functionally related to 'his social behavior in the community.'" Although Morris residents denied the existence of multiple classes in their midst, Hollingshead found that, in practice, they delineated five classes. Selecting thirty families, he then asked twenty-five respondents to stratify them. After dropping ten families about whose status there was no agreement, Hollingshead asked twelve long-time residents of Morris to determine the class standing of the remaining twenty families. A number of social scientists preferred Hollingshead's "elegantly simple" procedure to Warner's "intuitive," less "systematic" method.[95]

By 1949, Warner's views had not only gained wide currency among social scientists but were spreading to larger audiences. In September of that year, *Life* magazine published a "picture essay" on Rockford, Illinois, another community that had been studied by researchers from the Committee on Human Development. The essay illustrated use of the ISC with brief biographies and Margaret Bourke-White's photos of six persons, each of whom represented one of Rockford's social classes. ISC scores for the six ranged from a low of 12 points scored by the matriarch of an old family to a high of 74 scored by a high-school dropout and transient worker. Unable to afford a house, the latter lived with his wife and daughter in a trailer, yet dreamt of upward mobility. If the transient worker overcame his "educational handicap" by availing himself of "an air-conditioning training program in Chicago," *Life*'s editors suggested, he would "have begun the slow but feasible climb upward." Indeed, the editors considered "social 'mobility,'" "the opportunity to move rapidly upwardly through the levels of society," "the distinguishing characteristic of U.S. democracy." American democracy was thus like a ladder that anyone could climb. On this ladder were "already some who have reached the rungs above" and still others "coming up from below." (The editors, however, made no mention of downward mobility.)[96]

Warner, who was interviewed and photographed for the *Life* article, agreed that "the saving grace of the American social system" was that "our social positions" were not "fixed artificially." But in insisting that avenues of mobility be kept open, Warner rehearsed the reasons for his long-standing concern about blocked mobility: unionization had "slowed down" the individual worker's upward climb by putting the collective advancement of the working class ahead

[95] A. B. Hollingshead, *Elmtown's Youth: The Impact of Social Classes on Adolescents* (New York: Wiley, 1949); Joseph A. Kahl, *The American Class Structure* (New York: Holt and Rinehart, 1957), 36, 39.

[96] "An American Sociologist Looks at an American Community," *Life*, 12 September 1949, 108–109.

of the individual worker's mobility; mechanization was eroding the "hierarchy of increasing skill" that once existed in factories; and specialization in hiring resulted in the graduates of technical and engineering schools and universities, and not men coming up from below, filling "top jobs in industry." Although counseling "the prudent mobile man" to "prepare himself by education if he [wished] to fulfill an important job," Warner was not so sure that American public schools facilitated mobility. He drew on the research he had done during the war. With two colleagues from the Committee on Human Development, Robert Havighurst and Martin Loeb, he had investigated why so few lower-class high school graduates went on to college. Family finances, of course, kept many from going on, but so, too, did their teachers. Of predominantly middle-class background, teachers tended to underestimate the intelligence of working-class students, frequently tracking them into vocational courses and dead-end jobs. "Despite our free schools," Warner told *Life*'s editors, "the educational belt drops many lower-class children at the bottom of the route and carries those from the higher classes a longer distance."[97] In the Sachs Lectures at Columbia Teachers College in 1945–1946, James Bryant Conant, Harvard president, broadcast Warner's fear of blocked mobility to wider audiences.[98]

Warner achieved even greater notoriety when he served as the prototype for the anthropologist Malcolm Bryant in John P. Marquand's 1949 novel of social manners, *Point of No Return*. Fresh from "a call on the head-hunters" of Borneo, Bryant shows up in "Clyde," the fictional Newburyport, to survey what appeared to be "a beautiful, static, organized community," its "way of life" having "just the continuity" for which he had been looking. With the assistance of students from Harvard and Radcliffe, the industrious Bryant soon discovers the existence of "very definite and crystallized social strata," a class system. But Charles Gray, one of Bryant's informants, dismisses all Bryant's "talk about classes." "Nobody thinks about classes," he insists, "because every-one in Clyde knows he's as good as everyone else." Gray, however, eventually discovers that Bryant has been right all along when he is unable to marry his upper-upper-class sweetheart. Clyde, he finally admits, is "as full of blind instinct as a beehive." Still, Bryant's clumsy attempt to capture the complex reality of Clyde in "diagrams and geometric curves and a mass of static, regimented fact" puts Gray off. "Your categories and groupings bother me," he tells Bryant. "I like individuals, not groupings." Gray also resents the thinly disguised portrait of the Grays as a typical lower-upper-class family in *Yankee Persepolis*, so titled because it is where Yankees worship memories.[99]

[97] W. Lloyd Warner, quoted in "An American Sociologist Looks at an American Community," 118–119; W. Lloyd Warner, Robert J. Havighurst, and Martin B. Loeb, *Who Shall Be Educated? The Challenge of Unequal Opportunities* (New York: Harper, 1944).
[98] Ellen Condliffe Lagemann, *The Politics of Knowledge: The Carnegie Corporation, Philanthropy, and Public Policy* (1989; repr., Chicago: University of Chicago Press, 1992), 192–195.
[99] John P. Marquand, *Point of No Return* (Boston: Little, Brown, 1949), 244, 266, 58, 307, 524, 42, 62, 308, 65.

Reviews of *Point of No Return* suggested that ethnographies of the American scene had come full circle by 1949. Twenty years earlier, many readers had deemed the Lynds' *Middletown* superior to Sinclair Lewis's *Main Street* and *Babbitt* because of its "scientific" authority. Now more than one reader questioned whether social scientists were better than novelists at capturing the "elusiveness of [American] class lines." The literary critic Granville Hicks, who discovered only two classes in *Home Town* (1946), his study of Grafton, New York, thought that Marquand had "a better understanding of the class structure of American society than Lloyd Warner and all his advisers, colleagues, and assistants put together."[100] The historian Oscar Handlin agreed. Handlin charged that Warner used the techniques of the novelist but without the novelist's "imagination" or "insight."[101]

THE LIMITATIONS OF ANTHROPOLOGICAL METHODS

Curiously, Warner was unable to convince some of his fellow anthropologists that social class was a valid category in analyzing American society. Margaret Mead, who viewed the American social structure as a "pecking order" that could be described without mentioning class, preferred to talk about the "premium on success" and the "will to succeed." Although Geoffrey Gorer, like Warner, viewed class hierarchies as "local," and not "nation-wide," he saw competition for social status limited to the top 10 percent to 12 percent of Americans – those who belonged to Warner's three classes above the level of the common man – and club women as the "fiercest competitors." Warner's studies did convince Alfred Kroeber that Americans were "socially stratified in spite of wanting to believe that [they were] not," but Kroeber wondered how far the "levels" demarcated in Yankee City series represented "natural segregations, distinctions, existing de facto in the society and culture." Kroeber preferred the simple distinction that Carl Withers drew between an upper class and a lower class in *Plainville, U.S.A.* (1945), his ethnography of the "relatively isolated and still 'backward'" farming town of Wheatland, Missouri.[102]

---

[100] Granville Hicks, *Small Town* (New York: Macmillan, 1946); Granville Hicks, "Marquand of Newburyport," *Harper's*, April 1950, 101–108, on 104, 102; Michael Harrington, "Granville Hicks' Small Town," *Dissent* 4 (1957): 243–249.

[101] Oscar Handlin, review of *The Social Life of a Modern Community* and *The Status System of a Modern Community*, *New England Quarterly* 15 (1942): 556–557; Oscar Handlin, review of *The Social Systems of American Ethnic Groups*, *New England Quarterly* 18 (1945): 523–524.

[102] Margaret Mead, "The Class Handicap," in *And Keep Your Powder Dry* (1942; repr., New York: William Morrow, 1965), 54–69; Geoffrey Gorer, "More Equal than Others," in *The American People: A Study in National Character* (New York: Norton, 1948), 211–219; A. L. Kroeber, *Anthropology: Race, Language, Culture, Psychology, Prehistory* (New York: Harcourt, 1948), 272, 270; A. L. Kroeber, recommendation for Carl Withers to the John Simon Guggenheim Foundation, 4 December 1949, Kroeber Papers, reel 8; James West [pseudonym for Carl Withers], *Plainville, U.S.A.* (New York: Columbia University Press, 1945).

Although he acknowledged the existence of "class structures," consisting of "fairly stabilized social-intimacy groups" with "their own habits, definitions of life, and conceptions of their goals," in the East and the South, Clyde Kluckhohn played down their salience elsewhere in the United States. And though he admitted that a complex division of labor made "some form of class stratification almost inevitable," Kluckhohn insisted that class did not have "precisely the same meaning" in America that "it [had] in Europe." America, he said, remained an "open society" in which class lines were "still relatively fluid," everyone hoped to rise, and almost everyone subscribed to values that operated "to deny and tear down class divisions." Kluckhohn, however, changed his mind about the applicability of Warner's scheme to regions outside the East and the South when some of his students discovered the existence of six discrete social classes in the "frontier community" of Gallup, New Mexico. "Beaten by the facts," Kluckhohn then accepted Warner's "point of view."[103]

Sociologists were ambivalent about Warner. Some acknowledged their intellectual debts to him. William Foote Whyte, who studied Boston's Italian-American North End in *Street Corner Society* (1943), thought that Warner had helped to persuade sociologists to view a community as an "organized social system" rather than "in terms of social problems."[104] David Riesman credited Warner with documenting "the connection between class and leisure behavior," formulating the first theory "to take account of a consumer-oriented society," and showing "what goes together with what." If researchers knew what was in "the interior of a lower-upper class home," they could "make some pretty good guesses as to reading matter, child rearing, participation (or lack of it) in voluntary associations."[105]

[103] Clyde Kluckhohn, *Mirror for Man: The Relation of Anthropology to Modern Life* (1949; repr., Tucson: University of Arizona Press, 1985), 253–255; Clyde Kluckhohn, "Mid-Century Manners and Morals," in *Twentieth-Century Unlimited: From the Vantage Point of the First Fifty Years*, ed. Bruce Bliven (Philadelphia: Lippincott, 1950), 303–315; reprinted in *Culture and Behavior: Collected Essays of Clyde Kluckhohn*, ed. Richard Kluckhohn (New York: Free Press, 1962), 323–335, on 325; Clyde Kluckhohn, "Anthropological Studies of Human Relations," paper given at the Rockefeller Foundation Conference on Research in Human Relations, 27 February–1 March 1953, 11–12, folder 99, box 11, series 910, RG 3, Rockefeller Foundation Archives, RAC; Clyde Kluckhohn, "Student-Teacher," in *The People in Your Life: Psychiatry and Personal Relations by Ten Leading Authorities*, ed. Margaret M. Hughes (New York: Knopf, 1951), 170–171, 180–181. Kluckhohn's admission that he had been wrong about Warner's scheme prompted a letter from Warner, who was "much impressed with the courage [Kluckhohn] showed in print." Warner could "think of damn few people in social science with that kind of integrity." W. Lloyd Warner to Clyde Kluckhohn, 8 June 1953, HUG 4490.5, Kluckhohn Papers.

[104] William Foote Whyte, *Street Corner Society: The Social Structure of an Italian Slum*, 2nd ed. (Chicago: University of Chicago Press, 1955), 286–287. Whyte worked with Warner at Chicago, where he earned a Ph.D. in 1942.

[105] David Riesman, Memo to Kansas City Research Committee, 1 November 1952, Havighurst Papers, box 19; David Riesman, "Some Observations on Social Science Research," *Antioch Review* 11 (1951): 272. In 1952, eager to do fieldwork, Riesman seized the opportunity afforded by the Committee on Human Development's Kansas City Studies of Adult Life.

Other sociologists were sharply critical of Warner's approach. Drawing on Max Weber's terminology, C. Wright Mills criticized Warner's conflation of "status," the social axis of stratification, with "class," the economic axis, while ignoring "power" (or "party"), the political axis, altogether.[106] Gunnar Myrdal attributed what he regarded as Warner's exaggeration of "the rigor of the American class and caste system" and his overemphasis of "the role of purely social contacts" as an index to social class to the fact that he was challenging the "popular" theory of American classlessness, so deeply "anchor[ed] in the American Creed."[107]

Dissatisfaction mounted in the 1950s with attempts to extrapolate national patterns from "microcosms." Far from being as insular and self-sufficient as Warner implied, the typical American community was becoming part of an emergent mass society. No community could be considered a representative microcosm of America, and none could be studied in isolation from its neighbors or from the rest of the country. Warner himself admitted as much when he observed in 1953 that "the greatly extended economic and political hierarchies" of American life, with their "centers of decision" in New York and Washington, could "be only partly understood by [community] studies." Arthur Vidich and Joseph Bensman reflected this shift when, in their 1958 community study *Small Town in Mass Society*, they treated "Springdale," New York, not as a bounded, isolated, and self-sufficient place but rather as a dependent part of a larger system.[108]

Treating American communities as bounded and isolated also ignored the fact of geographical mobility, in- and out-migration, at a time when millions of Americans were moving from community to community in search of economic opportunity. As Florence Kluckhohn pointed out, the communities that Warner and his associates typically studied were not "expanding communities," but rather static ones consisting of those "who remained behind." Neither

[106] C. Wright Mills, review of *The Social Life of a Modern Community*, *American Sociological Review* 7 (1942): 263–271; Max Weber, "Class, Status, Party," in *From Max Weber: Essays in Sociology*, ed. Hans Gerth and C. Wright Mills (Oxford: Oxford University Press, 1946), 180–195. "Warner's failure to keep analytically separated the dimensions of *klass* and *stand* (status) makes it impossible for [Warner] to ask many very crucial (it seems to me) questions," Mills explained to Talcott Parsons in 1942. "One of the big advantages of Max Weber's terms for stratification phenomena lies precisely in the sharp distinction." "Maybe I am mistaken," Mills added, "but as different people begin increasingly to deal with *strata* I have become more and more convinced of the superiority of Weber's analysis and terminology as translated." W. Wright Mills to Talcott Parsons, 13 February 1942, HUG(FP) 15.2, box 19, Talcott Parsons Papers, Courtesy of the Harvard University Archives (hereafter Parsons Papers).

[107] Myrdal, *An American Dilemma*, 673, 670.

[108] Julian H. Steward, *Area Research: Theory and Practice* (New York: Social Science Research Council, 1950), 51, 132–333; W. Lloyd Warner, *American Life: Dream and Reality* (Chicago: University of Chicago Press, 1953), 34; Arthur J. Vidich and Joseph Bensman, *Small Town in Mass Society: Class, Power and Religion in a Rural Community* (Princeton, N.J.: Princeton University Press, 1958).

Newburyport nor Natchez, each with its "quite rigid status system," impediments to upward mobility, and stress on "lineage," could be regarded as "America in Microcosm."[109]

Finally, critics complained that Warner's methods were only "slightly historical," if not "ahistorical."[110] Oscar Handlin condemned Warner's decision not to consult any "previous summaries of data collected by anyone else (maps, handbooks, histories, etc.) until he had formed his own opinions of [Newburyport]." As Handlin pointed out, the "primitive peoples" that anthropologists normally studied had "no history," "only their traditions, myths, and rituals," all of which could be "examined by direct observation." But communities like Newburyport had documented histories. Warner's refusal to consult the historical record led to the "basic delusion" that Newburyport was predominantly "Yankee." Yet the vast majority of Newburyport's residents in the early 1930s were either foreign-born or the descendants of immigrants who hailed from elsewhere than England.[111]

Stephan Thernstrom rehearsed Handlin's criticisms in *Poverty and Progress* (1964), a study of working-class mobility in Newburyport from 1850 to 1880. In this refutation of "ahistorical social science," Thernstrom declared that Warner's "complete dependence" on observable behavior, informants' statements, and other "material susceptible to anthropological analysis" rendered him unable to distinguish the "actual past" from "current myths about the past." In fact, Warner's notions about Newburyport's past were "demonstrably false."[112]

FROM LAYER CAKE TO CONTINUUM

As class lines blurred in postwar America, social scientists moved away from Warner's conception of classes as "distinct" and "bounded" toward a

---

[109] Florence R. Kluckhohn, "Dominant and Substitute Profiles of Cultural Orientations: Their Significance for the Analysis of Social Stratification," *Social Forces* 28 (1950): 387–388. As Clifford Geertz scathingly remarked about "the Jonesville-is-the-USA 'microcosmic' model," "the notion that one can find the essence of national societies, civilizations, great religions, or whatever summed up in so-called 'typical' small towns and villages is palpable nonsense. What one finds in small towns and villages is (alas) small-town or village life." Clifford Geertz, "Thick Description: Toward an Interpretive Theory of Culture," in *The Interpretation of Cultures: Selected Essays* (New York: Basic Books, 1973), 21–22.

[110] Steward, *Area Research*, 39; Ruth Rosner Kornhauser, "The Warner Approach to Social Stratification," in *Class, Status, and Power*, 253–254.

[111] Handlin, review of *The Social Life of a Modern Community* and *The Status System of a Modern Community*, 556–557; Oscar Handlin, review of *The Social System of the Modern Factory, Journal of Economic History* 7 (1947): 277; Oscar Handlin, "Anthropology on Main Street," review of *American Life: Dream and Reality*, by W. Lloyd Warner, *New Leader*, 21 September 1953, 25–26.

[112] Stephan Thernstrom, *Poverty and Progress: Social Mobility in a Nineteenth Century City* (Cambridge, Mass.: Harvard University Press, 1964), 230; Stephan Thernstrom, "'Yankee City' Revisited: The Perils of Historical Naivete," *American Sociological Review* 30 (1965): 235.

conception of the American class system as a "status continuum." By 1958, according to Gerhard Lenski, Warner's influence had clearly waned among social scientists.[113]

Spurred by the rise of quantitative survey research, a behavioral revolution proceeded apace in the 1950s. Pioneered by Paul Lazarsfeld's radio research in the late 1930s and early 1940s, and exemplified by the multi-volume *The American Soldier* (1949), survey research was nominalist: it took the individual, and not the group, as its unit of analysis, and it studied nationally representative samples, not particular communities. Indeed, according to James S. Coleman, "the 1940s constituted a kind of watershed in empirical research in sociology." Before the watershed, the ethnographic approach was predominant among social scientists interested in studying the American class system; after the watershed, survey research was. Erving Goffman recalled that before *The American Soldier* was published, "one could still combine lots of different things," including qualitative ethnographic research and the quantitative. This was no longer true after the publication of *The American Soldier* stimulated both survey research and middle-range theory.[114]

In the wake of the behavioral revolution, social scientists placed renewed emphasis on occupation as the principal determinant of social standing. Indeed, by 1964, occupation had become "the single, most widely used variable" to place an individual in the American class system.[115] Use of occupational prestige scales, in turn, "reinforced" the tendency among social scientists to view the American class system in terms of a "status continuum."[116] This was especially true among social scientists who preferred "hard data to soft abstractions."[117] In his re-study of Wheatland, Missouri, in the mid-1950s, the same community that Carl Withers had studied in 1939–41, Art Gallagher placed townspeople along a status continuum rather than in the two social classes that Withers delineated. Social standing in Wheatland, Gallaher explained, no longer derived "from the acceptance of one value system as opposed to another," but rather flowed "from the possession of commonly desired symbols indicative of economic achievement."[118]

[113] Gerhard Lenski, "Social Stratification," in *Contemporary Sociology*, ed. Joseph S. Roucek (New York: Greenwood, 1958), 527–528.

[114] James S. Coleman, "Social Theory, Social Research, and a Theory of Action," *American Journal of Sociology* 91 (1986): 1313–1314, 1319–1320; Jef C. Verhoeven, "An Interview with Erving Goffman, 1980," *Research on Language and Social Interaction* 26 (1993): 333; Stein, "The Eclipse of Community," 216.

[115] Raymond J. Murphy, "Some Recent Trends in Stratification Theory and Research," *Annals of the American Academy of Political and Social Science* 356 (1964): 162.

[116] Reeve Vanneman and Fred C. Pampel, "The American Perception of Class and Status," *American Sociological Review* 42 (1977): 422.

[117] Leonard Reissman and Michael N. Halstead, "The Subject Is Class," *Sociology and Social Research* 34 (1970): 297.

[118] Art Gallaher, Jr., *Plainville Fifteen Years Later* (New York: Columbia University Press, 1961), 190–220, 222–224.

In the meantime, the functionalist sociologists Talcott Parsons, Kingsley Davis, Wilbert Moore, and Bernard Barber formulated a universal frame of reference in which any society could be compared with other societies without the detailed fieldwork required by "comparative sociology." Unlike Warner, who struggled to reconcile the existence of invidious social distinctions in typical American communities with Americans' egalitarian convictions, the functionalists maintained that some sort of social stratification was a general property of all social systems qua social systems. Stratification, in short, functioned as a "sorting mechanism" that "motivated" people to perform necessary tasks. Age and sex distinctions governed the allocation of tasks in primitive societies, "institutional inequality" performed the same function in complex societies. Thus stratification, Bernard Barber explained in 1957, resulted "from evaluation of functionally significant role differences."[119]

CLASS DISMISSED

After 1949, the Lynds' and Warner's fear that mobility was becoming harder to achieve in the United States gave way to celebrations of America as an "open society." Warner's conception of social mobility – hard-won, normally limited to movement from one class into an adjacent class, and frequently taking the form of increased prestige rather than dramatic material gains – proved to be an artifact of the interwar period. Growing evidence suggested that far from shrinking, as the Lynds and Warner feared, prospects for upward mobility in America were actually improving. At the same time, the lowering of status proscriptions against Jews and Catholics, the expansion of higher education spurred by the GI Bill, and the postwar boom all promoted social mobility.

In 1953, Oscar Handlin criticized Warner's assertion, "without the least substantiation," that the American worker could "no longer expect to advance and achieve success with anything like the same probability as did his father and grandfather."[120] By then, Warner himself was revising his views about social mobility in postwar America. In two books coauthored with James Abegglen that were published in 1955, Warner reported that prospects for upward mobility were increasing in the United States. Replicating F. W. Taussig and C. S. Joslyn's famous 1928 study of the origins of American business leaders, Warner and Abegglen found that although business leaders still came predominantly from the higher occupational levels in 1952, just as in 1928, mobility from the lower-middle and upper-lower classes into executive ranks was increasing, especially in large companies. Improving prospects for mobility

---

[119] Ely Chinoy, "Status," *New Society*, 2 November 1972, 264; Talcott Parsons, "An Analytical Approach to the Theory of Stratification," *American Journal of Sociology* 45 (1940): 841–862; Kingsley Davis and Wilbert Moore, "Some Principles of Stratification," *American Sociological Review* 10 (1945): 242–249; Bernard Barber, *Social Stratification: A Comparative Analysis of Structure and Process* (New York: Harcourt, 1957), 232.

[120] Handlin, "Anthropology on Main Street," 26.

reflected the great postwar expansion of higher education, corporations' adoption of impersonal selection procedures, and greater "emphasis upon competitive achievement." Warner and Abegglen's findings suggested that, more than ever before in American history, education was "the royal road to success."[121]

As class distinctions blurred and fears of blocked mobility receded, some social scientists began to question the applicability of the concept of social class to the American scene. In 1954, Robert E. L. Faris complained about "the unsatisfactory vagueness of a 'class-system' concept in American society." A class system, Faris explained, required the existence of "boundaries" between the several classes, with those boundaries serving as "official barriers to vertical mobility." In Faris's opinion, those boundaries did not exist in postwar America, which was fast "becoming a middle-class nation."[122] By 1955, Walter Goldschmidt had partially reversed his earlier views on the salience of class distinctions on the American scene. In *As You Sow* (1947), he had shown how agribusiness was replicating urban class distinctions in three farming towns in California's Central Valley. By 1955, however, Goldschmidt thought that the time had come for social scientists to go beyond "structural" and "static" analyses such as his own in *As You Sow* to take up the study of "status differentiation, whether or not these differences can be categorized into classes." Once an outspoken critic of American society, Goldschmidt now viewed it as "built upon mobility" and "without fixed positions."[123] In 1958, Arnold Rose urged that the "arbitrary" and diffuse concept of "class" be replaced by "simpler" concepts – such as occupation, income, and education – that had been in common use prior to publication of *Middletown*. In Europe, Rose explained, "class" designated "a power group with a certain group consciousness and characteristic 'life chances.'" In America, by contrast, most Americans considered themselves middle-class and there was "little empirical evidence that class differences" had "increased over the past generation." In 1959, Robert Nisbet announced that the "concept of class" had become "largely obsolete" because Americans were "living in a society governed by status, not class, values."[124]

Just how much social scientists' views of American social structure had changed by the late 1950s can be seen in their reaction to Vance Packard's 1959 best seller, *The Status Seekers*. Packard, a popularizer of social science,

[121] James C. Abegglen and W. Lloyd Warner, *Big Business Leaders in America* (New York: Harper, 1955); James C. Abegglen and W. Lloyd Warner, *Occupational Mobility in American Business and Industry* (Minneapolis: University of Minnesota Press, 1955).

[122] Robert E. L. Faris, "The Alleged Class System in the United States," *Research Studies of the State College of Washington* 22 (1954): 77–83, on 79, 80, 83. See also Robert E. L. Faris, "The Middle Class from a Sociological Viewpoint," *Social Forces* 39 (1960): 1–5.

[123] Walter R. Goldschmidt, *As You Sow* (New York: Harcourt, 1947); Goldschmidt, "Social Class and the Dynamics of Status in America."

[124] Arnold Rose, "The Concept of Class and American Sociology," *Social Research* 25 (1958): 53–69; Robert A. Nisbet, "The Decline and Fall of Social Class," *Pacific Sociological Review* 2 (1959): 11–17; Robert A. Nisbet, review of *Class in American Society*, by Leonard Reissman, *Commentary*, July 1960, 80.

argued that the increasing bureaucratization of American society (big business, big labor, and big government) was restricting opportunities for advancement and that both white-collar and blue-collar workers were deriving less social prestige, job satisfaction, and self-esteem from their labor. In response, Americans were becoming "status seekers" who seized every opportunity to dramatize their claims to prestige and to flaunt badges of status as compensation for lack of genuine advancement. Thus postwar affluence was "intensifying social striving" by strengthening the "barriers" and "humiliating distinctions" of social class.[125]

Many reviewers received much of what Packard had to say as old news. John Lydenberg dismissed *The Status Seekers* as "a shocker that doesn't shock." Lewis Coser disparaged *The Status Seekers* as "kitsch sociology" informed by "a guilty nostalgia for a supposedly less status-conscious and hence less anxiety-ridden past." Charles Rolo pronounced *The Status Seekers* "flawed" by Packard's "failure" to distinguish "between class, which is (usually) specific and immutable, and status, which is elusive and changeable." What existed in America was not "a class system in the conventional sense," Rolo explained, but "a hierarchy of prestige with a great many gradations of status."[126]

If earlier in the decade many American social scientists worried that class lines were hardening and social mobility decreasing, by 1959, the notion of blocked mobility seemed outdated. Indeed, some of Packard's critics retorted that status-seeking testified to the existence of an open society. If, "in a rigid class system, everyone 'knows his place,'" then "the frantic pursuit of status charted by Packard" suggested to Charles Rolo "the withering of the class system," not "its recrudescence." Warner's colleague Robert Havighurst also criticized Packard's views. In *Who Shall be Educated?*, Warner and Havighurst had pictured the public schools as impeding the mobility of lower-class students. Now, viewing American society as "open" and "fluid," Havighurst disputed Packard's belief that education tended "to harden the class structure by giving higher status children better treatment than lower-class children get." While admitting that the "evidence" for Packard's belief was "voluminous and convincing," Havighurst insisted that it was "only half of the truth." Although "a much smaller fraction of working-class youth [went] to college" in the late 1950s than did middle-class youth, "the important fact" was that a larger "minority of working-class youth" went to college in America than anywhere else. Thus American higher education worked "to make the society more fluid [and] to increase the amount of social mobility."[127]

[125] Vance Packard, *The Status Seekers* (New York: David McKay, 1959).
[126] John Lydenberg, "Veblen Updated," *New Leader*, 21 September 1959; Lewis Coser, "Kitsch Sociology," *Partisan Review*, Summer 1959, 482; Charles B. Rolo, "Class and Status," *Atlantic*, May 1959, 92. See also Daniel Horowitz, *Vance Packard and American Social Criticism* (Chapel Hill: University of North Carolina Press, 1994), esp. 166–171, 185–195.
[127] Rolo, "Class and Status," 92; Robert J. Havighurst, review of *The Status Seekers*, *Personnel and Guidance Journal* 38 (1960): 512–513.

Given the increasingly critical reception of social scientists to Warner's views, it is hardly surprising that class analysis did not figure prominently in American studies scholarship in the 1950s and 1960s. "America," David Potter declared in 1954, had "a greater measure of social equality and social mobility than any highly developed society in human history." However "real" and "difficult to break down" American social distinctions might be, they were "not based upon or supported by great disparities of wealth, in education, in speech, in dress, etc., as they [were] in the Old World." In 1957, Max Lerner celebrated America as an "open-class" society in which "classlessness" had "a different meaning" than in Europe. Classlessness in American usage, Lerner explained, did not mean "an absence of rank, class power, or prestige," but rather a "casteless" class system "characterized by great mobility and inter-penetration between classes." In postwar America, "class formations" were fluid; social mobility was "the rule rather than the exception"; and "class change" (social mobility) was "impressively obtainable." Denying that there had been "a creeping closure of mobility" in twentieth-century America, Lerner pointed to the impressive amount of vertical social mobility that had been "the most striking trait of the American class system." "The movement in America," Lerner concluded, had been neither "from classlessness to class" nor "from an open to a more rigid class system," but rather "from relatively clear divisions and modes of life to a situation where divisions [had] become more blurred," and "the stratification [had] become more subtle." The result was that American "modes of life" were then converging "in a large category of middle class living." Indeed, in the "democratic class struggle," "aspiration" to live the "good life" was at least as important as "disaffection" with one's social status.[128]

Class analysis receded even further in American studies after the 1970s as American studies scholars turned their attention to multiculturalism and emphasized race, ethnicity, and gender. In 1993, John Higham complained that multiculturalism was "absolutizing racial differences" and fostering "cultures of endowment" at the expense of "the broader inequalities of class."[129]

WARNER'S LEGACY

In 1959, Warner published *The Living and the Dead*, the fifth and last volume of the Yankee City series. In this study of the "symbolic life" of Americans, Warner sketched the career of "Biggy Muldoon," a legendary mayor of

---

[128] Larry J. Griffin and Larry W. Isaac, "Social Class," in *Encyclopedia of American Studies*, ed. George T. Kurian, Miles Orvell, Johnnella E. Butler, and Jay Mechling (New York: Grolier, 2001), 4:141; David M. Potter, *People of Plenty: Economic Abundance and the American Character* (Chicago: University of Chicago Press, 1954), 93–95, 101–102; Max Lerner, *America as a Civilization* (New York: Simon and Schuster, 1957), 467–540.

[129] John Higham, "Multiculturalism and Universalism: A History and a Critique" (1993), in *Hanging Together: Unity and Diversity in American Culture*, ed. Carl J. Guarneri (New Haven, Conn.: Yale University Press, 2001), 227–228.

Newburyport who rose from common man to "hero," before falling to "fool" and "traitor"; analyzed the forty-odd tableau-floats of a parade celebrating Massachusetts' tercentenary in 1930 as an example of the "ritualization of the past" in which the citizens of Newburyport "collectively state[d] what they believe[d] themselves to be"; and suggested that sacred symbols such as Memorial Day, the "modern cult of the dead," reconciled the "species behavior" that all men had in common with the normative demands of their respective cultures. Finally, advancing a general theory of symbols, Warner urged that social scientists pay more attention to myth, nonrational belief, and religion in modern life.[130]

In an inquiry cut short by his death in 1970, Warner delineated the "emergent American society" then coalescing around big business, the federal civil service, agribusiness, and other large-scale organizations. In *The Corporation in the Emergent American Society* (1961), he rehearsed the familiar themes that American communities had lost much of their autonomy and solidarity, that corporations were complicit in this development, and that a national labor market had developed in which there was extensive occupational and geographical mobility.[131] In *The American Federal Executive* (1963), Warner and coauthors Paul Van Riper, Norman Martin, and Orvis Collins found less occupational inheritance from father to son "among civilian and military executives" than in corporate ranks.[132] Finally, in the first volume of *Large-Scale Organizations* (1967), Warner, Darab Unwalla, and John Trimm examined big corporations, big government, big unions, and other large-scale organizations. A projected second volume, which was to have dealt with "processes" relating to "the realignment and centralization of power in various kinds of nationwide hierarchical institutions," was never published.[133]

Although interest in the ethnographies of the American scene had begun to recede even before Warner's death, his legacy remained alive for social scientists who continued to view social classes in cultural terms. In *Social Status in the City* (1971), Richard Coleman and Bernice Neugarten demonstrated that the concept of social class was applicable to a city as large as Kansas City. In fieldwork conducted by the Committee on Human Development from 1952 until 1962, Coleman and Neugarten modified the Index of Urban Status so that it took into account the education of both spouses, family income, church affiliation, and community association (including ethnicity). For Coleman and Neugarten, as for Warner, social mobility required "changes in life style – changes in associational patterns, in church affiliation, residential neighborhood – if gains

[130] W. Lloyd Warner, *The Living and the Dead* (New Haven, Conn.: Yale University Press, 1959).
[131] W. Lloyd Warner, *The Corporation in the Emergent American Society* (New York: Harper, 1961).
[132] Orvis Collins, Norman H. Martin, Paul P. Van Riper, and W. Lloyd Warner, *The American Federal Executive* (New Haven, Conn.: Yale University Press, 1963).
[133] John H. Trimm, Darab B. Unwalla, and W. Lloyd Warner, *Large-Scale Organizations*. Vol. 1: *The Emergent American Society* (New Haven, Conn.: Yale University Press, 1967).

in occupation, education, or marriage to a higher status partner were to be translated into social mobility."[134] To one reviewer, *Social Status in the City* illustrated "one of the hallmarks of the Warner tradition": "its followers' clear, lucid style of writing, that is enjoyable to read as well as intellectually stimulating."[135]

In *Social Standing in America* (1978), Richard Coleman and Lee Rainwater reported that although informants in Kansas City and in Boston associated money with "the idea of social class," money alone did not determine social standing in America. Indeed, Coleman and Rainwater's middle-class informants insisted on the importance of education, occupation, "moral standards, family history, community participation, social skills, speech, and physical appearance" as criteria of social standing. Coleman and Rainwater also reported that "psychological consequences" – in particular "snobberies engendered by status-related differences" – were "central" to social standing in America: being snubbed was "how 'class' really hits home."[136]

Like Warner, with whom he studied, Herbert Gans conceived of classes as "strata-with-subcultures," people's "responses" to "opportunities and deprivations." Also like Warner, Gans considered social mobility difficult to achieve because it required major changes in behavior and attitude. By converting Warner's "class-culture[s]" into "taste public[s]," Gans differentiated American audiences into subcultures conceived of as "aggregates of predisposition." Wherever "civic activity," an index of upper middle-class status, was found, "buying gourmet foods" and "reading a magazine like *Harper's*" were also likely to be present. Also like Warner, Gans thought of ethnicity in terms of cultural symbols. Indeed, he coined the concept of "symbolic ethnicity" to account for the resurgence of ethnic identification among fourth- and fifth-generation Euro-Americans in the 1970s.[137]

Lloyd Fallers, who was at work on a biography of Warner when he died in 1974, credited Warner with not only adding a "cultural dimension" to "the

[134] Richard P. Coleman and Bernice L. Neugarten, *Social Status in the City* (San Francisco: Jossey-Bass, 1971), vii–ix, 81, 253, 272–273, 248; Charles N. Glaab, Mark H. Rose, and William H. Wilson, "The History of Kansas City Projects and the Origins of American Urban History," *Journal of Urban History* 18 (1992): 371–394.

[135] Edward O. Laumann, review of *Social Status in the City*, by Richard P. Coleman and Bernice L. Neugarten, *American Journal of Sociology* 78 (1972): 270.

[136] Richard P. Coleman and Lee Rainwater, with Kent A. McClelland, *Social Standing in America: New Dimensions of Class* (New York: Basic Books, 1978), 22, 26, 29, 79–80, 294–295.

[137] Herbert J. Gans, "Relativism, Equality, and Popular Culture," in *Authors of Their Own Lives*, 432–451, on 439, 441, 447; Herbert J. Gans, *The Urban Villagers: Group and Class in the Life of Italian-Americans* (New York: Free Press, 1962), 24, 249, 253–254; Herbert J. Gans, *The Levittowners: Ways of Life and Politics in a New Suburban Community* (New York: Vintage, 1967), 24–25; Herbert J. Gans, *Popular Culture and High Culture: An Analysis and Evaluation of Taste* (New York, Basic Books, 1974), 71; Herbert J. Gans, "Symbolic Ethnicity: The Future of Ethnic Groups and Cultures in America," in *On the Making of Americans: Essays in Honor of David Riesman*, ed. Herbert J. Gans, Nathan Glazer, Joseph R. Gusfield, and Christopher Jenks (Philadelphia: University of Pennsylvania Press, 1979), 204.

study of social stratification," but with reviving concern with "inequality."[138] Like Warner, Fallers insisted that occupation, income, and other "objective" measures of inequality must be understood "in the context of their meaning to those involved in them." Grasping that meaning required that the researcher take into account the "evaluative standards and cognitive images" in which neighbors "evaluate[d]" each other on the basis of "style of life" and "symbols of status." Fallers, however, conceded that Warner "reified" class distinctions in Newburyport. It seemed to him unlikely that residents of Newburyport, even during the Depression, assigned their neighbors to "six clearly bounded, culturally distinguishable, stratified groups." He suggested that residents of Newburyport more likely conceived of their city's social hierarchy as "an unbroken status continuum" in which they regarded their neighbors as equals, superiors, or subordinates. It seemed to Fallers that what Warner delineated in the Yankee City series was less a class system than a "culture of inequality." And if "not exactly European," this culture of inequality revealed much more "continuity" with the "European culture of inequality" than Americans liked to acknowledge.[139]

Social class remains meaningful for Americans, as Fallers and, more recently, Sherry Ortner have demonstrated, in terms of "snobbery" and "humiliation." In 1991, Ortner complained of "the absence of any strong cultural category of 'class' in American discourse." "Rarely spoken of in its own right," social class was "displaced" on race, ethnicity, and even gender. In *New Jersey Dreaming* (2003), an ethnography of the class of '58 at Weequahic High School, Newark, New Jersey, Ortner insisted that social class was recognized by many Americans, who construe it "almost entirely as a matter of economic gradations and privileges" and who embed it "in narratives of snobbery and humiliation" inflicted by "invidious distinctions of money and privilege."[140]

Inaugurated by the Lynds, and developed by Warner and his many "associates," ethnographies of the American scene led to the discovery of distinct American social classes, thereby challenging a core belief of American exceptionalism. Whereas the Lynds conceived of social class in terms of occupation, income, and, eventually, power, Warner conceived of them as culture-based and status-obsessed. By making class distinctions more resistant to changes in occupation and income, the Warner school, and the market researchers who followed its lead, dissented from the prevailing view among social scientists that postwar America was becoming an increasingly middle class, and therefore classless, society. The Warner school both contributed to, and dissented from,

---

[138] Lloyd A. Fallers, *Inequality: Social Stratification Reconsidered* (Chicago: University of Chicago Press, 1973), ix; Lloyd A. Fallers, *The Social Anthropology of the Nation-State* (Chicago: Aldine, 1974), 17.

[139] Fallers, *Inequality*, 5–6, 19, 21–23, 25.

[140] Sherry B. Ortner, "Reading America: Preliminary Notes on Class and Culture," in *Recapturing Anthropology: Working in the Present*, ed. Richard G. Fox (Santa Fe: School of American Research Press, 1991), 169–170; Sherry B. Ortner, *New Jersey Dreaming: Capital, Culture, and the Class of '58* (Durham: Duke University Press, 2003), 10, 41–42, 51–52.

American exceptionalism. Its emphasis on the distinctive features of the American class system, features that were largely not shared by European social systems, was compatible with American exceptionalism. Yet, at the same time, the Warner school emphasized social hierarchy, and, to the extent that it viewed American class subcultures as little worlds, it largely cut classes off from one another. By delineating a culture of inequality, in which some Americans were exposed to snobbery and humiliation at the hands of other Americans, the Warner school suggested that, in this respect at least, the United States was not so different from Europe as many Americans had long believed.

As we have seen, many of Warner's fellow anthropologists resisted his discovery of the existence of social classes on the American scene. Much like early generations of American social scientists, they were impressed by the fluidity of the American scene. Hence their preference for the more dynamic term "status," as opposed to "class," with its connotation of fixity. Instead of classes, anthropologists such as Margaret Mead viewed the American social science hierarchy in terms of a pecking order. In Warner's studies of social structure, the "axis of organization," in Robert Redfield's words, was "the group," but the "typical individual" was the "axis" of the national character studies undertaken by anthropologists and other social scientists interested in culture and personality.[141]

[141] Robert Redfield, "Societies and Cultures as Natural Systems" (1955), in *Human Nature and the Study of Society: The Papers of Robert Redfield*, vol. 1, ed. Margaret Park Redfield (Chicago: University of Chicago Press, 1962), 126.

3

The Psychology of Culture and the American Character

In 1950, as he prepared his Walgreen Lectures at the University of Chicago on the impact of economic abundance on the American character, David M. Potter was "assailed by misgivings." Although the concept of the American character had been tarnished by its racial concomitants, few American historians failed to invoke the concept, "either occasionally or constantly, explicitly or implicitly," in their attempts to evoke the "total experience" of the American people. Yet, unless Americans could be regarded as "possessing distinctive traits and social adaptations," there would be no "unifying theme" in American history and the field would hold "little intellectual attraction" for historians. How, then, could the concept of national character be redeemed for its continued use by historians? In the published version of his lectures, *People of Plenty* (1954), Potter pointed out how the "behavioral scientists" Margaret Mead, Karen Horney, and David Riesman had not only freed the concept from "the curse of racism" but had documented the existence of "uniformities of [American] attitude and behavior." What the behavioral scientists had not done, though, was to identify the "determinants" of national character and to trace the development of the American character over time. This is where historians and American studies scholars were to come into the picture.[1]

The rehabilitation of the concept of national character was a product of culture and personality, an interdisciplinary collaboration between anthropologists (and other social scientists as well) and psychiatrists. It represented the application of psychological (and psychiatric) methods and viewpoints to anthropological material. Beginning in the late 1920s, what Clyde Kluckhohn called a "rapprochement" occurred between anthropology and psychiatry. Anthropologists turned to psychiatrists for insight into personality formation and socialization; psychiatrists looked to anthropologists for insight into the cultural conditioning of personality. By the late 1930s, cooperative seminars at Yale and Columbia were bringing together social scientists and psychiatrists to

---

[1] David M. Potter, *People of Plenty: Economic Abundance and the American Character* (Chicago: University of Chicago Press, 1954), vii, 7, 29, 57, 66.

118

devise new procedures for studying "culture *in* personality" and "personality *in* culture."

Culture and personality entered a new phase after war broke out in Europe in September 1939. Mobilized in defense of an embattled democracy, practitioners took up the problem of how individuals, given the malleability of human nature, embodied the culture in which they had been reared. Prevented from engaging in their customary fieldwork, anthropologists improvised "the study of culture at a distance." Using informants, films, and published sources, they delineated the national characters of the Germans, the Japanese, and other belligerents. In so doing, they gave "national character" a new lease on life.

Emboldened by their wartime access to policymakers, practitioners expected to play prominent roles in postwar reconstruction. With ample funding from philanthropic foundations and federal agencies, interdisciplinary teams of researchers attempted to put the study of culture at a distance on firmer footing as behavioral scientists entered a field previously dominated by economists, historians, and political scientists. But their efforts faltered amid mounting criticism of the scientific shortcomings of their approaches.

Yet, just at the moment when culture and personality was falling out of favor among social scientists, interest in national character spilled over into American history and American studies. Informed by a holistic approach to American life that glossed over class, ethnic, and regional differences, studies of the American character flourished until events in the 1960s shattered the postwar American consensus.

ANTHROPOLOGISTS, PSYCHOANALYSIS, AND THE AVANT-GARDE

In the 1910s and 1920s, Freudian depth psychology was an avant-garde movement in which lay proponents, bohemians, and members of the liberal intelligentsia broadcast Sigmund Freud's ideas to educated Americans, who, in turn, assimilated psychoanalysis into eclectic frameworks. In the process, they confounded psychoanalysis with the "revolt against civilization" and repression, concern about nervousness and neurosis, and the desire to expose "hidden motives." It is small wonder that the "Americanization" of psychoanalytic theory rendered it virtually unrecognizable to Freud himself.[2]

[2] Nathan G. Hale, Jr., *Freud and the Americans: The Beginnings of Psychoanalysis in the United States, 1876–1917* (New York: Oxford University Press, 1971), esp. 3–23; John C. Burnham, "The Influence of Psychoanalysis upon American Culture," in *American Psychoanalysis: Origins and Development*, ed. Jacques M. Quen and Eric T. Carlson (New York: Brunner/Mazel, 1978), 52–72; John C. Burnham, "From Avant-Garde to Specialism: Psychoanalysis in America," *Journal of the History of the Behavioral Sciences* 15 (1979): 128–134; John C. Burnham, "The New Psychology," in *1915, the Cultural Moment: The New Politics, the New Woman, the New Psychology, the New Art and the New Theatre in America*, ed. Adele Heller and Lois Rudnick (New Brunswick, N.J.: Rutgers University Press, 1991), 117–127; Fred H. Matthews, "The Americanization of Sigmund Freud: Adaptation of Psychoanalysis before 1917," *Journal of American Studies* 1 (April 1967): 39–62; Mari Jo Buhle, *Feminism and Its Discontents: A Century of Struggle with Psychoanalysis* (Cambridge, Mass.: Harvard University Press, 1998).

Until the late 1920s, anthropologists largely kept their distance from psychoanalysis. Franz Boas set the tone. In 1909, speaking on "Psychological Problems in American Anthropology" at a Clark University conference that Freud also attended, Boas emphasized the importance of "psychological anthropology," by which he meant the search for common psychological features among different cultures. Two years later, in *The Mind of Primitive Man*, Boas acknowledged the influence of socialization on custom, recognized the operation of unconscious processes (especially in language), and noted the formative influence of childhood experience. Yet, commenting in 1920 on Freud's efforts to establish an analogy between "primitive thought" and "individual psychic activity," Boas doubted that psychoanalytic methods could throw much light on cultures as historical growths or that Freud's theory of symbolism could explain primitive myths, taboos, and other cultural phenomena. Boas also questioned the cross-cultural validity of psychoanalysis.[3]

Alfred Kroeber felt even more ambivalent about psychoanalysis than Boas. Having studied psychology under James McKeen Cattell at Columbia, he closely followed developments in psychology and read Freud in German. In 1917, while recovering from the deaths from tuberculosis of both his first wife and of his Yana informant Ishi, and after suffering from an infection that left him permanently deaf in one ear, Kroeber was analyzed in New York. He then practiced as a lay analyst, first at the Stanford Clinic from 1918 until 1919, then in San Francisco until 1922. Although fascinated by the "insights" he gained into "symbolism" and "the human mind," Kroeber did not think that the experience helped him "to understand culture any better."[4] Yet, while critical of Freud for clinging to the discredited Lamarckian doctrine of inheritance of acquired characteristics, and put off by the "extravagance" of some of Freud's followers, Kroeber was convinced that psychoanalysis had "come to stay." In a 1920 review of *Totem and Taboo*, he acknowledged Freud's "contributions" to the psychology of culture, but took Freud to task for his out-of-date evolutionary framework, rejected Freud's belief in the "parallelism of savage and neurotic thought," and dismissed the Oedipus complex as a "Just-so story."

[3] Franz Boas, "Psychological Problems in Anthropology," *American Journal of Psychology* 21 (1910): 371–384; Franz Boas, *The Mind of Primitive Man* (New York: Macmillan, 1911); Franz Boas, "The Methods of Ethnology," *American Anthropologist* 22 (1920): 311–321; reprinted in *Race, Language, and Culture* (1940; repr., New York: Free Press, 1966), 281–289, on 288–289. See also George W. Stocking, Jr., "Polarity and Plurality: Franz Boas as a Psychological Anthropologist," in *Delimiting Anthropology: Occasional Inquiries and Reflections* (Madison: University of Wisconsin Press, 2001), 49–62.
[4] A. L. Kroeber to Edward Sapir, 14 July 1920, 17 January 1921, in *The Sapir-Kroeber Correspondence: Letters between Edward Sapir and A. L. Kroeber, 1905–1925*, ed. Victor Golla (Berkeley: University of California Survey of California and Other Indian Languages, 1984), 344, 363–364. See also Theodora Kroeber, *Alfred Kroeber: A Personal Configuration* (Berkeley: University of California Press, 1970), 101–119; Timothy Hans Hale Thoresen, "A. L. Kroeber's Theory of Culture; The Early Years" (Ph.D. diss., University of Iowa, 1971), 197.

When he revisited *Totem and Taboo* in 1939, Kroeber did not recant his earlier criticisms, but he did pay tribute to Freud's contributions to "general science."[5]

Alexander Goldenweiser also felt ambivalent about psychoanalysis. Although he told Edward Sapir in 1922 that as "we shed our deep-grained prepossessions, Freud's position tends to become more and more feasible." Goldenweiser suspected that Freud was "afflict[ed] with the philosopher's itch," which induced him to speculate far beyond what his clinical data supported. Believing that anthropology, "the science of man," was closely related to psychology, "the science of the mind," Goldenweiser mediated between anthropologists and the literary intellectuals whose contributions to the *Modern Quarterly* helped to promote the Americanization of Freud.[6]

THE PSYCHOLOGY OF CULTURE

Yet, from the mid-1920s on, anthropologists began to turn to psychiatrists for insight into personality formation, socialization, and character development. Leading the way was Edward Sapir, whose interest in psychoanalysis grew out of his long-standing concern with individual creativity. As early as 1915, Sapir was reading Freud, and from 1917 on, he was reviewing psychiatric literature for the *New Republic* and the *Dial*. Sapir welcomed psychoanalysis as "an entering wedge toward a physiology of mind," and gave it credit for throwing light on "the nature and functioning of the unconscious." Sapir was also beguiled by Carl Jung's "irreconcilable psychological types," "introvert" and "extravert," which he used to characterize friends, colleagues, and, as we shall see, cultures.[7]

[5] A. L. Kroeber, *The Nature of Culture* (Chicago: University of Chicago Press, 1952), 300; A. L. Kroeber, review of *Analytical Psychology*, by Carl Jung, *American Anthropologist* 20 (1918): 323–324; A. L. Kroeber, "Totem and Taboo: An Ethnologic Analysis," *American Anthropologist* 22 (1920): 48–55; A. L. Kroeber, "Totem and Taboo in Retrospect," *American Journal of Sociology* 45 (1939): 446–451; Theodora Kroeber, *Alfred Kroeber*, 101–102, 108, 154.

[6] A. Irving Hallowell, "On Being an Anthropologist," in *Contributions to Anthropology: Selected Papers of A. Irving Hallowell*, ed. Raymond D. Fogelson, Fred Eggan, Melford E. Spiro, George W. Stocking, Anthony F. C. Wallace, and Wilcomb E. Washburn (Chicago: University of Chicago Press, 1976), 4; Alexander Goldenweiser to Edward Sapir, 2 August 1922, quoted in Regna Darnell, *Edward Sapir: Linguist, Anthropologist, Humanist* (Berkeley: University of California Press, 1990), 140; Alexander Goldenweiser, *History, Psychology and Culture* (London: Kegan Paul, 1933), 71, 59; Buhle, *Feminism and Its Discontents*, 100, 94.

[7] Edward Sapir, "Psychoanalysis as a Pathfinder," review of *The Psychoanalytic Method*, by Oskar Pfister, *Dial*, 27 September 1917, 267–269; reprinted in *Selected Writings of Edward Sapir in Language, Culture, and Personality*, ed. David G. Mandelbaum (1949, repr., Berkeley: University of California Press, 1963), 523–524; Edward Sapir, "The Two Kinds of Human Beings," review of *Psychological Types, or the Psychology of Individuation*, by C. G. Jung, *Freeman*, 8 November 1923, 211–212; reprinted in *Selected Writings of Edward Sapir*, 529–532; Margaret Mead, *Blackberry Winter: My Earlier Years* (New York: William Morrow, 1972), 124.

In 1925, Sapir's appointment to the faculty of the University of Chicago brought him into contact with the political scientist Harold Lasswell and the psychiatrist Harry Stack Sullivan, both of whom were blessed, as was Sapir himself, "with the gift of tongues."[8] After being analyzed in Berlin in 1928–29, Lasswell championed the "prolonged interview" as "a method of investigating the unconscious substratum of personalities and situations." Adopting a Freudian perspective in *Psychopathology and Politics* (1930), he argued that individuals displaced their personal needs onto the political arena.[9] As we shall see, Sullivan pioneered "the fusion of psychiatry and social science," and his notion of "interpersonal relations" helped Sapir to reconcile the individual and society. Sullivan, in turn, was influenced by Sapir's emphasis upon the variability of personality in different cultural contexts. In 1930, he remarked that he was "so sympathetic" to Sapir's position on the individual in culture "that it seems almost unnecessary . . . to say anything." In 1933, Sapir told his wife that he "fit together" with Lasswell and Sullivan "in a curious and unpretentious way."[10]

Sapir's Chicago colleague William F. Ogburn was another enthusiastic proponent of psychoanalysis. Although Ogburn tried to make sociology more "scientific" by making it more quantitative and value-free, and although he tried to banish emotion from his own work, he was fascinated by Freud, was

My discussion of Sapir's role in culture and personality relies on Clyde Kluckhohn, "The Influence of Psychiatry on Anthropology in America during the Past One Hundred Years," in *One Hundred Years of American Psychiatry*, ed. J. K. Hall, G. Zilboorg, and E. A. Bunker (New York: Columbia University Press, 1944), 589–617, on 600–605; Milton Singer, "A Survey of Culture and Personality Theory and Research," in *Surveying Personality Cross-Culturally*, ed. Bert Kaplan (New York: Harper, 1961), 9–90, on 61–65; Regna Darnell, "Personality and Culture: The Fate of the Sapirian Alternative," in *Malinowski, Rivers, Benedict and Others: Essays on Culture and Personality*, ed. George W. Stocking, Jr. (Madison: University of Wisconsin Press, 1986), 156–183; Regna Darnell, *Edward Sapir: Linguist, Anthropologist, Humanist* (Berkeley: University of California Press, 1990).

[8] George W. Stocking, Jr., "Pedants and Potentates: Robert Redfield at the 1930 Hanover Conference," *History of Anthropology Newsletter* 5 (1978): 10.

[9] Harold D. Lasswell, "Afterthoughts: Thirty Years Later," in *Psychopathology and Politics* (1930; repr., New York: Viking, 1960), 269–319; Harold D. Lasswell, "What Psychiatrists and Political Scientists Can Learn from One Another," *Psychiatry* 1 (1938): 33–39; Harold D. Lasswell, "The Contribution of Freud's Insight Interview to the Social Sciences," *American Journal of Sociology* 45 (1939): 375–390; Bruce Lannes Smith, "The Mystifying Intellectual Influence of Harold D. Lasswell," in *Politics, Personality, and Social Science in the Twentieth Century: Essays in Honor of Harold D. Lasswell*, ed. Arnold A. Rogow (Chicago: University of Chicago Press, 1969), 41–105; Mark C. Smith, "Harold D. Lasswell and the Lost Opportunity of the Purposive School," in *Social Science in the Crucible: The American Debate over Objectivity and Purpose, 1918–1941* (Durham: Duke University Press, 1994), 212–252.

[10] Helen Swick Perry, *Psychiatrist of America: The Life of Harry Stack Sullivan* (Cambridge, Mass.: Harvard University Press, 1982), 242–250; Edward Sapir, "Why Cultural Anthropology Needs the Psychiatrist," *Psychiatry* 1 (1938): 7–12; reprinted in *Selected Writings of Edward Sapir*, 569–577; Edward Sapir to Jean Sapir, 16 September 1933, quoted in Darnell, *Edward Sapir*, 289.

analyzed, and helped to found the Chicago Institute for Psychoanalysis. And though he opposed the use of psychoanalytic concepts in social science, Ogburn thought that the same concepts could teach social scientists how to be less "unscientific" by illuminating how desires "disguise[d] themselves," "originate[d]," were "conditioned," and "form[ed] specific opinions."[11]

Stimulated by Chicago's interdisciplinary milieu, Sapir took the lead in exploring the relationship between culture and personality. In 1928, at the first of two American Psychiatric Association (APA) colloquia on "personality organization" that Sullivan convened for building bridges between psychiatrists and social scientists, Sapir speculated that if "culture" and "personality" were regarded as *"systems of ideas,"* there would be no conflict between the two systems: for "every individual acquires and develops his own 'culture'" and culture had "no psychological meaning until [it is] interpreted by being referred to personalities, or at the least, a generalized personality conceived as typical of a given society."[12]

At the second APA colloquium in 1929, Sapir outlined a "three-fold inquiry into personality" in which personalities would be analyzed, not as "isolated entities," but against "given backgrounds." He proposed that researchers study individual variation: first among Americans, then in "alien but not too distant cultures," and finally among "primitive man." While admitting that the inquiry he was proposing would require a certain amount of statistical work, Sapir urged researchers not to "lose sight of the fact" that their focus would be on "the actual individual studied." Indeed, Sapir considered the life history the "document *par excellence*" when it came to clarifying the "concept of personality." John Dollard later defined the life history as "an account of how a new person is added to the group and becomes an adult capable of meeting the traditional expectations of his society for a person of his sex and age."[13]

In 1930, Sapir discussed the "cultural approach to the study of personality" at the Hanover Conference. Hosted annually in Hanover, New Hampshire, from 1925 until 1930 by the Social Science Research Council, with funding

[11] Herman K. Haeberlin to Robert H. Lowie, 14 August 1917, Lowie Papers, box 7; Edward Sapir to A. L. Kroeber, 4 October 1920, in *The Sapir-Kroeber Correspondence*, 351; William F. Ogburn, "Bias, Psychoanalysis, and the Subjective in Relation to the Social Sciences," in *William F. Ogburn on Culture and Social Change*, ed. Otis Dudley Duncan (Chicago: University of Chicago Press, 1964), 301; Barbara Laslett, "Biography as Historical Sociology: The Case of William Fielding Ogburn," *Theory and Society* 20 (1991): 537n; Robert C. Bannister, *Sociology and Scientism: The American Quest for Objectivity, 1880–1940* (Chapel Hill: University of North Carolina Press, 1987), 162–163, 169; Darnell, *Edward Sapir*, 139.

[12] *Proceedings, First Colloquium on Personality Investigation, Held under the Auspices of the American Psychiatric Association, Committee on Relations with the Social Sciences* (Baltimore: Lord Baltimore Press, 1929), iii, 11, 26, 77, 79 (emphasis in original).

[13] *Proceedings, Second Colloquium on Personality Investigation, Held under the Auspices of the American Psychiatric Association, Committee on Relations of Psychiatry and the Social Sciences, and of the Social Science Research Council* (Baltimore: Johns Hopkins Press, 1930), 125, 123; John Dollard, *Criteria for the Life History: With Analyses of Six Notable Documents* (1935; repr., New York: Peter Smith, 1949), 3.

provided by the Rockefeller Foundation, the conference brought together "ped-ants" and "potentates," prominent social scientists and foundation officers, to chart agendas for American social science. Reviewing the "tangled field of personality and culture," Sapir criticized social scientists' reluctance to explore the "vast realm of human behavior" between the "culturalized part of conduct" and the "simpler somatic or psychological forms of behavior." Insisting that the "total personality" must be the "central point of reference" in the study of all "socialized patterns," Sapir emphasized the role the psychiatrist could play. More than any social scientist, the psychiatrist had tried "to rationalize as best he [could] the stubborn intuition of normal human beings" – an intuition that defied explanation "by any theories of conditioning" with which social scien-tists were then familiar. In the question-and-answer period that followed his paper, Sapir called attention to cross-cultural "parallels in the general person-ality gamut" that, in his opinion, overrode "all the determining forces of culture itself." In Sapir's opinion, the challenge then facing social scientists was how to account for those "variations in individual conduct" that could not be "explained by any kind of reference to anatomical facts."[14]

At the same Hanover Conference, Rockefeller Foundation officer Lawrence K. Frank hatched plans for a seminar on "the impact of culture on personality" to be held at the Yale Institute of Human Relations, which the foundation was then funding to study "human behavior in its individual and group relations."[15] Frank, whom Margaret Mead considered the inventor of "behavioral science," planned to bring a small number of foreign scholars to New Haven in 1931–32, where they would be inducted into culture and personality, and then return to their native lands to spread the word. Frank also expected the seminar to produce an "inventory" of the aspects of culture influenced by "the devel-opment of personalities," as well as to illuminate relations between the "demands" and "opportunities" of particular cultures and the "kinds of person-alities" found within them.[16]

At Clark Wissler's suggestion, the Rockefeller Foundation brought Sapir from Chicago to the Institute of Human Relations in 1931 to direct the seminar. Sapir was to be assisted by John Dollard, who had just earned his Ph.D. from the University of Chicago with a dissertation on the American family. When the

[14] Stocking, "Pedants and Potentates," 10; "Proceedings of the Social Science Research Council, Hanover Conference, Evening Sessions, August 29 – September 3, 1930" (Social Science Research Council, 1930), 73, 76, 79, 83–84, 89, 91, 95.

[15] James R. Angell to E. E. Day, 20 December 1928, quoted in Ellen Condliffe Lagemann, *The Politics of Knowledge: The Carnegie Corporation, Philanthropy, and Public Policy* (1989; repr., Chicago: University of Chicago Press, 1992), 155. On the Institute of Human Relations, see John Dollard, "Yale's Institute of Human Relations: What Was It?" *Ventures* 3 (1964): 32–40; Mark A. May, "A Retrospective View of the Institute of Human Relations at Yale," *Behavior Science Notes* 6 (1971): 141–172; J. G. Morawski, "Organizing Knowledge and Behavior at Yale's Institute of Human Relations," *Isis* 77 (1986): 219–242.

[16] Margaret Mead, "Lawrence Kelso Frank, 1890–1968," *American Sociologist* 4 (1969): 57–58; Lawrence K. Frank, "Memorandum on the Impact of Culture on Personality," 1931, folder 4828, box 408, series 200, RG 1.1, Rockefeller Foundation Archives, RAC.

seminar was postponed until 1932–33 because of difficulties encountered in recruiting foreign students, Dollard took advantage of a fellowship from the Social Science Research Council to study psychoanalysis with Hanns Sachs at the Berlin Psychoanalytic Institute.[17]

In the fall of 1932, thirteen students, hailing from eleven countries and representing eight disciplines, assembled in New Haven to study "the meaning of culture, its psychological relevance for personality, its value relativity and the problem of reconciling personality variations and cultural variations." They had prepared for the seminar by boning up on the extant literature on culture and personality in their native languages and by reading five books in English, including the Lynds' *Middletown*, as background for the "scientific projects" they were to undertake during breaks in the seminar. (Sapir, for his part, was mulling over a comparative study, modeled on *Middletown*, of two New Haven communities, one native-born, the other Italian-American.) Guest lecturers – including W. I. Thomas, Dorothy Thomas, and James Plant – supplemented Sapir's lectures on linguistic topics and Dollard's lectures on psychoanalytic topics. The seminar, however, failed to produce either the inventory that Frank was looking for or a "general outline of culture patterns from a psychological point of view" to guide future research. Disappointed by their investment in the seminar, which Ruth Benedict estimated at upward of $100,000, the officers of the Rockefeller Foundation refused to renew the fellowships of the eight students who applied to remain in the United States for another year.[18]

In addition to offering a continuing seminar at the Institute of Human Relations on "the psychology of culture," Sapir took a prominent part in interdisciplinary committees on culture and personality appointed by the Social Science Research Council and by the National Research Council. When the Social Science Research Council appointed him to a committee on culture and personality in 1930, Sapir suggested that studies of acculturation among American Indians would provide excellent opportunities for studying how culture contact affected personality development. But his proposal fell on deaf ears. In 1935, upon being made chairman of the National Research Council Division of Psychology and Anthropology, Sapir convened a small group at the American Museum of Natural History to map out "a research program in a field connecting psychology and anthropology." He regretted how much "material goes

[17] Darnell, *Edward Sapir*, 322–344; Neal E. Miller, "Dollard, John," *International Encyclopedia of the Social Sciences*, ed. David L. Sills (New York: Macmillan, 1979), 18:151.
[18] "Instructions to Fellows of Seminar on Impact of Culture and Personality," 30 March 1932, copy in Mead Papers, box G10; Edward Sapir, "Suggestions for the Culture and Personality Study of Two Selected New Haven Communities" (June 1932), folder 80, box 67, series 200, RG 1.1, Rockefeller Foundation Archives, RAC; Edward Sapir to Stacy May, 9 December 1932, folder 4829, box 408, series 200, RG 1.1, Rockefeller Foundation Archives, RAC; Stacy May to Edward Sapir, 8 June 1933; Stacy May to Tracy Kittredge, 6 June 1933, folder 4830, box 408, series 200, RG 1.1, Rockefeller Foundation Archives, RAC. The Mead Papers contain a list of some of the lectures given in the seminar. Estimates of the seminar's cost come from Ruth Benedict to Margaret Mead, 4, 10 March 1933, Mead Papers, box B14.

to waste in the anthropological field" because anthropologists, more attuned to "those types of behavior that throw light on the totality of pattern of behavior in a group," ignored "individual variations," even though those variations were easier to detect in a "primitive society" than in a more complex one. The Museum of Natural History conference led to the formation of two subcommittees: the first, chaired by A. Irving Hallowell, prepared a "handbook of psychological leads for ethnological field workers"; the second, headed by Harry Stack Sullivan, proposed a three-year training program in which young anthropologists would be analyzed before engaging in psychoanalytically-informed fieldwork. Although strongly backed by Sapir, the proposed training program elicited little interest at the National Research Council, perhaps because of its estimated cost of $70,000.[19]

Sapir made his chief contribution to culture and personality in a series of programmatic articles published between 1932 and his death in 1939. In "Cultural Anthropology and Psychiatry" (1932), he criticized "superorganic" conceptions of culture in which the individual was treated "as a more or less passive carrier of tradition [or culture]." The "genesis and development of cultural patterns," Sapir held, could not "realistically be disconnected" from "personality," which he defined as "those organizations of ideas and feelings which constitute the individual." Indeed, to Sapir, the "locus of culture" lay in the "interactions" of individuals and in the "world of meanings" they abstracted from those interactions.[20]

In "The Emergence of the Concept of Personality in a Study of Culture" (1934), Sapir urged social scientists to pay more attention to problems such as how the child acquired his or her culture. For "the more fully one tries to understand a culture, the more it seems to take on the characteristics of a personality organization." Instead of being "*given* to each individual," culture was "gropingly discovered." Indeed, "some parts of it are never acquired by individuals."[21] In an entry on "Personality" published in the *Encyclopedia of the Social Sciences* in the same year, Sapir characterized American culture as "definitely extraverted in character, with a greater emphasis on thinking and

[19] Edward Sapir to M. H. Britten, 8 February 1935; Minutes of the NRC Conference on Personality and Culture, 6 March 1935, 2, 8, National Research Council, A & P Conference on Personality and Culture, March 1935, National Academy of Sciences. On Hallowell, see A. Irving Hallowell, "On Being an Anthropologist," in *Contributions to Anthropology*, 3–14; George W. Stocking, Jr., "A. I. Hallowell's Boasian Evolutionism: Human Ir/rationality in Cross-Cultural, Evolutionary, and Personal Context," in *Significant Others: Interpersonal and Professional Commitments in Anthropology*, ed. Richard Handler (Madison: University of Wisconsin Press, 2004), 196–260.
[20] Edward Sapir, "Cultural Anthropology and Psychiatry," *Journal of Abnormal and Social Psychiatry* 27 (1932): 229–242; reprinted in *Selected Writings of Edward Sapir*, 509–521, on 512, 517–518.
[21] Edward Sapir, "The Emergence of the Concept of Personality in a Study of Cultures," *Journal of Social Psychology* 5 (1934): 408–415; reprinted in *Selected Writings of Edward Sapir*, 590–597, on 594–596 (emphasis in original).

intuition than on feeling." He fully expected social scientists to overcome their hostility to such "psychological characterizations of culture."[22]

In "The Contribution of Psychiatry to an Understanding of Behavior in Society" (1937), Sapir pointed to signs that "the sciences devoted to man as constitutive of society" were converging with psychiatry as social scientists began to turn their attention from "culture in the abstract" to "the actual day-to-day relations of specific individuals in a network of highly personal needs."[23] Sapir reiterated this point in "Why Cultural Anthropology Needs the Psychiatrist" (1938). "The dynamics of culture, of society, [and] of history," he maintained, could not be understood "without sooner or later taking account of the actual interrelationships of human beings."[24]

Finally, in "Psychiatric and Cultural Pitfalls in the Business of Getting a Living" (1939), Sapir staked the borderland between the "study of culture" and the "study of personality." The study of culture, he suggested, sprang from "the desire to lose oneself safely in the historically determined patterns of behavior." The study of personality, by contrast, proceeded from "the necessity which the ego feels to assert itself significantly."[25]

At the time of his death at the age of fifty-five in 1939, after a series of heart attacks, Sapir was convinced that future progress in culture and personality would be made by those researchers who took "seriously problems of personality organization and development." Indeed, he expected such work to lead eventually to "the recognition of certain fundamental normalities regardless of cultural differences."[26]

Sapir's plans for a psychology of culture, however, remained stillborn. Despite the opportunity to develop his ideas in a continuing seminar at Yale, Sapir never completed the book on psychology of the culture that he had promised to the publisher Alfred Harcourt. Although culture and personality continued to be pursued at Yale, it developed in ways that Sapir did not find congenial.[27] Sapir did leave a number of protégés, three of the most influential

[22] Edward Sapir, "Personality," *Encyclopedia of the Social Sciences*, ed. Edwin R. A. Seligman (New York: Macmillan, 1934), 12: 85–87; reprinted in *Selected Writings of Edward Sapir*, 560–563, on 563.

[23] Edward Sapir, "The Contribution of Psychiatry to an Understanding of Behavior in Society," *American Journal of Sociology* 42 (1937): 862–870.

[24] Edward Sapir, "Why Cultural Anthropology Needs the Psychiatrist," *Psychiatry* 1 (1938): 7–12; reprinted in *Selected Writings of Edward Sapir*, 569–577, on 569, 575.

[25] Edward Sapir, "Psychiatric and Cultural Pitfalls in the Business of Getting a Living," *Mental Health*, Publication of the American Association for the Advancement of Science (1939), 237–244; reprinted in *Selected Writings of Edward Sapir*, 578–589, on 585.

[26] Edward Sapir to Philip S. Selznick, 25 October 1938, quoted in George W. Stocking, Jr., "Sapir's Last Testament on Culture and Personality," *History of Anthropology Newsletter* 7 (1980): 9–10.

[27] Darnell, *Edward Sapir*, 132. Years later, Judith Irvine reconstructed Sapir's lectures on the psychology of culture from student notes. Edward Sapir, *The Psychology of Culture: A Course of Lectures*, ed. Judith T. Irvine (Berlin: Mouton de Gruyter, 1994).

of whom were Ruth Benedict, Margaret Mead, and John Dollard. All three, however, had grown estranged from Sapir before his death.

CONTINUITIES AND DISCONTINUITIES IN CHILD REARING

Ruth Benedict first became interested in personality formation when she tried to put her finger on what distinguished the Pueblo peoples from other Native American peoples in the Southwest. In "Psychological Types in the Cultures of the Southwest" (1930), she attributed the distinctiveness of the Pueblo people to the differences between their "psychological type" and those of neighboring tribes. It was precisely to evoke such a contrast that Benedict borrowed the terms "Apollonian" and "Dionysian" from Friedrich Nietzsche's *Birth of Tragedy*. To Benedict, the Apollonian ethos was one of "sobriety"; that of the Dionysian, "excess."[28]

By 1934, Benedict had turned her attention from the ethos of cultures to the relationship between cultures and their constituent personality types. When she characterized the Zuñi as sober, the Dobu as paranoid, and the Kwakiutl as megalomaniac in *Patterns of Culture*, Benedict did not investigate either the distribution of the dominant psychological type among each people or the socialization of individuals. Rather, she apparently considered human nature to be malleable enough so that it could be molded into almost any imaginable shape.[29] No wonder, then, that Sapir criticized her conflation of the "as-if" personality of a whole culture with the actual personalities of individuals. For Sapir, Benedict's characterization of cultures as sober, paranoid, and megalomaniac had "the value of literary suggestiveness," but "not of close personality analysis."[30]

After publishing *Patterns of Culture*, Benedict turned her attention to the "bridges" that cultures built between childhood and adulthood. American culture, she suggested, made the transition from adolescence to adulthood unnecessarily difficult by emphasizing discontinuities such as that between the adolescent's lack of responsibility and the adult's responsibility and that between the taboo against sex in adolescence and the expectation that adults would enjoy sex. By way of contrast, Benedict praised the "economy" of continuous conditioning in Zuñi culture. Although "impressed with the

[28] Ruth Benedict, "Psychological Types in the Cultures of the Southwest," *Proceedings of the Twenty-Third International Congress of Americanists* (Chicago: University of Chicago Press, 1930), 572–581; reprinted in *An Anthropologist at Work: Writings of Ruth Benedict*, ed. Margaret Mead (Boston: Houghton Mifflin, 1959), 248–261. My discussion of Benedict's interest in cultural and psychological types draws on Singer, "A Survey of Culture and Personality Theory and Research," 23–29.
[29] Franz Boas, introduction to *Patterns of Culture*, by Ruth Benedict (1934; repr., Boston: Houghton Mifflin, 1959), xvi.
[30] Sapir, "The Contribution of Psychiatry to an Understanding of Behavior in Society," 867; Sapir, *The Psychology of Culture*, 183–185; Alex Inkeles and Daniel J. Levinson, "National Character: The Study of Modal Personality and Sociocultural Systems," in *Handbook of Social Psychology*, ed. Gardner Lindzey (Reading, Mass.: Addison-Wesley, 1954), 987.

wickedness of premature sex experimentation," the Zuñi child, she explained, ran less risk than the American child "of associating the wickedness with sex itself rather than with sex at his age." In this way, continuity in cultural conditioning among the Zuñi lessened the storm and stress of adolescence.[31]

THE INDIVIDUAL IN CULTURE

Margaret Mead's three popular works on the South Pacific – *Coming of Age in Samoa, Growing Up in New Guinea,* and *Sex and Temperament in Three Primitive Societies* – made her well-known "in psychiatric circles." As was noted in Chapter 1, Mead marshaled telling evidence in all three books of the malleability of human nature while investigating the cultural conditioning of "character." Mead first became interested in psychology while a Barnard undergraduate. As she read the work of Freud and his followers in William F. Ogburn's "magnificent" class on "Psychological Factors in Culture," she began "to see real relationships between the way the minds of human beings worked and the cultures within which they were reared." Although she soon left psychology for anthropology, Mead thought that the question that the psychologist Robert S. Woodworth put to her, "When does an Indian become an Indian?," set the course of her career.[32]

In the summer of 1934, Mead was recruited into culture and personality at a conference organized by Lawrence Frank at Hanover, New Hampshire, to develop "an outline of our existing knowledge of human behavior for teaching adolescents." While working with John Dollard on the changing American family, Mead learned "how to handle the problem of character formation [in] a neo-Freudian way." She began to realize that before anthropologists could investigate "character formation in whole cultures," they must learn how to relate character formation systematically to "social structure."[33] Mead's newfound interest in Freudian theory was reinforced by her association with the German émigrés Erich Fromm and Karen Horney in the Zodiac Club, an informal network of like-minded psychoanalysts and social

[31] Ruth Benedict, "Continuities and Discontinuities in Cultural Conditioning," *Psychiatry* 1 (1938): 161–167.

[32] Kluckhohn, "Influence of Psychiatry on Anthropology," 600; Margaret Mead, *From the South Seas: Studies of Adolescence and Sex in Primitive Societies* (New York: William Morrow, 1939), xi–xii, vii; Margaret Mead, "Margaret Mead," in *A History of Psychology in Autobiography,* ed. Gardner Lindzey, vol. 6 (Englewood Cliffs, N. J.: Prentice-Hall, 1974), 310–311.

[33] Margaret Mead, "Letter for Larry's Seventy-fifth Birthday," 9 November 1965, Mead Papers, box M1; Margaret Mead, "Retrospects and Prospects," in *Anthropology and Human Behavior,* ed. Thomas Gladwin and William C. Sturtevant (Washington, D.C.: Anthropological Society of Washington, 1962), 126–128; Margaret Mead to Lawrence K. Frank, n.d.; "II. American Culture: Institutionalized Channels of Its Transmission," 21 August 1935; Section II of the Outline on Human Relations, n.d., Mead Papers, box F32.

scientists organized around Harry Stack Sullivan after he moved to New York in 1931.[34]

Before fleeing Germany in 1934 to set up private practice in New York, Erich Fromm took an active part in the efforts of the Frankfurt Institut für Sozialforschung (Institute for Social Research) to interpret political and historical developments from a Freudian perspective. Fromm was to combine Freudian and Marxian schema to account for fascism's appeal in his 1941 best seller *Escape from Freedom*.[35]

After coming to America in 1932 to serve as associate director of the Chicago Institute for Psychoanalysis, Karen Horney postulated instinctual femininity to counter Freud's concept of penis envy. In 1934, having irrevocably damaged her working relationship with Franz Alexander, the Institute's director, Horney moved to New York. At the Hanover Conference that summer, she charted what Mead described as a "multi-front operation" in which she located the source of neurosis, not in the Oedipus complex, but in "cultural conditions." Not only female sexuality but also motherhood, Horney held, were cultural formations. With the publication of *The Neurotic Personality of Our Time* in 1937, Horney became a public intellectual. In this widely discussed book, she attributed the neuroses Americans were then suffering from to the anxiety and hostility that ensued from their competition for material success and personal recognition – anxiety and hostility exacerbated by the greater likelihood of individual failure in this competition in the depths of the Depression.[36] Robert Lynd elaborated on Horney's critique in *Knowledge for What?*. After reiterating her point about how "individual competitive aggressiveness against one's fellows" isolated Americans and heightened their anxiety, Lynd quipped that "any candid person" who read *The Neurotic Personality of Our Time* found "himself brought up short at point after point with the thought, 'But she's talking about me and my friends.'"[37] Horney thus recast in psychological terms the familiar critique of the competition, hyper-individualism, aggression, and drive for material success of American culture, all of which were held to breed anxiety and frustration.[38]

[34] Perry, *Psychiatrist of America*, 344, 354–355; Buhle, *Feminism and Its Discontents*, 114–115.

[35] H. Stuart Hughes, *The Sea Change: The Migration of Social Thought, 1930–1965* (1975; repr., New York: McGraw-Hill, 1977), 80–81; Neil G. McLaughlin, "Why Do Schools of Thought Fail? Neo-Freudianism as a Case Study in the Sociology of Knowledge," *Journal of the History of the Behavioral Sciences* 34 (1998): 113–134; Wilfred M. McClay, *The Masterless: Self and Society in Modern America* (Chapel Hill: University of North Carolina Press, 1994), 198–199, 207–208.

[36] Karen Horney, "Culture and Neurosis," *American Sociological Review* 1 (1936): 221–230; Karen Horney, *The Neurotic Personality of Our Time* (New York: Norton, 1937); Buhle, *Feminism and Its Discontents*, 85–86, 111–119.

[37] Robert S. Lynd, *Knowledge for What? The Place of Social Science in American Culture* (1939; repr., Princeton, N.J.: Princeton University Press, 1970), 71, 230.

[38] Dennis H. Wrong, "The Functional Theory of Stratification: Some Neglected Considerations," *American Sociological Review* 24 (1959): 780n; Howard Brick, *Transcending Capitalism: Visions of a New Society in Modern American Thought* (Ithaca: Cornell University Press, 2006), 86–120.

In 1935, having been commissioned by the Social Science Research Council to study "competitive and cooperative habits" from a cross-cultural perspective, Mead supervised a small group of Columbia graduate students as they investigated cooperation and competition in thirteen "primitive" cultures. Mead summed up their findings in the introduction to *Cooperation and Competition among Primitive Peoples* (1937). The social structures of what she labeled "competitive" cultures tended to encourage individual initiative, value property "for individual ends," and subscribe to a "single scale of success." The social structures of "cooperative" cultures, by contrast, were characterized by a "faith in an ordered universe," placed little emphasis on "rising in status," and assured individuals "a high degree of security." It therefore seemed necessary to Mead to go beyond "patterned relations of items of social behavior" to attend to the ways in which a child was "added to the group" and "a given type of culture [was] laid down in the [child]."[39]

CULTURE AND PERSONALITY AT YALE

At the same time the Social Science Research Council commissioned Mead to study cooperative and competitive habits from a cross-cultural perspective, it commissioned John Dollard "to canvass the life-history literature." After examining six such documents – three clinical case histories, two sociological studies, and one autobiography – Dollard concluded that the life history placed the individual front and center: "the person is 'there,'" he wrote, "in full emotional reality."[40]

In the summer of 1935, Dollard went to Indianola, Mississippi, to collect life histories that would throw light on the development of personality among African-Americans. He quickly realized, however, that "whites and whiteness form[ed] an inseparable part of the mental life of the Negro." Adopting Lloyd Warner's caste–class framework, Dollard devoted much of his ethnography of Indianola, published in 1937 under the title *Caste and Class in a Southern Town*, to a discussion of the economic, sexual, and prestige gains that whites derived from belonging to the superior caste, the strains African Americans experienced from being consigned to the inferior caste, and the psychic gains lower-class blacks enjoyed thanks to their immunity from middle-class inhibitions.[41]

Dollard's subsequent research "centered in the psychological field" as he joined in the efforts of his colleagues at the Institute of Human Relations to integrate stimulus-and-response learning theory, Freud's theories of character

[39] Margaret Mead, ed., *Cooperation and Competition among Primitive Peoples* (1937; repr., Boston: Beacon Press, 1961), ix, 460–461, 510–511.
[40] Dollard, *Criteria for the Life History*, iii, 3, 5.
[41] John Dollard, *Caste and Class in a Southern Town* (1937; repr., Madison: University of Wisconsin Press, 1988), 1; Walter Jackson, *Gunnar Myrdal and America's Conscience: Social Engineering and Racial Liberalism, 1938–1987* (Chapel Hill: University of North Carolina Press, 1990), 97. See also Christopher Lasch, *Haven in a Heartless World: The Family Besieged* (New York: Basic Books, 1977), chap. 2.

development, and social scientists' emphasis upon social setting. In *Frustration and Aggression* (1939), Dollard and his colleagues tested a "basic principle of human and animal behavior" that Dollard derived from his reading of Freud and then took into the field in Indianola with him: specifically, that "aggression is always a consequence of frustration." In *Children of Bondage* (1940), Dollard collaborated with Allison Davis on a study of the impact of caste and class on the personalities of African-American youth in New Orleans and Natchez, Mississippi. In *Social Learning and Imitation* (1941), he and Neal Miller inquired into the "principles" on which, and the "conditions" under which, a human being "learns." Finally, in *Personality and Psychotherapy* (1950), which Dollard considered his best book, he and Miller analyzed neurosis from the perspective of the Yale fusion of psychoanalysis and learning theory.[42]

TWO ENGLISH RECRUITS

In 1935–36, the circle around Mead, Benedict, and Dollard expanded to incorporate two English recruits. The first was Gregory Bateson, who became Mead's husband in 1936. The son of the distinguished English geneticist William Bateson, Bateson had studied with the zoologist A. C. Haddon at Cambridge, then lived among the Iatmul of New Guinea from 1927 to 1930. Returning to New Guinea in 1932 for another season of fieldwork, he met Mead and her then-husband, the New Zealand anthropologist Reo Fortune, on the Sepik River. After their wedding, Mead and Bateson engaged in two years of joint fieldwork in Bali, studying "the way in which" the Balinese, "as living persons, moving, standing, eating, sleeping, dancing, and going into trance, embody that abstraction which (after we have abstracted it) we technically call culture." They took "notes on [Balinese] behavior" in some twenty-five thousand of still photographs that Bateson snapped and Mead annotated.[43]

[42] Dollard, *Caste and Class in a Southern Town*, xiii, xiv, 267; John Dollard to Margaret Mead, 7 June 1937, Mead Papers, box C2; John Dollard, Leonard W. Doob, Neal E. Miller, O. Hobart Mowrer, and Robert R. Sears, *Frustration and Aggression* (New Haven, Conn.: Yale University Press, 1939); Allison Davis and John Dollard, *Children of Bondage: The Personality Development of Negro Youth in the Urban South* (1940; repr., New York: Harper, 1964); Neal E. Miller and John Dollard, *Social Learning and Imitation* (New Haven, Conn.: Yale University Press, 1941); John Dollard and Neal E. Miller, *Personality and Psychotherapy: An Analysis in Terms of Learning, Thinking, and Culture* (New York: McGraw-Hill, 1950). On Dollard, see Steven Weiland, "Life History, Psychoanalysis, and Social Science: The Example of John Dollard," *South Atlantic Quarterly* 86 (1987): 269–281; Nadine Weidman, "Dollard, John," *American National Biography*. Supplement Six, ed. John A. Garraty and Mark C. Carnes (New York: Oxford University Press, 1999), 708–710; Rebecca Lemov, *World as Laboratory: Experiments with Mice, Mazes, and Men* (New York: Hill and Wang, 2005), 107–124, 131–135, 138–140.
[43] Gregory Bateson and Margaret Mead, *Balinese Character: A Photographic Analysis* (New York: New York Academy of Sciences, 1942), xii; Margaret Mead to Franz Boas, 19 May 1941, quoted in Gerald Sullivan, *Margaret Mead, Gregory Bateson, and Highland Bali: Fieldwork Photographs of Bayung Gedé, 1936–1939* (Chicago: University of Chicago Press, 1999), 3. On Bateson, see David Lipset, *Gregory Bateson: The Legacy of a Scientist* (Boston: Beacon, 1982).

The second English recruit, Geoffrey Gorer, had been educated at Cambridge, the Sorbonne, and the University of Berlin. After publishing two well-received travelogues, *Africa Dances* (1935) and *Bali and Angkor* (1936), Gorer went to New York to collect materials on burlesque theaters and their audiences for his next book, *Hot Strip Tease, and Other Notes on American Culture.* After Mead and Benedict gave him a crash course in anthropology, Gorer went to Sikkim for fieldwork among the Lepcha. Although he passed this rite of passage with flying colors, Gorer suffered a bad fall that ruled out any further fieldwork.[44]

Becoming interested in the changes "the Western European character" had undergone over the previous 150 years, Gorer secured a fellowship from the Rockefeller Foundation that enabled him to study psychoanalysis, behaviorist psychology, and the impact of the movies and radio on the American people at the Institute of Human Relations. The Yale researchers' frustration-aggression hypothesis, he soon came to believe, would make it possible to put psychology and sociology on a "fairly strict and controllable scientific basis."[45] By December 1939, Gorer had assimilated enough anthropology to expound the culture concept at the annual meetings of the American Historical Association. In his exposition, Gorer emphasized "character formation," or "the process by which the newborn animal is fitted into his culture." After rehearsing Ruth Benedict's argument that individual "potentialities" and "temperament types" were "culturally produced," Gorer went on to assert that "relatively uniform methods of infant rearing" produced "relatively uniform adult characters."[46]

Forming a more or less congenial circle, Mead, Benedict, Dollard, Bateson, and Gorer explored child-rearing patterns and personality development. They did not, however, follow Sapir's lead in locating culture in the individual. Nor did they develop an approach that could be used in the field. Culture and personality was not to be put into practice until operational concepts were developed in a cooperative seminar at Columbia.

[44] Geoffrey Gorer, *Africa Dances: A Book about West African Negroes* (New York: Knopf, 1935); Geoffrey Gorer, *Bali and Angkor: Or, Looking at Life and Death* (Boston: Little, Brown, 1936); Geoffrey Gorer, *Hot Strip Tease, and Other Notes on American Culture* (London: Cresset, 1937), 3–5; Geoffrey Gorer to Margaret Mead, 17 February, 17 April 1937, Mead Papers, box B15; Geoffrey Gorer, "Foreword to the First Edition" in *Himalayan Village*, 2nd ed. (New York: Basic Books, 1967), 11–12; obituary of Gorer, (London) *Times*, 29 May 1985.

[45] Geoffrey Gorer to Margaret Mead, 18 November [1938], 6 August 1939, 24 June 1936, Mead Papers, box B15.

[46] Geoffrey Gorer, "Society as Viewed by the Anthropologist," in *The Cultural Approach to History*, ed. Caroline F. Ware (1940; repr., New York: Gordon Press, 1974), 20–33, on 29. While praising Gorer's exposition of the culture concept, Melville Herskovits questioned the extent to which Gorer had "overload[ed] the bag of conceptual tools with psychological instruments." Herskovits wished that Gorer had "stressed the institutional patterning of culture" more and the psychological implications less. Melville J. Herskovits, review of *The Cultural Approach to History*, ed. Caroline F. Ware, *Annals of the American Academy of Political and Social Science* 216 (1941): 217.

CULTURE AND PERSONALITY AT COLUMBIA

In 1933, Abram Kardiner inaugurated a seminar on "The Application of Psychoanalysis to Problems in Mythology, Religion, and Ethnology" at the New York Psychiatric Institute. Some two decades earlier, Kardiner had briefly studied anthropology with Boas at Columbia before deciding to become a psychiatrist and undergoing an analysis in Vienna with Freud himself.[47]

Although Kardiner's seminar initially enrolled only two students, it soon attracted Cora Du Bois. While majoring in history at Barnard College, Du Bois took a course in anthropology jointly taught by Boas and Benedict. After earning an M.A. from Columbia in medieval history in 1928, she decided to pursue a Ph.D. in anthropology at the University of California, where Lowie's "theoretical" approach supplemented Kroeber's "factual" one. In 1935–36, a fellowship from the National Research Council allowed Du Bois to work with Henry A. Murray at the Harvard Psychological Clinic and to attend Sapir's lectures on the psychology of culture at the Institute of Human Relations. Then, in New York, she presented ethnographic material on the Trobriand Islanders and Kwakiutl to Kardiner's seminar. "Enthralled to discover" that a group of young analysts would "sit thru 2 solid hours of Trobriand social organization without protest," Du Bois began to see her participation in Kardiner's seminar as "missionary work" and to look for opportunities in which she could promote the "rapprochement between psychology and anthropology."[48] Convinced of the need to test Kardiner's theories in the field, Du Bois got a "phenomenal break" when he "stak[ed]" her to two years of fieldwork on the island of Alor in the Netherlands East Indies.[49]

In the meantime, Kardiner's seminar piqued the curiosity of other anthropologists. In the spring of 1937, Sapir and Dollard both came down from New Haven, and Benedict led three sessions on the "Constellation of Competition and Rivalry in Primitive Society."[50] Then, in the spring of 1938, Ralph Linton, Boas's successor at Columbia, gave detailed accounts of his fieldwork among the Marquesans of Polynesia and the Tanala of Madagascar. In 1939, Linton invited Kardiner to Columbia, where the two men offered a joint seminar on the "Psychological Analysis of Primitive Cultures."[51]

[47] My account of the Kardiner seminar relies on William C. Manson, "Abram C. Kardiner and the Neo-Freudian Alternative in Culture and Personality," in *Malinowski, Rivers, Benedict and Others*, 72–94.
[48] Cora Du Bois to Ruth Benedict, 27 January 1929, 6 February 1936, Benedict Papers, box 28, folder 284; Cora Du Bois to Robert H. Lowie, 24 April 1936, Lowie Papers, box 6; Cora Du Bois, *The People of Alor: A Social-Psychological Study of an East Indian Island* (1944; repr., New York, Harper, 1961), viii; Cora Du Bois, "Some Anthropological Hindsights," *Annual Review of Anthropology* 9 (1980): 1–2; Cora Du Bois, "Some Anthropological Perspectives on Psychoanalysis," *Psychoanalytic Review* 24 (1937): 252.
[49] Cora Du Bois to Margaret Mead, 12 September 1938, 13 May 1937, Mead Papers, box C2; Cora Du Bois to Robert H. Lowie, 6 April 1937, Lowie Papers, box 6.
[50] Margaret M. Caffrey, *Ruth Benedict: Stranger in This Land* (Austin: University of Texas Press, 1989), 242–243.
[51] Manson, "Abram C. Kardiner and the Neo-Freudian Alternative in Culture and Personality," 79–84.

Kardiner, who considered his meeting with Linton not only a "very lucky stroke" but a turning point in the development of his own thought, began to realize that "certain innovations" needed to be made in psychoanalytic theory.[52] Accordingly, in *The Individual and His Society* (1939), he developed the concepts of "primary institution," "secondary institution," and "basic personality structure." In place of the conventional Freudian emphasis on the libido, Kardiner emphasized the ego's relation to the institutions of his or her society. He considered those institutions, such as family organization and the sexual division of labor, that structured the relations between parents and children to be "primary" institutions. Primary institutions shaped the basic personality structure, which, in turn, integrated the "projective systems" manifested in such "secondary" institutions as religion, myth, folklore, and ritual. Ralph Linton was just as surprised as "any of the students" in the seminar by "the psychological coherence of institutions which emerged in the course of [Kardiner's] analyses." Small wonder that Clyde Kluckhohn, in 1944, pronounced *The Individual and His Society* as "the outstanding integration of anthropology psychiatry to date." Even Ruth Benedict, who did not consider Kardiner's distinction between primary and secondary institutions "a sharp tool of methodological analysis," admitted that students of "the dynamics of human behavior" would in the future have to follow Kardiner's lead in giving "more weight to culturally standardized experiences brought to bear on individuals."[53]

Soon after returning from Alor, Du Bois presented her findings to the Kardiner-Linton seminar. Kardiner interpreted her findings from a psychoanalytical perspective, then the Rorschach expert Emil Oberholzer undertook a "blind analysis" of her protocols. Oberholzer's analysis was, as Du Bois told Robert Lowie, "a knock out." It not only confirmed Kardiner's interpretation of her findings, but established the validity of the Rorschach test as a tool in the cross-cultural study of personality.[54] In *The People of Alor* (1944), Du Bois presented the eight life histories that she had collected on Alor together with Kardiner's interpretation and Oberholzer's analysis. As a statistical substitute for basic personality structure, Du Bois expounded the concept of "modal personality." It referred to the most frequent type of personality encountered in a society.[55]

[52] Abram Kardiner, quoted in Manson, "Abram Kardiner and the Neo-Freudian Alternative," 81.

[53] Abram Kardiner, *The Individual and His Society: The Psychodynamics of Primitive Social Organization* (New York: Columbia University Press, 1939), 18, 126–134, 467–487; Ralph Linton, foreword to ibid., xviii; Kluckhohn, "The Influence of Psychiatry on Anthropology," 611; Ruth Benedict to Thelma Herman, 12 July 1944, Benedict Papers, box 12, folder 115.

[54] Cora Du Bois to Robert H. Lowie, 10 May [1940], Lowie Papers, box 6.

[55] Du Bois, *The People of Alor*; Colin McPhee, "Clinic in the South Seas," review of *The People of Alor*, *New York Times Book Review*, 17 September 1944.

THE STUDY OF CULTURE AT A DISTANCE

Culture and personality entered a new phase after war broke out in Europe in September 1939. The war spurred the development of the study of culture at a distance, in which practitioners of culture and personality took up the study of national character. As Margaret Mead later pointed out, national character studies took "their form and methods from the exigencies of the post-1939 world political situation." Indeed, the Second World War provided practitioners with access to policymakers, inspired "messianic" ambitions to rebuild the postwar world, and opened up new sources of financial support.[56]

In 1940, Margaret Mead, Ruth Benedict, Gregory Bateson, and Geoffrey Gorer all joined the Committee for National Morale, a "pressure group" whose members, convinced that social scientific techniques could be used to promote American morale, did what they could to assure that "as many of [their] ideas" as possible "would get 'stolen' by the government."[57] Unable to engage in their customary fieldwork, the anthropologists among them drew on interviews with foreign travelers and resident aliens, fiction, and even films, to study culture at a distance.[58]

Once the war began, culture-and-personality researchers quickly turned their attention to the national characters of America's enemies, the Germans and the Japanese. Even before America entered the war, Erich Fromm had published *Escape from Freedom*, a psychiatrically informed account of the German character. Rapid economic change, Fromm argued, had released Germans from "traditional bonds" while intensifying their "feeling of powerlessness and aloneness." This newfound freedom engendered "a compulsive quest for certainty" and "desperate escape from anxiety" that impelled individuals, in particular lower-middle-class Germans, to surrender their freedom to a "leader." Complete submission to some stronger person or thing, plus hatred and cruelty toward the weak, constituted what Fromm called "the authoritarian character."[59]

---

[56] Margaret Mead, "National Character," in *Anthropology Today: An Encyclopedic Inventory*, ed. A. L. Kroeber (Chicago: University of Chicago Press, 1953), 642; Robert Endleman, "The New Anthropology and Its Ambitions: The Science of Man in Messianic Dress," *Commentary*, October 1949, 284–291.

[57] Memo from Gregory Bateson and Margaret Mead, 5 September 1941, Mead Papers, box F1; Gregory Bateson to Beatrice Bateson, 30 March 1941, quoted in Virginia Yans-McLaughlin, "Science, Democracy, and Ethics: Mobilizing Culture and Personality for World War II," in *Malinowski, Rivers, Benedict and Others*, 196.

[58] Minutes of General Meeting of the Committee for National Morale, 6 March 1941, Mead Papers, box F1; Margaret Mead, "Anthropological Contributions to National Policies during and immediately after World War II," in *The Uses of Anthropology*, ed. Walter R. Goldschmidt (Washington, D.C.: American Anthropological Association, 1979), 148–149.

[59] Erich Fromm, *Escape from Freedom* (1941; repr., New York: Avon Books, 1965), 77, 92, 123, 207–208; Margaret Mead, "The Choice Offered Us," review of *Escape from Freedom*, *New York Herald Tribune Books*, 21 September 1941; "The Flight from Freedom," *TLS*, 10 October 1942.

Still other wartime analysts of the German character rooted German authoritarianism not in anomie, but rather in the patriarchal nature of the German family. Diagnosing the German character as "paranoid," the psychiatrist Richard Brickner prescribed "a vast educational program" for postwar Germany. The historian Helen Peak likened "the Nazi virus" to a "disease." Mapping the "areas in which the infection rate was highest," Peak suggested, would allow researchers to identify "the predisposing causes of this social pathology." The "personality profile" that the English psychiatrist Henry Dicks constructed from his interviews with German prisoners of war classified the Nazis among them as sado-masochists who repressed "tender tie[s]" to their mothers and "homo-sexual (extra-punitive) relation[s]" with their fathers. The German people, Dicks concluded, had "an ambivalent compulsive character structure with the emphasis on submissive/dominant conformity."[60]

Gregory Bateson, analyzing German movies for clues about "what makes the Nazis tick," distinguished between "complementary" motifs that stimulated the individual "to greater assertiveness by the comparative weakness of his enemy," characteristic of the German people, and "symmetrical motifs" that stimulated the individual "to make positive assertive efforts in response to the great strength or assertiveness shown by his enemy." The latter was characteristic of the American people.[61]

The Danish émigré psychoanalyst Erik H. Erikson likened "Hitlerized Germany" to "a not uncommon type of adolescent who turns delinquent." In the "infantile imagery" of Hitler's *Mein Kampf* and "much of German idealism," he detected a "peculiar combination of paternal dominance and filial rebellion and submission." Indeed, "in many respects," the Third Reich was "a magnificent realization of certain collective adolescent fantasies."[62]

While wartime commentators emphasized German submissiveness to authority, either to the *Führer* or to a patriarchal father, they pictured the Japanese character as formed by severe toilet-training practices. Geoffrey Gorer set the tone when, early in the war, he depicted the Japanese as a "compulsive"

[60] Richard M. Brickner, "The German Cultural Paranoid Trend," *American Journal of Orthopsychiatry* 12 (1942): 544–545; Richard M. Brickner, *Is Germany Incurable?* (Philadelphia: Lippincott, 1943); Helen Peak, "Observations on the Characteristics and Distribution of German Nazis," *Psychological Monographs* 59 (1945): 3; Henry Dicks, "Personality Traits and National Socialist Ideology: A War-Time Study of German Prisoners of War," *Human Relations* 3 (1950): 111–154, on 111, 113–114.

[61] Gregory Bateson, "Morale and National Character," in *Civilian Morale*, ed. Goodwin Watson (New York: Reynal and Hitchcock, 1942), 84–85; Gregory Bateson and Margaret Mead, "Principles of Morale Building," *Journal of Educational Sociology* (1941): 216; Gregory Bateson, "Some Systematic Approaches to the Study of Culture and Personality," *Character and Personality* 11 (1942): 76–82.

[62] Erik H. Erikson, "On Nazi Mentality" (1940), in *A Way of Looking at Things: Selected Papers from 1930 to 1980*, ed. Stephen Schlein (New York: Norton, 1987), 341–345; Erik H. Erikson, "Comments on Anti-Nazi Propaganda" (1942), copy in Mead Papers, box M32; Erik Erikson, "Hitler's Imagery and German Youth," *Psychiatry* 5 (1942): 475–493; Lawrence J. Friedman, *Identity's Architect: A Biography of Erik H. Erikson* (New York: Scribner, 1999), 163–176.

people whose indifference to "regularity of meals or of diet," "excessive fear of soiling and dirt," and obsession with "neatness and tidiness" stemmed from "drastic toilet training." The Japanese, Gorer suggested, bifurcated the world into "male" countries, to be "followed and obeyed," and "female" countries, "to be forced to yield to aggression or threats of aggression." The Japanese "fear of criticism from strangers," Gorer added, led to both "conformity" and a "constant urge to control the environment as completely as possible."[63]

To Weston La Barre, the Japanese seemed "probably the most compulsive people in the world ethnological museum." La Barre attributed Japanese compulsiveness to a harsh regime of toilet training in which the child relinquished "primary gratifications" and took on the "culturally colored conditioning of the sphincter."[64]

John Embree agreed with Gorer and La Barre that the "early period" of Japanese childhood was formative in shaping "adult personality." The twin "shock[s]" of drastic toilet training and the mother's withdrawal of her affection upon the birth of her next child, Embree suggested, produced a Japanese adult who compensated for lack of self-assurance by becoming "almost paranoiac."[65] Embree's analysis of the Japanese character was echoed in 1943 by an anonymous author in the *New York Times Magazine* who attributed the truculence and vengefulness of the "Jap soldier" to the fact that he was petted "inordinately" from his birth "until the arrival of his little sister," then dismissed by his mother and turned over to "the indifferent care of servants." The Japanese adult never got "over the shock" to "his nervous system."[66]

To the specialists who attended a conference held under the auspices of the Institute of Pacific Relations in December 1944, Japanese behavior resembled that of American adolescents. Conformists "without conviction," the Japanese were rebelling against "conformity to all standards." Hence the specialists recommended that, after Japan was defeated, the United States should act like an "elder brother" and bring the wayward "younger brother" back into the "family of nations."[67]

[63] Geoffrey Gorer, "Themes in Japanese Culture," *Transactions of the New York Academy of Sciences* 5 (1943): 106–124, on 107, 115–116, 118–120, 122–123. In this article Gorer condensed a memorandum on "Japanese Character Structure," prepared in 1942 for the Council on Intercultural Relations. A capsule summary appeared in *Time* under the title, "Why Are Japs Japs?" *Time*, 7 August 1944, 66. My account of wartime studies of Japanese character draws on John W. Dower, *War without Mercy: Race and Power in the Pacific War* (New York: Pantheon, 1986), chap. 6. Dower contends that the wartime national character studies reinforced popular stereotypes of the Japanese.

[64] Weston La Barre, "Some Observations on Character Structure in the Orient: The Japanese," *Psychiatry* 8 (1945): 319–342, on 326, 327, 340.

[65] John F. Embree, *The Japanese* (Washington, D.C.: Smithsonian Institution, 1943), 23.

[66] "Jap Bullies," *New York Times Magazine*, 1 August 1943, 17.

[67] Excerpts from "Provisional Analytic Summary of the Institute of Pacific Relations Conference on Japanese Character Structure, December 16–17, 1944," quoted in Dower, *War without Mercy*, 131–133.

Perhaps Douglas Haring said the last word when he suggested that if the word "Japanese" were substituted everywhere Karen Horney had used "neurotic" in *The Neurotic Personality of Our Time*, the result would be "the most perfect description of the Japanese."[68]

Emphasis on German authoritarianism and Japanese toilet training, however, receded in postwar analyses of America's former enemies. In *Postwar Germany* (1948), based on five months of fieldwork in the largely Protestant German state of Hesse in 1945 and interviews with more than 150 Germans, many of them former Nazi sympathizers, David Rodnick reported that German children generally experienced happy childhoods that made their adulthoods seem lonely and insecure. Whereas American children were rewarded "when they act[ed] like adults," German children were rewarded "when they act[ed] like children." Hence German adults who craved a return to the protective womb of childhood followed leaders who rewarded their obedience.[69]

The authoritarian family did not figure at all in either of Robert Lowie's two books on postwar Germany. In *The German People: A Social Portrait to 1914* (1945), Lowie depicted the Germans as a heterogeneous people divided by mutually unintelligible dialects.[70] In *Toward Understanding Germany* (1954), he judged German families to be less patriarchal than those of the German-speaking Swiss. Convinced that much of what had, during the war, been labeled German was in reality either European or generically human, Lowie found marked class distinctions the only "highly distinctive" German feature. Moderately optimistic about the future of Germany, Lowie thought it "possible" that Germany would "achieve democracy of a sort, not through alien imposition, but by the democratic faith of its working class and as yet only moderately large group of intellectuals."[71]

An even more profound reevaluation of the Japanese character occurred when Ruth Benedict published the *The Chrysanthemum and the Sword* in 1946. Benedict's book grew out of her wartime service in the Foreign Morale Analysis Division of the Office of War Information. As a psychological warrior, she prepared detailed studies of Thai and Romanian behavior, a memorandum on Burma, and brief studies of the Netherlands, Finland, Denmark, and Norway. In what she called "the social anthropology of Europe and Asia," Benedict attempted to persuade American foreign policymakers "to take into account different habits and customs of other parts of the world" by identifying not only "specific weaknesses" that could be exploited during the

[68] Douglas Haring, quoted in Dower, *War without Mercy*, 134–135.
[69] David Rodnick, *Postwar Germans: An Anthropologist's Account* (New Haven, Conn.: Yale University Press, 1948).
[70] Robert H. Lowie, *The German People: A Social Portrait to 1914* (New York: Farrar and Rinehart, 1945).
[71] Robert H. Lowie, *Toward Understanding Germany* (Chicago: University of Chicago Press, 1954).

war but also "specific strengths" that could be tapped to promote postwar reconstruction.[72]

After being asked in 1944 to "use all the techniques" at her disposal "to spell out what the Japanese were like," Benedict "saturated" herself in literary materials and interviewed Japanese-American informants to prepare memos on suicide, myths, behavior patterns, ethics, and the emperor. In the last memo she seconded the recommendations of both Geoffrey Gorer and John Embree that the emperor be kept on the throne as a "Good Father" or "sacred chief" during postwar reconstruction.[73]

Benedict's wartime memos set the stage for *The Chrysanthemum and the Sword*. Shortly after the war ended, Benedict's editor at Houghton Mifflin, Ferris Greenslet, asked her to write a book on Japan. "Adamant about having a title on the order of 'Black Lamb and Grey Falcon,'" Rebecca West's acclaimed account of prewar Yugoslavia, Greenslet chose a title for Benedict's book that would evoke the stark contrast between the aesthetic and the militaristic aspects of the Japanese character. Benedict's aim, however, was to domesticate the "alien" Japanese in American eyes. She thus set out to show how the "assumptions" on which the Japanese built their culture also served as the "lenses" through which they viewed their "existence." When viewed from this perspective, the "violent swings" of Japanese behavior that had long puzzled Western observers could be seen as "integral parts" of the Japanese character. Maintaining that "in warfare as well as in peace, the Japanese acted in character," Benedict focused on "all the ways in which the Japanese departed from Western conventions of war" as clues to understanding their character.[74]

In her attempt to make Japanese culture intelligible, Benedict juxtaposed strange and seemingly paradoxical Japanese customs with familiar American customs, defamiliarizing the latter.[75] Where Americans prized equality, the

---

[72] Ruth Benedict to Charles D. Anderson, 7 March 1944, Benedict Papers, box 12, folder 112; Ruth Benedict to Rev. Richard Henry, 8 August 1946, Benedict Papers, box 14, folder 135. Guy Pauker, a Romanian national, criticized Benedict's assumption of "a degree of cultural homogeneity throughout the social structure of the Old Kingdom [of Romania] which does not fit reality." Guy J. Pauker, "The Study of National Character Away from That Nation's Territory," *Harvard Studies in International Affairs* 1 (1951): 81–103, on 87.

[73] Ruth Benedict, "Japanese Behavior Patterns," 15 September 1945; Ruth Benedict, "What Shall be Done about the Emperor," Benedict Papers, box 90, folder 1123. As John Dower has pointed out, American policymakers apparently heeded the recommendation that the Emperor be left in place out of fear that dethroning him would stiffen Japanese resistance to the postwar occupation. Yet other recommendations made by wartime students of the Japanese character fared less well. Neither their conclusion that Japanese morale had begun to crack as early as 1944 nor their suggestion that "situational ethics" explained the surprising willingness of Japanese prisoners of war to divulge information about their units affected American policy. Dower, *War without Mercy*, 143.

[74] Ruth Benedict to Clyde Kluckhohn, 19 August 1946, HUG 4490.3, Kluckhohn Papers; Ruth Benedict, *The Chrysanthemum and the Sword: Patterns of Japanese Culture* (1946; repr., Cleveland: World, 1967), 1, 17, 5.

[75] Clifford Geertz, "Us/Not-Us: Benedict's Travels," in *Works and Lives: The Anthropologist as Author* (Stanford: Stanford University Press, 1988), 102–128.

Japanese emphasized hierarchy, "taking one's proper station," in both domestic and foreign affairs. Where Americans celebrated individualism and self-reliance, the Japanese enmeshed themselves in tightly-knit webs of reciprocal obligations. The Japanese, like Americans, cultivated strict self-discipline, but they did so, not out of any abstract sense of good and evil, but rather out of a belief that self-discipline was necessary to carry out their obligations. Although the Japanese were certainly austere, they were not Puritans; they did not proscribe sex, alcohol, or other physical pleasures. But they did insist that these pleasures be "kept in their place." Where Americans worshiped competition, the Japanese went to elaborate lengths to minimize direct competition so as not to shame those who lost. Finally, where Americans relied on guilt as their principal social sanction, the Japanese relied on shame.[76]

Benedict then turned her cross-cultural comparison on its head by showing how, in a number of key respects, the Japanese resembled Americans. The fundamental "discontinuity" between childhood and adulthood in the two cultures meant that both Japanese and Americans paid "high price[s]" for their distinctive ways of life. Benedict traced the violent swings in mood and apparent "contradictions" in Japanese behavior to the fact that their "arc of life" was "plotted" in quite a different manner from America: Japanese culture permitted maximum freedom and indulgence to the young and to the old; American culture, to adults in the prime of their lives. Indeed, the dramatic contrast between the "privilege and psychological ease in babyhood," when the Japanese "did not know shame," and the "circumspection and 'knowing shame'" of adulthood was the source of their dualistic "outlook on life." Determined to be accepted by their peers, yet acutely sensitive to "threats of ostracism and detraction," the Japanese "denied themselves simple freedoms which Americans count upon as unquestionably as the air they breathe." Americans were touchiest when someone challenged their "principles of freedom"; the Japanese, when they detected "an insult or a detraction."[77]

At the end of *The Chrysanthemum and the Sword*, Benedict expressed confidence that their "culturally conditioned character" would allow the Japanese to "sail a new course" after the war. She warned American occupation forces against using "techniques of humiliation," which would only incite the Japanese to seek revenge.[78]

Ironically, given her empathy in *Patterns of Culture* with those whose congenial responses fell outside the arc of behavior capitalized by their culture, Benedict had surprisingly little to say about Japanese misfits and deviants. She also glossed over class, generational, and regional differences. Moreover, to heighten the contrast between Japan and America, Benedict played down the presence among Americans of some of the very traits that she labeled Japanese.

---

[76] Benedict, *Chrysanthemum and the Sword*, 43, 177–178, 222–223, 153–155.
[77] Benedict, *Chrysanthemum and the Sword*, 286–287, 254, 293–294.
[78] Benedict, *Chrysanthemum and the Sword*, 299, 304, 306–307.

She also exaggerated the contrast between Japan as a shame society and America as a guilt society.[79]

Yet, in *The Chrysanthemum and the Sword*, Benedict produced what John Bennett hailed as "a tour de force." Without ever having visited Japan, Benedict "reduce[d] a great national society to a single cultural expression." *The Chrysanthemum and the Sword* made Alfred Kroeber "proud to be an anthropologist." When Clyde Kluckhohn went to Japan in 1946–47 as a consultant to American occupation forces, he was "astonished to discover the extent to which [he] knew what was coming in unformalized situations or contexts not covered by [his] reading." Before he went to Japan, Kluckhohn's "admiration for" *The Chrysanthemum and the Sword* was "great." Afterwards, it was "enormous."[80]

COLD WAR PSYCHOLOGICAL WARRIORS

After 1945, practitioners of the study of culture at a distance turned their attention to understanding the Russian character. Ruth Benedict led the way. Convinced that "serious study of learned cultural behavior" would promote "better international understanding" and reduce "mistakes in international communication," Benedict set out to refine the methods that had been hurriedly improvised during the war. With support from two small grants, she planned to offer a seminar at Columbia in which foreign students would study American culture from their perspective as outsiders (much as students in the Seminar on the Impact of Culture on Personality had done in 1932–33). Her plans changed dramatically, however, after the Office of Naval Research, which had become interested in sponsoring "peacetime research in cultural patterns," awarded her $90,000 in 1946 for the first year of the two-year project entitled "A Cultural Study of American Minorities of Foreign Origin."[81]

[79] Benedict, *Chrysanthemum and the Sword*, 108; Benedict, *Patterns of Culture*, 258. See the reviews of *Chrysanthemum and the Sword* by John Morris, *New Statesman* 33 (1947): 416, and *Pacific Affairs* 20 (1947): 210; Peter Lawrence, *Nature* 161 (1948): 78; Gordon Bowles, *Harvard Journal of Asiatic Studies* 10 (1947): 237–241. See also Milton B. Singer, "Shame Cultures and Guilt Cultures," in Gerhart Piers and Milton B. Singer, *Shame and Guilt: A Psychoanalytic and a Cultural Study* (1953; repr., New York: Norton, 1971), 59–100.

[80] John W. Bennett, "Supplement: A Note on the Critique of Benedict's *Chrysanthemum and the Sword* by Japanese Scholars," in *Classic Anthropology: Critical Essays, 1944–1996* (New Brunswick, N.J.: Transaction Publishers, 1998), 373; Alfred Kroeber, review of *The Chrysanthemum and the Sword*, *American Anthropologist* 49 (1947): 469; Clyde Kluckhohn, in *Ruth Fulton Benedict: A Memorial* (New York: Viking Fund, 1949), 18–19.

[81] Ruth Benedict, "Remarks on Receiving the Annual Achievement Award of the American Association of University Women," 1946, quoted in Mead, *An Anthropologist at Work*, 430–431; Benedict to Kluckhohn, 16 May 1946; Caffrey, *Ruth Benedict*, 329. Until the creation of the National Science Foundation in 1950, the Office of Naval Research was the principal federal agency supporting "basic" rather than "applied" research. George W. Stocking, Jr., "'Do Good, Young Man': Sol Tax and the World Mission of Liberal Democratic Anthropology," in *Excluded Ancestors: Inventible Traditions: Essays toward a More Inclusive History of Anthropology*, ed. Richard Handler (Madison: University of Wisconsin Press, 2000), 180.

From April 1947 until 1951, Benedict's project, which came to be known as the Columbia University Research in Contemporary Cultures, mobilized some 120 researchers, drawn from sixteen nationalities and fourteen disciplines, in studying the cultures of Czechoslovakia, Poland, China, France, and Syria, pre-Bolshevik Russia, and pre-Holocaust Eastern European Jewry. Although some fieldwork was undertaken in Czechoslovakia and Poland, most of the research took place in the New York metropolitan area, "a rich laboratory of foreign-background communities," where researchers, seeking information on "the persistence and modifications of [foreign] traits," interviewed émigrés, then checked the information gleaned from these interviews against historical and sociological sources, projective tests, and thematic analyses of literature, folklore, and films. Although Benedict knew full well that years of detailed work would be required before their "central hypotheses" about each culture could be "corrected by region, occupation, class, sex, and age groups, and by periods," she nonetheless thought that the Columbia researchers could quickly arrive at the "basic themes" of the cultures they were studying. Anthropological concepts and methods dominated Research in Contemporary Cultures, but researchers also made liberal use of insights gleaned from learning theory and psychoanalysis.[82]

By July 1947, Benedict was thinking about writing a book about the contributions anthropologists could make to improving international relations. Her book would focus on what other peoples' "habits and values" could teach Americans. "However strange," the customs of foreigners were, Benedict contended, "only variant solutions, of the same problems" then facing Americans. Benedict also hoped that identifying the "cultural regularities" of selected countries would ameliorate "problems in human relations" – problems that, she believed, lay at the roots of international misunderstanding.[83]

Accordingly, the Columbia researchers focused on how peoples characterized their nations as wholes – for example, the uses to which the French put their national symbol Marianne. They assumed that in every society there existed a "cultural character structure," "regularities in the intrapsychic organization" that could be traced to socialization practices. In their search for such regularities, the Columbia researchers treated child-rearing practices as clues to adult character. One such clue was the swaddling of infants. Although a common practice in Eastern Europe, the meaning of swaddling, what the practice "communicated," varied from country to country. In Russia, where swaddling persisted despite the best efforts of Soviet officials to suppress it, parents

---

[82] Ruth Benedict to A. J. Leigh, 10 September, 17 December 1947, Mead Papers, box G4; "A Lady of Culture," *Science Illustrated* 3 (1948): 25–27; Weston La Barre, "Columbia University Research in Contemporary Cultures," *Scientific Monthly* 58 (1948): 239–240; Margaret Mead, "Research in Contemporary Cultures," in *Groups, Leadership and Men: Research in Human Relations*, ed. Harold Guetzkow (Pittsburgh: University of Pittsburgh Press, 1951), 106–118.

[83] Ruth Benedict to Grayson Kirk, 17 July 1947, Mead Papers, box G2.

swaddled babies to keep them from doing violence to themselves. Polish parents, by contrast, swaddled infants considered "exceedingly fragile." Swaddling had thus been "revamped to conform to the values of" each group.[84] By the spring of 1948, the Columbia researchers had produced a portrait of the pre-Bolshevik Russian character, identified the basic themes of the French character, recovered the culture of Eastern European Jewry, and confirmed the Freudian notion that infancy was indeed the formative period in the development of adult character.[85] Worried that Research in Contemporary Cultures was becoming seriously overextended, Benedict contracted with the Rand Corporation for a study of Soviet "conflicts with authority."[86] The Studies in Soviet Culture project, which Margaret Mead directed after Benedict's death in September 1948, culminated in the publication of *Soviet Attitudes toward Authority* in 1951. Among the hypotheses that Mead and her collaborators advanced about Soviet "patterns" and "regularities" was the suggestion that present-day Russian behavior could be understood, in part, as a product of the Soviet attempt to counteract deeply rooted tendencies in the historic Russian character.[87]

With help from Rhoda Métraux, Mead summed up the accomplishments of Research in Contemporary Cultures in *The Study of Culture at a Distance* (1953). This "training manual" included theoretical essays, illustrations of team research methods, sample interviews, and interpretations of literary texts and films. Integral to what Mead called the "psychocultural approach" was the concept of cultural character structure. It designated the "psychodynamic regularities" found in individuals who grew up in the same culture.[88]

BECOMING AMERICAN

In renewing interest in national character studies, the study of culture at a distance spurred social scientists to join the long-standing debate over the American character that had raged ever since the Frenchman Hector St. Jean de Crèvecoeur asked in 1782, "What is this new man, the American?"

In 1942, Margaret Mead published *And Keep Your Powder Dry* as a "pioneer venture" assessing both the strengths and the weaknesses of "the American character." Mead's aim was to help Americans win the Second World War the "American way," which, to her mind, was also the "democratic way." On this

---

[84] Ruth Benedict, "Child Rearing in Certain European Countries," *American Journal of Orthopsychiatry* 19 (1949): 342–348; reprinted in Mead, *An Anthropologist at Work*, 449–458, on 452–453, 458.

[85] Margaret Mead to Peter P. Jonstis, 11 February 1949, Mead Papers, box G3.

[86] Mead, *An Anthropologist at Work*, 436; Margaret Mead to Hans Speier, 15 October, 2 December 1948, Mead Papers, box G76.

[87] Margaret Mead, *Soviet Attitudes toward Authority* (New York: McGraw-Hill, 1951), 10.

[88] Margaret Mead and Rhoda Métraux, eds., *The Study of Culture at a Distance* (Chicago: University of Chicago Press, 1953).

"job of social engineering," Mead brought to bear insights from her fieldwork in the South Pacific.[89]

Mead answered Crèvecoeur's question by saying that Americans were what they were "because they [had] been reared in America by parents with certain ways of behaving." To understand how Americans were made, one must study "character formation," the "consistencies and regularities in which new-born babies grow up and assume the attitudes and behavior patterns of their elders." Not surprisingly, given Mead's emphasis on socialization, the American family figured prominently in *And Keep Your Powder Dry*, for it was the office of parents, siblings, and close relatives to mediate between the child and the "great configuration of American culture."[90]

Viewing the American family from a cross-cultural perspective brought out its distinctive features. The nuclear American family isolated parents and children from "paternal and maternal lines of kindred." American children, moreover, grew up with what Mead called a "third-generation" character structure in which they were expected to achieve more than their "out-of-date" fathers so as to earn their mothers' "conditional" love. Just as American parents relied on child-rearing manuals for guidance in raising their children, so, too, did they rely on "externals" to validate their children's success. Indeed, success was relative in American culture.[91]

American culture was as moral as it was competitive. Americans, Mead explained, characteristically saw "life in terms of moral behavior and its rewards." It was for this reason that any analysis of the American character "must simply bristle with words like *good* and *bad*." American morals also explained why Americans handled "the problem of aggression" with a "chip on [their] shoulder." They insisted that their opponent be equal to them, that their own effort was permissible only against a "strong" enemy, and that the other fellow had to start the fight.[92]

In an echo of John Dewey's query in *Freedom and Culture*, Mead asked, "is not science, itself the child of democracy, the child of freedom to think and inquire?" Like science, democracy prized flexibility and inventiveness. If Americans were "to draw upon the dynamics of American culture" in waging war and to rebuild the postwar world "in accordance with the dictates of democracy," they could not "make a finished blueprint into which [they would] force other people to fit." Rather, Americans should consult social scientists who were equipped to "set in motion forces" that would "implement human freedom." The postwar world, then, should be reconstructed "scientifically, on an engineering basis."[93]

[89] Margaret Mead, *And Keep Your Powder Dry* (1942; repr., New York: William Morrow, 1965), 327, 24, 176. See also Richard Handler, "Boasian Anthropology and the Critique of American Culture," *American Quarterly* 42 (1990): 252–273.

[90] Mead, *And Keep Your Powder Dry*, 120–121, 21, 38.

[91] Mead, *And Keep Your Powder Dry*, 83, 39, 52, 109, 111, 95.

[92] Mead, *And Keep Your Powder Dry*, 10, 60, 138–139, 143–144.

[93] Mead, *And Keep Your Powder Dry*, 177, 217, 182, 249.

In *The American People* (1947), Geoffrey Gorer extended Mead's discussion of "inter-personal relations" beyond the family to include "business and labor, majority to minorities, [and] nationals to foreigners."[94] Drawing on seven years' residence in the United States, visits to forty American states, and studies of public opinion polls as a fellow at the Institute of Human Relations, he attempted to convey to English readers American "differentness" by approaching Americans as though they were "Eskimos, Lepchas or Chinese." In England, popular response to Gorer's book prompted the BBC to broadcast a series of six programs on national character on the home service. In the United States, a 4,000-word précis of Gorer's book appeared in *Life* magazine, followed by an American edition in 1948.[95]

In *The American* People, Gorer identified a number of themes in American life. First and foremost was the rejection of patriarchal authority. As Benedict and Mead had done before him, Gorer emphasized the role that discontinuities played in the formation of the American character. Gorer, unlike Mead, dated "the American mutation," the rejection of the father "both as a model and as a source of authority," in the second generation. Just as Freud had traced the origins of civilization to the Oedipus complex, the sons' ritual slaying of the primal father, so did Gorer trace the American rejection of patriarchal authority to the colonists' renunciation of their allegiance to George III in the 1770s. The effects of this renunciation were long-lasting. Because the father's authority in the American family was "vestigial," the child grew up internalizing an "ethical, admonitory, censorious mother" who had to be propitiated on Mother's Day. A second theme that Gorer identified in American life reflected the influence of an "immigrant psychology" that made the father a "cipher," the mother the "arbiter of social standards," and the child the "hero of the American Dream." Like Mead, Gorer viewed the American mother's love for her children as "conditional," contingent on their keeping up with, if not surpassing, their peers in growth, development of motor skills, and precocity in teething and talking. Thus, for the American child, the question "Am I successful?" meant "Am I loved?" Gorer added a wrinkle to this picture of the American family when he suggested that the world in which American children grew up was a bifurcated one in which idealism, benevolence, and friendliness were considered feminine traits, and independence, "know-how," and "technological genius" were considered masculine traits. It was this bifurcated world, Gorer thought, that accounted for American men's "panic fear of homosexuality." It also explained why the class distinctions that Lloyd Warner documented often felt so "unreal and meaningless" to Americans. For "class hierarchies" in the United States were "fundamentally feminine," with social standing dependent on "maternal lines of descent" and arbitrated by clubwomen.[96]

[94] Geoffrey Gorer to Ruth Benedict, 27 May 1947, Mead Papers, box O39.
[95] Geoffrey Gorer, "The American People," *Life*, 18 August 1947, 94–112.
[96] Gorer, *The American People: A Study in National Character*, rev. ed. (New York: Norton, 1964), 17, 26–27, 56, 63, 125, 153, 157, 231; Buhle, *Feminism and Its Discontents*, 147–148.

Gorer's interpretation of the American character aroused considerable skepticism. Alfred Kroeber chided him for leaving "historical factors" out of his portrait of the "national psychology." Although Ralph Linton praised Gorer's "penetrating, intuitive observations," he denied that *The American People* was scientific. Clyde Kluckhohn condemned Gorer's "essentially literary approach" for its "cavalier disregard" of both "evidence" and "the facts of American history." Hortense Powdermaker called attention to "the absence of anything even faintly resembling a sample." Milton Singer predicted that, owing to its lack of "verification," Gorer's account of "how the American got his character" would be read as anthropologists read Freud's *Totem and Taboo* – as "a 'Just-so story.'" Although Margaret Mead acclaimed *The American People* in print, she took Gorer to task in private correspondence for his "lack of documentation," which left historians feeling "cheated."[97] One historian who felt cheated was Richard Hofstadter. "The study of national character," Hofstadter wrote in a review of *The American People*, had not yet "reached a point at which the methods of social science have outmoded the impressionistic essay."[98]

OVERREACHING ON NATIONAL CHARACTER

Criticism of *The American People*, however, paled in comparison with the controversy that erupted over Gorer's next book, *The People of Great Russia*, coauthored with the psychiatrist John Rickman and published in 1949. According to Gorer and Rickman, swaddling was a clue to the Russian character. Swaddling, they argued, threw light on the sudden and unpredictable swings of mood that had long puzzled observers of Russian life. Feeling this "constraint" to be "extremely painful and frustrating," Russian infants responded to swaddling "with intense and destructive rage" directed more at the constraint itself than at those who constrained them. Unswaddling infants so that they could be "suckled and petted" made this rage more tolerable.[99]

[97] A. L. Kroeber, review of *The American People, Journal of Abnormal and Social Psychology* 43 (1948): 554–555; Ralph Linton, review of *The American People, Scientific American* 178 (1948): 59; Clyde Kluckhohn, review of *The American People, Psychosomatic Medicine* 10 (1948): 304–305; Hortense Powdermaker, review of *The American People, American Anthropologist* 50 (1948): 666; Milton Singer, "How the American Got His Character," *Ethics* 60 (1949): 66; Margaret Mead, review of *The American People, American Journal of Orthopsychiatry* 106 (1949): 157; Margaret Mead to Geoffrey Gorer, 3 January 1950, Mead Papers, box B15.
[98] Richard Hofstadter, review of *The American People, Political Science Quarterly* 63 (1948): 441–442; Richard Hofstadter to Margaret Mead, 16 November 1950, Mead Papers, box I49.
[99] Geoffrey Gorer and John Rickman, *The People of Great Russia* (1949; repr., New York: Norton, 1962), 189, 168–169, xxxi–xxxiii. Gorer distilled the swaddling hypothesis in an article that he went to great lengths to place in a professional journal where it would be read by social scientists. Geoffrey Gorer, "Some Aspects of the Psychology of the People of Great Russia," *American Slavic and East European Review* 8 (1949): 155–166; Margaret Mead to Irving Goldman, 18 October 1950, Mead Papers, Box C21.

At least a few readers of *The People of Great Russia* interpreted swaddling as more a cause of, rather than a clue to, the Russian character. As Paul Wohl explained, Gorer and Rickman's hypothesis was that "the Russian national character [had] been caused and conditioned through the centuries by the tight swaddling of Russian babies." Still other critics took Gorer and Rickman to task for reducing the complexities of the Russian character to child-rearing practices. Bertram Wolfe attributed Gorer and Rickman's "unhistorical method" to the fact that it had originally been developed to treat "closed, fossilized, tribal societies."[100] Irving Goldman considered Gorer and Rickman's stress on the "psychological determinants" of the Russian character "inevitably misleading." Not only did Gorer and Rickman fail to study "a statistically significant sample of the Russian population," but their neglect of "history" and their "exclusive emphasis upon the child-rearing situation" led to "cultural stereotypes of doubtful validity."[101]

In a review of the "reception" of the swaddling hypothesis in the *American Anthropologist* in 1954, Margaret Mead attempted to rehabilitate both Gorer's reputation and the psychocultural approach. She explained that Gorer held "history constant" because his concern was less with the "origins" of the Russian character than with how Russians learned their culture. The "usefulness" of the swaddling hypothesis, Mead suggested, lay in whether it led to the formulation of "a coherent theory of Russian personality."[102]

Mead, however, was unable to prevent critics from satirizing national character studies as "diaperology" that featured an "oral-anal" approach. But even if Gorer had not pushed the approach to "unnecessary lengths," it seems likely that national character studies would have been called into question on account of their alleged scientific shortcomings.[103]

---

[100] Gorer, "Some Aspects of the Psychology of the People of Great Russia," 159n; Paul Wohl, "Without the Imponderables," *Christian Science Monitor*, 30 September 1950. Bertram D. Wolfe, "The Swaddled Soul of the Great Russians," *New Leader*, 29 January 1951, 15–18; Patrick Mullahy, review of *The People of Great Russia*, *New Republic*, 11 September 1950, 18; John Golden, review of *The People of Great Russia*, *American Anthropologist* 54 (1952): 415.

[101] Irving Goldman, "Psychiatric Interpretation of Russian History: A Reply to Geoffrey Gorer," *American Slavic and East European Review* 9 (1950): 151–161, on 151, 161, 154, 156.

[102] Margaret Mead, "The Swaddling Hypothesis: Its Reception," *American Anthropologist* 56 (1954): 395–409, on 396, 404, 397–398, 402–403. Mead had rushed to Gorer's aid in private correspondence as early as 1949, defending him from those "who are unable to distinguish between the statement that certain methods of child rearing are used to perpetuate certain social institutions and the statement that such methods are the *cause* of such social institutions." Gorer, she added, "specifically disclaim[ed]" any "statement" to the effect that "the Russian character is caused by the way in which Russian babies are swaddled." Indeed, he "merely used the methods of swaddling as a clue to the way in which Great Russian character is formed." Margaret Mead to J. Enrique Zanetti, 8 November 1949, Mead Papers, box G3 (emphasis in original).

[103] Morroe Berger, "'Understanding National Character' – and War: The Psychological Study of Peoples," *Commentary*, April 1951, 383; Mead, "The Swaddling Hypothesis: Its Reception," 404; Harold Orlansky, "Destiny in the Nursery: Child-Rearing Techniques and Adult Personality," *Commentary*, June 1948, 563.

By 1954, national character studies had come under heavy criticism from critics.[104] Harold Orlansky thought that "the rigidity of character structuring during the first year or two of life [had] been greatly exaggerated."[105] David Schneider noted that students of national character had made little effort toward verifying either the "empirical generalizations" or the "series of deductions following from them" in their studies. National character studies, moreover, were "based on an elaborate but implicit theoretical scheme" that so long as it remained implicit could neither be "examined critically" nor "checked against empirical findings."[106] John Thurston and Paul Mussen reported that they had been "unable to find any relationship between feeding gratification or nongratification" and "adult personality."[107] To Alfred Lindesmith and Anselm Strauss, the use of projective tests such as the Rorschach in non-Western societies suggested "an illusory precision." "Western biases," they suggested, "must inevitably find expression in the inferences made about the psychological characteristic of given peoples."[108]

Anthony F. C. Wallace summed up much of this criticism when he pointed out that culture-and-personality scholars had been primarily concerned with the "replication of uniformity," the process by which a culture reproduced itself, to the neglect of the "organization of diversity," or the ways in which "various individuals organized themselves culturally into orderly, expanding, changing societies."[109] Still other critics criticized what they regarded as the lack of adequate samples in many national character studies. Margaret Mead tried to rebut this criticism by maintaining that "anthropological sampling" was "*simply a different kind of sampling*," the "validity" of which depended less on the number of cases than on "the proper specification" of informants.[110]

Yet, despite falling out of favor among social scientists, the concept of national character studies spilled over into American history and American studies, where it was appropriated by scholars such as David Potter.

[104] George D. Spindler, "General Introduction," in *The Making of Psychological Anthropology*, ed. George D. Spindler (Berkeley: University of California Press, 1978), 3.

[105] Harold Orlansky, "Infant Care and Personality," *Psychological Bulletin* 46 (1949): 38.

[106] David M. Schneider, review of *The People of Great Russia*, Man 50 (1950): 128–129.

[107] John R. Thurston and Paul H. Mussen, "Infant Feeding Gratification and Adult Personality," *Journal of Personality* 19 (1951): 457.

[108] Alfred Lindesmith and Anselm Strauss, "A Critique of Culture-Personality Writings," *American Sociological Review* 15 (1950): 593. In 1961, Bert Kaplan, who had administered the Rorschach test to Navajo, Hispanic Americans, Mormons, and Texans in western New Mexico, acknowledged that the "difficulties" of using projective tests in anthropology were "enormous." "Only a modicum of validity and value," he concluded, could be "obtained from" their use. Bert Kaplan, "Personality and Social Structure," in *Studying Personality Cross-Culturally*, 252.

[109] Anthony F. C. Wallace, *Culture and Personality* (New York: Random House, 1961), 26–29.

[110] Otto Klineberg, "Recent Studies of National Character," in *Character and Personality*, ed. S. Stanfeld Sargent and W. Marian Smith (New York: Viking Fund, 1949), 130, 136; David G. Mandelbaum, "On the Study of National Character," *American Anthropologist* 55 (1953): 182; Mead, "National Character," 654–655 (emphasis in original).

AMERICAN IDENTITY

Two books, both published in 1950, were instrumental in popularizing the concept of national character among historians and American studies scholars. In *Childhood and Society*, Erik Erikson drew on "specimen situations" derived from his varied experience as a clinician in private practice, collaborator with Scudder Mekeel in fieldwork among the Oglala Sioux and with Alfred Kroeber in fieldwork among the Yurok, and consultant for the Committee for National Morale to devise a developmental model of "identity." Because psychiatrists were then shifting their emphasis from "the conditions which blunt and distort the individual ego" to "the ego's roots in social organization," Erikson focused on the ego's "relation" to "society." Although intended "to supplement the psychiatric education of American physicians, psychologists, and social workers," *Childhood and Society* quickly became required reading for a generation of college students and helped to garner Erikson an appointment to Harvard.[111]

In a chapter entitled "Reflections on the American Identity," Erikson proposed that since an "equally characteristic opposite" could be found for each "truly American trait," the American national identity derived from the ways in which "opposite potentialities" such as migratory/sedentary, individualistic/standardized, competitive/cooperative, and pious/free-thinking had been "counterpointed" in American history. He traced this "extreme polarization" to the American frontier. As molded by the frontier legacy, the American was a "freeborn child."[112]

Erikson pictured the American family as both a "school for democracy" and "a training ground" that promoted "the tolerance of individual interests." By nurturing "undogmatic people" who were "ready to drive a bargain and to compromise," the American family militated against authoritarianism. Yet "role diffusion" threatened the ability of male adolescents to establish "a dominant positive ego identity." "Bewildered" by the roles "forced on" them by "inexorable standardization," they ran away "in one form or another," seeking to avoid "neurotic anxiety" by scaling back their ambition and setting "limited goals" for themselves "with circumscribed laws." "Self restriction" was thus the "dominant defense mechanism" among American male adolescents.[113]

American male adolescents, moreover, grew up wrestling with the question of "freedom for what, and at what price?" Although they embodied the "fruit[s] of American education" – the "combination of native mechanical ability, managerial autonomy, personalized leadership, and unobtrusive tolerance" – they struck Erikson as politically apathetic, "strangely" uninterested "in the running of the nation." Erikson traced this apathy to "Momism" – the "dominant place" that mothers occupied in the American family, education, and cultural life – and to "bossism" – the "autocracy of irresponsibility"

---

[111] Erik H. Erikson, *Childhood and Society* (1950; repr., New York: Norton, 1985), 16–17, 13.
[112] Erikson, *Childhood and Society*, 285–286, 293, 299.
[113] Erikson, *Childhood and Society*, 310, 316–318, 305–308.

embodied in machine politics. He looked forward for a "counterpart in a political rejuvenation."[114]

THE CONTINENTAL PUEBLO

The Lonely Crowd: A Study of the Changing American Character, by David Riesman, Nathan Glazer, and Reuel Denney, also popularized national character studies among historians and American studies scholars. Although Riesman and his coauthors deliberately wrote their book for a popular audience, even they were astounded by the phenomenal success enjoyed by what originated as "a study of the relation between political apathy and character structure." In 1954, after *The Lonely Crowd* had been as much discussed as the Lynds' *Middletown* had been during the Depression, the reticent Riesman became the first sociologist to grace the cover of *Time* magazine, with the caption inquiring, "What is the American character?" In 1958, he was appointed to an endowed chair at Harvard.[115]

Although he agreed with Mead and Gorer that childhood was "of great importance in molding character," Riesman did not believe that childhood could be isolated from social structure. He focused instead on the way in which any society "ensures some degree of conformity" among its members by either encouraging or frustrating the "mode" that had been "built" into them as children. To this end, Riesman employed Erich Fromm's concept of "social character."[116] According to Fromm, for any society to function smoothly, its members had to acquire "the kind of character" that made them "want to act in the way they *have* to act." Simply put, "they have to *desire* what objectively is *necessary* for them to do so." Fromm, then, described a situation in which authority was internalized, in which "outer force" gave way to "inner compulsion." Thus, when Riesman spoke of social character in *The Lonely Crowd*, he had in mind that "part of 'character'" that was "shared among significant social groups" – whether "classes," "groups," "regions," or "nations."[117]

[114] Erikson, *Childhood and Society*, 321–324.
[115] David Riesman to Margaret Mead, 12 July 1948, Mead Papers, box C19; David Riesman to Hannah Arendt, 14 June 1949, quoted in Wilfred M. McClay, "The Strange Career of *The Lonely Crowd*: or, the Antinomies of Autonomy," in *The Culture of the Market: Historical Essays*, ed. Thomas L. Haskell and Richard F. Teichgraeber III (New York: Cambridge University Press, 1993), 411.
[116] Riesman underwent several years of analysis with Fromm, "not because [he] thought [he] needed it," but "to please [his] mother, who wanted to be able to talk with [him] during the time she was an analysand of Karen Horney, who had recommended Fromm to her for [him]." David Riesman, "Becoming an Academic Man," in *Authors of Their Own Lives: Intellectual Autobiographies by Twenty American Sociologists*, ed. Bennett M. Berger (Berkeley: University of California Press, 1990), 45–46.
[117] David Riesman, Nathan Glazer, and Reuel Denney, *The Lonely Crowd: A Study of the Changing American Character*, abridged ed. (New Haven, Conn.: Yale University Press, 1961), 3–4; Erich Fromm, "Individual and Social Origins of Neurosis," *American Sociological Review* 9 (1944): 381 (emphasis in original).

On the basis of in-depth interviews, sociological surveys, and analyses of books and films, Riesman documented changes in social character among "the metropolitan, American upper-middle class." In what proved to be the most controversial section of *The Lonely Crowd*, Riesman linked changes in the American character to long-term demographic changes. The "tradition-directed" type, he contended, was characteristic of societies of "high growth potential"; the "inner-directed" type, who early in life "internalized" a "set of goals," predominated in societies of "transitional population growth"; finally, the "other-directed" type, who was "sensitized to the expectations and prefer-ences of others," appeared in societies of "incipient population decline." Riesman went on to suggest that the American character was then changing, at least among upper-middle-class Americans, from the inner-directed to the other-directed type. No longer guided by a "psychological gyroscope," the American was now guided by "radar" tuned to signals from peers. These meta-phors reflected Riesman's wartime service as a consultant for the Sperry Corporation, developer of radar.[118]

The circumscription of parental authority to the preschool years accompa-nied the shift from the inner- to the other-directed type of social character. After children entered school, teachers and peers began to serve as "proxy parents." Earlier generations of American children had felt guilty; children in postwar America felt a "diffuse anxiety." Rechanneling their drive for achievement into a drive for peer approval, they aimed to get along rather than to make their own ways as rugged individualists. Failure to conform in the postwar United States resulted in "anomie," or maladjustment. Riesman, however, celebrated those "autonomous" Americans who freely chose "whether to conform or not." The postwar United States, he suggested, allowed "larger possibility" for "autonomy" to develop "out of other direction." Although autonomy did not depend on class standing, Riesman believed that it was most likely to be attained by upper-middle-class Americans.[119]

In perhaps the most interesting chapter of *The Lonely Crowd*, Riesman recounted his experience when he asked students at the University of Chicago to assign themselves to one of the three cultures that Ruth Benedict had delineated in *Patterns of Culture*. Most of his students, who viewed Americans "as individualists, primarily interested in the display of wealth and status," chose the Kwakiutl. The "politically more radical" among them, emphasizing "the sharp practices of American business life" and the "great jealousy and bitterness in family relations," likened themselves to the Dobu. Riesman him-self, however, thought that "the tone of Pueblo life, with its insistence on equal-ity, cooperation, and emotional restraint," seemed "most like the American peer group, with its insulting 'You think you're big.'" To the extent that his students sought "social security" rather than "great achievement," and "approval" rather than "fame," they were already living in a Pueblo-like culture. Perhaps

[118] Riesman, *The Lonely Crowd*, 5–8, 16, 25.
[119] Riesman, *The Lonely Crowd*, 55–57, 64–66, 76, 80, 240–242, 260, 328, 404.

this is why Riesman gave some thought to calling *The Lonely Crowd* "The Continental Pueblo."[120]

Although Margaret Mead praised *The Lonely Crowd* as intellectually stimulating, she criticized Riesman's "use of history" as "too second hand." Geoffrey Gorer agreed. Gorer, who had himself been criticized for his ahistorical approach to the study of the American character, considered *Childhood and Society* an example of "how social scientists should not (repeat not) use history. If they are going to reinterpret historical material they must go back to the sources." To Gorer, the use of "stereotypes from other people's historical studies" seemed not only "useless," but "dangerous," for it threatened to bring "the whole question of sociological/anthropological analysis into disrepute." Someone had "to tackle historical material some time" – a prospect that Gorer looked on as "a damnable bore."[121]

THE AMERICAN CHARACTER

Although it fell out of favor among social scientists in the 1950s, the concept of national character migrated into American intellectual history and American studies, where scholars put it to good use in constructing a "consensus" view of the postwar United States.

By the fall of 1950, there was enough interest in anthropology among American historians and American studies scholars for Edmund Morgan to invite Margaret Mead to give a paper at a conference on American studies at Brown University. Morgan told Mead that he thought that historians had "more to learn from anthropology than from any other field of study." In her paper Mead reviewed "where we have got to in the last 11 years" since Geoffrey Gorer expounded the culture concept at the annual meetings of the American Historical Association in 1939.[122] She began by emphasizing the affinity between anthropologists and historians. Both anthropologists and historians, according to Mead, had "a special relationship to their concrete materials" – the "sequence of rites performed at a particular ceremony" and the "particular document," respectively. Both anthropologists and historians prized the particular, "the unique event in all its uniqueness." Once kept apart by their respective preoccupations with "primitive peoples" and "past periods," anthropologists and historians were coming closer together out of a common interest in the "contemporary problems of the great civilizations of the world – including our own." Increasingly, anthropologists and historians were

---

[120] Riesman, *The Lonely Crowd*, 225–235; Rupert Wilkinson, ed., *American Social Character: Modern Interpretations from the '40s to the Present* (New York: Harper, 1992), 392.

[121] Margaret Mead to Geoffrey Gorer, 6 March 1951; Geoffrey Gorer to Margaret Mead, 2 June 1951, Mead Papers, box B15.

[122] Edmund Morgan to Margaret Mead, 13 October 1950; Margaret Mead to Geoffrey Gorer, 19 October 1950, Mead Papers, box I49; Margaret Mead, "Anthropologist and Historian: Their Common Problems," *American Quarterly* 3 (1951): 3–13, on 4n.

working with "wholes" – "whole societies," "whole persons," and "whole periods."[123]

Yet important "methodological differences" remained between anthropologists and historians. Mead traced these differences to their customary sources, informants and documents, respectively. To "bridge the gap" between the two disciplines, she proposed that anthropologists and historians undertake a joint research project modeled on the historian Robert K. Lamb's investigation of entrepreneurial strategies in early twentieth-century Fall River, Massachusetts. In Mead's proposed project, anthropologists would develop a "working model" of the "whole community" and the "whole culture," while historians would be responsible for maintaining "the sense of trend, of movement over time."[124]

It was against this convergence of interest between some anthropologists and some historians that David Potter assayed national character as a "frontier" between history and the behavioral sciences. He devoted the first two chapters in *People of Plenty* to showing how behavioral scientists had "rehabilitated" the concept of the American character after historians had "used and abused" it. In the rest of the book Potter gave examples of what historians could contribute to the study of the American character. His own contribution took the form of examining how the "historical factor" of "economic abundance" had "impinged" on American culture. Equating American culture with American nationality, Potter invoked the immanent tendency of any culture "to realize itself politically through the process of national unification." When this occurred, the "culture group" became, "for all practical purposes," a "national group," and "cultural character" became "national character."[125] Potter's elision of the distinction between culture and nationality was as curious as it was unsatisfactory, for he had long been critical of "the forcing of history into national compartments." Indeed, in 1962, Potter criticized historians' tendency to overemphasize "the culture component as the one master key to nationality" and their assumption of "too simple an equation between nationality and culture."[126]

Rehabilitated by behavioral scientists and championed by historians and American studies scholars, inquiries into the American character flourished

[123] Mead, "Anthropologist and Historian," 3–6, 8–9.
[124] Mead, "Anthropologist and Historian," 9–12; Robert K. Lamb, "Entrepreneurship in the Community," *Explorations in Entrepreneurial History* 2 (1950): 114–127; Robert K. Lamb, "Family and Community in Fall River, Massachusetts," course handout for Economics 14.81, Massachusetts Institute of Technology, Fall 1950, Mead Papers, box I49.
[125] Potter, *People of Plenty*, xviii–xix, xvii, 13–14.
[126] David M. Potter, quoted in Don E. Fehrenbacher, Howard R. Lamar, and Otis A. Pease, "David M. Potter: A Memorial Resolution," *Journal of American History* 58 (1971): 308; David M. Potter, "The Historian's Use of Nationalism and Vice Versa," *American Historical Review* 67 (1962): 933; Walter P. Metzger, "Generalizations about National Character: An Analytical Essay," in *Generalization in the Writing of History*, ed. Louis Gottschalk (Chicago: University of Chicago Press, 1963), 95–96.

in the 1950s and 1960s. In *Virgin Land* (1950), Henry Nash Smith noted how every generation of Americans addressed Crèvecoeur's question about American identity, "but the varying national self-consciousness they have tried to capture always escapes final statement." Venturing his own expression of national self-consciousness, Smith reexamined Frederick Jackson Turner's frontier thesis, which held that the American character had been "shaped by the pull of a vacant continent drawing population westward." For Turner, the West was a tangible entity; for Smith, it was country of the mind.[127] In *The American Adam* (1955), R. W. B. Lewis traced the "Adamic theme" in American thought – the "myth" of the new man, the reborn European, free, innocent, and unburdened with a past.[128] In *Andrew Jackson: Symbol for an Age* (1955), John William Ward showed how Jackson symbolized the American values of nature, providence, and will.[129] The American character, declared Max Lerner in *America as a Civilization* (1957), was "a doctrine not of blood but of culture"; it comprised the "body of values, social habits, attitudes, [and] traits held in common by most members of [American] culture." Lerner located the American character "at the point where cultural norms in America shape personality." In *The Burden of Southern History* (1958), C. Vann Woodward invoked the American character as a foil against which to set off Southern distinctiveness. After enumerating a number of definitions of the American character "to which the South proves an exception," Woodward concluded that whereas "the South once thought of itself as a 'peculiar people,' set apart by its eccentricities," perhaps "in many ways modern America better deserves that description." In 1959, while conceding that the American character was "a hazy expression," Marcus Cunliffe invoked the concept to argue that the "assemblage of beliefs and patterns" regarded by Americans and non-Americans alike as distinctively American was in place as early as 1837.[130]

By the mid-1950s, according to Reuel Denney, scholarly views of the American character largely coincided with those of the general public. Neither scholars nor educated Americans were really quite sure that the American character existed "in some highly definable sense," yet both groups were sure "that it [was]

[127] Henry Nash Smith, *Virgin Land: The American West as Symbol and Myth* (1950; repr., Cambridge, Mass.: Harvard University Press, 1970), 3; Robert F. Berkhofer, Jr., "Space, Time, Culture and the New Frontier," *Agricultural History* 38 (1964): 24–25. In *People of Plenty* (pp. 22–23), Potter also deployed the concept of culture in his argument against Turner's frontier thesis.

[128] R. W. B. Lewis, *The American Adam: Innocence, Tragedy, and Tradition in the Nineteenth Century* (Chicago: University of Chicago Press, 1955).

[129] John William Ward, *Andrew Jackson: Symbol for an Age* (New York: Oxford University Press, 1955).

[130] Max Lerner, *America as a Civilization* (New York: Simon and Schuster, 1957), 64, 68–69; C. Vann Woodward, "The Search for Southern Identity" (1958), in *The Burden of Southern History*, rev. ed. (1968; repr., New York: New American Library, 1969), 17–31, on 29, 31; Marcus Cunliffe, "The American Character," in *The Nation Takes Shape, 1789–1837* (Chicago: University of Chicago Press, 1959), 186–187.

'better' than many intellectuals thought it was two decades ago." Thus, to Denney, "American interest in the application of national-character theories to America" indexed American "self-identification." George W. Pierson had no doubts that an American character existed. "The most intelligent thinkers and observers have thought so," he pointed out in 1962, "and have kept on thinking so, across the years."[131]

For American historians and American studies scholars, then, the American character was like Voltaire's God: Had the concept not existed, they would have invented it. They invoked the American character to emphasize American homogeneity and consensus, the transcendent whole greater than the manifold class, ethnic, racial, and regional divisions that had run through the American experience since the first European settlements. In 1964, Michael McGiffert acknowledged that national character was something of an "ideal-type," less "an exact empirical description" than "a construction designed for conceptual clarity and analytical utility." Sometimes, as in R.W. B. Lewis's *The American Adam* or John William Ward's *Andrew Jackson: Symbol for an Age*, it even had "the appearance of myth." Yet, despite all the "blurring [of] detail," if not "distortion," often found in studies of the American character, McGiffert thought that continued use of the concept was justified on the grounds that it captured "the distinctive qualities of a nation's people." Echoing David Potter, McGiffert added that "when the findings of the behavioral scientists are illuminated by a knowledge of history it becomes evident that never before has there been better hope and more adequate intellectual equipment for discovering what the American is, has been, and may become."[132]

Consensus historians and American studies scholars appropriated the concept of the American character to explain the "homogeneity" of the American people, the "durability" of American society and its institutions, and the "continuity" of American history in what John Higham characterized as their "quest for a national definition" and "achievement of national identity."[133] Yet both consensus history and the myth-symbol approach to American studies lost credibility during the 1960s as the concept of national character, on which their

[131] W. Reuel Denney, "How Americans See Themselves (1954)," in *Studies in American Culture: Dominant Ideas and Images*, ed. Joseph J. Kwiat and Mary C. Turpie (Minneapolis: University of Minnesota Press, 1960), 16–26, on 17, 25–26; George W. Pierson, "The M-Factor in American History," *American Quarterly* 14 (1962): 275–276.

[132] Michael McGiffert, "Foreword to the First Edition" (1964), in *The Character of Americans: A Book of Readings*, rev. ed., ed. Michael McGiffert (Homewood, Ill.: Dorsey, 1970), ix–xii; Michael McGiffert, "Selected Writings on American National Character," *American Quarterly* 15 (1963): 272.

[133] John Higham, "The Cult of the 'American Consensus': Homogenizing Our History," *Commentary*, February 1959, 56; John Higham, "The Study of American Intellectual History" (1961), in *Writing American History: Essays on Modern Scholarship* (Bloomington: Indiana University Press, 1970), 67–68; John Higham, introduction to *New Directions in American Intellectual History*, ed. John Higham and Paul K. Conkin (Baltimore: Johns Hopkins University Press, 1979), xi–xii.

"entire conceptual foundation" rested, "crumbled away," and as two assumptions closely associated with national character studies – the first, that "societies tend to be integrated"; the second, that "a shared culture maintains that integration" – "came under withering attack."[134] As Michael McGiffert acknowledged in 1969, the "culture-and-personality approach" had "fallen on dry days." This reflected, in part, "deepening misgivings" about the validity of national character, but also the "upheavals" of the 1960s. As belief in the existence of a unitary American culture declined, so, too, did the existence of an American character appear increasingly problematic.[135]

Yet the appeal of national character has remained. In 1979, Alex Inkeles emphasized the element of "continuity" that he detected in the American character over more than two centuries.[136] As Clifford Geertz commented, "the persistence of a significant part of a people's cultural character, of the feel and pressure of their lives, across enormous, even discontinuous historical changes" was "one of the deeper mysteries of the human sciences."[137]

Since the 1970s, there have been efforts to revive culture and personality. Francis L. K. Hsu proposed that the field of culture and personality be renamed "psychological anthropology," yet conceded that researchers in the field had failed "wholeheartedly and systematically to include the large literate societies and cultures in [their] intellectual deliberations." Richard Schweder also wanted to rename the field. To get rid of the "stigma" associated with culture and personality because of its association with "national character studies," Shweder proposed the name "cultural psychology" to signal "rebirth [of the field] without stigma." Unlike "culture *and* personality," "cultural psychology" did not imply that one term was the independent variable and the other term the dependent variable; nor did it imply that "cultural things and psychological things [could] be neatly separated from each other."[138]

[134] Higham, introduction to *New Directions in Intellectual History*, xii.
[135] Michael McGiffert, "Selected Writings on American National Character and Related Subjects to 1969," *American Quarterly* 21 (1969): 330–331; Thomas L. Hartshorne, "Recent Interpretations of the American Character," in *Sources for American Studies*, ed. Jefferson B. Kellogg and Robert H. Walker (Westport, Conn.: Greenwood Press, 1983), 307. For critiques of national character by American studies scholars, see Murray G. Murphey, "An Approach to the Historical Study of National Character," in *Context and Meaning in Cultural Anthropology*, ed. Melford E. Spiro (New York: Free Press, 1965), 144–163; David Stannard, "American Historians and the Idea of National Character," *American Quarterly* 23 (1971): 202–220.
[136] Alex Inkeles, "Continuity and Change in the American National Character," in *The Third Century: America as a Post-Industrial Society*, ed. Seymour Martin Lipset (Stanford: Hoover Institution Press, 1979), 390–391.
[137] Clifford Geertz, preface to the French edition of *Bali* (Paris: Gallimard, 1983), 9, quoted in Olivier Zunz, "Producers, Brokers, and Users of Knowledge: The Institutional Matrix," in *Modernist Impulses in the Human Sciences, 1870–1930*, ed. Dorothy Ross (Baltimore: Johns Hopkins University Press, 1994), 365n.
[138] George W. Stocking, Jr., "Essays on Culture and Personality," in *Malinowski, Rivers, Benedict and Others*, 9; Francis L. K. Hsu, "Psychological Anthropology in the Behavioral Sciences," in *Psychological Anthropology*, ed. Francis L. K. Hsu (Cambridge: Schenkman, 1972), 13; Richard A. Shweder, "Why Cultural Psychology?" *Ethos* 27 (1999): 62–63 (emphasis in original).

The study of national character grew out of anthropologists' interest, honed in collaboration with neo-Freudian psychoanalysts, in developing an understanding of the individual as the locus of culture and their interest in how culture is passed on to children and, in the process, shapes their personality. These interests, in turn, spawned the study of culture at a distance during the Second World War and various theories about how different child-rearing practices shaped the national characters of various peoples. It spread after the war to American historians and American studies scholars interested in finding a way to talk about a unified national character and to view the American people as homogeneous. Thus the study of national character represented an early, perhaps pioneering, effort on the part of anthropologists to study big, modern, complex societies.[139] As the study of national character came to be seen as "impressionistic" and "psychologistic" by many anthropologists as well as by social scientists in cognate disciplines, anthropologists developed other approaches for dealing with, and comparing, complex societies. Well aware of just how woolly the concept of national character had become by the late 1940s, Clyde Kluckhohn turned his attention from culture and personality to the scientific study of values.

[139] Sidney Mintz, "The Localization of Anthropological Practice: From Area Studies to Trans-nationalism," *Critique of Anthropology* 19 (1998): 128–129. For another complaint about the "psychological reductionism" of the postwar national character studies, see Richard G. Fox, Introduction to *Nationalist Ideologies and the Production of National Cultures*, ed. Richard G. Fox (Washington, D.C.: American Anthropological Association, 1990), 1–16.

4

The Drift of American Values

In 1949, Clyde Kluckhohn published *Mirror for Man: The Relation of Anthropology to Modern Life*. His book, which won a $10,000 prize offered by McGraw-Hill for the best popular book on science, was a "manifesto" of "the New Anthropology." Popularized by Ruth Benedict and Margaret Mead, the New Anthropology was, in the words of a critic, "anthropology with a message" – the message that anthropologists now commanded "the knowledge needed to reform the world."[1]

Anthropology, Kluckhohn announced, was "no longer just the science of the long-ago and far-away," it was "an aid to useful action." Thanks to the "all-embracing" or holistic character of their discipline, anthropologists occupied "a strategic position" to determine which "factors" would "create a world community of distinct cultures and hold it together against disruption." Only those experts who were "singularly emancipated from the sway of the locally accepted" could surmount the apparently "unbridgeable gap" between "competing ways of life" by laying bare "the principles that undergird each culture."[2] On the heels of the publication of *Mirror for Man*, Kluckhohn appeared on the cover of the *Saturday Review of Literature*, proclaiming that anthropologists now possessed "the beginnings of a science whose principles are applicable to any human situation."[3]

As a prophet of the New Anthropology, Kluckhohn captured anthropologists' postwar exuberance and heady optimism, born of their wartime mobilization on behalf of an embattled democracy, that they would play prominent parts in rebuilding a shattered world.[4] No longer practitioners of what Clifford Geertz described as "an obscure, isolate, even reclusive, lone-wolf sort of

[1] Robert Endleman, "The New Anthropology and Its Ambitions: The Science of Man in Messianic Dress," *Commentary*, October 1949, 285.

[2] Clyde Kluckhohn, *Mirror for Man: The Relation of Anthropology to Modern Life* (1949; repr., Tucson: University of Arizona Press, 1985), 286–287.

[3] Clyde Kluckhohn, quoted in the *Saturday Review of Literature*, 29 January 1949, 11.

[4] Bernard Mishkin, review of *Mirror for Man*, *New York Times Book Review*, 30 January 1949, 15.

discipline," they would increasingly participate in "multi- (or inter-, or cross-) disciplinary work" and "team projects," lavishly funded by philanthropic foundations and federal agencies, dedicated to solving "the immediate problems of the contemporary world."[5] This enthusiasm proved infectious. For a brief moment, anthropology loomed as the "reigning social science" in the eyes of many political scientists, family therapists, historians, and American studies scholars.[6]

This chapter follows Kluckhohn's multifaceted campaign to make anthropologists more self conscious and thereby to enhance their scientific standing. Early in his career, Kluckhohn took anthropologists (and archaeologists) to task for not making their premises and procedures more explicit. His work in culture and personality, in particular his development of the concept of "implicit culture" to designate those aspects of a culture of which carriers were largely unaware, explored the nonrational, affective dimension of culture. At the same time, he collaborated with Alfred Kroeber, the dean of American anthropology after Franz Boas's death, on arriving at a consensual meaning of culture that could be easily conveyed to non-anthropologists. As a founding member of the Harvard Department of Social Relations, the first director of the Harvard Russian Research Center, as well as the author of a prize-winning introduction to anthropology, Kluckhohn became one of the discipline's most prominent ambassadors to non-anthropologists. In an attempt to bring the study of values within the fold of social science, he designed the ambitious Comparative Study of Values in Five Cultures. Seeking to model anthropology on linguistics, he searched for the cultural equivalent of the phoneme, the most basic unit of language. His hope was that comparing the basic units of culture would eventually lead not only to the formulation of cultural "grammars," but also to the discovery of "pan-cultural verities," universals or near universals that could serve as moral anchors in an unsettled world. Joining in the postwar American quest for national purpose, Kluckhohn essayed several linguistically informed analyses of changing American values before his death in 1960.

DISCOVERING ANTHROPOLOGY

Born in LeMars, Iowa, in 1905, Clyde Kay Maben Kluckhohn came to anthropology by a "roundabout road." In 1922, while recuperating on a

[5] Clifford Geertz, "An Inconstant Profession: The Anthropological Life in Interesting Times," *Annual Review of Anthropology* 31 (2002): 3.
[6] Lucian W. Pye, "Culture and Political Science: Problems in the Evaluation of the Concept of Political Culture," in *The Idea of Culture in the Social Sciences*, ed. Louis Schneider and Charles Bonjean (Cambridge: Cambridge University Press, 1973), 65; Deborah F. Weinstein, "Culture at Work: Family Therapy and the Culture Concept in Post-World War II America," *Journal of the History of the Behavioral Sciences* 40 (2004): 23–46; Robert F. Berkhofer, Jr., "Clio and the Culture Concept: Some Impressions of a Changing Relationship in American Historiography," in *The Idea of Culture in the Social Sciences*, 77–100.

ranch in western New Mexico from the rheumatic fever that had cut short his freshman year at Princeton, he became interested in the small band of Navajo who lived near Ramah. His academic interests then lay in the classics; he had studied Latin at the Culver Military Academy and the Lawrenceville School. Quickly becoming "fascinated" by the Navajo, Kluck-hohn explored their country on a 3,000-mile pack-horse trip that he chronicled in the 1927 travelogue *To the Foot of the Rainbow*. Resuming his education at the University of Wisconsin, he majored in Greek, edited the campus news-paper, and was elected senior class president. During summer breaks, he led classmates on pack-horse trips to Navajo country that he described in a second travelogue, *Beyond the Rainbow*, published in 1933. Awarded a Rhodes Schol-arship in 1928, Kluckhohn read Greek and Latin literature in the Greats Pro-gram in Corpus Christi College, Oxford. After briefly attending Harvard Law School, he traveled extensively on the Continent, learned French and German, and studied anthropology at the University of Vienna with Father Wilhelm Schmidt and other members of the *Kulturkreis* school, diffusionists who emphasized migrations from early cultural centers in Asia. While in Vienna, Kluckhohn was analyzed by Eduard Hitschmann, one of Freud's earliest dis-ciples, after John Dollard, his Wisconsin classmate, told him that he would be a "fool" if he did not avail himself of the opportunity for an "excellent" but inexpensive analysis. Royalties from *To the Foot of the Rainbow* paid for his analysis.[7]

After further work with R. R. Marett, E. B. Tylor's successor at Oxford, Kluckhohn married the aspiring sociologist Florence Rockwood and, in 1932, began teaching physical anthropology at the University of New Mexico. During the summers, he supervised archaeological work at Jemez and Chaco Canyon. In 1934, Kluckhohn took advantage of a fellowship from the Rockefeller Foun-dation to pursue a Ph.D. in anthropology at Harvard. Switching his interests from physical anthropology and archaeology to cultural anthropology, Kluck-hohn cut such a brilliant figure that he was appointed instructor after Lloyd Warner left for Chicago. Acceding to Alfred Tozzer's "command," he expanded a colloquium paper on the *Kulturkreislehre* into a library-based dissertation on "Contemporary Theory in Cultural Anthropology," which he defended in 1936. Appointed assistant professor in 1937, Kluckhohn was promoted to associate professor in 1940. In 1946, having become a full professor, he joined the sociologist Talcott Parsons, the clinical psychologist Henry A. Murray, and

---

[7] Anne Roe, transcript of interview with Clyde Kluckhohn, March 1952, Anne Roe Papers, American Philosophical Society (B/R621) (hereafter Anne Roe Papers); Clyde Kluckhohn, "Autobiographical Sketch," ca. 1946, HUG 4490.7, Kluckhohn Papers; Evon Z. Vogt, *Field-work among the Maya: Reflections on the Harvard Chiapas Project* (Albuquerque: University of New Mexico Press, 1994), 18; Melville J. Herskovits, "Clyde Kay Maben Kluckhohn," *Biographical Memoirs of the National Academy of Sciences* 37 (1961): 129–153; Talcott Parsons and Evon Z. Vogt, "Clyde Kay Maben Kluckhohn, 1905–1960," *American Anthro-pologist* 64 (1962): 140–161. On the *Kulturkreis* school, see Robert H. Lowie, *The History of Ethnological Theory* (New York: Holt, 1937), 177–195.

the social psychologist Gordon Allport in founding the Harvard Department of Social Relations.[8]

CLARIFYING CULTURE THEORY

Early in his career, Kluckhohn, who always regarded himself as a "refiner" whose mission was to bring "concept[ual] integration [and] synthesis" to anthropology, joined Ralph Linton in an attempt to clarify culture theory.[9] In a series of articles published between 1936 and 1939, he contrasted the "healthy insistence upon strenuous criticism of sources" and "attention to written sources" of the members of the *Kulturkreis* school with what seemed to him American anthropologists' lack of concern about "canons of procedure" and "almost morbid avoidance of theory." Anthropological method and theory, Kluckhohn contended, were "so intimately and immediately related" that anthropologists could no longer afford the luxury of continuing to collect facts while dismissing theory as "speculation." Indeed, until they made their "postulates" and "propositions" more explicit, and hence subject to "systematic criticism," anthropology would not be recognized by the practitioners of cognate disciplines as a science.[10] Similarly, Kluckhohn criticized the classification schemes and taxonomy of archaeologists working in the American Southwest, and the antiquarianism of Maya scholars who, to his mind, wallowed in detail and operated without explicit theoretical or conceptual formulations.[11]

As we have seen, Kluckhohn even took his "anthropological god," Franz Boas, to task for his failure to throw more light on anthropologists' suppositions and operations. Given the small number of American

[8] Roe, transcript of interview with Kluckhohn; Clyde Kluckhohn to Paul H. Buck, 3 February 1949, HUG 4490.5, Kluckhohn Papers; Florence Kluckhohn to Talcott Parsons, 21 December 1964, HUG(FP) 15.4, box 10, Parsons Papers.
[9] Roe, transcript of interview with Kluckhohn; George W. Stocking, Jr., "Ideas and Institutions in American Anthropology: Thoughts toward a History of the Interwar Years," in *The Ethnographer's Magic and Other Essays in the History of Anthropology* (Madison: University of Wisconsin Press, 1992), 145–147.
[10] Clyde Kluckhohn, "Some Reflections on the Method and Theory of the 'Kulturkreislehre,'" *American Anthropologist* 38 (1936): 157–158; Clyde Kluckhohn, "The Place of Theory in Anthropological Studies," *Philosophy of Science* 6 (1939): 328–344, on 333, 330. Desley Deacon labels Kluckhohn the "enfant terrible" of American anthropology in *Elsie Clews Parsons: Inventing Modern Life* (Chicago: University of Chicago Press, 1997), 372–373.
[11] Richard Woodbury, "Clyde Kay Maben Kluckhohn, 1905–1960," *American Antiquity* 26 (1961): 407–409; Clyde Kluckhohn, "The Conceptual Structure in Middle American Studies," in *The Maya and Their Neighbors*, ed. C. L. Hays, R. L. Linton, et al. (1940; repr., Salt Lake City: University of Utah Press, 1962), 41–51; Gordon R. Willey and Jeremy A. Sabloff, *A History of American Archaeology*, 2nd ed. (San Francisco: Freeman, 1980), 131–133; Bruce Trigger, *A History of Archaeological Thought* (Cambridge: Cambridge University Press, 1989), 275, 302.

anthropologists – fewer than 400 in the 1930s – their work remained "too much in the family tradition." It was precisely because they took so much for granted that anthropologists handled such important matters as fieldwork techniques "largely on the basis of implicit agreement or on the basis of informal, oral discussion."[12]

THE RAMAH PROJECT

In 1936, Kluckhohn embarked on a long-term study of the Ramah band of Navajo that continued until 1949 and involved seventeen other researchers. "Assured" by his advisors that "Navaho culture was already well known," he saw his original task as describing "local variations" and "the Ramah situation." Soon realizing that he had not yet grasped either the "basic patterns" or the "cultural dynamics" of the Navajo, he conferred with Donald Scott, director of the Peabody Museum, who impressed on him the importance on continuously observing "the same persons in the same environment." Inspired by John Dollard and by Edward Sapir, who tutored him in Navajo linguistics in 1936–37, Kluckhohn decided to follow a representative sample of forty-eight Navajo children (approximately one-third of the children at Ramah) through time as they "acquired" their culture in "a needed experiment" to correct what he regarded as "the flat, one-dimensional quality" of "even the best of anthropological monographs." Kluckhohn thus became one of the pioneers of "long-term field research" in American anthropology.[13]

Most of Kluckhohn's fieldwork took place during summer vacations at Harvard, but in 1939–40 he spent nine months in the field and another six months in 1946.[14] Although bored by kinship and social organization, Kluckhohn paid close attention to ceremonialism, personality development, and witchcraft. Concerned with both general Navajo patterns and individual variations from those patterns, he meticulously recorded the frequency of the behavior he observed, attempted to determine the extent of individual participation in ceremonies, and indicated whether his sources were informants or his own observations. In his published reports on the Navajo, Kluckhohn presented his material in such a way that it was easy for readers to distinguish "fact" from "inference." Although Kluckhohn was, like Dollard and Sapir, strongly oriented toward the life-history method, he acknowledged the usefulness of

[12] Clyde Kluckhohn, "Bronislaw Malinowski, 1884–1942," *Journal of American Folklore* 56 (1943): 210–211.
[13] Clyde Kluckhohn, "The Ramah Project," in Alexander H. Leighton and Dorothea Leighton, *Gregorio, the Hand-Trembler* (Cambridge: Harvard University Peabody Museum of American Archaeology and Ethnology, 1949), v; George M. Foster, Thayer Scudder, Elizabeth Colson, and Robert V. Kempfer, introduction to *Long-Term Field Research in Social Anthropology*, ed. George M. Foster, Thayer Scudder, Elizabeth Colson, and Robert V. Kemper (New York: Academic Press, 1979), 7–8.
[14] Clyde Kluckhohn to E. A. Hoebel, 7 February 1957, HUG 4490.5, Kluckhohn Papers.

statistical analysis, and, whenever possible, quantified his generalizations.[15] Convinced that "multiple observations" and "multiple approaches" would eliminate "distortions" stemming from the researcher's personal bias or the "stereotyped fashions" of his discipline, he entered into a number of cross-disciplinary collaborations. With the physiologist Leland Wyman, he compiled a taxonomy of Navajo rituals. With the psychiatrist Dorothea Leighton, he produced two books on the Navajo for the Indian Education Research Project. And with the biological anthropologist James Spuhler, he studied "inbreeding coefficients" among the Ramah Navajo.[16] Kluckhohn's many collaborations, and his creation at Ramah of a summer field school for graduate students in anthropology, helped to make the 1940s and 1950s "the Kluckhohn era" in anthropological studies of the Navajo.[17]

In his work among the Navajo, Kluckhohn employed what he described as a "modified functionalism." Although no admirer of the British functionalists Bronislaw Malinowski and A. R. Radcliffe-Brown, he did credit them with having demonstrated the "intricate interdependence" of the various aspects of culture and with having driven home the point that the "organization" of a culture was just as important as its content.[18] Yet, to avoid some of the "ambiguities" he discerned in functionalist theory, Kluckhohn adopted O. Hobart Mowrer's distinction between "adaptive" behavior, which ensured the "survival" of an individual or a society, and "adjustive" behavior, which removed the stimulus to action. Thus suicide was adjustive, but not adaptive. Kluckhohn also adopted the sociologist Robert K. Merton's distinction between "manifest" functions, which were planned or intended, and "latent" functions, which were not.[19]

[15] Clyde Kluckhohn, rejoinder to "Sociological Mirror for Cultural Anthropologists," by Jessie Bernard, *American Anthropologist* 51 (1949): 678; David F. Aberle, "Clyde Kluckhohn's Contributions to Navaho Studies," in *Culture and Life: Essays in Memory of Clyde Kluckhohn*, ed. Walter W. Taylor, John L. Fischer, and Evon Z. Vogt (Carbondale: Southern Illinois University Press, 1973), 85–87; Louise Lamphere, "The Long-Term Study among the Navajo," in *Long-Term Field Research in Social Anthropology*, 21–28.
[16] Kluckhohn, "The Ramah Project," vi; Clyde Kluckhohn and Leland Wyman, *An Introduction to Navaho Chant Practice with an Account of the Behaviors Observed in Four Chants* (Menasha, Wisc.: American Anthropological Association, 1940); Clyde Kluckhohn and Dorothea Leighton, *The Navaho* (Cambridge, Mass.: Harvard University Press, 1946); Dorothea Leighton and Clyde Kluckhohn, *Children of the People* (Cambridge, Mass.: Harvard University Press, 1947); James N. Spuhler and Clyde Kluckhohn, "Inbreeding Coefficients of the Ramah Navaho Population," *Human Biology* 25 (1953): 295–317.
[17] Gary Witherspoon, *Navajo Kinship and Marriage* (Chicago: University of Chicago Press, 1975), ix.
[18] Kluckhohn, "Bronislaw Malinowski," 216; Clyde Kluckhohn to Hortense Powdermaker, 13 October 1943, HUG 4490.3, Kluckhohn Papers; Clyde Kluckhohn to Hiram Haydn, 16 January 1950, HUG 4490.5, Kluckhohn Papers; Kluckhohn, "Place of Theory in Anthropological Studies," 337; Clyde Kluckhohn, "The Limitations of Adaptation and Adjustment as Concepts for Understanding Cultural Behavior," in *Adaptation*, ed. John Romano (Ithaca: Cornell University Press, 1949), 99–113, on 104, 99–100.
[19] Kluckhohn, "The Limitations of Adaptation and Adjustment," 100–105.

These two conceptual refinements informed Kluckhohn's 1944 monograph *Navaho Witchcraft*, in which he tested the hypothesis that myths and rituals provided "a cultural storehouse of adjustive responses for individuals." Although neither he nor any other anthropologist had ever observed a Navajo practicing witchcraft or using "witchcraft paraphernalia," Kluckhohn maintained that the existence of witchcraft could be inferred from "a whole assemblage of behavior patterns" that would "only make sense on the basis of [Navajo] 'belief' in witchcraft as a force to be feared." Witchcraft, he contended, had both manifest and latent functions for the Navajo. Its manifest functions included opening an "avenue to supernatural power," providing "answers" to "perplexing" and "disturbing" questions, and maintaining "conviction in the efficacy of curing ceremonials." Its latent functions included serving as "a device for getting attention," expressing "anti-social tendencies," and, in Kluckhohn's version of the frustration-aggression hypothesis, "displacing hostile impulses" from relatives and white Americans onto culturally approved "scapegoats." Insofar as witchcraft "dramatically defin[ed] what is bad" and reinforced "familism" (the cultural expectation that wealthy Navajo would share their wealth with poorer relatives), it strengthened "solidarity." Yet insofar as it projected aggression and discouraged able individuals from shouldering the "burdens of leadership," witchcraft also exacted a steep "cost." Still, the "euphoric effects" of witchcraft seemed to outweigh the "dysphoric effects."[20]

After publishing *Navaho Witchcraft*, however, Kluckhohn gradually distanced himself from functionalism. In 1945, he pointed out how "functional" definitions of culture disregarded "the fact that cultures create needs as well as provide a means of fulfilling them."[21] In 1949, elaborating on his critique of functionalism, Kluckhohn charged that functionalists ignored the "cost" of adaptation and adjustment, lost sight of the individual as a "concrete human organism," were unable to deal with "culture change" and "process," and invoked an overly simple and culture-bound "relief-from-tension formula" to account for human motivation. Above all, functionalists failed to acknowledge the ways in which cultures mediated between individuals and the stimuli to which they responded. For all these reasons, Kluckhohn looked forward to the development of a new way of thinking, one that would take into account the "pull of expectancies," recognize "instability" as a source of "growth and creativity," and emphasize "culturally created values."[22]

[20] Clyde Kluckhohn, "Myths and Rituals: A General Theory," *Harvard Theological Review* 35 (1942): 65; Clyde Kluckhohn, *Navaho Witchcraft* (1944; repr., Boston: Beacon Press, 1989), 81–83, 85, 98, 110–111, 120–121, 67. It is no wonder that Talcott Parsons thought that without the "encouragement" of "the Yale group," Kluckhohn would not have been able to have written *Navaho Witchcraft*. Talcott Parsons, "Clyde Kluckhohn and the Integration of Social Science," in *Culture and Life*, 47.

[21] Clyde Kluckhohn and William H. Kelly, "The Concept of Culture," in *The Science of Man in the World Crisis*, ed. Ralph Linton (New York: Columbia University Press, 1945), 81.

[22] Kluckhohn, "The Limitations of Adaptation and Adjustment," 105, 108, 111–113.

KLUCKHOHN'S TURN TO PSYCHIATRY

For help in fulfilling what he considered anthropology's job – providing "a factually established and rigorously formulated description of human nature" – Kluckhohn turned to psychiatry. As an undergraduate, he took his first course in psychology from Norman A. Cameron – then a "brass instrument" behaviorist who had little use for psychoanalysis but who later underwent analytic training. Although Kluckhohn "stopped ranting about Freud's anthropological errors" after he discovered the "unconscious" during his analysis in Vienna, he remained ambivalent about psychoanalysis, most likely because of the hostility of some of his Harvard colleagues.[23] In 1939, after some hesitation, Kluckhohn accepted a fellowship from the Carnegie Corporation that allowed him to study psychology and psychiatry with Ralph Linton, present some of his Navajo material in the Kardiner-Linton seminar at Columbia, and participate in Sandor Rado's seminar on psychoanalytic theory at the New York Psychoanalytic Institute.[24]

Upon his return to Harvard, Kluckhohn teamed up with O. Hobart Mowrer and Henry A. Murray to offer a cooperative seminar on "socialization" modeled on the Kardiner-Linton seminar. Kluckhohn and Mowrer, an experimental psychologist who joined the Harvard faculty in 1940 after six years as a research associate at the Yale Institute of Human Relations, subsequently developed a "conceptual scheme" for culture and personality that fused "concepts" and "postulates" drawn from anthropology, learning theory, and psychoanalytic theory. The two men, however, did not "see eye to eye on all points."[25]

Kluckhohn found the clinician Henry Murray, director of the Harvard Psychological Clinic and developer of the Thematic Apperception Test, more congenial than Mowrer. He was much taken with Murray's distinction between the "alpha press," the "temporal gestalt of stimuli" ascertainable by a fieldworker, and the "beta press," the informant's interpretation. He followed Murray, whom he admired as a "humanist," in construing social science as the systematic study of "the whole man." In 1948, in the hope of teaching "social science to psychiatrists," Kluckhohn and Murray brought out *Personality in Nature,*

---

[23] Roe, transcript of interview with Kluckhohn; Parsons, "Clyde Kluckhohn and the Integration of Social Science," 30.

[24] Charles Dollard to Clyde Kluckhohn, 3 March 1939; Ralph Linton to Clyde Kluckhohn, 9, 13 February, 26 March 1939, HUG 4490.3, Kluckhohn Papers; Kluckhohn, *Navaho Witchcraft*, 237n; Ellen Condliffe Lagemann, *The Politics of Knowledge: The Carnegie Corporation, Philanthropy, and Public Policy* (1989; repr., Chicago: University of Chicago Press, 1992), 166. On Cameron, see Ralph M. Crowley, "A Memorial: Norman Alexander Cameron, Ph.D. M.D.," *Journal of the American Academy of Psychoanalysis* 7 (1979): 469–472.

[25] O. Hobart Mowrer and Clyde Kluckhohn, "Dynamic Theory of Personality," in *Personality and the Behavior Disorders*, ed. J. McV. Hunt (New York: Ronald Press, 1944), 69–135; Clyde Kluckhohn and O. Hobart Mowrer, "Culture and Personality: A Conceptual Scheme," *American Anthropologist* 46 (1944): 1–29; Clyde Kluckhohn to Norman A. Cameron, 24 October 1944, HUG 4490.3, Kluckhohn Papers; Margaret Mead to Clyde Kluckhohn, 10 December 1943; Clyde Kluckhohn to Margaret Mead, 28 December 1943, Mead Papers, box C10.

Society, and Culture, the first collection of readings from the periodical literature in culture and personality.[26]

When, in 1944, the American Psychiatric Association invited Kluckhohn to assess psychiatry's impact on anthropology, he credited Ruth Benedict, Margaret Mead, and Edward Sapir with having promoted a "rapprochement" between the two disciplines. In Benedict's work, he said, there was an "attitude" that could "only be described as 'psychiatric.'" Kluckhohn ascribed Mead's high standing among psychiatrists to her "field data," tests of psychiatric problems in the field, and an "idiom" that psychiatrists "found intelligible." It was Sapir, however, who had "made possible some real fusion between the two disciplines." The "tough insights" that Sapir drew from psychiatry had "forced" anthropologists to reconstruct their "postulates." Thanks to the "conceptual refinements" that Sapir had introduced, anthropologists could no longer regard individuals as the "more or less passive carrier[s] of tradition," nor could they regard culture any longer as "a superorganic, impersonal whole."[27]

In 1945, evaluating the use of personal documents in anthropology for the Social Science Research Council's Committee on Appraisal of Research, Kluckhohn drew on his collaboration with Dorothea Leighton to emphasize the "interpersonal" aspects of fieldwork. Anthropologists, he said, should "take more account of the 'human' side of their materials." One way in which they could do so would be to follow the example of the psychiatrist and act as "a blank screen" on which informants could project their own lives. Kluckhohn was convinced that until anthropologists learned how to "deal rigorously with the 'subjective factors' in the lives of 'primitives,'" their work would remain "flat and insubstantial."[28]

Kluckhohn was also convinced of the existence of certain "affinities" between the anthropologist and the psychiatrist. Both were interested in "total personality" and "the whole man." The disciplines of both were not only "innocent of statistics," but also primarily "observational" rather than "experimental." Then, too, fieldwork was as "fundamentally revealing" of the relationship between the anthropologist and his informant as analysis was of the

[26] Clyde Kluckhohn to Henry A. Murray, 18 July 1944, quoted in Forrest G. Robinson, *Love's Story Told: A Life of Henry A. Murray* (Cambridge, Mass.: Harvard University Press, 1992), 294–295; Clyde Kluckhohn and Henry A. Murray, eds., *Personality in Nature, Society, and Culture* (New York: Knopf, 1948); Clyde Kluckhohn to Roger Shugg, 8 May 1948, HUG 4490.3, Kluckhohn Papers.

[27] Clyde Kluckhohn, "The Influence of Psychiatry on Anthropology in America during the Past One Hundred Years," in *One Hundred Years of American Psychiatry*, ed. J. K. Hall, G. Zilboorg, and E. A. Bunker (New York: Columbia University Press, 1944), 589–617, on 597, 600–603.

[28] Clyde Kluckhohn, "The Personal Document in Anthropological Science," in Louis Gottschalk, Clyde Kluckhohn, and Robert Angell, *The Personal Document in History, Anthropology, and Sociology* (New York: Social Science Research Council, 1945), 79–174, on 86, 122, 162–163; Ira Bashkow, "The Dynamics of Rapport in a Colonial Situation: David Schneider's Fieldwork on the Islands of Yap," in *Colonial Situations: Essays on the Contextualization of Ethnographic Knowledge*, ed. George W. Stocking, Jr. (Madison: University of Wisconsin Press, 1991), 189–190.

relationship between the psychiatrist and his analysand. Exposure to psychiatry, moreover, had made anthropologists self-conscious. In investigating such topics as "the individual in culture" and the "transmission of culture through child-training," borrowing such psychiatric concepts as ambivalence and identification, and supplementing their traditional "question-and-answer method" of fieldwork with "passive interviews" and "controlled observations," they had begun to alter their postulates and "sharply refashion" their "whole thinking about the individual informant as a cultural specimen." As a result, they were gradually abandoning "the false antinomy of 'the individual vs. society'" as well as revising their "assumptions as to relative proportions of rational, non-rational, and irrational elements in human behavior."[29]

What Kluckhohn was looking for from psychiatrists was "a theory of raw human nature." Earlier in his career, when he still regarded Freudian theory as "strongly culture-bound," he had found the work of the neo-Freudian psychoanalysts Erich Fromm and Karen Horney congenial. By the late 1940s, however, his views were converging with those of the more orthodox Freudian Géza Róheim. Kluckhohn had come to believe that the neo-Freudians went too far in discounting the influence of biology. In addition, they were more interested in cultural differences than in the "universals" of culture. Besides, Kluckhohn's fieldwork among the Navajo had convinced him of the "astonishing correctness" with which Freud had depicted a number of universal "themes in motivational life." While the "expression" and "manifest content" of these themes varied from culture to culture, there was, he believed, an "underlying psychologic drama" that "transcend[ed] cultural difference." It was now time for anthropologists to turn their attention from the differences among cultures to the similarities.[30]

Before anthropologists could come up with their own theory of raw human nature, however, they had to determine the limits of human malleability and to distinguish the "cultural" products of "local variations in time and space" from the "universal" products of "man's unchanging biology and the unshakable 'givens' of the human situation." The "invariant points of reference supplied by [these] givens," in turn, made possible "valid cross-cultural comparison." It was on this basis that Kluckhohn attempted to construct what his student

---

[29] Clyde Kluckhohn, "An Anthropologist Looks at Psychology," *American Psychologist* 3 (1948): 440–441; Clyde Kluckhohn, "The Impact of Freud on Anthropology," *Bulletin of the New York Academy of Medicine* 32 (1956): 906; Kluckhohn, "The Influence of Psychiatry on Anthropology," 596, 616–617; Clyde Kluckhohn, "Anthropological Studies of Human Relations," paper given at the Conference on Research in Human Relations sponsored by the Rockefeller Foundation, 27 February–1 March 1953, 1–2, folder 99, box 11, series 900, RG 3, Rockefeller Foundation Archives, RAC.

[30] Clyde Kluckhohn and William Morgan, "Some Notes on Navaho Dreams," in *Psychoanalysis and Culture: Essays in Honor of Géza Róheim*, ed. G. B. Wilbur and Warner Muensterberger (New York: International Universities Press, 1951), 120–131; reprinted in *Culture and Behavior: Collected Essays of Clyde Kluckhohn*, ed. Richard Kluckhohn (New York: Free Press, 1962), 350–363, on 350–351; Eric R. Wolf, *Anthropology* (1964; repr., New York: Norton, 1974), 36, 39.

Clifford Geertz termed a *consensus gentium* (a consensus of all mankind) enshrining the Enlightenment notion that "there are some things that all men will be found to agree upon as right, real, just, or attractive, and that these things are, therefore, in fact right, real, just, or attractive."[31]

When his heart condition kept him out of the military, Kluckhohn devoted himself to "psychological warfare." While working alongside Ruth Benedict in the Foreign Morale Analysis Division of the Office of War Information in 1944–45, he came to appreciate her uncanny ability to "saturate" herself in library materials and grasp "the essential dynamics of Japanese personality and culture" without engaging in fieldwork.[32]

After the war was over, Kluckhohn joined Benedict in attempting to put the study of culture at a distance, hastily improvised during the war, on permanent peacetime footing. In 1948, he became the first director of the Harvard Russian Research Center, which had been established with the help of $840,000 in grants from the Carnegie Corporation for the purpose of bringing the methods and insights of the behavioral sciences – anthropology, sociology, and psychology – to bear on "problems of Russian behavior." Kluckhohn was appointed not because of his expertise on Russia – he had not studied Russian affairs and did not have a command of Russian – but because of his interdisciplinary background, wartime experience in psychological warfare, and long-time friendship with Charles Dollard, John's brother, who was then president of the Carnegie Corporation. From the inception of the Russian Research Center, Kluckhohn fostered research designed to be interdisciplinary, experimental, and "cumulative." In the Émigré Interview Project, he and the sociologists Alex Inkeles and Raymond Bauer analyzed more than 400 life histories and 2,000 questionnaires that had been collected from Soviet refugees. They found that the Soviet system was more stable than many American observers liked to believe. Its stability rested on the "nice balance" maintained between Soviet "powers of coercion" and the Russian citizens' "adjustive habits." Despite Kluckhohn's best efforts to promote the behavioral sciences at the Russian Research Center, their methods and insights took a back seat to those of history, economics, and political science.[33]

[31] Clyde Kluckhohn, "Universal Categories of Culture," in *Anthropology Today: An Encyclopedic Inventory*, ed. A. L. Kroeber (Chicago: University of Chicago Press, 1953), 520–521; Clifford Geertz, "The Impact of the Concept of Culture on the Concept of Man," in *The Interpretation of Cultures: Selected Essays* (New York: Basic Books, 1973), 33–54, on 38–39.

[32] Clyde Kluckhohn, in *Ruth Fulton Benedict: A Memorial* (New York: Viking Fund, 1949), 18–19. On psychological warfare, see Ellen Herman, *The Romance of American Psychology: Political Culture in the Age of Experts* (Berkeley: University of California Press, 1995).

[33] Clyde Kluckhohn, "Russian Research at Harvard," *World Politics* 1 (1949): 267–272; Lagemann, *The Politics of Knowledge*, 174–175; Alex Inkeles, "Clyde Kluckhohn's Contribution to Studies of Russia and the Soviet Union," in *Culture and Life*, 58–70; David C. Engerman, "The Ironies of the Iron Curtain: The Cold War and the Rise of Russian Studies," in *The Humanities and the Dynamics of Inclusion since World War II*, ed. David A. Hollinger (Baltimore: Johns Hopkins University Press, 2006), 318.

By 1954, Kluckhohn could proudly point to the "considerable improvement in communication" that had occurred between psychiatrists and anthropologists since the late 1920s. While admitting that work in culture and personality "suffered" from being too "fashionable," notably in such "hasty, overly schematic, and indeed naïve" publications as Geoffrey Gorer and John Rickman's *The People of Great Russia*, the "underlying notions" of the field still seemed to Kluckhohn "basically sound." Yet he left the field. Even though he continued to review work in culture and personality for professional journals, and for the *New York Times* and the *New York Herald Tribune*, his "central interests" took a pronounced linguistic turn as he endeavored to bring the study of values within the fold of social science.[34]

EXPLORING IMPLICIT CULTURE

Kluckhohn turned to a linguistically informed study of values out of an abiding interest in describing the "patterns" of culture as rigorously and as parsimoniously as possible.[35] He did so without having received any linguistic training at Harvard. He did study Navajo linguistics with Edward Sapir, however, and he also closely followed the work of the anthropological linguists Benjamin Whorf and Dorothy Lee.

Kluckhohn drew on linguistics to develop what he considered his most important theoretical contribution, the concept of "implicit culture" (which, until 1945, he called "covert culture").[36] In "Patterning as Exemplified in Navaho Culture," published in a 1941 Sapir *festschrift*, Kluckhohn followed Sapir and Benedict in regarding all cultural behavior as "patterned." Yet he believed that Benedict had unwittingly sown confusion among anthropologists when she used the word "pattern" to refer at one and the same time to "specific modalities of ideals and behavior" and "generalized configurations." To clear up this ambiguity, Kluckhohn proposed that "pattern" be limited to overt or observable phenomena, while the term "configuration" designate the phenomena of "covert culture." By covert culture, Kluckhohn had in mind that sector of a culture of which individuals within the culture were only minimally aware or completely unaware. Where "pattern" was "a generalization *of* behavior," he explained, "configuration" was "a generalization *from* behavior." The anthropologist observed a pattern, but he inferred the existence of a configuration. A pattern was thus a "form"; a configuration, by contrast, designated the "inter-relationship" between forms.[37]

---

[34] Clyde Kluckhohn, "Culture and Behavior," in *Handbook of Social Psychology*, ed. Gardner Lindzey (Cambridge: Addison-Wesley, 1954); 921–976, on 961; Clyde Kluckhohn, "Southwestern Studies of Culture and Personality," *American Anthropologist* 56 (1954): 693.

[35] John L. Fischer, "Linguistic Models and the Study of Culture: Clyde Kluckhohn's Approach," in *Culture and Life*, 156.

[36] Herskovits, "Clyde Kay Maben Kluckhohn," 130.

[37] Clyde Kluckhohn, "Patterning as Exemplified in Navaho Culture," in *Language, Culture, and Personality: Essays in Memory of Edward Sapir*, ed. Leslie A. Spier, A. Irving Hallowell, and Stanley S. Newman (Menasha, Wisc.: Sapir Memorial Publication Fund, 1941), 109–130, on 109, 112, 114, 124, 126 (emphasis in original).

Kluckhohn derived the concept "implicit culture" from a number of different sources. The first and most influential was Edward Sapir. As Dell Hymes pointed out, Sapir showed anthropologists how to treat patterning rigorously, but without aping the methods of natural science. Sapir's "methodology," moreover, enabled anthropologists "to go beyond" describing the patterns of overt culture to inferring the configurations of implicit culture. Then, too, Sapir searched for "linguistic universals."[38] Finally, Sapir invoked linguistics as a source of method for anthropologists. "Human beings," Sapir explained, "do not live in the objective world alone," but were "very much at the mercy of the particular language" of their group. The "real world" as the individual grasped it was thus "to a large extent unconsciously built upon [his or her group's] language habits."[39]

Kluckhohn also "derived a major part of his theoretical orientation" from Ruth Benedict. The concept of implicit culture echoed not only Sapir's notion of "unconscious sound patterning" but also Benedict's notion of "unconscious canons of choice." Then, too, Kluckhohn's stress on the "regularity," as opposed to the randomness, of pattern was "consonant" with Benedict's view that pattern was "summative in a culture."[40]

Ralph Linton's unpublished lectures were yet a third source of Kluckhohn's conception of implicit culture. For Linton, the difference between overt and covert culture largely boiled down to the difference between the "tangible" and the "intangible" aspects of culture. Where for Linton, covert culture designated "the whole range of psychological phenomena ordinarily included in the culture concept," for Kluckhohn, it designated the "elements existing in the deeper levels of personality."[41]

Kluckhohn was also influenced by the work of Benjamin Lee Whorf. A chemical engineer and fire insurance investigator who had studied linguistics with Sapir at Yale, Whorf conceived of languages as integrated "fashions of speaking," the "categories" of which shaped the ways in which their speakers "dissect[ed] nature and [broke] up the flux of experience into objects and entities to construct propositions about." Distinguishing between "overt" and "covert" categories, Whorf called the latter "cryptotypes" to designate "elusive,

---

[38] Dell H. Hymes, "Linguistic Method in Ethnography: Its Development in the United States," in *Essays in the History of Linguistic Anthropology* (Amsterdam: John Benjamins, 1983), 165–168, 178–180.

[39] Edward Sapir, "The Status of Linguistics as a Science," *Language* 5 (1929): 207–214; reprinted in *Selected Writings of Edward Sapir in Language, Culture and Personality*, ed. David G. Mandelbaum (1949; repr., Berkeley: University of California Press, 1963), 160–168, on 162; Dell H. Hymes, "Morris Swadesh: From the First Yale School to World Prehistory," in *Essays in the History of Linguistic Anthropology*, 291.

[40] Kluckhohn in *Ruth Fulton Benedict*, 18–19; Hymes, "Linguistic Method in Ethnography," 165–168.

[41] Clyde Kluckhohn to Ralph Linton, 10 December 1942; Ralph Linton to Clyde Kluckhohn, 7, 15 December 1942, HUG 4490.3, Kluckhohn Papers; Clyde Kluckhohn, "Covert Culture and Administrative Problems," *American Anthropologist* 45 (1943): 217–218; Ralph Linton, *The Cultural Background of Personality* (New York: D. Appleton-Century, 1945), 38.

hidden, but functionally important meaning[s]." Covert categories, Whorf added, were "apt to be more rational than overt ones."[42]

A fifth and final source of Kluckhohn's conception of implicit culture was the anthropological linguist Dorothy D. Lee, who had been Alfred Kroeber's student. Kluckhohn liked to quote Lee's point that "grammar contains in crystallized form the accumulated and accumulating experience, the *Weltanschauung* [worldview] of a people." Indeed, he often spoke of the "Whorf-Lee hypothesis," by which he had in mind a linguistic tradition, stretching back to Wilhelm von Humboldt, that "distinctive language habits predispose different peoples to certain modes of sensory perception and thought."[43]

Although Kluckhohn borrowed the concept of implicit culture from others, he quickly made it his own.[44] In 1943, he emphasized the organizational property of culture. "Every culture," he said, had a "structure." Although anthropologists still lacked a "coherent theory" of covert culture, Kluckhohn thought that its "configurations" could be studied scientifically.[45] In 1945, Kluckhohn substituted "implicit culture" for "covert culture" in order to avoid any connotation of secrecy or concealment. In an essay coauthored with William Kelly in *The Science of Man in the World Crisis*, a volume edited by Ralph Linton that expressed the hopes of American social scientists who looked forward to playing prominent parts in postwar reconstruction, Kluckhohn defined culture as "an historically defined system of explicit and implicit designs for living, which tends to be shared by all or specially designated members of a group."

[42] Benjamin Lee Whorf, "Languages and Logic," in *Language, Thought, and Reality: Selected Writings of Benjamin Lee Whorf*, ed. John B. Carroll (Cambridge: MIT Press, 1956), 233–245, on 239; Benjamin Lee Whorf, "Grammatical Categories," ibid., 89, 92; Benjamin Lee Whorf, "Thinking in Primitive Communities," ibid., 80.

[43] Kluckhohn and Kelly, "The Concept of Culture," 101; Dorothy D. Lee, "Conceptual Implications of an Indian Language," *Philosophy of Science* 5 (1938): 89; E. F. Konrad Koerner, "The Sapir-Whorf Hypothesis: A Preliminary History and a Bibliographical Essay," *Journal of Linguistic Anthropology* 2 (1992): 173–198. In 1941, Kluckhohn called Whorf's attention to the "extraordinary convergence" between Lee's work and Whorf's own work. Clyde Kluckhohn to Benjamin L. Whorf, 25 February 1941, HUG 4490.3, Kluckhohn Papers. After Whorf's death, Lee told Kluckhohn that Whorf "did not speak my language, but his work is much beyond mine." Her own work, Lee explained, came "about purely as a response to" the "very uncomfortable questions" posed by her husband, the philosopher Otis Lee. Lee had "never studied with a linguist, and, to [her] shame," had never met Sapir. Dorothy D. Lee to Kluckhohn, 30 July 1942, HUG 4490.3, Kluckhohn Papers. In 1950, Kluckhohn urged Jeremiah Kaplan, publisher of The Free Press, to publish Lee's papers, "most of [which] are already regarded as small classics." Clyde Kluckhohn to Jeremiah Kaplan, 4 August 1950, HUG 4490.5, Kluckhohn Papers.

[44] Clyde Kluckhohn, comment on "The Problem of Communication between Cultures seen as Integrated Wholes," by Carl J. Friedrich, in *Approaches to National Unity: Fifth Symposium*, ed. Lyman Bryson, Louis Finkelstein, and Robert M. MacIver (New York: Harper, 1945), 633–634. See also Clyde Kluckhohn, "Covert or Implicit Culture," in *A Dictionary of the Social Sciences*, ed. Julius Gould and William L. Kolb (New York: Free Press, 1964), 145–146.

[45] Kluckhohn, "Covert Culture and Administrative Problems," 217–218, 222–223.

Culture, for Kluckhohn, was thus an abstraction or logical construct that did not refer to either behavior or artifacts.[46]

FIXING THE MEANING OF CULTURE

Early in 1947, Kluckhohn visited Berkeley to persuade Alfred Kroeber, who had recently become professor emeritus, to teach in Harvard's new Department of Social Relations. Established the preceding year, "Soc Rel" grew out of conversations, which began before the Second World War, among the "Levellers," a small, interdisciplinary group that included Kluckhohn and his wife, Henry Murray, Hobart Mowrer, Talcott Parsons, and Gordon Allport.

The Levellers' initiatives to advance "basic social science" at Harvard came to fruition in 1946 when the Department of Social Relations was established and authorized to award graduate degrees in anthropology, sociology, clinical and social psychology. Clifford Geertz captured the spirit of the new department when he said that it represented "social science in full cry; headier and more confident than before or since."[47]

When Kroeber joined the Soc Rel faculty in the fall of 1947, he and Kluckhohn embarked on their compendium on culture. After Kroeber left Harvard for Columbia in 1948, the two men "operate[d] almost entirely by correspondence, getting together only very occasionally, for a few hours on it." Kluckhohn's duties as director of the Russian Research Center, however, limited his "contribution" to "the odd moments [he] could snatch over these years evenings and weekends."[48]

Both Kluckhohn and Kroeber were convinced that the "extension and clarification" of culture had been American anthropologists' "most significant accomplishment." Both men also agreed that the "study of values" was "a proper and necessary part of the study of culture." In addition, both men believed in the existence of "pan-cultural verities." As Clifford Geertz pointed out, Kroeber's pan-cultural verities were "mostly about messy creatural matters like delirium and menstruation, Kluckhohn's about messy social ones like lying and killing within the in-group." The two men's belief in pan-cultural verities expressed "a much vaster concern," the notion "that if something isn't anchored everywhere nothing can be anchored anywhere."[49]

---

[46] Ralph Linton, "The Scope and Aims of Anthropology," in *The Science of Man in the World Crisis*, 3; Kluckhohn and Kelly, "The Concept of Culture," ibid., 100–101.

[47] Lagemann, *The Politics of Knowledge*, 166–171; Clifford Geertz, *After the Fact: Two Countries, Four Decades, One Anthropologist* (Cambridge, Mass.: Harvard University Press, 1995), 100.

[48] Clyde Kluckhohn to Raymond Firth, 6 April 1953, HUG 4490.5, Kluckhohn Papers; Theodora Kroeber, *Alfred Kroeber: A Personal Configuration* (Berkeley: University of California Press, 1970), 206–207, 212–213.

[49] A. L. Kroeber, "A Half-Century of Anthropology," *Scientific American* 183 (1950): 87–94; reprinted in *The Nature of Culture* (Chicago: University of Chicago Press, 1952), 139–143, on 139; A. L. Kroeber, "Values as a Subject of Natural Science Inquiry," *Proceedings of the Natural Academy of Sciences* 35 (1949): 261; Clifford Geertz, "Anti Anti-Relativism," in *Available Light: Anthropological Reflections on Philosophical Topics* (Princeton, N.J.: Princeton University Press, 2000), 45–46.

The two men's theoretical views, however, diverged on three points. Kluckhohn believed that Kroeber's superorganic conception of culture reified culture and ignored individual variation.[50] The two men also disagreed on the ontological status of cultural universals. Although Kroeber did not dispute the existence of invariant points of reference, he denied that these constants were "the same as culture," and, instead, assigned them to "the subcultural level." Finally, where Kluckhohn suspected that a number of "categories" and "structural principles," the cultural equivalents of the phoneme (the smallest unit of speech that distinguishes one word, or utterance, from another in the same language), could be discovered "in all cultures," Kroeber thought that the discovery of such "constant elemental units" was "highly unlikely."[51]

In tracing the development of the culture concept since its origins in early nineteenth-century German thought, Kroeber and Kluckhohn hoped to fix its meaning. By the late 1940s, at least 164 formal definitions of culture in its technical anthropological sense had been propounded, and countless partial definitions. Hence the need for "stock-taking" and "comparing of notes" lest the concept become "so diffuse as to promote confusion rather than clarity."[52]

After arranging the formal definitions that they had collected in an exhaustive library search in rough chronological order, Kroeber and Kluckhohn classified them into six categories: enumeratively descriptive, historical, normative, psychological, structural, and genetic. By so grouping the varying notions that had "accreted" around the culture concept, Kroeber and Kluckhohn hoped to "cross-relate" the "interconnections." Next, they compiled "a thesaurus of representative or significant statements on culture theory." This thesaurus consisted of passages on the nature, components, and distinctive properties of culture, and on culture's relations to psychology, language, society, individuals, environment, and artifacts. Finally, Kroeber and Kluckhohn identified the general features of culture. These included "integration," "historicity," "uniformity," "causality," and "values." "Every culture," the two men agreed, "possesse[d] a considerable degree of integration of both its content and its forms," although integration was "never perfect or complete." Every culture, moreover, was "a precipitate of history."[53]

[50] Clyde Kluckhohn, review of *Configurations of Culture Growth*, by A. L. Kroeber, *American Journal of Sociology* 51 (1946): 336–341.
[51] A. L. Kroeber to Clyde Kluckhohn, 28 April 1951, HUG 4490.9, Kluckhohn Papers; A. L. Kroeber, comment on "Universal Categories of Culture," by Clyde Kluckhohn, in *An Appraisal of Anthropology Today*, ed. Sol Tax, Loren C. Eisely, Irving Rouse, and Carl F. Voegelin (1953; repr., Chicago: University of Chicago Press, 1976), 119.
[52] A. L. Kroeber and Clyde Kluckhohn, *Culture: A Critical Review of Concepts and Definitions* (Cambridge: Harvard University Peabody Museum of American Archaeology and Ethnology, 1952): 4.
[53] Kroeber and Kluckhohn, *Culture*, 41–42, 83, 159.

Although neither Kroeber nor Kluckhohn anticipated "the discovery of cultural laws," both saw in the ongoing search for the common denominators and universals of culture the promise of "parsimonious description and 'explanation' of cultural phenomena." Moreover, both men insisted that any inquiry into the nature of culture must include values, since, to their minds, the scientific study of values represented "the only basis for the fully intelligible comprehension of culture." Kroeber and Kluckhohn concluded their compendium by qualifying their commitment to the untrammeled cultural relativism of the interwar period, which the horrors of the Second World War had called into question. "The inescapable fact of cultural relativism," they said, did "not justify the conclusion that cultures [were] in all respects utterly disparate monads and hence strictly noncomparable entities." Declaring that "relativity exist[s] only within a universal framework," Kroeber and Kluckhohn held out the hope that "true universals or near universals," although "apparently few in number," could be discovered.[54]

By 1952, as the publication of Kroeber and Kluckhohn's monograph attested, anthropologists commanded "a fairly well-delineated concept" of culture, the "conceptual elements" of which could be enumerated. But anthropologists still lacked a "full theory of culture." Kroeber and Kluckhohn pinned their hopes for "a dynamic and generalized conceptual model" of culture on further investigation of cultural forms and individual variability. Although they stopped short of claiming that the culture concept provided "a complete explanation of human behavior," the two men nonetheless insisted that "a cultural element" existed "in most human behavior" and that "certain things in behavior" made "most sense when seen through culture." In their eyes, their history of the culture concept told "the story of the emergence of an idea that was gradually strained out of the several connotations of an existing word" – a process they tried to accelerate by defining culture as a logical construct and enumerating its properties.[55]

In stressing the autonomy of culture, Kluckhohn and Kroeber hoped to forestall any attempt by Kluckhohn's colleague Talcott Parsons "to absorb culture within social system" in his all-encompassing "general theory of action."[56] Influenced by Max Weber, about whom Kluckhohn felt "notably negative," Parsons proposed that anthropologists specialize in the study of culture, defined narrowly as the realm of ideas, values, and symbols. Parsons's narrower conception of culture eventually prevailed, not only within the Department of Social Relations but also within American social science. In an entente that Parsons reached with Kroeber in 1958, culture was restricted

[54] Kroeber and Kluckhohn, *Culture*, 163, 167, 173, 175–176, 178.

[55] Kroeber and Kluckhohn, *Culture*, 180–181, 186, 145.

[56] Clyde Kluckhohn to François Bourricaud, 5 May 1953, HUG 4490.5, Kluckhohn Papers; Clyde Kluckhohn to Talcott Parsons, 24 October 1953, HUG 4490.7, Kluckhohn Papers; Clyde Kluckhohn, "Toward a Comparison of Value-Emphases in Different Cultures," in *The State of the Social Sciences*, ed. Leonard D. White (Chicago: University of Chicago Press, 1956), 129; Kroeber and Kluckhohn, *Culture*, 15, 134–136.

in its application to "values, ideas, and [symbols]" while the social system designated "interaction" and "social action."[57]

While many social scientists endorsed Kroeber and Kluckhohn's conception of culture as a logical construct, the outspoken "culturologist" Leslie White complained that, far from clarifying the concept of culture, Kroeber and Kluck-hohn had "run head on into such ontological problems as the nature of culture, its reality, its abstract or concrete character, and so on, without quite knowing how to handle them." In a review of Kroeber and Kluckhohn's compendium, White expressed his disappointment that the two men failed to "distinguish clearly between things and events in the external world" and the "verbal con-cepts with which these phenomena are represented." Opposing "the shift from 'concrete-mindedness' to traffic in abstractions," White demanded that the term "culture" be defined "in terms of concrete, objective observable things and events in the external world."[58]

Similarly, the philosopher-turned-anthropologist David Bidney criticized Kroeber and Kluckhohn for conflating the "logical construct" of culture with "actual, existential culture." "Human behavior," Bidney insisted, was more than a "precondition" from which culture was abstracted. As "a patterned process," human behavior constituted "actual culture."[59]

Ultimately, the biggest problem with Kroeber and Kluckhohn's attempt to codify culture was that their definition included too much. As we shall see in the Epilogue, Kluckhohn's students Clifford Geertz and David Schneider attempt-ed, as Geertz put it, to cut "the culture concept down to size" so as to ensure "its continued importance" as "a narrowed, specialized, [and] theoretically more powerful concept."[60]

---

[57] Talcott Parsons to David Schneider, 21 January 1965, HUG(FP) 15.60, box 3, Parsons Papers; A. L. Kroeber and Talcott Parsons, "The Concepts of Culture and of Social System," *American Sociological Review* 23 (1958): 582–583; Talcott Parsons, "Culture and Social System Revisited," in *The Idea of Culture in the Social Sciences*, 33–46; Adam Kuper, *Culture: The Anthropologists' Account* (Cambridge, Mass.: Harvard University Press, 1999), 68–70.

[58] Leslie A. White, review of *The Nature of Culture*, by A. L. Kroeber, and *Culture: A Critical Review of Concepts and Definitions, American Anthropologist* 56 (1954): 462, 464, 465. Earlier, White and Kluckhohn had squabbled over "culturology." Although he agreed "entirely" with White that "the cultural field is a field in its own right," Kluckhohn was "unhappy" that White apparently wanted "to build such a tight fence about it." Kluckhohn justified his interest in psychology, which White criticized, on the ground that he could not "understand the origin of another culture (which always has been my central interest) without overstepping arbitrary boundaries between the disciplines erected by accidents of history." Clyde Kluckhohn to Leslie A. White, 27 July 1947, HUG 4490.5, Kluckhohn Papers.

[59] David Bidney, review of *Culture: A Critical Review of Concepts and Definitions, American Journal of Sociology* 59 (1954): 489.

[60] Clifford Geertz, "Thick Description: Toward an Interpretive Theory of Culture," in *The Inter-pretation of Cultures*, 4; Roger M. Keesing, "Theories of Culture," *Annual Review of Anthro-pology* 3 (1974): 73.

INVESTIGATING VALUES

Well aware of just how diffuse the culture concept had become, Kluckhohn began to investigate values. By values he meant the "total apperceptive mass" that mediated between individuals and the stimuli to which they responded. "Except under conditions of extreme physiological stress," Kluckhohn explained, individuals did not respond directly to stimuli, but rather to their "interpretations" of those stimuli. Their interpretations, in turn, were based, "consciously or unconsciously," upon culturally derived values.[61] Insisting that any culture must be conceived of as "an organized system of meanings," Kluckhohn located the essence of a culture in its "selectivity." This selectivity, in turn, could be reduced to the "value system" – that is, to a culture's "tacit and explicit premises and categories." If anthropologists wanted to go beyond enumerating the contents of cultures to grasping cultures as organized wholes, they had to identify the values of each culture. The identification of values thus promised to make possible succinct statements of cultural logic and the parsimonious comparison of cultures.[62]

In urging anthropologists to study values, Kluckhohn testified to the impact of the Second World War on the untrammeled cultural relativism of the interwar period.[63] The war had caused Ruth Benedict herself to wonder whether her professional ethic as an anthropologist prohibited her from making value judgments. Must anthropologists "in this conflict of value systems," she asked in 1942, "take a professional stand of cultural relativity"? Qualifying her own commitment to cultural relativism, Benedict proposed that anthropologists go "beyond relativity" to search for "the ways and means of social cohesion – the scientific study of aspects of society which *do* correlate with social cohesion and so with minimizing individual aggression and frustration."[64]

Another reason why Kluckhohn qualified his belief in cultural relativism was that, in its untrammeled version, it seemed to rule out "comparative appraisals." Denying that values were always "culture-bound," or "completely relative to the cultures from which they derive," he posited the existence of universals stemming from "similarities in the human situation throughout time and space." Indeed, "a considerable number of categories and of structural

[61] Clyde Kluckhohn, "Anthropology and the Study of Values," unpublished abstract of paper delivered to the Viking Fund Supper-Conference for Anthropologists, 31 March 1950, 3, HUG 4490.34, Kluckhohn Papers.
[62] Clyde Kluckhohn, quoted in *An Appraisal of Anthropology Today*, 123, 326; Clyde Kluckhohn to Leland C. DeVinney, 8 January 1951, folder 4365, box 510, series 200, RG 1.2, Rockefeller Foundation Archives, RAC.
[63] Wolf, *Anthropology*, 20–21; Peter Novick, *That Noble Dream: The "Objectivity Question" and the American Historical Profession* (New York: Cambridge University Press, 1988), 283–285.
[64] Ruth Benedict, "Ideologies in the Light of Comparative Data," in *An Anthropologist at Work: The Writings of Ruth Benedict*, ed. Margaret Mead (Boston: Houghton Mifflin, 1959), 383, 385 (emphasis in original); Virginia Heyer Young, *Ruth Benedict: Beyond Relativity, Beyond Pattern* (Lincoln: University of Nebraska Press, 2005).

principles," he said, could be "found in all cultures." Some were "givens" reflecting human biology.[65] Others reflected "the generalities of the human situation" because human behavior, unlike animal behavior, was not wholly, or even largely, instinctive.[66] Viewing cultures as "somewhat distinct answers to essentially the same questions posed by human biology and by the generalities of the human situation," Kluckhohn believed in the existence of a "generalized framework."[67]

Kluckhohn also agreed with the philosopher F. S. C. Northrop that "scientific means" could "hasten the re-emergence of universal values." Kluckhohn considered *The Meeting of East and West* (1946), in which Northrop searched for a "scientifically grounded philosophy" that would synthesize the best of the Orient and the Occident, "one of the really important books of our time." Northrop, he thought, was "on the right track" in employing methods derived from the behavioral sciences to examine the "underlying primitive postulates" of cultures. The use of such methods, Kluckhohn held, would allow researchers to compare "value systems on an objective basis."[68] Kluckhohn also endorsed the view propounded by the mathematical biologist Anatol Rapoport that the scientific outlook, far from being the "by-product" of Western civilization, constituted "the essence of a culture which has not yet been established – a culture-studying culture."[69]

BRINGING VALUES WITHIN THE FOLD OF SOCIAL SCIENCE

The confluence of three currents after 1945 heightened interest in the social scientific study of values. The first was the hope that inquiries into values would promote a convergence between anthropology and the humanities by overcoming the distinction between "fact" and "value." Ruth Benedict spoke to this issue in her presidential address before the American Anthropological Association in 1947 when she called attention to the similarity between the "nature of the problems posed and discussed in the humanities" and "those in anthropology." For both anthropologists and humanists were concerned with "man and

---

[65] Clyde Kluckhohn, "An Anthropological Approach to the Study of Values," *Communication* 4 (1951): 3.

[66] Clyde Kluckhohn, "Values and Value-Orientations in the Theory of Action," in *Toward a General Theory of Action*, ed. Talcott Parsons and Edward A. Shils (1951; repr., New York: Harper, 1962), 388.

[67] Clyde Kluckhohn, "Universal Values and Anthropological Relativism," in *Modern Education and Human Values* (Pittsburgh: University of Pittsburgh Press, 1952), 102.

[68] Clyde Kluckhohn, "The Special Character of Integration in an Individual Culture," in *The Nature of Concepts, Their Inter-Relation and Role in Social Structure* (Stillwater: Oklahoma A & M College, 1950), 87; Clyde Kluckhohn, quoted in E. Z. Vogt and Ethel Albert, Memo, Flagstaff Conference, 27 October 1954, HUG(FP) 42.25, box 1, Parsons Papers. Kluckhohn attended the Stillwater Conference because of his "personal loyalty to and affection for" Northrop. Clyde Kluckhohn to Alan Gregg, 23 April 1951, HUG 4490.5, Kluckhohn Papers.

[69] Clyde Kluckhohn, "Science as a Possible Source of New Moral Values," *Humanist* 14 (1954): 214; Anatol Rapoport, *Science and the Goals of Man* (New York: Harper, 1950), 232–233.

his works and his ideas and his history." Benedict was convinced that the "scientific" and "humanistic" traditions, far from being incompatible, complemented each other.[70]

In a second development, social scientists were becoming more self-conscious about their methods and about how normative and moral considerations affected their research.[71] As early as 1933, the German sociologist of knowledge Karl Mannheim had argued that, instead of excluding evaluations from their work, social scientists should "control" them "through critical awareness." In 1936, the sociologist Louis Wirth endorsed Mannheim's call for a sociology of knowledge. As Wirth noted, social scientists' "choice of areas for research," "selection of data," "method of investigation," "organization of materials," and "formulation of [their] hypotheses and conclusions" were all informed by "explicit or implicit assumption[s] or scheme[s] of evaluation." In *Knowledge for What?* (1939), Robert Lynd demanded that social scientists "make explicit [their] tacit criteria of the 'significant,'" lest they permit the "*de facto* leaders of the culture" to determine what the findings of their researches meant. Finally, in *An American Dilemma* (1944), Gunnar Myrdal dismissed the possibility of "value-free" social science, and proposed that researchers explicitly state their "value premises" as a way of mitigating their "biases" and laying a "rational basis" for stating "theoretical problems and the practical conclusions."[72]

The third and final current flowing into postwar interest in values was the possibility that the social sciences would become eligible for substantial financial support from philanthropic foundations and the federal government. The possibility of external support raised the question of whose criteria, the pedant's or the potentate's, would granting agencies use to assess "the importance of different problems" and to choose the projects they would support?[73]

[70] Ruth Benedict, "Anthropology and the Humanities," *American Anthropologist* 50 (1948): 585–593; reprinted in *An Anthropologist at Work*, 459–470.

[71] Daniel Lee Kleinman and Mark Solovey, "Hot Science/Cold War: The National Science Foundation after World War II," *Radical History Review* 63 (1995): 119.

[72] Karl Mannheim, quoted in Mark Solovey, "Riding Natural Scientists' Coattails onto the Endless Frontier: The SSRC and the Quest for Scientific Legitimacy," *Journal of the History of the Behavioral Sciences* 40 (2004): 401; Louis Wirth, preface to *Ideology and Utopia*, by Karl Mannheim, trans. Louis Wirth and Edward A. Shils (Chicago: University of Chicago Press, 1936), xiii–xxxi; reprinted in *Louis Wirth on Cities and Social Life*, ed. Albert J. Riess, Jr. (Chicago: University of Chicago Press, 1964), 125–145, on 135; Robert S. Lynd, *Knowledge for What? The Place of Social Science in American Culture* (1939; repr., Princeton, N.J.: Princeton University Press, 1970), 186–187; Gunnar Myrdal, with the assistance of Richard Sterner and Arnold Rose, *An American Dilemma: The Negro Problem and Modern Democracy* (1944; repr., New York: Pantheon, 1974), 2:1045; Mark Smith, *Social Science in the Crucible: The American Debate over Objectivity and Purpose, 1918–1941* (Durham: Duke University Press, 1994).

[73] Louis Wirth, quoted in Recorder's Notes of the Sub-Committee on Social Science and Values of the Committee on Commissions of Inquiry, Division of the Social Sciences, University of Chicago, 9 February 1949, 1–2, Milton Singer Papers, Special Collections Research Center, University of Chicago (hereafter Singer Papers), box 54.

This question of the relationship between the sponsor and the researcher came to a head in the late 1940s during the congressional debate over whether the social sciences should be included within the purview of what became in 1950 the National Science Foundation. To the dismay of many social scientists, the social sciences were largely excluded from the new foundation on the grounds that their work was more "socialistic" than "scientific."[74]

In 1949, with funding provided by a small grant from the Rockefeller Foundation, the Social Science Research Council sponsored a series of faculty seminars at universities across the country to discuss the relation between "value problems and social science research." By then, as Council President Pendleton Herring explained, most American social scientists recognized that concern about "ethical issues" raised questions not only about their research but also about the application of their findings to "practical problems." Herring thought that social scientists could best "advance an understanding of ethical issues and values problems," not by specifying "the values that should govern human conduct," but rather by analyzing "the process whereby values are determined" and "the circumstances that give rise to conflict or frustration."[75]

At Cornell a faculty seminar discussed the conceptual status of values. It was led by the sociologist Robin M. Williams, Jr., who viewed values as "recurring ideal patterns" that constituted the "structures" of American society.[76] The Cornell researchers, however, stopped short of formulating "any general definition of value," which, they feared, "was likely to be too general to be highly valuable." But they did agree that "all science begins with and rests upon value-elements," that any science that dealt with human behavior had to "confront values" as either its "data" or "actual subject matter," and that the study of values would promote the "convergence" of the several social sciences and their "integration" with the humanities.[77]

---

[74] Samuel Z. Klausner and Victor M. Lidz, eds., *The Nationalization of the Social Sciences* (Philadelphia: University of Pennsylvania Press, 1986); Solovey, "Riding Natural Scientists' Coattails onto the Endless Frontier."

[75] Pendleton Herring to Joseph H. Willits, 28 October 1948; Memo on "Conference on Value Problems and SS Research," 24 June 1949, folder 4728, box 399, series 200, RG 1.1, Rockefeller Foundation Archives, RAC.

[76] Robin M. Williams, Jr. to Pendleton Herring, 23 June 1949, copy in folder 4729, box 400, series 200, RG 1.1, Rockefeller Foundation Archives, RAC. Earlier, at the annual meetings of the American Sociological Society in December 1948, Williams argued that, far from being "epiphenomenal," values, "considered as variables in social systems," were "legitimate and necessary objects for sociological study." Robin M. Williams, Jr., "Some Problems in the Sociological Study of Values," 29 December 1948, 4, 11, copy in folder 4728, box 399, series 200, RG 1.1, Rockefeller Foundation Archives, RAC.

[77] Robin M. Williams, Jr. to Clyde Kluckhohn, 13 October 1950, HUG 4490.5, Kluckhohn Papers; Robin M. Williams, Jr., "Summary of Discussions by the Cornell Value-Study Group," 11 June 1949, 1–2, 6–7, copy in folder 4728, box 399, series 200, RG 1.1, Rockefeller Foundation Archives, RAC. See also Robin M. Williams, Jr., *American Society: A Sociological Interpretation* (New York: Knopf, 1952).

At Harvard a faculty seminar concentrated on "ideology," or "the articulate justification of conduct." Led by the legal historian Robert G. McCloskey, who was interested in the "value-infused" area of American attitudes toward the Supreme Court, the Harvard researchers proposed that the Social Science Research Council sponsor a study of "the process of self-justification" developed for the "free-enterprise society" in late-nineteenth-century America.[78]

And at the University of Chicago a faculty seminar debated whether or not the social sciences could furnish a "basis of ethics." If, as Louis Wirth held, values could not be banished from either social scientists' discourse or from their policy-making, what was implicit could at least be made more explicit. Indeed, Wirth thought that social scientists could help to defuse the Cold War by bringing "out into the open" the values then "at issue" between America and Russia.[79]

In June 1949, each group of researchers prepared a memorandum for a two-day conference in Princeton, New Jersey, that brought together researchers from Cornell, Harvard, and Chicago with representatives from Yale, Rockefeller Foundation officers, and Pendleton Herring. At first, each group defended "its own point of view against that of the others," reported Rockefeller Foundation officer Norman Buchanan, but the "solid front" soon disappeared, as did any "irreconcilable differences" among the groups. After the meeting, one of the researchers who attended told Buchanan that despite "the complexity and diversity of the subject," he had been stimulated by the "opportunity to exchange ideas with persons from other institutions." Yet the Social Science Research Council decided not to pursue the scientific study of values and, in November 1949, returned the unspent portion of its grant to the Rockefeller Foundation. It had not proved "feasible," Pendleton Herring explained, to synthesize the various reports prepared in "a single, overall statement." Moreover, despite general agreement on the importance of social scientists' ongoing study of values, "no obvious person nor obvious mode of attack" then appeared "ready at hand."[80]

---

[78] [Robert McCloskey], "Values," June 1949, 1, 4, 10, 15, 23–25, copy in folder 4729, box 400, series 200, RG 1.1, Rockefeller Foundation Archives, RAC. See also Robert G. McCloskey, "The American Ideology," in *Continuing Crisis in American Politics*, ed. Marion D. Irish (Englewood Cliffs, N.J.: Prentice-Hall, 1963), 10–25.

[79] Recorder's notes, Sub-Committee on Social Science and Values, Committee on Commissions of Inquiry, Division of the Social Sciences, University of Chicago, 9 February 1949, 2; Louis Wirth, "On Making Values Explicit" (1949), in *Louis Wirth on Cities and Social Life*, 157–161, on 161.

[80] Memo on "Conference on Value Problems and SS Research"; Pendleton Herring to Norman S. Buchanan, 7 November 1949; Norman S. Buchanan and Leland C. DeVinney, notes from interview with Pendleton Herring, 10 October 1949, folder 4729, box 400, series 200, RG 1.1, Rockefeller Foundation Archives, RAC.

COMPARING VALUES IN NEW MEXICO

Yet, even before the Social Science Research Council decided against any further pursuit of values, the Rockefeller Foundation awarded the Harvard Department of Social Relations a three-year grant of $100,000 for the scientific study of values, which was renewed for another three years in 1952. As the officer Leland C. DeVinney told the Foundation's trustees, values were "the standards a man lives by," "the criteria which determine his actions." For this reason, DeVinney and his fellow officers considered "the study of values" to be "the most fundamental of all studies of competing cultures."[81]

From 1949 until 1953, thirty-seven fieldworkers, representing Harvard and nine other institutions and practicing a dozen different disciplines, compared the value systems of the Navajo, Zuñi, Mexican-Americans, Mormons, and Texans who lived near Ramah, New Mexico. What came to be known as the Comparative Study of Values in Five Cultures built on Clyde Kluckhohn's long-term, multidisciplinary work in the area. It also reflected his interest in extending researches "beyond the Navaho to encompass a comparative dimension." In addition, the Values Study spoke to Kluckhohn's conviction that "a fairly ambitious empirical investigation of values by social science methods was badly needed."[82]

The researchers' immediate objective was to understand why the values of each culture differed, even though all five cultures had adapted to the same arid environment, responded to the same streams of diffusion from "generalized" American culture, and interacted with each other for at least a generation. In explaining why the values of the five cultures differed, the researchers hoped to develop a "unified theory" of values and a common "set of methods" for studying them.[83]

As Kluckhohn's duties at the Russian Research Center kept him in Cambridge, supervision of the fieldworkers devolved upon John M. Roberts and Evon Z. Vogt, both of whom had already done fieldwork in the area.[84] Because Kluckhohn was adamant that there be no "party line" to which everyone had to adhere, the fieldworkers were permitted to follow their own hunches and leads.[85] Most, however, took as their point of departure one of the two provisional definitions of value that Kluckhohn formulated. In 1948, he defined

[81] Monthly Report to the Trustees, March 1951, folder 4365, box 510, series 200, RG 1.2, Rockefeller Foundation Archives, RAC.

[82] Clyde Kluckhohn, "A Comparative Study of Values in Five Cultures," in E. Z. Vogt, *Navaho Veterans: A Study of Changing Values* (Cambridge: Harvard University Peabody Museum of American Archaeology and Ethnology, 1951), vii.

[83] Evon Z. Vogt and Ethel M. Albert, "The 'Comparative Study of Values in Five Cultures' Project," in *People of Rimrock: A Study of Values in Five Cultures*, ed. Evon Z. Vogt' and Ethel M. Albert (1966; repr., New York: Atheneum, 1970), 1–5.

[84] Vogt, *Fieldwork among the Maya*, 46–52.

[85] Clyde Kluckhohn to Evon Z. Vogt, 11 April 1950, HUG 4490.20, Kluckhohn Papers.

value as "a selective orientation toward experience, characteristic of an individual and/or of a group, which influences the choice between possible alternatives in behavior."[86] Quickly realizing that this definition did not do enough to "set values apart from the totality of culture," Kluckhohn ventured a second definition in *Toward a General Theory of Action* (1951), the "Yellow Book" that Talcott Parsons tried to make Soc Rel's "official doctrine." Kluckhohn now defined value as "a conception, explicit or implicit, distinctive of an individual or characteristic of a group, of the desirable which influences the selection from available modes, means, and ends of action." A value was not just a preference, but a preference that was felt to be justified.[87] Kluckhohn's second definition reduced, but did not completely eliminate, the substantial overlap between value and culture.

In emphasizing evaluation, and in distinguishing the desirable from the desired, Kluckhohn followed John Dewey's lead in *Theory of Valuation* (1939). "Valuations," Dewey had contended, "exist in fact and are capable of empirical observation." Dewey, moreover, had focused on preferential behavior. Valuation thus involved desiring. In so doing, Dewey rejected the "emotivist" stance that values could not be empirically verified because they expressed emotions or attitudes.[88]

Kluckhohn's approach also reflected the influence of the philosopher Charles W. Morris. Morris, a pragmatist, set out to develop the "scientific axiology," or "verifiable theory of preferential behavior," that Dewey had shown to be possible. The aim of such an axiology was to arrive at "laws" that would "tell us who prefers what under what conditions." After giving up his tenured position at the University of Chicago because he did not think he had "much more to gain in straight philosophy work," Morris spent three semesters at Harvard in the early 1950s working on "experiential humanities." In *Varieties of Human Value* (1956), he compared the ways of life of college students in America, China, India, Japan, and Norway. By putting the pragmatist position to

[86] [Department of Social Relations], "Request for a grant of $38,000 per year for five years to make *A Comparative Study of Values in Five Cultures*," December 1948, folder 4364, box 510, series 200, RG 1.2, Rockefeller Foundation Archives, RAC.

[87] Kluckhohn, "Values and Value-Orientations in the Theory of Action," 395; George Caspar Homans, *Coming to My Senses: The Autobiography of a Sociologist* (New Brunswick, N.J.: Transaction Publishers, 1984), 302–303.

[88] Kluckhohn, "Values and Value-Orientations in the Theory of Action," 396–400, 422; John Dewey, "The Field of 'Value,'" in *Value: A Cooperative Inquiry*, ed. Ray Lepley (New York: Columbia University Press, 1949), 64ff; John Dewey, *Theory of Valuation* (Chicago: University of Chicago Press, 1939), 58, 2; Edward A. Purcell, Jr., *The Crisis of Democratic Theory: Scientific Naturalism and the Problem of Value* (Lexington: University Press of Kentucky, 1973), 42–43; Robert B. Westbrook, *John Dewey and American Democracy* (Ithaca: Cornell University Press, 1991), 404–408; J. O. Urmson, "Emotivism," *Encyclopedia of Ethics*, ed. Lawrence C. Becker and Charlotte B. Becker (New York: Garland, 1992), 304–305; Robert F. Berkhofer, Jr., *A Behavioral Approach to Historical Analysis* (New York: Free Press, 1969), 101.

empirical test, Morris hoped to bring "the socio-humanistic disciplines within the scope of the program of unified science."[89]

In 1953, hoping to impart philosophical rigor to the Values Study, Kluckhohn recruited Ethel Albert, whose interests lay in "methodology," "value theory," and other "areas in which philosophy and social science overlap." Reviewing the work of the Values Study, Albert found that researchers defined values in vague, culture-bound, and circular ways. Still, she thought, many of their hypotheses could be tested empirically.[90]

As it turned out, the "loose" tone of the Values Study militated against the development of common methods and a common theory for the social scientific study of values. Kluckhohn himself likened the Values Study to a "series of 'fishing expeditions.'"[91] When researchers met in Flagstaff, Arizona, in September 1954 to discuss plans for the publication of a final report to be published in two volumes in 1959 and 1960, respectively, Rockefeller Foundation officer Charles B. Fahs reported that they took pride in the "modest progress" they had "made in dealing with such a refractory subject." But having "intentionally" made "no effort to force a common approach," they had not arrived at any "clear solutions." Still, Kluckhohn was convinced that the researchers had demonstrated both the feasibility and the significance of the scientific study of values. Observing that values were then "being made explicit on a greater scale" than in any previous period, he noted the parallel between contemporary Americans and the ancient Greeks. Unlike the Greeks, whose "intellectual apparatus afforded no systematic way to deal with the rational and irrational," Americans, thanks to the behavioral sciences, were developing an unprecedented "kind of understanding" for dealing with those opposing categories.[92]

In addition to affording fieldworkers extensive training in both crosscultural and interdisciplinary research, the Values Study issued more than

[89] Charles W. Morris, "Axiology as the Science of Preferential Behavior," in *Value: A Cooperative Inquiry*, 211–222, on 211–212, 219–220, 222; Charles W. Morris to Clyde Kluckhohn, 5 February 1948, 17 April 1949, HUG 4490.5, Kluckhohn Papers; Charles W. Morris and Lyle V. Jones, "Value Scales and Dimensions," *Journal of Abnormal and Social Psychology* 51 (1955): 523; Charles W. Morris, *Varieties of Human Value* (1956; repr., Chicago: University of Chicago Press, 1973), vii–viii, 184.

[90] Ethel M. Albert to Charles B. Fahs, 20 October 1954, folder 110, box 16, series 200, RG 2–1954, Rockefeller Foundation Archives, RAC; Ethel M. Albert, "Theory and Method in the Comparative Study of Values in Five Cultures: An Analysis and Assessment," November 1953, 14, 52, 59, 65, quoted in Willow Roberts Powers, "The Harvard Five Cultures Values Study and Post War Anthropology" (Ph.D. diss., University of New Mexico, 1997), 210–216.

[91] Clyde Kluckhohn, "The Scientific Study of Values," in *Three Lectures. University of Toronto Installation Lectures, 1958* (Toronto: University of Toronto Press, 1959), 31.

[92] Clyde Kluckhohn, quoted in Vogt and Albert, Memo, Flagstaff Conference, 51–52. For assessments of the Values Study, see Nicolas C. Vaca, "The Comparative Study of Values in Five Cultures Project and the Theory of Value," *Aztlan* 12 (1981): 89–120; Powers, "The Harvard Five Cultures Study and Post War Anthropology."

sixty-five papers and monographs. Among the more notable publications were Richard Hobson's study of the accumulation of wealth among the Navajo, Watson Smith and John Roberts's analysis of Zuñi judicial cases, David McAllester's examination of Navajo music, Robert Rapoport's use of projective tests to study the impact of Christian missions among the Navajo, John Roberts's evocation of "the flow of Zuñi life," and Otto von Mering's exploration of value-patterns through focus-group discussions.[93] In addition, Bert Kaplan administered the Rorschach test to Navajo, Mexican-American, Mormon, and Texan informants.[94] Byproducts of the Values Study included Kaspar Naegele's examination of "the main values which constitute the system of American values," and, in "a sort of dry-run for the kind of field research – comparative, collaborative, and addressed to questions of meaning and significance – that [he] would spend the rest of [his] life pursuing," Clifford Geertz analyzed the "differential responses" of the five cultures to such common "problems" as "drought, death, and alcohol."[95]

The two most noticed studies that issued from the Values Study were Evon Z. Vogt's *The Homesteaders* (1955) and John Ladd's *The Structure of a Moral Code* (1957). Vogt identified five "core American values" of the pinto-bean farmers who had migrated from Texas to Ramah in the 1930s: individualism, mastery of nature, faith in the future, a suitable balance between working and "loafing," and a complex combination of feelings of superiority toward their Zuñi, Navajo, and Mexican-American neighbors and feelings of inferiority toward the Mormons. By the mid-1950s, Vogt contended, the Texans' "frontier" values, "precipitates" of their history, had grown "maladaptive" and threatened the survival of their community.[96]

Although John Ladd's research had not been sponsored by the Harvard Values Study, Kluckhohn told Leland C. DeVinney that "the project [was]

[93] Richard Hobson, *Navaho Acquisitive Values* (Cambridge: Harvard University Peabody Museum of American Archaeology and Ethnology, 1954); Watson Smith and John M. Roberts, *Zuñi Law: A Field of Values* (Cambridge: Harvard University Peabody Museum of American Archaeology and Ethnology, 1954); David P. McAllester, *Enemy Way Music: A Study of Social and Esthetic Values as Seen in Navaho Music* (Cambridge: Harvard University Peabody Museum of American Archaeology and Ethnology, 1954); Robert N. Rapoport, Changing *Navaho Religious Values: A Study of Christian Missions to the Rimrock Navahos* (Cambridge: Harvard University Peabody Museum of American Archaeology and Ethnology, 1954); John M. Roberts, *Zuñi Daily Life* (Lincoln: University of Nebraska Laboratory of Anthropology, 1956); Otto von Mering, *A Grammar of Human Values* (Pittsburgh: University of Pittsburgh Press, 1961).

[94] Bert Kaplan, *A Study of Rorschach Responses in Four Cultures* (Cambridge: Harvard University Peabody Museum of American Archaeology and Ethnology, 1954).

[95] Kaspar Naegele, "From de Tocqueville to Myrdal: A Research Memorandum on Selected Studies of American Values" (Cambridge: Harvard University Department of Social Relations, 1949); Geertz, "An Inconstant Profession," 5–6.

[96] Evon Z. Vogt, *The Homesteaders: The Life of a Twentieth-Century Frontier Community* (Cambridge, Mass.: Harvard University Press, 1955). Earlier, in *Navaho Veterans*, Vogt had studied the reintegration into Ramah of fourteen Navajo veterans and one non-veteran after the Second World War.

proud to have had a part of it." In 1951, Ladd, a philosopher who taught at Brown University, spent two months engaging in intensive dialogue, mediated by an interpreter, with the Navajo elder The Son of Many Beads, whose ideas seemed to him "as rationally coherent and systematic as any to be found in the moral codes of our culture." Ladd thought that this dialogue demonstrated "the possibility of a scientific descriptive ethics." Kluckhohn hailed Ladd's work as filling the "void left by American philosophy" after it "abdicated its role as the general critic of abstractions and its function as the integrator of systematic information."[97]

Ultimately, the import of the Values Study depended on the reception of its final report.[98] But Kluckhohn's many commitments and his death in 1960 delayed the publication of the summary statement until 1966, when it appeared as a single volume under the title *People of Rimrock*.[99] As Evon Vogt and Ethel Albert acknowledged in their introduction to the final report, four methodological and conceptual problems plagued the Values Study throughout its brief history. First, the data the fieldworkers collected were not uniform. Second, unable to resolve the "conflict" between "faithful description" of each culture and "cross-cultural comparison," the fieldworkers ended up comparing itemized features from each culture rather than the cultures as wholes.[100] Third, the fieldworkers' discovery of microenvironmental niches, such as those determined by the availability of water, suggested that the adaptations made by each culture to the arid environment of western New Mexico were not wholly determined by their values. And fourth, the fieldworkers' conceptions of values were so broad that values became almost coterminous with culture. As a result, the fieldworkers never were able to "stabilize" the class of phenomena to which the term "value" referred.[101]

Yet, despite what Kluckhohn admitted was the "incompleteness, imprecision, and crudity" of some of its work, the Values Study spawned three promising lines of research.[102] In the first, Ethel Albert modified European

[97] Clyde Kluckhohn to Leland C. DeVinney, 16 January 1957, folder 4366, box 511, series 200, RG 1.2, Rockefeller Foundation Archives, RAC; John Ladd, *The Structure of a Moral Code: A Philosophical Analysis of Ethical Discourse Applied to the Ethics of the Navaho Indians* (Cambridge, Mass.: Harvard University Press, 1957); Clyde Kluckhohn, foreword to *The Structure of a Moral Code*, xiii–xiv; Bruce Kuklick, "Philosophy and Inclusion in the United States, 1929–2001," in *The Humanities and the Dynamics of Inclusion since World War II*, 164–167.
[98] Leland C. DeVinney, notes from interview with Clyde Kluckhohn, 27 March 1958, in unprocessed, Harvard (F-L), series 200, RG 2-GC 1958, Rockefeller Foundation Archives, RAC.
[99] On Kluckhohn's overextension, see Evon Vogt to Clyde Kluckhohn, 15 July 1957, HUG 4490.5, Kluckhohn Papers; Geertz, "An Inconstant Profession," 4.
[100] Vogt and Albert, "The 'Comparative Study of Values in Five Cultures,'" 5, 11–12; Louis Dumont, "On Values," *Proceedings of the British Academy* 66 (1980): 212–215.
[101] Vogt and Albert, "The 'Comparative Study of Values in Five Cultures' Project," 23–24; Theodore D. Graves, review of *People of Rimrock*, *American Anthropologist* 69 (1967): 751.
[102] Kluckhohn, "The Scientific Study of Values," 31–32.

philosophical categories so that they could be applied to nonliterate, non-European cultures. In an attempt to develop a "behavioral scientific and philosophical inquiry in ethics," she classified values in a "logico-semantic" manner designed to be neither culture-bound nor coterminous with culture. Sharply critical of "apriorism" (a priori speculation), Albert insisted that ethical terms and judgments be analyzed in their "conceptual context" – that is, in terms of the "cultural world-view" and the value system of the people who subscribed to them.[103]

In the second line of research, Florence Kluckhohn developed "a systematic conceptual framework" in which she analyzed "variations in culture value orientations," both between and within cultures. Distrustful of "absolutes" and "thinking in simple either-or terms," she strove to cultivate an appreciation of "variation."[104] On the basis of the responses to the questionnaires that she had distributed to approximately twenty persons in each of the five cultures, Kluckhohn constructed a grid comparing "value orientations" in terms of how each culture "patterned" or "rank-ordered" solutions to the common problems of human nature, man's relationship to nature, time, activity, and man's relation to other men. Assisted by Fred Strodtbeck, who had studied interactions among Mexican-American, Mormon, and Texan couples, Kluckhohn compared the "core values" of the five cultures. In *Variations in Value Orientations* (1961), she and Strodtbeck reported that solutions to "common human problems," although "neither limitless nor random," did vary. Every society, moreover, not only had "a dominant profile of value orientations," but had "numerous variant or substitute profiles" as well.[105]

In the third and final line of research, Clyde Kluckhohn compared "value-emphases" in terms of binary oppositions or "distinctive features." He was inspired, in part, by the French anthropologist Claude Lévi-Strauss, who, he believed, was well on the way toward isolating "elementary units" comparable to linguistic phonemes. Lévi-Strauss's method of identifying "significant discontinuities" not only allowed researchers to make explicit "the relations between the elements of a culture pattern," but also pointed the way to a

[103] Albert to Fahs, 20 October 1954; Ethel M. Albert, "The Classification of Values: A Method and Illustration," *American Anthropologist* 58 (1956): 222; Ethel M. Albert to Clyde Kluckhohn, 24 August 1955, HUG 4490.5, Kluckhohn Papers.

[104] Florence Kluckhohn to Donald Biddle, 5 October 1962, HUG(FP) 81.10, Florence Rockwood Kluckhohn Papers, Courtesy of Harvard University Archives (hereafter Florence Kluckhohn Papers); Florence R. Kluckhohn to Kenneth Thompson, 22 October 1963, unprocessed, Harvard University (J-L), subseries 200, series GC 1963, RG 2, Rockefeller Foundation Archives, RAC; Florence R. Kluckhohn, "Dominant and Substitute Profiles of Cultural Orientations," *Social Forces* 28 (1950): 376–393.

[105] Florence R. Kluckhohn and Fred L. Strodtbeck, *Variations in Value Orientations* (Evanston: Row, Peterson, 1961), 3, 10. Several readers thought that Kluckhohn and Strodtbeck had succeeded in putting the anthropological study of values on a scientific basis for the first time. James E. Ritchie, review of *Variations in Value Orientations, Journal of the Polynesian Society* 71 (1962): 284–287; Gordon Allport to Florence Kluckhohn, 29 August 1961, HUG(FP) 81.45, Florence Kluckhohn Papers.

"grammar of culture." [106] Kluckhohn was also inspired by the work of the linguist Roman Jakobson, whose use of "distinctive features" analysis suggested a way in which researchers could go "beyond developing configurational terms," after the manner of Ruth Benedict, to analyzing "whole-culture patterns" in terms of "universal binary dimensions," the existence of which were "independent of particular cultures." Distinctive features had the further advantage of being "rigorous," but without involving the use of statistics. [107]

STEPPING ONTO THE PUBLIC STAGE

By the time of his death of a heart attack in 1960, Kluckhohn had become one of American anthropology's most prominent public intellectuals. As George Peter Murdock put it in an obituary, "If Margaret Mead typifie[d] anthropology to the general public, Clyde Kluckhohn represented the subject to his professional colleagues." Indeed, Kluckhohn was convinced that scientists had a "responsibility to communicate" not only "their personal findings" but "the total scientific outlook" to the educated public. [108]

Kluckhohn first stepped onto the public stage as a public intellectual in 1941 when he joined the historian Rushton Coulborn and the writer John Peale Bishop, two other "thinkers who are prophets too," in a symposium on "The American Culture" organized by the literary intellectual John Crowe Ransom. Kluckhohn began by pointing out that although its "basic elements" were still "largely European," the American "way of life" was "no longer a colonial culture." He identified six "macroscopic features" that distinguished American culture from its European antecedents: biological and cultural heterogeneity, urban and regional patterns, technological and materialistic "orientations," "frontier spirit," "relatively strong trust in 'science' and 'education'" combined with "relative indifference to 'religion,'" and "considerable personal insecurity." Like a host of other American intellectuals between the world wars, Kluckhohn traced the insecurity that many Americans then felt to the poor "fit" between the "theory" and "practice" of their culture. Because Protestantism was "essentially dead" and Roman Catholicism was characterized by what Kluckhohn regarded as "persistent infantile fixations," Americans needed to formulate a "sturdy creed" for the future. He recommended that this new creed

---

[106] Clyde Kluckhohn to Kenneth Setton, 27 October 1959, HUG 4490.6, Kluckhohn Papers; Clyde Kluckhohn, "Culture," in *A Dictionary of the Social Sciences*, 165; Claude Lévi-Strauss, "Social Structure," in *Anthropology Today*, 536; Hymes, "Linguistic Method in Ethnography," 193–194, 207; Dell H. Hymes, "Directions in (Ethno-) Linguistic Theory," *American Anthropologist* 66 (1964): 15, 45n.

[107] Hymes, "Notes toward a History of Linguistic Anthropology," 24; John L. Fischer and Evon Z. Vogt, introduction to *Culture and Life*, 9–11; Fischer, "Linguistic Models and the Study of Culture: Clyde Kluckhohn's Approach," 143–145.

[108] George Peter Murdock, "Clyde Kluckhohn (1905–1960)," *Behavioral Science* 6 (1961): 4; Clyde Kluckhohn to Ralph Brown, 19 July 1956, HUG 4490.5, Kluckhohn Papers.

be informed by "scientific humanism, internationally minded."[109] As a lapsed Protestant who had "flirted" with becoming an Episcopalian priest and had even given some thought to converting to Catholicism, Kluckhohn now stood firmly opposed to revealed religion. Moreover, he was only one of many Protestant and Jewish intellectuals who then worried about the threat that Catholicism posed to "American freedom."[110]

During the Second World War, Kluckhohn took an active part in the annual symposia of the Conference on Science, Philosophy and Religion in Their Relation to the Democratic Way of Life. Founded in 1940 by religiously minded Americans in response to the rise of totalitarianism abroad, the Conference searched for "a consensus concerning the universal character of truth." Although some of its founders, put off by what they regarded as the Conference's "religious" orientation, soon withdrew to form a more secular organization of their own, Kluckhohn found the Conference's emphasis on the relation between "ethical values" and "the democratic way of life" congenial.[111]

The Conference's annual symposia provided Kluckhohn with a forum in which to try out a number of ideas for which he would become better known after the war. The first and foremost was his belief in the American need for a secular religion. Replying to a conference questionnaire in December 1942, Kluckhohn identified the principal "evil" facing "our world" as the "lack of a faith" that "could be believed in by a reasonable man familiar with what we have learned of our world by 'scientific methods.'" Such a naturalistic faith was necessary, Kluckhohn believed, because Americans were sorely in need of "a central, common purpose" not based on "supernatural sanctions."[112] As an anthropologist, Kluckhohn did not deny "the existence of 'absolutes' in and for human conduct," but he did insist that such absolutes be "validated by empirical observation."[113] He saw a "fundamental conflict" between those who, like himself, tried "to understand experience in naturalistic terms" and those who insisted on bringing supernaturalism into the picture.[114]

[109] John Crowe Ransom to Clyde Kluckhohn, 26 November 1940, HUG 4490.3, Kluckhohn Papers; Clyde Kluckhohn, "The Way of Life," *Kenyon Review* 3 (1941): 160–179.
[110] Roe, notes from interview with Kluckhohn; John T. McGreevy, *Catholicism and American Freedom: A History* (New York: Norton, 2003), 166–188.
[111] Van Wyck Brooks, "Conference on Science, Philosophy and Religion in Their Relation to the Democratic Way of Life," in *Science, Philosophy and Religion: A Symposium* (New York: Harper, 1941), 1–2; Ordway Tead, "Survey and Critique of the Conference on Science, Philosophy and Religion," in *Approaches to National Unity*, 785.
[112] Clyde Kluckhohn, reply to questionnaire from the Conference on Science, Philosophy and Religion dated 7 December 1942, Mead Papers, box E59; Clyde Kluckhohn to William D. Geer, 27 January 1943, HUG 4490.5, Kluckhohn Papers.
[113] Clyde Kluckhohn, "Anthropological Research and World Peace," in *Approaches to World Peace*, ed. Lyman Bryson, Louis Finkelstein, and Robert M. MacIver (New York: Harper, 1944), 143–152.
[114] Clyde Kluckhohn, comment on "Some Contributions of Science to the Easing of Group Tensions, by Harry A. Overstreet," in *Approaches to National Unity*, 83.

Second, Kluckhohn envisioned an international world made safe for differences. In "A Declaration of Interdependence: A Creed for Americans as World Citizens," a "manifesto" that he circulated among friends in the winter of 1942–43, he envisioned a postwar world in which people would be guaranteed the right to "live according to their own values and traditions." His new world order thus bore no resemblance to Henry Luce's vaunted American Century, which he regarded as a prescription for "imperialistic American domination of the world." Rather, Kluckhohn demanded that Americans choose between Luce's example of beating "a frightened retreat to some single standard" and reorganizing American culture around the principle of "orchestrated heterogeneity."[115] Here he echoed Margaret Mead's words in the preface to *From the South Seas* (1939): "We are at a crossroads," Mead wrote, "and must decide whether to go forward towards a more ordered heterogeneity, or make a frightened retreat to some single standard which will waste nine-tenths of the potentialities of the human race in order that we may have a too dearly purchased security."[116]

A third point Kluckhohn rehearsed in the wartime conferences was scientific tough-mindedness. Anthropologists, he contended, were "tough-minded" social scientists who insisted upon "the stupidity of any unilinear attack upon the bases for world peace" while criticizing any attempt to view problems "too exclusively in the light of reason." For "the nonlogical elements in action" – sentiments, unconscious assumptions, and other intangibles – could not be ignored.[117] Indeed, Kluckhohn was convinced that the contributions of behavioral scientists – anthropologists, sociologists, and psychologists – "bearing upon the nonrational and irrational aspects of human behavior" would have "the most significance in the long run."[118]

Fourth, Kluckhohn reiterated his belief in the existence of cultural universals. Drawing on material from his fieldwork among the Navajo, he suggested that "the conditions for universal sociopsychological processes" could be found "in the uniformities of human neurological equipment and in the universality of the great dramas of human life (birth, renewed dependency, death)." Although the forms varied culturally, the processes, he maintained, were "identical."[119] Opposed to any international order based on "universal adherence" to

[115] Clyde Kluckhohn, "A Declaration of Interdependence: A Creed for Americans as World Citizens," version 1b, 17 January 1943, HUG 4490.3, Kluckhohn Papers.

[116] Margaret Mead, "1925–1939," in *From the South Seas: Studies of Adolescence and Sex in Primitive Societies* (New York: William Morrow, 1939), xxx–xxxi. "Orchestrated heterogeneity" seems to have been Kluckhohn's own phrasing. Dorothy Lee thought it "particularly felicitous." Dorothy D. Lee to Clyde Kluckhohn, 6 November 1944, HUG 4490.3, Kluckhohn Papers.

[117] Kluckhohn, "Anthropological Research and World Peace," 143–152.

[118] Clyde Kluckhohn, "Implicit and Explicit Values in the Social Sciences Related to Human Growth and Development," *Merrill-Palmer Quarterly* 1 (1955): 139.

[119] Clyde Kluckhohn, "Group Tensions: Analysis of a Case History," in *Approaches to National Unity*, 222–231.

traditional values, Kluckhohn insisted that individuals and groups be "encouraged to fulfill themselves in diverse ways." It was for this reason that he strenuously objected to the notion that the "integration" of mankind could be achieved only if "*all* men" were subordinated "to values which are *all* the same." Specifically, he denounced the claim of "official Christianity" to being "the *only* perfect faith."[120]

Fifth and finally, Kluckhohn prefigured his shift from culture and personality to the social scientific study of values when he held out the hope that anthropologists could arrive at the "major bents" or "single integrating principles" of culture. The key, he thought, lay in working "up from the bottom" and then "dissect[ing] out" the "phenomena of patterning in the explicit culture." Before such "a coherent theory of 'the logics' of any culture" could be "formulated," however, researchers needed to develop "a whole array of new conceptual instruments" that would allow them to test and validate their "assertions about cultural structure."[121]

In pitting America in ideological combat with Russia, the Cold War heightened the urgency that Kluckhohn felt for articulating a new American creed. Such a "positive, clearly defined national faith" seemed to him essential to offset Communism's appeal as a "secular religion."[122] Kluckhohn had become aware of the need for such a creed while in Japan in 1946–47. There, Japanese "of many classes" complained to him of their inability to understand what American democracy stood for.[123]

In 1950, Kluckhohn invoked the example of the Founding Fathers, declaring that the time had come for Americans to "take stock of [their] own position," to state "explicitly what America is" and "what [they] want America to become." He feared that Americans, in arming themselves "with the technology of 1950 . . . but with the ideas of 1850," ran the risk of losing "the cold war and, in the long run, a possible hot war."[124] Kluckhohn's analysis owed a lot to an earlier article, "The Ideological Combat," in which the Russian specialist Geroid Tanquary Robinson spoke of the lag between "American theory" and "American practice." "Without benefit of philosophy," Robinson wrote, "we are backing

---

[120] Clyde Kluckhohn, comment on "Theses on Group Tensions," by Pitirim Sorokin, in *Approaches to National Unity*, 216–217 (emphasis in original); Clyde Kluckhohn, comment on "Some Requisites for Better Understanding between the East and the West," by Taraknath Das, ibid., 297–298 (emphasis in original).

[121] Kluckhohn, comment on "The Problem of Communication between Cultures seen as Integrated Wholes," by Carl J. Friedrich, in *Approaches to National Unity*, 628–634 (emphasis in original).

[122] Clyde Kluckhohn, "Mid-Century Manners and Morals," in *Twentieth Century Unlimited: From the Vantage Point of the First Fifty Years*, ed. Bruce Bliven (New York: Lippincott, 1950), 303–315; reprinted in *Culture and Behavior*, 323–335, on 328–329.

[123] Kluckhohn, *Mirror for Man*, 229, 231–232, 259–260.

[124] Clyde Kluckhohn, "The Dynamics of American Democracy," *Babson Institute of Business Education Bulletin* 2 (1950), no pagination.

tail-first into the future." Americans were "facing the crisis of 1949 with the military equipment of 1950 and the ideological equipment of 1775."[125]

In thus invoking the Founding Fathers, Kluckhohn and Robinson were in the forefront of an "urgent inquiry into national purpose" that took place in the 1950s, an inquiry born of the sense of concern felt by American intellectuals about "American purpose and purposefulness." In their attempts to "discover, define, and invent an American ideology" that would compete with "communist dogma," they held up the Founding Fathers as exemplars of Americans who had a clear sense of national purpose.[126]

The press of his many administrative duties at the Russian Research Center kept Kluckhohn from developing his thoughts about American values until after he stepped down from the directorship in 1954. Even then, he was preoccupied with writing up his material on the Navajo. In 1957, though, an invitation to chart the trajectory of "value changes" in the postwar United States at a Conference on American Values and the American Performance hosted by the M.I.T. Center for Institutional Studies gave him an opportunity to reflect on, if not synthesize, an enormous mass of material on shifts in American values over the course of the previous generation.

In Kluckhohn's view, American values, which had been "remarkably stable" from the colonial period through the early twentieth century, had changed so dramatically since the Depression that he thought that he detected the emergence of "a 'new' set of values." It now seemed to him that the "Puritan ethic," with "its demands for exhibitionistic achievement, unbridled 'individualism,' and competition," was giving way to David Riesman's "other-directed" personality. Here Kluckhohn echoed Riesman, William H. Whyte, Jr. (author of *The Organization Man* [1956]), and other commentators who had announced the decline of the Puritan (or Protestant) ethic. Taking its place were sensitivity "to the approval of others," the desire "to be liked," and respect for "the standards of [one's own] group." Like Riesman, Kluckhohn welcomed "today's kind of conformity" as marking "a step toward more genuine individuality." He traced postwar conformity to Americans' dawning "realization of the uncertainty of things" and "recognition of the implacable necessities of gigantic corporations."[127]

Commenting on Kluckhohn's paper, the historian Richard Hofstadter observed how the shift from the Puritan ethic to an "ethic of adjustment" had spawned political apathy. To Hofstadter, the "socialized, adjusted personality" of Americans in the 1950s made a mockery of whatever notions critics of

---

[125] Geroid Tanquary Robinson, "The Ideological Combat," *Foreign Affairs* 27 (1949): 525–539.

[126] John W. Jeffries, "The 'Quest for National Purpose' of 1960," *American Quarterly* 30 (1968): 451–470.

[127] Clyde Kluckhohn, "Have There Been Discernible Shifts in American Values during the Past Generation?" in *The American Styles: Essays in Value and Performance*, ed. Elting E. Morison (New York: Harper 1958), 145–217, on 152, 204, 185, 187, 189. A shorter version of Kluckhohn's essay, entitled "The Evolution of Contemporary American Values," was published in *Daedalus* 87 (1958): 78–109.

American "competitive individualism" had held during the Depression. Hofstadter viewed the prospect of a "fully employed, incredibly rich, well-adjusted, complacent, and apathetic" postwar America as "a tacky Utopia."[128]

In the lively discussion that followed Hofstadter's commentary, no one dissented from Kluckhohn's prediction that never "again in the foreseeable future" would Americans place the Puritan ethic "at the very center of their value system." No one dissented, either, from Kluckhohn's assessment that the Puritan ethic, once almost as integral to the American character as "the Hapsburg lip," had disappeared.[129]

Kluckhohn said his last word on changing American values in a review of Max Lerner's *America as a Civilization*. Although he praised Lerner's synthesis of the findings of a legion of social scientists who had studied America since 1950, Kluckhohn criticized Lerner's assumption that "core American values" had remained fairly stable. He also regretted that Lerner had dealt only "briefly and cursorily" with "the [American] quest for new standards." Reiterating "the importance of primitive concepts and of abstract premises," Kluckhohn declared that "the first fundamental shift in American values in our history" had taken place since the Depression. "The most essential thing to say about life and thought" in postwar America, he insisted, was "that some value premises have already changed radically and others are in rapid process of change."[130]

Kluckhohn's evidence, however, did not convince Talcott Parsons that Americans' "fundamental values" had changed since the Depression.[131] In a manuscript left unfinished at the time of his death in 1979, Parsons and coauthor Winston White credited Kluckhohn with having provided "probably the best empirical survey and interpretive analysis [of American values] in the recent literature," but they criticized his "blanket categorization" of values for obscuring "the fact of pattern stability."[132]

Nor was the sociologist Seymour Martin Lipset convinced by the evidence Kluckhohn marshaled. When Lipset examined "the role of values" in the evolution of America from the colonial period until the early 1960s, he saw no evidence that "the achievement motive" and "the Protestant ethic" were "dying." The "historical record," he wrote in *The First New Nation* (1963),

---

[128] Richard Hofstadter, "Commentary: Have There Been Discernible Shifts in American Values during the Past Generation?" in *The American Style*, 354–357.

[129] Elting Morison, "The Course of the Discussion," in *The American Style*, 407.

[130] Clyde Kluckhohn, "Shifts in American Values," review of *America as a Civilization*, *World Politics* 11 (1959): 251, 254–256. Lerner feared that Kluckhohn had "overdone any emphasis of" his on the "stability" of values. *America as a Civilization*, he pointed out, was "riddled with 'revolution' concepts." Max Lerner to Clyde Kluckhohn, 31 July 1959, HUG 4490.6, Kluckhohn Papers.

[131] Talcott Parsons to Clyde Kluckhohn, 5 December 1957, HUG 4490.20, Kluckhohn Papers.

[132] Talcott Parsons and Winston White, "The Values of American Society," unpublished ms., 2–3, HUG(FP) 42.45.2, box 8, Parsons Papers. Earlier, White had taken issue with Kluckhohn's interpretation in *Beyond Conformity* (New York: Free Press, 1961).

suggested "more continuity than change with respect to the main elements in the national value system."[133]

KLUCKHOHN'S LEGACY

Kluckhohn's position at Harvard, where the first American studies program had been founded in 1937, prominence as a public intellectual, and frequent attempts to chart American values all influenced American studies scholars. With the exception of Margaret Mead, Kluckhohn's work was more "helpful" than any of the other "strictly ethnological analyses of culture" that Richard Huber had consulted while undertaking "an historical-sociological study of the idea of success in America." It was certainly "the most accurate." Louis Filler asked Kluckhohn whether his "experience with the [Russian Research] Center furnishe[d] any suggestions for comparable treatment with respect to the United States." William G. McLoughlin named Kluckhohn "the man for the job" of persuading "rather hostile" graduate students in the Harvard's American Civilization program that they had something to learn from the newer social sciences, in particular anthropology. George W. Pierson had been "impressed" by both the bibliography and "the range and variety of attack" of Kluckhohn's 1957 paper on shifts in American values. So, too, had David Potter.[134]

Kluckhohn's concern with fact and value was paralleled, within American studies, by Henry Nash Smith's search for a method that would overcome the separation between "social facts" and "aesthetic values." As Smith pointed out in 1957, content analysis and the other research techniques then favored by many social scientists made it difficult "to deal with the states of consciousness embodied in serious literature." At the same time, those humanists who, like the New Critics, analyzed texts apart from their contexts "cut aesthetic value loose from social fact." Thinking that the culture concept "embrace[d] the concepts 'society' and 'art,'" Smith turned to anthropology to resolve this dualism, only to discover that when anthropologists studied complex societies, they adopted positivistic assumptions about the relation of fact to value.[135]

[133] Seymour Martin Lipset, "Socialism and Sociology," in *Sociological Self-Images: A Collective Portrait*, ed. Irving Louis Horowitz (Beverly Hills: Sage, 1969), 143–175, on 162–163, 173–174; Seymour Martin Lipset, *The First New Nation: The United States in Historical and Comparative Perspective* (New York: Basic Books, 1963), 102–103, 123–124.

[134] Richard Huber to Clyde Kluckhohn, 12 March 1952; Louis Filler to Clyde Kluckhohn, 21 November 1952; William G. McLoughlin to Clyde Kluckhohn, 16 April 1953; David M. Potter to Clyde Kluckhohn, 30 October 1957, HUG 4490.5, Kluckhohn Papers; George W. Pierson to Clyde Kluckhohn, 20 December 1957, HUG 4490.6, Kluckhohn Papers.

[135] Henry Nash Smith, "Can 'American Studies' Develop a Method?" *American Quarterly* 9 (1957): 197–208; reprinted in *Locating American Studies: The Evolution of a Discipline*, ed. Lucy Maddox (Baltimore: Johns Hopkins University Press, 1999), 1–12, on 10–11; Giles Gunn, "American Studies as Cultural Criticism," in *The Culture of Criticism and the Criticism of Culture* (New York: Oxford University Press, 1987), 158–159.

The split between social fact and aesthetic value that Smith wished to over-come tore apart an interdisciplinary American studies seminar on American values held at the University of Pennsylvania in 1954–55. Led by the business historian Thomas Cochran and the literary historian Robert Spiller, faculty members and students engaged in "an interdisciplinary study" of American values from 1890 until 1915. A "deep schism," however, soon pitted those who, like Cochran, were "primarily concerned with the nature of society itself as the embodiment of a culture" against those who, like Spiller, were "con-cerned with the expression of the culture in mass media or individual art." It eventually got to the point that neither the humanists nor the social scientists in the seminar were willing "to admit the validity of the [others'] method." Where the social scientists insisted on subjecting literary masterpieces to content anal-ysis, the humanists demanded special treatment for the same works.[136]

Kluckhohn's distinction between overt and covert culture left a longer legacy among American studies scholars, although their understanding of covert cul-ture sometimes retained the connotation of secretiveness that had impelled him to substitute "implicit" for "covert." When a faculty seminar at the University of Minnesota discussed "covert culture" in 1955, the participants defined the concept as consisting of those "traits of culture rarely acknowledged by those who possess them" because they were either "ignore[d]" or "repress[ed]."[137] David Potter invoked the distinction between overt and covert culture in an informal seminar held at the Center for Advanced Study in the Behavioral Sciences in the spring of 1958. Where the historian "working with change" attended to "the overt, consciously stated," the historian "working with con-stants" attended to "the covert and implicit." When it came to studying the Civil War, the historian who attended to the overt would accordingly empha-size the explicit "points of disagreement" between the North and the South; the historian who attended to the covert, by contrast, the "implicit points of agree-ment."[138]

Potter was an example of a historian who shared Kluckhohn's self-consciousness. In his 1954 book *People of Plenty*, he spoke of how "in its headlong, *ad hoc* assault upon the record of human experience, history [had] built its narrative upon an extraordinary mélange of unstated premises, random

---

[136] Thomas C. Cochran to Clyde Kluckhohn, 14 February 1957, HUG 4490.7, Kluckhohn Papers; Syllabus, American Civilization 900, Fall Term 1954–1955, "Problems in American Civiliza-tion: Values as Index to Twentieth Century American Civilization," folder 233, box 36, series 200, RG 2–1955, Rockefeller Foundation Archives, RAC; Robert E. Spiller, "Value and Method in American Studies," in *The Second Dimension: Studies in Literary History* (New York: Macmillan, 1963), 207–208.

[137] Bernard Bowron, Leo Marx, and Arnold Rose, "Literature and Covert Culture," in Leo Marx, *The Pilot and the Passenger: Essays on Literature, Technology, and Culture in the United States* (New York: Oxford University Press, 1988), 127–138. Bowron et al.'s article was first pub-lished in the *American Quarterly* in 1957.

[138] David M. Potter, quoted in transcript of informal seminar on comparative civilizations, Center for Advanced Study in the Behavioral Sciences, spring 1958, copy in Singer Papers, box 96.

assumptions, untested hypotheses, and miscellaneous notions about the nature of man, the workings of society, and the causation of historical change." Historians had not "recognized," much less "confronted," the "anomalous nature of [their discipline's] conceptual foundation." Nine years later, as a member of the Committee on Historical Analysis of the Social Science Research Council, Potter argued that historians must systematically examine the "implicit assumptions" that shaped their "explicit data" in the committee's report, *Generalization and the Writing of History.*[139]

The historian Robert F. Berkofer, Jr., who found "valuable" anything written by Kluckhohn, attempted to reorient the practice of history around "the new knowledge of men's behavior" then issuing from the behavioral sciences. In *A Behavioral Approach to Historical Analysis* (1969), he proposed, that in reconstructing the cultures of men in the past, historians adopt the idea of a continuum running from explicit, self-conscious culture at one end to unconscious culture at the other. Berkhofer, however, went beyond Kluckhohn when he emphasized the importance of the culture concept for "causation" as well as for "analysis."[140]

Kluckhohn also influenced several prominent cultural historians, which is hardly surprising, since as Donald Kelley tells us, anthropology "has always served as a source of inspiration if not a model" for cultural history. In 1968, the historian of slavery David Brion Davis suggested that if American historians paid more attention to the "distinctions and relationships between cultures and subcultures" explored in the publications of the Comparative Study of Values in Five Cultures, they might be more cautious in generalizing about "what 'Americans' believed or thought." Davis, who had begun his study of of slavery "with little awareness of its cultural dimension," soon discovered that the controversy "involved values and associations deeply embedded in the heritage of American culture." In *The Problem of Slavery in the Age of Revolution* (1976), he identified a new humanitarian sensibility or "moral perception" at the heart of opposition to slavery.[141]

John William Ward drew on Kluckhohn's 1942 article in which he formulated a general theory of "myths and rituals" in treating Andrew Jackson as a "symbol" for how antebellum Americans "avoid[ed] the disadvantages of both

[139] David M. Potter, *People of Plenty: Economic Abundance and the American Character* (Chicago: University of Chicago Press, 1954), x; David M. Potter, "Explicit Data and Implicit Assumptions in Historical Study," in *Generalization in the Writing of History: A Report of the Committee on Historical Analysis of the Social Science Research Council,* ed. Louis Gottschalk (Chicago: University of Chicago Press, 1963), 178–194.

[140] Berkhofer, *A Behavioral Approach to Historical Analysis,* 1, 5, 84n, 135, 160; Thomas L. Haskell, "Farewell to Fallibilism: Robert Berkhofer's *Beyond the Great Story* and the Allure of the Postmodern," *History and Theory* 37 (1998): 347, 355.

[141] Donald R. Kelley, "The Old Cultural History," *History of Human Sciences* 9 (1996): 102; David Brion Davis, "Some Recent Directions in American Cultural History," *American Historical Review* 73 (1968): 696–707, on 698, 705; David Brion Davis, "Intellectual Trajectories: Why People Study What They Do," *Reviews in American History* 37 (2009): 148–159.

extreme civilization and savage nature." From the writings of Kluckhohn and other anthropologists Ward derived the notion that man's ability to make himself "by making culture" was what set mankind apart from "other animals." Defining culture as "the organization of social experience in the minds of men made manifest in symbolic action," Ward urged cultural historians to look on history as "the study of past culture."[142] Yet, in a review of Ward's 1969 collection of essays, *Red, White, and Blue*, Alan Trachtenberg asked whether culture history informed by the culture concept had not "run its course." For, given the upheavals of the 1960s, American society could no longer be presumed to be "a whole society, based on 'widely shared values.'"[143]

The folklorist Alan Dundes, who was, like Kluckhohn, interested in both psychoanalysis and structuralism, echoed Kluckhohn when he insisted that cultural relativism "must not preclude the recognition and identification of transcultural similarities and potential universals." Kluckhohn's conviction that biological, psychological, and sociological "givens" were "manifested in myth" suggested to Dundes the possibility that fieldwork could empirically verify "a theory of universal symbolism." Kluckhohn's writings on worldview reinforced Dundes's belief that in folklore "implicit worldview principles and themes" were often made "explicit." In a parallel to Kluckhohn's search for "elemental units" as the cultural equivalents of the phoneme, Dundes searched for "oicotypes" (minimal structural units) in folklore. Perhaps Kluckhohn's interest in a people's "unstated assumptions" inspired Dundes's interest in "folk ideas," or "traditional notions that a group of people have about the nature of man, of the world, and of man's life in the world." In any event, Dundes assigned to the folklorist the "task" of identifying "the various underlying assumptions held by members of a given culture."[144]

Kluckhohn's search for distinctive American values, which paralleled searches for the American character by anthropologists, historians, and

[142] John William Ward, *Andrew Jackson: Symbol for an Age* (New York: Oxford University Press, 1955), 13; John William Ward, "Looking Backward: *Andrew Jackson: Symbol for an Age*," in *The Historian's Workshop*, ed. L. P. Curtis, Jr. (New York: Knopf, 1970), 207, 219n; John William Ward, "History and the Concept of Culture," in *Red, White, and Blue: Men, Books, and Ideas in American Culture* (Oxford: Oxford University Press, 1969), 3–17, on 9, 16–17.

[143] Alan Trachtenberg, "The Relevance of the Historian," review of *Red, White, and Blue*, by John William Ward, *Carleton Miscellany* (1970): 109–110.

[144] Alan Dundes, "Earth-Diver: Creation of the Mythopoeic Male," *American Anthropologist* 64 (1962): 1032–1051, on 1036, 1048; Alan Dundes, "The Psychological Study of Folklore in the United States, 1880–1980," *Southern Folklore* 98 (1991): 97–120, on 108–109; Alan Dundes, "Folk Ideas as Units of Worldview," *Journal of American Folklore* 84 (1971): 93–103; Alan Dundes, "From Etic to Emic Units in the Structural Study of Folktales," *Journal of American Folklore* 75 (1962): 95–105; Alan Dundes, "Structuralism and Folklore," *Studia Fennica* 20 (1976): 75–93; Alan Dundes, "Thinking Ahead: A Folkloristic Reflection of the Future Orientation in American Worldview," *Anthropological Quarterly* 42 (1969): 53–71, on 53–54; Simon J. Bronner, "Introduction: The Analytics of Alan Dundes," in *The Meaning of Folklore: The Analytical Essays of Alan Dundes*, ed. Simon J. Bronner (Logan: Utah State University Press, 2007): 1–50.

American studies scholars, reflected not only the Cold War, which pitted the United States in an ideological conflict against the Soviet Union, but also the postwar backlash against cultural relativism, which fueled a search for cultural universals or common denominators.[145] If, in John Higham's words, the "collapse of the idea of progress" during and after the Second World War, "together with the terrible anxieties and rigidities created by the Cold War," impelled intellectual historians and American studies scholars to search for "an ideological foundation, a moral anchor," it impelled Kluckhohn's search for an orchestrated heterogeneity that would at once take the place of attenuated supernatural sanctions and diminish Communism's appeal as a secular religion.[146] Like so many other members of the liberal American intelligentsia, Kluckhohn sought refuge from ethnic and religious parochialism in affirmations of the universalism of science.[147] And like so many other intellectuals of the interwar generation, Kluckhohn was sharply critical of the "competitive individualism" enshrined in the American value system.[148] Where Kluckhohn parted company from many, though by no means all, intellectuals of his generation was in his receptivity to the "publicly standardized 'group values'" and desire for "respectable and stable group security." Instead of worrying about the flaccidity of a predominantly middle-class and unprecedentedly affluent society, he welcomed its alleged "conformity" as signaling greater tolerance for diversity. At least in Kluckhohn's case, this was perhaps less reasoned scientific judgment than affirmation of faith.

Quite aware of the fuzziness or woolliness of the concept of national character, Kluckhohn left culture and personality in the early 1950s for the social scientific study of values. His taking up the study of values signaled a shift of interest from socialization to the tacit assumptions and organizing principles of "implicit culture." For help in studying values scientifically, Kluckhohn turned to linguistics, which provided him with a "tough-minded" analytic framework in which he could compare cultures without risk of ethnocentrism. His turn to linguistics reflected, in part, the impact of the new "rigorism" in the social sciences, for linguistics was, to his mind, the most rigorously scientific of the humanities.[149]

For Kluckhohn, the scientific study of values continued Sapir's and Benedict's inquiries into the selectivity of cultures. If, as he wrote in 1957, most

[145] George Peter Murdock, "The Common Denominator of Cultures," in *The Science of Man in the World Crisis*, 123–143; Wolf, *Anthropology*, 20–23; Novick, *That Noble Dream*, 283–285.
[146] John Higham, "The Study of American Intellectual History" (1961), in *Writing American History: Essays on Modern Scholarship* (Bloomington: Indiana University Press, 1970), 67–68.
[147] David A. Hollinger, "Ethnic Diversity, Cosmopolitanism, and the Emergence of the American Liberal Intelligentsia," in his *In the American Province: Studies in the History and Historiography of Ideas* (Bloomington: Indiana University Press, 1985), 56–73.
[148] Dennis Wrong, "The Functional Theory of Stratification: Some Neglected Considerations," *American Sociological Review* 24 (1959): 780.
[149] Parsons, "Culture and Social System Revisited," 45.

anthropologists agreed that the "distinctiveness of cultures rests upon their principles of selectivity, in terms of which certain 'paths' are consistently selected from the many that are 'objectively' open," those principles could be understood only by grasping "the key values of each culture" and seeing them "in the context of those broad panhuman values that are universals or near-universals."[150] The Harvard Values Study, he believed, had "proven" the "feasibility" of describing "the preferred paths of behavior that take their direction from varying conceptions of the desirable."[151] In a world in which "varied peoples and cultures now find themselves in uncomfortably close contact," the "primary intellectual function of anthropology" was now "to supply, on a small scale and in a scientific manner, the perspective which philosophy [had] traditionally attempted [to supply] in a global and unscientific manner."[152] For Kluckhohn, "to speak of values" was "one way of saying that human behavior is neither random nor solely instinctual," but that it was instead anchored.[153] In studying values, he joined the debate over what constituted the "good life" in postwar America, thereby serving not only as a public intellectual but as a public moralist as well.

As we have seen, in following a representative sample of Navajo children over time, Kluckhohn became one of the pioneers of long-term field research in American anthropology. He criticized Margaret Mead for the absence of an historical perspective in her *And Keep Your Powder Dry* and Geoffrey Gorer for his failure to steep "himself in the facts of American history." Moreover, in 1952, he told Milton Singer, "I couldn't agree with you more when you say 'History is an essential to adequate comparison of cultures as comparison is to the writing of history.'"[154] As we shall see in the next chapter, anthropologists took a historical turn after 1945 as they became increasingly interested in studying peasants, complex societies, and even civilizations. Just as anthropologists acknowledged the indispensability of history in comparing cultures, so, too, did they press the necessity of comparison upon professional historians.

[150] Clyde Kluckhohn, foreword to *Cultural Foundations of Education: An Interdisciplinary Exploration*, Theodore B. H. Brameld (New York: Harper, 1957), xiii.
[151] Clyde Kluckhohn, "The Scientific Study of Values and Contemporary Civilization," *Proceedings of the American Philosophical Society* 102 (1958): 473.
[152] Clyde Kluckhohn, "Developments in the Field of Anthropology in the Twentieth Century," *Journal of World History* 3 (1957): 777.
[153] Kluckhohn, "The Scientific Study of Values and Contemporary Civilization," 474.
[154] Clyde Kluckhohn and Florence Kluckhohn, review of *And Keep Your Powder Dry*, by Margaret Mead, *American Anthropologist* 45 (1943): 623–624; Clyde Kluckhohn, review of *The American People*, by Geoffrey Gorer, *Psychosomatic Medicine* 10 (1948): 304–305; Clyde Kluckhohn to Milton Singer, 28 November 1952, 4490.6, Kluckhohn Papers.

5

America as a Civilization

In *America as a Civilization* (1957), Max Lerner, a former journalist and pundit who was teaching American civilization at Brandeis University, asserted that "for good or ill, America is what it is – a culture in its own right, with many characteristic lines of power and meaning of its own, ranking with Greece and Rome as one of the great distinctive civilizations of history." Lerner's choice of title exposed him to the quips of friends who, astonished, asked, "Do we have one?" For the book's title begged an issue that had long troubled American intellectuals: the distinctiveness, intrinsic worth, and creativity of American culture. By 1957, few observers, either at home or abroad, would have objected to Lerner's claim that there was a distinctive American culture. Why, though, did Lerner feel the need to proclaim America a civilization rather than just a culture? His answer was that when a "culture," which he defined, following contemporary anthropological usage, as a "design for living" or "set of blueprints for a society," had not only grown "highly complex" but also "cut a wide swath in history in the minds of men," then one searched "for a term more highly charged with the overtones of these meanings." Civilization was just such a term. For it connoted a "way of life" and "world view" that had left "a deep imprint" on human experience. Moreover, because of its connotations of "total pattern" and "total impact," civilization was an even more holistic term than was culture.[1]

In treating civilization as a subset of culture, rather than as its foil or antithesis, Lerner reflected the transvaluation of the term civilization that had taken place not only among American anthropologists but also among American intellectuals in general since the 1920s. In the aftermath of the First World War, anthropologists such as Edward Sapir had drawn a sharp contrast between an external, instrumental, and even spurious "civilization" and an

---

[1] Max Lerner, *America as a Civilization: Life and Thought in the United States Today* (New York: Simon and Schuster, 1957), 58–61; Max Lerner, "Our Country and Our Culture," in *America and the Intellectuals: A Symposium* (New York: Partisan Review, 1953), 65.

internal, expressive, and genuine "culture."[2] The Second World War, however, taught anthropologists what Eric Wolf described as "a lesson in cultural dominance on a scale never seen before." As a result, they repressed their romantic impulses, tempered their cultural relativism, and became more interested in the "on-going process of civilization." At the same time, anthropological horizons rapidly expanded beyond North America to the rest of the world, and the sites of anthropologists' fieldwork shifted from "primitive isolates" to peasantries, complex societies, and even historic civilizations, as anthropologists played prominent parts in interdisciplinary area studies of the non-Western parts of the world.[3]

America as a Civilization also testified to what John Higham described as "the general postwar reconciliation between America and its intellectuals." In the 1920s, intellectuals had commonly condemned American civilization for such failings as worship of the machine, spiritual poverty, hypocrisy, and colonial mentality. The gulf in American thought between culture and civilization, however, narrowed during the 1930s and 1940s. Amid the heightened cultural nationalism of the Great Depression, intellectuals searched for "the roots of American culture" that would explain how the American people hung together while complex societies elsewhere fragmented. With the onset of the "democratic revival" of the late 1930s, many of these same intellectuals began to view American culture as a normative democratic culture. "No idea," neither "democracy" nor "the American way of life," Charles and Mary R. Beard declared in 1942, "expresse[d] the American spirit so

---

[2] Edward Sapir, "Culture, Genuine and Spurious," in *Selected Writings of Edward Sapir in Language, Culture and Personality*, ed. David G. Mandelbaum (1949; repr., Berkeley: University of California Press, 1963), 308–331; Eric R. Wolf, *Anthropology* (1964; repr., New York: Norton, 1974), 18–19.

[3] Wolf, *Anthropology*, 13, x–xii; Sidney Mintz, "The Localization of Anthropological Practice: From Area Studies to Transnationalism," *Critique of Anthropology* 18 (1998): 128–129; George W. Stocking, Jr., "'Do Good, Young Man': Sol Tax and the World Mission of Liberal Democratic Anthropology," in *Excluded Ancestors, Inventible Traditions: Essays Toward a More Inclusive History of Anthropology*, ed. Richard Handler (Madison: University of Wisconsin Press, 2000), 179; David G. Mandelbaum, "The Study of Complex Civilizations," in *Current Anthropology: A Supplement to Anthropology Today*, ed. William L. Thomas, Jr. (Chicago: University of Chicago Press, 1956), 203–225. By the mid-1950s, according to Robert F. Murphy, a majority of American anthropologists were no longer studying primitive peoples. Robert F. Murphy, "Introduction: A Quarter Century of American Anthropology," in *Selected Papers from the "American Anthropologist," 1946–1970*, ed. Robert F. Murphy (Washington: American Anthropological Association, 1976), 6. On the central role that anthropologists played in area studies of the non-Western parts of the world, see William Nelson Fenton, *Area Studies in American Universities* (Washington, D.C.: American Council on Education, 1947), 82; Julian H. Steward, *Area Research: Theory and Practice* (New York: Social Science Research Council, 1950); Robert E. Ward and Bryce Wood, "Foreign Area Studies and the Social Science Research Council," *Items* 28 (1974): 54–55; Robert A. McCaughey, *International Studies and Academic Enterprise: A Chapter in the Enclosure of American Learning* (New York: Columbia University Press, 1984).

coherently, comprehensively, and systematically as [did] the idea of civilization."[4]

If the Beards' assertion that civilization had become the keyword of American discourse seemed premature in 1942, the word was on the lips of many American intellectuals only ten years later. In introducing the *Partisan Review* symposium "Our Country and Our Culture," William Phillips and Philip Rahv announced that "the wheel [had] come full circle," that the United States was no longer that "raw and unformed land of promise from which men of superior gifts like [Henry] James, [George] Santayana, and [T. S.] Eliot departed," and that American intellectuals no longer viewed Europe as a "sanctuary" offering "that rich experience of culture which inspired and justified a criticism of American life." Indeed, by 1952, in the eyes of many American intellectuals, it was now the United States, and no longer Europe, that was the "protector of Western civilization." By then, programs dedicated to the study of what was variously called American studies and American civilization were proliferating on campuses at home and abroad. At the core of these programs was the notion that America now possessed a high culture equal to, if not more vital than, the more historic high cultures of Europe to which educated Americans had long been in the habit of unfavorably comparing their own culture.[5]

Yet, in taking up the study of peasants (many of whom had recorded histories), complex societies, and historic civilizations, anthropologists felt handicapped by their lack of experience in working with written documents. Customarily, they had worked with what Alfred Kroeber termed "made" documents – materials elicited in "face-to-face interviews" and "observations." Their reliance on such made documents often led to the publication of what Clyde Kluckhohn admitted were "needlessly a-historical" ethnographies.[6] As anthropologists turned toward history, they learned how to use written documents, to adopt more diachronic approaches, and even to enter into collaborations with historians.[7] They also moved closer to historians and other humanists by taking up the study of values, emphasizing creativity, using expressive documents, and evaluating cultures as better or worse. In the

[4] John Higham, "Beyond Consensus: The Historian as Moral Critic" (1962), in *Writing American History: Essays on Modern Scholarship* (Bloomington: Indiana University Press, 1970), 144; Charles A. Beard and Mary R. Beard, *The American Spirit: A Study of the Idea of Civilization in the United States* (New York: Macmillan, 1942), 672.

[5] "Editorial Statement," in *America and the Intellectuals*, 1–5.

[6] A. L. Kroeber, "The Delimitation of Civilizations," in *An Anthropologist Looks at History* (Berkeley: University of California Press, 1963), 4; A. L. Kroeber, "History and Anthropology in the Study of Civilizations," ibid., 160; Clyde Kluckhohn, "Anthropological Studies of Human Relations," paper given at a Conference on Research in Human Relations sponsored by the Rockefeller Foundation in February 1953, 5, folder 99, box 56, series 6, RG 3, Rockefeller Foundation Archives, RAC.

[7] McKim Marriott, "An Indian Civilization Course," in *The Teaching of Anthropology*, ed. David G. Mandelbaum, Gabriel W. Lasker, and Ethel M. Albert (Berkeley: University of California Press, 1963), 214.

process, their notion of culture as a way of life moved closer to the venerable humanistic conception of culture emphasizing sophistication and refinement.

Alfred Kroeber and Robert Redfield both played prominent parts in promoting anthropologists' historical turn. Before his death in 1960, Kroeber adumbrated a "natural history of civilizations" in which he construed civilizations as "historical growths" amenable to empirical study. Much as Carolus Linnaeus had paved the way for Charles Darwin by classifying the flora and fauna of the world, so would Kroeber pave the way for the comparative study of civilizations by compiling a roster of the civilizations of the world. Likening his attempt to delimit civilizations in space to historians' periodization of historical phenomena in time, Kroeber extended the concept of style from fashion and the fine arts to intellectual achievements, organic life, and, ultimately, "total cultures." He also pressed historians to engage in more comparative work. Where Kroeber approached civilizations from the top down, Redfield approached them from the bottom up. In the aftermath of the Second World War, Redfield, who had previously shown little interest in history and viewed civilization as the antithesis of culture, acquired a newfound interest in history and a new appreciation for the civilizing process. Before his death in 1958, he outlined a "social anthropology of civilizations" in which he construed civilizations as the products of conversations between literati with their "little traditions" and cosmopolitan intellectuals with their "great traditions." With the help of grants from the Ford Foundation, Redfield brought together humanists and social scientists in seminars at the University of Chicago to fuse textual and contextual approaches toward the study of the historic civilizations of China, India, and Islam. The convergence between Kroeber's natural history approach and Redfield's social anthropological approach to the study of civilizations paved the way for such pioneer works in world history as William McNeill's *The Rise of the West* (1963), Marshall Hodgson's *The Venture of Islam* (1974), and Eric Wolf's *Europe and the People without History* (1982).

CULTURAL HISTORIAN OF ABORIGINAL NORTH AMERICA

Although Alfred Louis Kroeber's multifaceted career spanned six decades, it was "remarkably 'of a piece.'" Throughout, he pursued what he described as a "prevalently macroscopic, long-range, historical" approach, "purely on the cultural level, impersonal, and non-psychological." As a "humanistically tinged natural historian," Kroeber classified anthropology as "only partly social science." Its roots, he held, lay far deeper in the natural sciences and the humanities.[8] Indeed, in his view, anthropology combined natural scientists' concern with "scientific description, narration, and classification" with humanists' concern with "discernment, formulation, comparison, and history of values."

---

[8] Theodora Kroeber, *Alfred Kroeber: A Personal Configuration* (Berkeley: University of California Press, 1970), vii; A. L. Kroeber to Bernard Berelson (draft), 16 September 1956, Kroeber Papers, reel 10; A. L. Kroeber to Sol Tax, 13 August 1959, Kroeber Papers, reel 12.

Then, too, anthropologists studied "culture," long the subject matter of the humanities.[9]

As we have seen, Kroeber staked anthropology's claim to being a "third field" between biology and history in his 1917 exposition of a "superorganic" conception of culture. Yet, until that field was "surveyed, fenced, and improved," Kroeber was content to classify anthropology as a "historical science" that aimed at knowing "the relations of social facts to the whole of civilization." Because civilization was "an entity in itself," history, as Kroeber defined it, was concerned with the "interrelations" of civilization, not with its component individuals. Uninterested in either individual creativity or agency, Kroebert abandoned the search for both origin and causation to search instead for patterns.[10]

From the early 1900s until 1918, when he completed most of the *Handbook of the Indians of California* (the publication of which financial exigencies delayed until 1925), Kroeber mapped the culture areas of aboriginal California. He grouped more than fifty Native American "nations" into four "culture provinces," each of which had a "center," or "hearth," where "the most intensive development or greatest specialization of culture" had occurred. Although the four provinces occupied quite different natural environments, none was environmentally determined. Rather, Kroeber located the antecedents of each province in cultural phenomena. Given the absence of recorded history and time depth in archaeology, the "geographical factor" necessarily loomed larger in Kroeber's version of California culture history than did the "element of time." Still, Kroeber insisted that in trying to "reconstruct" a record of events in the *Handbook*, he was writing "history." Yet, by history, Kroeber here meant 'process,' recurrence, and the search for regularities in history, not historians' concern with chronology, or the ordering of events.[11]

In his next book, *Cultural and Natural Areas of Native North America*, largely completed by 1931 but not published until 1939, Kroeber synthesized the culture history of the North American continent. He delineated eighty-four "growth[s] of culture" in each of which culture was "relatively uniform."

---

[9] A. L. Kroeber, *The Nature of Culture* (Chicago: University of Chicago Press, 1952), 57; A. L. Kroeber to P. W. Bridgman, 18 May 1956, Kroeber Papers, reel 10.

[10] A. L. Kroeber, "Eighteen Professions," *American Anthropologist* 17 (1915): 283–288, on 283–284, 287; Thomas Buckley,"'The Little History of Pitiful Events'; The Epistemological and Moral Contexts of Kroeber's Californian Ethnology," in *"Volksgeist" as Method and Ethic: Essays on Boasian Ethnography and the German Anthropological Tradition*, ed. George W. Stocking, Jr. (Madison: University of Wisconsin Press, 1996), 263.

[11] A. L. Kroeber, *Handbook of the Indians of California* (Washington: U.S. Government Printing Office, 1925), v 898–899, 918; James L. Newman, "The Culture Area Concept in Anthropology," *Journal of Geography* 70 (1971): 9. See also A. L. Kroeber, "American Culture and the Northwest Coast," *American Anthropologist* 25 (1923): 1–20; A. L. Kroeber, "Native Culture in the Southwest," *University of California Publications in American Archaeology and Ethnology* 23 (1928): 375–398. My account of Kroeber as a cultural historian draws on Harold E. Driver, "The Contribution of A. L. Kroeber to Culture Area Theory and Practice," *Indiana University Publications in Anthropology and Linguistics* 18 (1962): 1–28.

Grouping those growths into six larger culture areas, Kroeber then correlated the culture areas with natural areas formed by drainage, elevation, landform, climate, and plant cover. Although he found numerous "correspondences" between the culture and natural areas, Kroeber concluded that the "causes of culture" were cultural, not environmental. Well aware of the indeterminate boundaries of the cultural areas he delineated, Kroeber coined the concept of "culture climax" to designate "peak[s]" of intensity. Because he considered the richer, "high-intensity" cultures to be more highly differentiated than "low-grade" cultures, Kroeber thought it possible to develop an "objective measure" of cultural intensity.[12]

From 1934 until 1938, Kroeber's search for such an objective measure of cultural intensity spawned the ambitious, although ultimately abortive, University of California Culture Elements Survey. Kroeber, who had long encouraged his students to develop more "objective" (that is to say, statistical) methods with which to delimit culture areas, used a coefficient developed by Harold Driver to quantify "cultural relationships." Kroeber's collaboration with Driver, in turn, attracted the notice of the Polish anthropologist Stanislaw Klimek, who spent two years in Berkeley on a fellowship from the Rockefeller Foundation devising statistical techniques with which to "analyze" aboriginal California cultures. Although Klimek's statistical work largely validated Kroeber's more intuitive classifications of California's culture areas, it also revealed that the "data" were too "uneven" to allow "reliable and large-scale comparison."[13]

To ensure the "empirical definability" of culture elements, Kroeber secured money from the Rockefeller Foundation to dispatch thirteen fieldworkers who, armed with survey questionnaires, recorded the presence or absence of cultural traits among some 254 Indian tribes west of the Rocky Mountains. Instead of laying the foundation for an authoritative taxonomy of North American cultures, as Kroeber hoped, the resulting surveys were largely dismissed by other anthropologists as mere inventories of cultural traits.[14] While a chastened

---

[12] A. L. Kroeber, *Cultural and Natural Areas of Native North America* (Berkeley: University of California Press, 1939), 1–2, 205, 222–223, 225.

[13] Forrest E. Clements, Sara M. Schenck, and T. K. Brown, "A New Objective Method for Showing Special Relationships," *American Anthropologist* 28 (1926): 585–604; Harold E. Driver and A. L. Kroeber, "Quantitative Expression of Cultural Relationships," *University of California Publications in American Archaeology and Ethnology* 31 (1932): 211–256; Stanislaw Klimek, "The Structure of California Indian Culture," *University of California Publications in American Archaeology and Ethnology* 37 (1935): 1–70; Amanda L. Golbeck, "Quantification in Ethnology and Its Appearance in Regional Culture Trait Distribution Studies," *Journal of the History of the Behavioral Sciences* 16 (1980): 228–240.

[14] A. L. Kroeber to Edmund E. Day, 2 October 1935, Kroeber Papers, reel 6; A. L. Kroeber, "Culture Element Distributions: XI. Tribes Surveyed," *Anthropological Record* 1 (1939): 435–440; Kroeber, *The Nature of Culture*, 263–264; Driver, "Contribution of A. L. Kroeber to Culture Area Theory and Practice," 17–18; Clyde Kluckhohn, quoted in transcript from the Rockefeller Foundation Conference on Research in Human Relations, 241, folder 100, box 11, series 910, RG 3.1, Rockefeller Foundation Archives, RAC.

Kroeber quickly turned to other interests, Harold Driver continued work on a statistical method for delineating culture areas.[15]

In 1935, Kroeber's use of inferential techniques in historical reconstruction precipitated an open clash with Franz Boas.[16] In a review of Boas's book *Primitive Art*, Kroeber labeled his former teacher a "spiritual physicist" who, "with one or two brief and hesitant exceptions," did not do "history."[17] For Kroeber, doing history meant engaging in what he called "descriptive integration"; that is, situating cultural phenomena in their spatial and temporal contexts.[18] Rejecting Kroeber's "interpretation" of his work, Boas pointed out that, ever since his 1887 article on "The Study of Geography," he had aligned himself with researchers "motivated by the affective appeal of a phenomenon that impresses us as a unit" and had endeavored to understand culture as a "historical growth." Yet, at the same time, Boas demanded "a high degree of probability" for the indirect evidence on which anthropologists relied to reconstruct the histories of cultures without written histories. To Boas, Kroeber's reliance on intuition, and the less rigorous demands he made of his evidence, seemed an "Epicurean" position, not a scientific one.[19]

In response, Kroeber explained that what he was about was to make the best case he could for "a valid phenomenological approach" that preserved phenomena "intact" to complement the "analytic" scientific approach that "decompose[d]" the same phenomena. Although both approaches were valuable, Kroeber considered the analytic method better suited to inorganic phenomena and the historical method to cultural phenomena.[20]

AN INDUCTIVE SPENGLER

After completing *Cultural and Natural Areas of Native North America*, Kroeber turned his attention to historic civilizations with written histories. In *Configurations of Culture Growth*, which he completed in 1938 but whose length (846 pages) delayed its publication until 1944, Kroeber investigated why "cultural florescences" – aesthetic and intellectual accomplishments – tended to "cluster" in both space and time. His inspiration in this undertaking was *The Decline of the West*, in which Oswald Spengler delimited eight historic

[15] H. E. Driver and W. C. Massey, "Comparative Studies of North American Indians," *Transactions of the American Philosophical Society* 47 (1957): 165–460; Newman, "The Culture Area Concept in Anthropology," 11.

[16] David Bidney, "The Contribution of A. L. Kroeber to Contemporary Anthropology," in *Theoretical Anthropology*, 2nd ed. (New York: Schocken, 1967), 472.

[17] A. L. Kroeber, review of *Primitive Art*, by Franz Boas, *American Anthropologist* 31 (1929): 139–140.

[18] A. L. Kroeber, "History and Science in Anthropology," *American Anthropologist* 37 (1935): 539–569; part of which is reprinted in *The Nature of Culture*, 63–65.

[19] Franz Boas, "History and Science in Anthropology: A Reply," *American Anthropologist* 38 (1936): 137–141; reprinted in *Race, Language, and Culture* (1940; repr., New York: Free Press, 1966), 305–307; Franz Boas to A. L. Kroeber, 5 August 1935, Boas Papers.

[20] A. L. Kroeber to Franz Boas, 28 August 1935, Boas Papers.

cultures, then intuitively characterized their fundamental patterns. Western civilization, for example, was "Faustian," characterized by relentless striving. Although Kroeber admired Spengler's marked "powers of characterization" and insistence that a culture be understood "in its own terms," he balked at what he regarded as Spengler's "needless exaggerations, dogmatism, vehemence of conviction, blind spots, [and] inability to balance evidence." In addition, Kroeber rejected Spengler's fatalism. Where, for Spengler, "civilization" marked the terminal stage in the life history of a culture, for Kroeber, it marked the "florescence" of a culture.[21]

Kroeber set out to substitute empirical investigation for Spengler's intuition. "Cheerfully renounc[ing the] search for causes," he traced the "order," "death," and "symmetry" of the "growth curves" of the historic civilizations of the world. Had civilizations, he asked, been alike in producing their "highest manifestations"? To compare the florescences of civilizations empirically, Kroeber examined their "roster[s] of genius," their most talented and creative individuals as identified in encyclopedias, textbooks, and other sources of "conventional opinion." Although he canvassed an enormous amount of material on philosophy, science, philology, sculpture, painting, drama, literature, and music (but not religion, since he was not sure he could estimate the growth of an activity that depended on "emotional tendency"), Kroeber did not discover anything "cyclical, regularly repetitive, or necessary" in the history of civilizations. Nor was he able to identify the "causes" of the rise and fall of civilizations. Rather, the conclusions he arrived at were more modest: "cultures do not necessarily age or progress, but they do undergo variations in vigor"; cultures, moreover, vary in vigor owing to their "adherence" to a "set of patterns" that, once fulfilled, "exhaust" themselves; exhaustion leads to either the "breakdown" of the civilization or the "abandonment" and "reformulation" of the exhausted patterns. Finally, in "higher civilizations," aesthetic and intellectual achievements not only overlap but "preponderantly realize themselves in temporary bursts." Because of the absence of any "more precisely denotative terms," Kroeber employed such "recurring metaphors" as "growth," "saturation," "realization," "pulse," and "dissolution," but he deliberately avoided use of the term "cycle."[22]

Configurations of Culture Growth received mixed reviews from anthropologists and historians who, although impressed by Kroeber's erudition, were dismayed by the tentativeness of his findings and objected to some features of his "macroscopic" approach. Clyde Kluckhohn complained that Kroeber's lack of interest in human agency precluded any "satisfactory theory of culture change." The Islamist G. L. Della Vida objected to Kroeber's cultural determinism. Whether or not "freedom of will" was true, Della Vida reminded Kroeber, the historian had to act "as if [he] believed in it." The historian Rushton

[21] A. L. Kroeber, *Configurations of Culture Growth* (Berkeley: University of California Press, 1944), 825–828; A. L. Kroeber, *Style and Civilizations* (Ithaca: Cornell University Press, 1957), 84.
[22] Kroeber, *Configurations of Culture Growth*, 761–763, 822.

Coulborn regretted the "powerful curb" that inhibited Kroeber's "subjective, intuitive interpretations" of his material.[23] Kroeber, however, was unwilling to concede that he had somehow "failed" because he had not "emerged" from his researches "with something bigger." He told Leslie White, who accused him of confounding history (the "temporal sequence of unique events") with evolution (the "temporal sequence of forms"), that he had "had a fine time satisfying an inner need." Later, however, Kroeber admitted that *Profiles of Culture Growth* would have been a better title for his book.[24]

Publication of *Configurations of Culture Growth* provoked an exchange of letters between Kroeber and the philosopher-turned-anthropologist David Bidney. Kroeber, who claimed to be "really unread in formal philosophy," declared that he was more interested in the "formal" causes of cultural phenomena than in such "efficient" causes as individual agency. He described his approach as one in which the "time element" was held "constant for a moment." Kroeber admitted that anthropologists "must recognize in [their] analysis of culture something like 'creativity.'" By applying the historical method to the subject matter of the natural sciences, and by rooting values in nature, Kroeber went beyond the neo-Kantian philosopher of history Heinrich Rickert.[25]

NATURAL HISTORIAN OF CIVILIZATIONS

Kroeber's contacts with the Rockefeller Foundation, standing as the dean of American anthropology, and emeritus status after 1946 all allowed him to preside over developing interest in the comparative study of civilizations and cultures. As we shall see, he formulated concepts that helped anthropologists and historians apprehend civilizations as wholes, organized conferences on comparative history, and rounded up financial support for promising comparative historians.[26]

Even before retirement, Kroeber added a new wrinkle to anthropologists' understanding of diffusion when he formulated the concept of "stimulus diffusion," or the transmission of "the idea of the complex or system" rather than its "concrete content." As a case in point, Kroeber cited Sequoyah's development of the Cherokee alphabet. Without exposure to the Roman

---

[23] Clyde Kluckhohn, review of *Configurations of Culture Growth*, *American Journal of Sociology* 51 (1946): 336–341; G. L. Della Vida, review of *Configurations of Culture Growth*, *Journal of the American Oriental Society* 65 (1945): 207–210; G. L. Della Vida to A. L. Kroeber, 20 February 1946, Kroeber Papers, reel 34; Rushton Coulborn, review of *Configurations of Culture Growth*, *American Historical Review* 51 (1945): 92–95.

[24] A. L. Kroeber to Leslie A. White, 11 September 1945, Kroeber Papers, reel 7; A. L. Kroeber to Leslie A. White, 11 February 1946, White Papers, box 2; A. L. Kroeber, "Configurations, Causes, and St. Augustine," *American Anthropologist* 53 (1951): 281.

[25] A. L. Kroeber to David Bidney, 26 March 1945, Kroeber Papers, reel 7; A. L. Kroeber to David Bidney, 11 May 1953, Kroeber Papers, reel 9; A. L. Kroeber to David Bidney, 18 December 1946, Kroeber Papers, reel 7.

[26] A. L. Kroeber to Clark Kerr, 20 May 1953, Kroeber Papers, reel 9.

alphabet, Kroeber suggested, Sequoyah "would certainly never had had the objective or goal of a system of writing arise in his mind." Stimulus diffusion, then, combined "development within a culture" and "influence from outside." Its occurrence, as Sequoyah's case illustrated, was "inferred" from its "effects."[27]

In 1946, Kroeber revived the concept of the *Oikoumenê* (ecumene), which the ancient Greeks had used to designate "the inhabited," that "web of culture growth" stretching from China in the east to Gibraltar in the west. Within the ecumene, "people lived in cities in organized states, plowed their fields and raised cattle, worked iron, and knew letters." Also within the ecumene, new "cultural materials" and "ways of thinking" were propagated, "sometimes rapidly, almost like a wave or pulsation." "Primitive" cultures within the ecumene, moreover, coalesced through "selective reduction," either preserving "old elements largely discarded elsewhere" or doing "without elements which their retardation [made] them unable or unwilling to accept." Kroeber proposed that the term ecumene designate the "total area reached by traceable diffusion influences from the main higher centers of Eurasia." Could the history of "higher civilization," he wondered, be written as "a unitary process, as a single, large-scale, long-term event"?[28]

After being coaxed out of retirement by Clyde Kluckhohn to teach at Harvard in 1947–48, Kroeber taught at Columbia from 1948 until 1952. Living on the East Coast allowed Kroeber to get to know three men who shared his interest in "macrohistory," all of whom, he thought, were "aiming at essentially the same goal" as he was.[29] The first man was the philosopher F. S. C. Northrop, who taught at Yale. Although Kroeber welcomed Northrop as the first "Anglo-Saxon" philosopher to concern "himself with culture in the concrete," he did not share Kluckhohn's high opinion of *The Meeting of East and West*. Northrop's book, Kroeber commented, was "a programmatic thesis book with a problem and a solution." Northrop had written not so much a "natural history of civilizations" as a book revolving "around a dualism of principles" and "slanted by a desire to head off world catastrophe."[30]

The second man was the sociologist Pitirim Sorokin, who taught at Harvard. In his four-volume *Social and Cultural Dynamics* (1937–41), Sorokin did not delimit civilizations in either space or time, but rather traced the development of three "supersystems" – the "ideational," the "idealistic," and the "sensate" – that, he believed, had predominated in fairly uniform succession in the

[27] A. L. Kroeber, "Stimulus Diffusion," *American Anthropologist* 42 (1940): 1–20; reprinted in *The Nature of Culture*, 344–357.

[28] A. L. Kroeber, *The Ancient Oikoumenê as a Historic Culture Aggregate: The Huxley Memorial Lecture for 1945* (London: Royal Anthropological Institute of Great Britain and Ireland, 1946); reprinted in *The Nature of Culture*, 379–395.

[29] A. L. Kroeber to F. S. C. Northrop, 2 October 1947, Kroeber Papers, reel 7.

[30] F. S. C. Northrop, *The Meeting of East and West: An Inquiry Concerning Human Understanding* (New Haven, Conn.: Yale University Press, 1947); A. L. Kroeber, review of *The Meeting of East and West*, *American Anthropologist* 49 (1947): 306–309; Kroeber, *Style and Civilizations*, 111.

development of civilizations. According to Sorokin, the Western world was then in the twilight of a sensate (this-worldly, utilitarian, relativistic) dispensation that had dominated it since the sixteenth century. Kroeber found Sorokin more "stimulating in the flesh" than his "inflated if not turgid" writing suggested. And, for a sociologist, Sorokin commanded "a great deal of actual history." Still, in Kroeber's view, Sorokin's "systematizing approach" precluded any treatment of civilizations as "historic entities" that had both unity and integration.[31]

The third man was the English metahistorian Arnold J. Toynbee. In the first six volumes of *The Study of History* (1934–39), Toynbee sketched a universal history that featured twenty-odd "civilizational entities." Awed by the "staggering mass of Toynbee's varied and subtle historical material," Kroeber praised his "endeavor to grapple empirically" with a problem that Spengler had only "intuited," the delimitation of civilizations. Toynbee not only dealt "with concrete material," but "test[ed] his hypotheses step by step against evidence." And like Kroeber, he treated "events and personalities" as "expressions or indices." Yet, though he agreed with Toynbee that civilizations, and not nation-states, were the "intelligible field of historical study," Kroeber was put off by Toynbee's public guise as a prophet. Still, he urged his fellow anthropologists to familiarize themselves with *The Study of History* so that they might overcome their "timidity" toward dealing with "documented," as opposed to "self-recorded," material. It was precisely this timidity that kept anthropologists from entering "the fertile domain of comparison" – a field that historians, with the conspicuous exception of Toynbee, had shown "little inclination to occupy."[32]

In February 1948, after by a "very stimulating but all too short" session with Northrop and Sorokin, Kroeber proposed to his old friend, the physicist J. Robert Oppenheimer, director of the Institute for Advanced Study, that the Institute play host to a small group of scholars who were interested in promoting the comparative study of civilizations at a meeting timed to coincide with Toynbee's residence there on a fellowship from the Rockefeller Foundation. Kroeber believed that such a conference would promote the cause of

[31] Pitirim A. Sorokin, *Social and Cultural Dynamics*, 4 vols. (1937; repr., New York: Bedminster Press, 1962); A. L. Kroeber to Arnold J. Toynbee, 20 April 1948, Kroeber Papers, reel 8; Kroeber, *Style and Civilizations*, 132–135. Sorokin, in turn, criticized Kroeber for the "vagueness" of some of the concepts in *Configurations of Culture Growth*, use of the clustering of genius as an index of cultural creativity, and failure to distinguish both between sensate and ideational "cultures and periods." Still, Sorokin thought that "the bulk of Kroeber's procedures and results" coincided with his own results. Pitirim A. Sorokin, *Social Philosophies of an Age of Crisis* (Boston: Beacon Press, 1950), 260–266.

[32] A. L. Kroeber, review of *The Study of History*, by Arnold J. Toynbee, vols. 1–6, *American Anthropologist* 45 (1943): 294–299; reprinted in *The Nature of Culture*, 373–378. Toynbee considered Kroeber the "most illuminating and helpful, as well as the most generous and kindly" of his many critics. Arnold J. Toynbee to A. L. Kroeber, 17 February 1960, Kroeber Papers, reel 45.

comparative history by "defining the relations of our basic concepts." Stimulated by this meeting, which took place in April 1948, Kroeber returned to Harvard to give two lectures on "Civilizations as a Field of Comparative History": the first entitled "Spengler and Predecessors"; the second, "Toynbee and His Successors."[33]

A second conference, organized at the initiative of the Dutch historian Jan Romein, took place at the Institute for Advanced Study in May 1949. Romein distinguished "theoretical history," which compared "developments" and "concepts" in different times and places, from "practical history," which dealt with subjects having a temporal or spatial "unity."[34] The theme of this second conference was the "Interpretation of History." Accordingly, the conferees discussed the morphology of civilizations, the distinction between the "repetitive" and the "non-repetitive" in history, and "pattern" if not "rhythm" in the "succession of events." After Toynbee discussed how "prophets" beheld in "encounters between civilizations" opportunities for "creating something new on the plane of Religion," the conferees then addressed five questions that Kroeber had circulated in advance. All five pertained to his natural history of civilizations. Did the search for recurrent forms and processes in civilizations, construed as "natural, empirical segments of history," necessitate the use of such metaphorical terms as "cycle," "wave," "pendulum-beat," and "fixed duration"? Which term – "culture," "society," "events," or "psychology and character" – best captured the "total forms" of civilizations? Did the natural history of civilizations rule out attention to individuals "except as exemplifications of superindividual currents or formations"? What were the criteria for delimiting civilizations? Finally, could civilizations be construed as "style-assemblage[s]" or "superstyle[s]" characterized by "a one-way and limited course"?[35]

Among those who attended the May 1949 conference was the German émigré musicologist Curt Sachs. Sachs's attempt to formulate "a philosophy of how styles grow and change" in *The Commonwealth of Art* (1946) piqued Kroeber's curiosity about how far scholars could formulate "regularity" in terms of "recurrent growth," "saturation," and "disintegration of style patterns." Convinced that "the basic problems of art styles" were also "problems of cultural anthropology," Kroeber looked forward to a fruitful collaboration between art historians and anthropologists in which art historians would

[33] A. L. Kroeber to J. Robert Oppenheimer, 27 February 1948, Kroeber Papers, reel 7; Kroeber to Toynbee, 20 April 1948.

[34] Jan Romein to A. L. Kroeber, 5 January 1949, Kroeber Papers, reel 8; A. L. Kroeber to David H. Stevens, 7 February 1949, folder 2543, box 263, series 200, RG 1.2, Rockefeller Foundation Archives, RAC; Jan Romein, "Theoretical History," *Journal of the History of Ideas* 9 (1948): 53–64, on 54–55, 58.

[35] Arnold J. Toynbee, abstract of "Encounters between Civilizations," Kroeber Papers, reel 45; Rushton Coulborn, rapporteur, "Report on a Conference on The Interpretation of History," 12–13 May 1949, folder 2544, box 264, series 200, RG 1.2, Rockefeller Foundation Archives, RAC.

contribute their "richer humanism" and "sensitively trained perceptiveness"; anthropologists, their "genuine natural science discipline."[36]

Also attending the May 1949 conference was another German émigré, the philosopher of history Paul Schrecker. In *Work and History: An Essay on the Structure of Civilization* (1948), which the Rockefeller Foundation supported with grants-in-aid, Schrecker construed civilizations as "integrations of results of human work" distinguished by the correspondence of six "provinces": the state, science, religion, aesthetics, the economy, and language.[37]

In addition, the historian Ralph E. Turner, who taught at Yale, attended the conference. In a session devoted to the cultural approach of history at the annual meetings of the American Historical Association in 1939, Turner employed an anthropological "frame of reference" to examine the "industrial city" as a "center of cultural change." Two years later, in *The Ancient Cities* and *The Classical Empires*, the first two volumes of a projected six-volume history of *The Great Cultural Traditions*, Turner traced the diffusion of cultural traits from the great cities of Mesopotamia, India, Egypt, and Crete to the European continent, their coalescence in "the Western High Intellectual Tradition," and their "imperial phase and decline" down to the sixth century A.D. Supported by grants-in-aid from the Rockefeller Foundation, Turner was then working on a book on "The Meaning of the Twentieth Century."[38]

Serving as the rapporteur of the conference was Rushton Coulborn, an Englishman who taught at Atlanta University. Coulborn hoped to place universal history on firmer footing by replacing Toynbee's religious "prejudices" with "critically established data" informed by anthropology. He had embarked on a history of "how civilization began" in seven "primary" civilizations. Unlike Kroeber, Coulborn thought that "causes" could be discovered in history.

---

[36] A. L. Kroeber, review of *The Commonwealth of Art: Style in the Fine Arts, Music, and Dance,* by Curt Sachs, *American Anthropologist* 49 (1947): 485–487; Kroeber to Toynbee, 20 April 1948.

[37] John Marshall, notes from interview with Paul Schrecker, 2 November 1942, folder 650, box 54, series 200, RG 1.1, Rockefeller Foundation Archives, RAC; Paul Schrecker, prospectus for book (1944), folder 651, box 54, series 200, RG 1.1, Rockefeller Foundation Archives, RAC; Paul Schrecker, *Work and History: An Essay on the Structure of Civilization* (Princeton, N.J.: Princeton University Press, 1948).

[38] Ralph E. Turner, "The Industrial City: Center of Cultural Change," in *The Cultural Approach to History,* ed. Caroline F. Ware (New York: Columbia University Press, 1940), 228–242; Ralph E. Turner, *The Great Cultural Traditions.* Vol. 1: *The Ancient Cities;* Vol. 2: *The Classical Empires* (New York: McGraw-Hill, 1941); Grant Action RF 48081, 18 June 1948, folder 4040, box 473, series 200, RG 1.2, Rockefeller Foundation Archives, RAC. In 1951, Turner was appointed chairman of the editorial board planning the UNESCO (United Nations Educational, Scientific, and Cultural Organization) multivolume *Cultural History of Mankind.* Gilbert Allardyce, "Toward World History: American Historians and the Coming of the World History Course," *Journal of World History* 1 (1990): 27–28, 32–36.

He expected that one of these causes would explain the "rise and fall" of civilizations.[39]

The May 1949 conference generated enough interest in comparative history for a third conference to be held at the Institute for Advanced Study in October 1950. Sponsored by the American Council of Learned Societies and the Rockefeller Foundation, and chaired by Kroeber, the conference discussed "uniformities in history." Eight papers, all prepared in advance, inquired into whether the "methods of feudalism" – notably, vassalage and fief-holding – had been "applied" anywhere outside Europe. The conferees concluded that Japan was the only non-European civilization in which feudal elements were also present. To the revised versions of the papers published in 1956 under the title *Feudalism in History*, Coulborn contributed a long essay in which he analyzed feudalism as a "developmental uniformity."[40]

Although Kroeber was encouraged by the outcome of the third conference, the American Council of Learned Societies decided against the further pursuit of comparative history. If comparative history was to be pursued, it would be under different auspices.

STUDENT OF STYLE

In addition to organizing conferences on the comparative study of civilizations, Kroeber pressed historians to compare more. In a paper delivered at the annual meeting of the American Historical Association in December 1951, he invited historians to join him in a "comparative attack" on "civilizations as wholes" and "uniformities in history" by enumerating the criteria by which civilizations could be delimited. These included discontinuity in time and space; salient differences of language, religion, politics, armed forces, economy, or technology; and, Kroeber's preference, "style." By style, Kroeber had in mind not only the fields of fashion and the fine arts, but also intellectual activities that exhibited "historical behavior." Kroeber favored style because the activities it encompassed were the most "overtly 'creative,'" the most "markedly qualitative," and the "most transient on the whole."[41]

Kroeber's interest in style stemmed from at least four sources. The first was his long-standing interest in what the study of fashion could reveal about

[39] Rushton Coulborn, "Survival of the Fittest in the Atomic Age," *Ethics* 57 (1947): 236; Rushton Coulborn to A. L. Kroeber, 2 June 1951, Kroeber Papers, reel 20; Rushton Coulborn, "Causes in Culture," *American Anthropologist* 54 (1952): 112–116; Rushton Coulborn, *The Origin of Civilized Societies* (Princeton, N.J.: Princeton University Press, 1959), 185, 383, 364.

[40] Charles E. Odegaard to Charles B. Fahs, 6 April 1950; John Marshall, "Conference on Uniformities in History," 6 November 1950, folder 2544, box 264, series 200, RG 1.1, Rockefeller Foundation Archives, RAC; Rushton Coulborn, ed., *Feudalism in History* (Princeton, N.J.: Princeton University Press, 1956), 3–4, 185; Clifford Geertz, "Politics Past, Politics Present: Some Notes on the Uses of Anthropology in Understanding the New States," in *The Interpretation of Cultures: Selected Essays* (New York: Basic Books, 1973), 329.

[41] A. L. Kroeber, "The Delimitation of Civilizations," *Journal of the History of Ideas* 14 (1953): 264–275; reprinted in *An Anthropologist Looks at History*, 3–17.

regularities in history. In an article published in 1919, he reported that he had discovered an "underlying pulsation" in European women's dress fashion over the course of the previous century that suggested that, despite fashion's well-known capriciousness, "the major proportions of dress change with a slow majesty." This "regularity in social change" attested to "the principle of civilizational determinism" because it had so little to do with "the fortuitous appearance of personalities gifted with this taste or that faculty." Then in a 1940 article co-authored with Jane Richardson, Kroeber traced the basic dimensions of women's dress over three centuries. He found that such "primary features" as the length and width of skirts alternated "with fair regularity." The "near-regularity in periodicities," in turn, pointed to the existence of a "basic pattern" toward which European culture "tended as an ideal." When studied as super-organic phenomena, fashion styles exemplified order, regularity, and recurrence in civilization.[42]

Archaeology was a second source of Kroeber's interest in style. In 1916, after sorting the potsherds he had collected at a number of Zuñi sites along the lines of differences in color and decorative techniques, Kroeber developed a seriation series that he converted into a temporal sequence with which archaeologists could date artifacts. In 1942, he coined the term "horizon style" to describe the rough chronology that could be derived from the distribution of the stylistic features of material culture.[43]

Language was yet a third source of Kroeber's interest in style. "Every human language," he held, had a "patterned style" better known as "grammar." Although the speakers of any language were largely unaware of them, grammatical principles could be "discovered" and "formulated." Although "never total," the "coherence" of any grammar exceeded any "catalogue of [the] random items" of the language. To be sure, cultures were "larger, more varied and complicated sets of phenomena" than were languages; they were "more substantive and less autonomous" as well. Still, Kroeber thought that the "structure" of a culture, like the structure of a language, could be described "in terms of an over-all patterning."[44]

[42] A. L. Kroeber, "On the Principle of Order in Civilization as Exemplified by Changes of Fashion," *American Anthropologist* 21 (1919): 235–263, on 257–258, 260–261; A. L. Kroeber, "Study of Cultural Phenomena," 25 August 1927, transcript of the proceedings of the Hanover Conference, 15–30 August 1927, 220–234, folder 700, box 66, series 3.6, Laura Spelman Rockefeller Memorial, RAC; A. L. Kroeber and Jane Richardson, "Three Centuries of Women's Dress Fashions: A Quantitative Analysis," *University of California Anthropological Records* 5 (1940): 111–153.

[43] A. L. Kroeber, "Zuñi Potsherds," *Anthropological Papers of the American Museum of Natural History* 18 (1916): 1–37; A. L. Kroeber, *Peruvian Archaeology in 1942* (New York: Viking Fund, 1944); Gordon R. Willey and Jeremy A. Sabloff, *A History of American Archaeology*, 2nd ed. (San Francisco: Freeman, 1980), 56–57, 95–96, 173–174; Bruce G. Trigger, *A History of Archaeological Thought* (Cambridge: Cambridge University Press, 1989), 200–202.

[44] Kroeber, *Style and Civilizations*, 106–107; Dell H. Hymes, "Alfred Louis Kroeber: Linguistic Anthropologist," in *Essays in the History of Linguistics* (Amsterdam: John Benjamins, 1983), 245–272.

Art was the fourth and most important source of Kroeber's interest in style. His doctoral dissertation had been on Arapaho decorative art, and, after his retirement, he often talked to his wife and children about a book on art that he wanted to write. While teaching at Columbia, he had had long conversations with art historian Meyer Schapiro, whom he invited to give a paper on "Style" at the 1952 Wenner-Gren Symposium on Anthropology Today. In a paper widely considered to be one of the highlights of the conference, Schapiro defined "style" as "a manifestation of the culture as a whole, the visible sign of its unity." Yet Schapiro thought that more insight into "the principles of form construction and expression" was required before an adequate "theory of style" could be formulated.[45]

Kroeber adumbrated his own theory of style in *Style and Civilizations* (1957), the published version of the Messenger Lectures on the Evolution of Civilization that he had delivered the preceding year at Cornell. Defining "style" as the characteristic set of forms that both integrated a civilization and set it apart from other civilizations, Kroeber drew on his inquiries into the periodicity of women's dress fashion to posit "developmental flow" as one of style's "most characteristic features." He went on to note the "doubleness of creativity," the coincidence of aesthetic and intellectual achievements that he had documented in *Configurations of Culture Growth*. After reiterating his conviction that "gifts of genius" depended upon "cultural setting" for their realization, Kroeber suggested that "analogues" of style could be found in organic life. As an example, he cited the "coherence and congruence of form-quality" that distinguished a greyhound from a bulldog.[46]

Kroeber devoted the remainder of *Style and Civilizations* to assessing the "schemes" of other comparative historians. To Spengler, Sorokin, and Toynbee, Kroeber added the name of the Russian botanist Nikolai Danilevsky, who pioneered the natural history of civilizations when he delimited a dozen "culture-historical types" in *Russia and Europe* (1869).[47] Danilevsky, like Spengler, Sorokin, and Toynbee in part, pictured European civilization in irreversible decline. Kroeber, however, thought that European civilization was reconstituting itself – much as Graeco-Roman civilization gave way during the Dark Ages to modern European civilization. But whether European civilization was then disintegrating or reconstituting itself seemed less important to Kroeber than the tone in which the comparative study of civilizations was conducted. It could

[45] Hymes, "Alfred Louis Kroeber," 261; Meyer Schapiro to A. L. Kroeber, 14 February 1953, Kroeber Papers, reel 41; Meyer Schapiro, "Style," in *Anthropology Today: An Encyclopedic Inventory*, ed. A. L. Kroeber (Chicago: University of Chicago Press, 1953), 287, 311.
[46] Kroeber, *Style and Civilizations*, 1, 70, 9, 21, 33–34, 57–58, 61, 58–59, 77.
[47] H. Stuart Hughes, *Oswald Spengler* (1952; repr., New Brunswick, N.J.: Transaction Publishers, 1992), 44–49; Robert Redfield, "Civilization," in *Human Nature and the Study of Society: The Papers of Robert Redfield*, vol. 1, ed. Margaret Park Redfield (Chicago: University of Chicago Press, 1962), 406.

not become a "truly scientific or scholarly" activity "until it divest[ed] itself of emotional concern about crisis, decay, collapse, extinction, and doom." Kroeber urged that the comparative study of civilizations be expanded beyond "a small number of highly contrastive great cultures" to include "minor, derivative, and even humbler cultures." Toynbee had pointed the way in delimiting twenty-odd civilizations, but Kroeber thought it possible to go much further. Indeed, in his opinion, the schemes of other comparative historians suffered less from their being "intuitively subjective" than from their "inadequacy of content and coverage."[48]

Kroeber's treatment of style, however, disappointed Meyer Schapiro. Kroeber, Schapiro explained, approached civilizations less as characteristic sets of forms than in terms of their "complex qualit[ies] or disposition[s]." In thus holding that "infinity" characterized European civilization, Kroeber ignored the large domain not "marked" by infinity. In addition, Kroeber gave far more emphasis to the aesthetic and intellectual aspects of civilizations than he did to their economic, political, moral, and familial aspects. In short, Kroeber's conception of style fell short of being "a principle of integration of the culture at a point in time and space."[49]

In 1957, Kroeber began work on a "classificatory roster" intended to serve as "a sort of checklist of the known principal civilizations and cultures of the world." In the fragments of the *Roster* he completed before his death in October 1960, he treated the terms "culture" and "civilization" as virtually synonymous. The slight difference between the two terms that Kroeber acknowledged was that "civilization" designated the "larger and richer cultures" treated in his roster.[50]

Kroeber's death cut short his development of a natural history of civilizations. Even had he lived long enough to complete his roster, Kroeber would probably have been hampered by what Eric Wolf characterized as his "natural-scientific positivism." Kroeber's insistence that his formulations be

[48] Kroeber, *Style and Civilizations*, 100–102, 155, 157–160.

[49] Meyer Schapiro, review of *Style and Civilizations*, *American Anthropologist* 61 (1959): 304–305.

[50] A. L. Kroeber, *A Roster of Civilizations and Culture* (New York: Wenner-Gren Foundation for Anthropological Research, 1962), 9–10, 12, 16–17. In the last year of his life, Kroeber stressed "the need for taxonomy" in language as in culture. "The dominant historical interest in the past century," he explained, had been "microdynamic." "More macrodynamics, bolstered by a better taxonomy," were needed. "The situation is made more difficult," Kroeber pointed out, "by the fact that anthropologists still tend to value personal expertise, technical virtuosity, cleverness in novelty, and do not clearly recognize the fundamental value of the humble but indispensable task of classifying – that is, structuring – our body of knowledge, as biologists did begin to recognize it two hundred years ago." A. L. Kroeber, "Evolution, History, and Culture," in *Evolution after Darwin*, vol. II: *The Evolution of Man*, ed. Sol Tax (Chicago: University of Chicago Press, 1960), 14; A. L. Kroeber, "Statistics, Indo-European, and Taxonomy," *Language* 36 (1960): 19–21; Driver, "The Contribution of A. L. Kroeber to Culture Area Theory and Practice," 20.

verified by correspondence with an external reality that he presupposed was "out there" led him, as Rushton Coulborn had shrewdly observed in his review of *Configurations of Culture Growth*, to curb his powerful intuition. Despite his "remarkable ability for recall and retention of data," Kroeber never attained the stature of a Spengler or a Toynbee as "a poet of historical interpretation." Then, too, there was Kroeber's lack of interest in human agency. Indeed, as Wolf pointed out, there were "no people" in Kroeber's natural history of civilizations.[51]

Yet Kroeber gave encouragement to several historians who, Darwin-like, engaged in comparative history. One was Philip Bagby, who shortly before his untimely death at the age of forty in 1958, published *Culture and History: Prolegomena to the Study of Civilizations*. Bagby dedicated his manifesto on the "science of history" to Kroeber, who had tried to secure a subvention for his work. As its title suggested, Bagby's book gave pride of place to the culture concept. History, Bagby argued, would "become intelligible" only if historians treated "historical events" as "instances of cultural regularities" and pursued their inquiries "on the level of culture."[52]

H. Stuart Hughes was yet another historian who acknowledged an intellectual debt to Kroeber. In *Consciousness and Society: The Reorientation of European Social Thought, 1890–1930*, a landmark account of the "intellectual revolution" wrought by the turn-of-the-century "revolt against positivism," Hughes treated Émile Durkheim, Sigmund Freud, Vilfredo Pareto, Max Weber, and other early twentieth-century European social scientists as constituting a "cluster of genius." In letters to Kroeber, Hughes thanked Kroeber for encouraging him to persist in writing an intellectual biography of Oswald Spengler, despite some of his colleagues' "ill-concealed condescension," and deemed Kroeber's reflections on Toynbee "by far the fairest judgment" he had "encountered anywhere."[53]

Then, too, there was Kroeber's protégé Rushton Coulborn. In *The Origin of Civilized Societies* (1959), Coulborn traced the origins of seven primary civilized societies – Egypt, Mesopotamia, India, Crete, China, Middle America, and Andes – to post-glacial desiccation, which compelled primitive farmers to migrate to river flood plains in search of "a reliable water supply." In each of these civilized societies, farmers developed "new religions" based on water

[51] Coulborn, review of *Configurations of Culture Growth*, 93; Hughes, *Oswald Spengler*, 181–182; Kluckhohn, review of *Configurations of Culture Growth*, 339; Eric R. Wolf, "Alfred L. Kroeber," in *Totems and Teachers: Key Figures in the History of Anthropology*, ed. Sydel Silverman, 2nd ed. (Walnut Creek, Cal.: AltaMira Press, 2004), 42.

[52] Philip H. Bagby, *Culture and History: Prolegomena to the Comparative Study of Civilizations* (1958; repr., Berkeley: University of California Press, 1959), 7–8, 20, 156.

[53] H. Stuart Hughes to A. L. Kroeber, 20 March 1952, 21 August 1957, Kroeber Papers, reel 30; H. Stuart Hughes, *Consciousness and Society: The Reorientation of European Social Thought, 1890–1930*, rev. ed. (New York: Vintage, 1977), 17–18; H. Stuart Hughes, "The Historian and the Social Scientist," *American Historical Review* 66 (1960): 20–46.

worship. All seven societies were characterized by a common pattern of cyclic rise and fall, to Coulborn's mind the primary difference between civilized and primitive societies.[54]

In addition, Kroeber supported Sylvia Thrupp's efforts to launch the journal *Comparative Studies in Society and History* "to bring fresh historical material to bear on a related series of problems that lend themselves to comparative study." When Thrupp solicited his opinion for fleshing out the prospective journal's title, Kroeber suggested adding "in History" to "Comparative Studies." For "the word [history]," he explained, "no longer means mere story-telling to scholars." To Kroeber, the new journal's prospects looked good, because "humanistic scholarship in the U.S.A." seemed "on the verge of a great rising tide." His great hope was that the new journal would spur historians to "compare more."[55]

Kroeber, then, championed a plural conception of civilizations, criticizing other comparative historians – Danilevsky, Spengler, Sorokin, and Toynbee – for delimiting too few civilizations. In his magnum opus, *Configurations of Culture Growth*, he attempted to put Spengler's intuition on solid footing by finding objective and tangible indices. Kroeber's own positivism, however, constrained his intuition and insight. Kroeber, who regarded delimitation in space (if not also in time) as the equivalent for the anthropologist of periodization for the historian, pressed historians to compare more, and to search for regularities, recurrences, and, above all, patterns in history. In addition to developing the concept of stimulus diffusion, he revived the concept of the ecumene, which, as we shall see, became a matrix in the developing field of world history. Resisting the quantitative, statistical turn taken by many American social scientists after 1945, Kroeber emphasized the nonquantitative and the intuitive. He also held up biology, and not physics, as his natural-science model. Optimistic about both the future and the role that the discipline of anthropology would play in it, Kroeber looked forward to the creation of a world culture and the formation of an international pool of styles.

THE FOLK

Robert Redfield was, in many ways, Kroeber's opposite; yet the two men held each other in great esteem. Redfield's trajectory took him from the margins of anthropology in the 1930s to its philosophical center at the time of his death in 1958. Concerned throughout his career with the relationship

---

[54] Coulborn, *The Origin of Civilized Societies*, 19–20, 158–159, 5–6, 24.
[55] Sylvia Thrupp to A. L. Kroeber, 10 December 1955, Kroeber Papers, reel 44; A. L. Kroeber to Sylvia Thrupp, 14 May 1956, Kroeber Papers, reel 10; A. L. Kroeber to Sylvia Thrupp, 2 December 1958, Kroeber Papers, reel 11; Sylvia Thrupp, "Alfred L. Kroeber," *Comparative Studies in Society and History* 3 (1961): 351–352.

between "culture" and "civilization" and with the incorporation of people on the peripheries into "modern industrial civilization," Redfield developed "the folk–urban continuum" on which "culture" and "civilization" were polar opposites. Yet, after acquiring a newfound appreciation for archaeology, history, and civilization, Redfield substituted civilization for urban culture on the folk–urban continuum. Where Kroeber approached civilizations from a macrohistorical and aesthetic perspective, Redfield approached them processually as the products of interaction between the great traditions of the reflective few and the little traditions of the unreflective many. For Redfield, then, the civilizing process was both a cognitive and moral phenomenon.

Born in 1897 to a "real go-getting" attorney and the "fastidious" daughter of Chicago's Danish consul, Redfield studied biology and Latin at the University of Chicago before rashly volunteering to drive an ambulance in France in 1917. Left "very much confused and disorganized," and something of a pacifist, by his wartime experience, Redfield floundered until he accepted his father's offer to "stake" him to law school. After earning a J.D. in 1921, he practiced municipal law. Soon becoming bored and restless, however, Redfield and his wife, Margaret, the daughter of the sociologist Robert Park, "recklessly" took off for a month-long vacation in Mexico, where he grew fascinated by the villages they saw. In January 1924, at Park's suggestion, he enrolled in the University of Chicago's joint program in sociology and anthropology.[56]

Redfield was strongly attracted by Robert Park's vision of a generalizing and processual "science of society" that was more concerned with attitudes than events, and that revolved around "concepts," middle-level generalizations that enabled the researcher to glimpse "the universal in the particular." Inducted by Park into the long-running debate among social scientists on both sides of the Atlantic over the "Great Transformation," the wrenching series of changes that transformed Europe from a small-scale, rural society to a large-scale urban civilization, Redfield found himself "stirred" by the work of Henry Maine, who described the Great Transformation in terms of a shift from "status" to "contract," and by that of Émile Durkheim, who searched for an "organic solidarity" to take the place of an attenuated "mechanical solidarity." He was also influenced by Ferdinand Tönnies's antithesis between *Gemeinschaft* (community) and *Gesellschaft* (society). Groomed by his father-in-law to be an interdisciplinary figure, Redfield constantly strove to fuse the "different emphases" that sociology and anthropology gave to "common problems" such as assimilation/culture-borrowing. Also reflecting his father-in-law's influence, Redfield deemed

[56] Anne Roe, transcript of interview with Robert Redfield, 1950, Roe Papers. See also Clifford Wilcox, *Robert Redfield and the Development of American Anthropology* (Lanham, Md.: Lexington Books, 2004).

"guiding formulations" more important than what Kroeber called descriptive integration.[57]

Like Kroeber, Redfield worked within the parameters of the German distinction between history as a particularizing, descriptive method and science as a generalizing, explanatory method. Indeed, Park invoked this distinction to define sociology. Unlike Kroeber, Redfield leaned more toward science than he did toward history, and praised A. R. Radcliffe-Brown's introduction of "a strictly non-historical, scientific method" into American anthropology. Indeed, until the Second World War, Redfield did not concern himself with such "historical problems" as inferring historical sequences from the spatial distribution of cultural phenomena, rescuing "survivals" from aboriginal culture, or determining the provenance of cultural traits.[58] Redfield's preference for studying social and cultural processes "as they happened" was to render his work before the Second World War, as his teacher Edward Sapir put it, "somewhat marginal to the main work of American anthropologists."[59]

In 1925, as part of his practicum, Redfield studied Chicago's small but rapidly growing Mexican colony. When he discovered that the migrants' self-consciousness, arising from their feeling that native-born Americans looked down on them as "inferior," made it difficult for him to "gain their confidence," Redfield decided that it would be far better to study the migrants in their home communities in Mexico. To the end of obtaining "an intimate view of their

[57] Robert Redfield, "Anthropology, A Natural Science?" *Social Forces* 4 (1926): 715–721; reprinted in *Human Nature and the Study of Society*, 3–11; Robert E. Park and Ernest W. Burgess, *Introduction to the Science of Sociology* (Chicago: University of Chicago Press, 1921), 12–24; Robert E. Park, "Experience and Race Relations: Opinion Attitudes, and Experience as Types of Human Behavior," *Journal of Applied Sociology* 9 (1924): 18–24; reprinted in *Race and Culture* (Glencoe, Ill.: Free Press, 1950), 152–157, on 153; Robert Redfield to Margaret Park Redfield, 10 July [1928], Redfield Papers, box 1, folder 3; Robert Redfield to Armand Winfield, 3 May 1948, Redfield Papers, box 42, folder 6; Robert Redfield to Joseph H. Willits, 8 June 1945, Redfield Papers, box 27, folder 10; Robert Redfield, introduction to *Magic, Science and Religion and Other Essays*, by Bronislaw Malinowski (1948; repr., Garden City, N.Y.: Doubleday, 1954), 11; Wilcox, *Robert Redfield and the Development of American Anthropology*, 27–28, 38n. On the Great Transformation, see Robert A. Nisbet, "Community," in *The Sociological Tradition* (New York: Basic Books, 1966), 47–106; and Thomas Bender, *Community and Social Change in America* (1978; repr., Baltimore: Johns Hopkins University Press, 1982), chap. 2. On Robert Park, see Fred H. Matthews, *Quest for an American Sociology: Robert E. Park and the Chicago School* (Montreal: McGill-Queens University Press, 1977).
[58] Robert Redfield, introduction to *Social Organization of North American Tribes*, ed. Fred Eggan (Chicago: University of Chicago Press, 1937), vii–xii; reprinted in *Human Nature and the Study of Society*, 17–21, on 20; *Sociol* (1926): Robert Redfield, introduction to *Tepoztlán, a Mexican Village: A Study of Folk Life* (1930; repr., Chicago: University of Chicago Press, 1973), 10–14; Robert Redfield to Duncan Strong, 12 July 1939, Redfield Papers, box 33, folder 10; Robert Redfield to W. Lloyd Warner, 12 July 1939, Redfield Papers, box 40, folder 4.
[59] Edward Sapir to Robert H. Lowie, 3 July 1933, in *Letters from Edward Sapir to Robert H. Lowie*, ed. Luella Cole (Berkeley: privately published, 1965), 64.

life," he proposed to study, in a "typical" Mexican village, "that type of social process known to the sociologist as assimilation and to the anthropologist as culture-borrowing." Awarded a fellowship by the Social Science Research Council, Redfield engaged in seven months of fieldwork in 1926–27 in Tepoztlán, a Morelos village of about 4,000 inhabitants, almost all of them "Indians of pure blood."[60]

In his ethnography of the village, published in 1930 under the title *Tepoztlán, a Mexican Village: A Study of Folk Life,* Redfield attempted to reconcile the two "academic viewpoints" in which he had been trained: anthropology and sociology. Anthropologists studied primitive peoples; sociologists, city dwellers. The villagers of Tepoztlán were neither one nor the other. They were "peasants," a new cultural type that, Redfield believed, had been brought into existence by the rise of the city.[61] Although their rural culture remained homogeneous, the villagers had "long since reached an adjustment with Western civilization": they used money, wore commercially made clothes when they traveled to other villages, in some cases knew how to read and write, and had adopted some of the rituals of Catholicism. Their music, dominated by *corridos* (ballads), was transitional. Although orally transmitted, the *corridos* were set down in copybooks and functioned, in this largely illiterate community, as a kind of "news organ," much as newspapers functioned in Chicago.[62] The villagers' medical practices were also transitional, reflecting the extension of "rational conduct" at the expense of "magical behavior."[63]

[60] Fay-Cooper Cole, "Investigation of Mexican Immigration," in "Report of Joint Conference of the Committee on Problems and Policy of the Social Science Research Council Meeting with Other Representatives of the Social Sciences in Attendance upon the Dartmouth Conference of Social Sciences and Allied Groups," 31 August 1925, 33–34, folder 711, box 68, series 3, Laura Spelman Rockefeller Memorial, RAC; Robert Redfield, "Statement of the Nature of the Fieldwork Proposed" [summer 1925], Redfield Papers, box 1, folder 4.

[61] Redfield discussed the reconciliation of the "complementary" viewpoints of anthropology and sociology in "The Folk Society and Culture," a paper that he read at the tenth anniversary of the Social Science Research Building at the University of Chicago in December 1939, and was published in the *American Journal of Sociology* 45 (1940): 731–742. Redfield expressed similar views in his 8 June 1945 letter to Joseph Willits.

[62] Redfield, *Tepoztlán*, 9–10, 185–193. While the Redfields were in Mexico in 1923, Park urged them to "dig up" as many *corridos* as they could so that they would "be able to clearly define the role in which these popular ballads play in the politics of the country." Park, who suspected that the *corridos* had never been "sociologically interpreted," suggested that the Redfields investigate "the manner in which they extend the fame of a popular hero" such as Emilio Zapata and "give him prestige and eventually power." Robert E. Park to Margaret Park Redfield, 16 November 1923, Park Papers, box 2, folder 5.

[63] Redfield, *Tepoztlán*, 166–167. In his application to the Social Science Research Council, Redfield quoted a passage from Park's article "Magic, Mentality and City Life," in which Park suggested that "magic may be regarded . . . as an index in a rough way, not merely of the mentality, but the general cultural levels of races, peoples, and classes." Robert E. Park, "Magic, Mentality and City Life," *Publications of the American Sociological Society* 18 (1924): 109.

Struck by the pronounced differences among villagers with respect to "degree of civilization," Redfield mapped the distribution of "cultural types." In the process, he identified *los correctos* (the "correct") – the secular, Spanish-speaking villagers (among whom were his principal informants) living near the plaza at the center of the village – and *los tontos* (the "ignorant") – the more traditionally minded villagers living in *barrios* (neighborhoods) on its periphery. Among *los correctos*, Redfield glimpsed "an intelligentsia who lived in two worlds," and who were, for that reason, "restless and often unhappy." As such, they resembled Robert Park's "marginal men." Redfield was intrigued by the "double aspect" of the personality of *los correctos*: on the one side, their "intelligence, detachment, secularity"; on the other, their "self-consciousness, restlessness, malaise." Like Park, he believed that it was in the "mind" of such marginal men, "where the changes and fusions of culture are going on," that "the processes of civilization and of progress" could best be studied.[64]

Tepoztlán pioneered what came to be known, after the Second World War, as peasant studies. In a review, Alfred Kroeber announced that "social change" was the "theme" of Redfield's book. Less interested in "how things came to be" in Tepoztlán than in "how they interact now," Redfield eschewed "archival documentation" and touched on history and geography "as lightly as possible."[65]

THE FOLK-CULTURE CONTINUUM

Redfield's commitment to anthropology as a generalizing science deepened after A. V. Kidder enlisted him in 1929 in the Carnegie Institution of Washington's "panscientific attack" on Yucatan. Resisting Kidder's pressure to search for relics of pre-Columbian custom as a sort of "epilogue to the history of the ancient Maya," Redfield seized the opportunity afforded by the peninsula's relatively small space and wide range of cultural types – everything from the "tribal Indian" in the remote Quintana Roo to European-educated city-dwellers in Merida, the state capital – to study the ongoing incorporation of a "people on the margins" into "modern industrial civilization." Proposing to treat Yucatan "as a single entity," Redfield recruited fieldworkers who would simultaneously record the "culture" in four sample communities. Over the course of the 1930s, Redfield, the Mexican schoolteacher-turned-anthropologist Alfonso Villa Rojas, and the sociologist Asael Hansen studied the "process

[64] Robert Redfield to Robert E. Park, 16 February, 15 March, 10 May 1927, Redfield Papers, box 1, folder 2; Redfield, *Tepoztlán*, 209, 213; Robert Redfield, "What Is Cultural Marginality?" undated notes for a seminar presentation, Redfield Papers, box 61, folder 16; Robert Redfield, "The Regional Aspect of Culture," *Publications of the American Sociological Society* 24 (1930): 33–41; reprinted in *Human Nature and the Study of Society*, 145–151, on 151; Robert E. Park, "Human Migration and the Marginal Man," *American Journal of Sociology* 33 (1928): 881–893; reprinted in *Race and Culture*, 345–356, on 355–356.

[65] A. L. Kroeber, review of *Tepoztlán*, *American Anthropologist* 33 (1931): 236–238.

of becoming civilized" in more or less simultaneous fieldwork in Merida, the *mestizo* (mixed-blood) town of Dzitas, the peasant village of Chan Kom, and the tribal settlement of Tusik.[66]

Renouncing any attempt to distinguish customs and artifacts of Indian from those of Spanish provenance, Redfield delineated Yucatan's "folk culture," an "integrated and unified mode of life" in which Indian and Spanish elements had fused so thoroughly in the four hundred years since the Spanish conquest that "nothing is entirely Indian, nothing is entirely Spanish." He thus concentrated on observing the changes taking place before his eyes as Yucatecan folk culture came into contact and communication with "civilization" – "schools, roads, and economic exploitation." To capture the processes involved in the "transition from one fundamental type of social organization to another," Redfield adopted Robert Park's suggestion that he employ "ideal concepts, to which perhaps nothing real actually conforms, but to which every type of society tends to conform," as working hypotheses.[67]

The "folk society" was best approximated by Tusik. It was an isolated, culturally homogeneous, integrated community, with only a simple division of labor. "Closely adjusted to its local milieu," the folk society was characterized by "personal" relationships and "familial" institutional controls. It also had a "moral order" – consensual judgments "as to what is right" – the sanctions of which were "prevailingly sacred." In contrast, "urban society," typified by Merida, was mobile and culturally heterogeneous, its way of life "less closely integrated," and its "group-habits" compartmentalized. Relationships in urban society were impersonal and family organization attenuated. Urban life was also secularized: individuals acted "from constraint or convenience," not "from deep moral conviction." Early in his research, Redfield designated the tribal way of life "culture," and the urban way of life "civilization." The transition from the tribal to the urban way of life thus described a process of "deculturalization." But because these terms denied "culture" to the "life-ways of city man," Redfield substituted "folk culture" and "city culture" for culture and civilization as the two poles of the folk–urban continuum.[68]

In 1941, Redfield synthesized a decade of fieldwork in Yucatan. Dedicated to Robert Park, *The Folk Culture of Yucatan* illustrated what Redfield considered the "mainspring of advance in social science" – the "interaction between concept and new particular type" – by reporting the results that he and his co-workers had obtained when they tested generalizations about the process of becoming civilized that had been put forward by Henry Maine, Lewis Henry

[66] A. V. Kidder, "Division of Historical Research," *Year Book* of the Carnegie Institution of Washington 29 (1930): 91–118; Robert Redfield, "A Plan for the Study of the People of Present-Day Yucatan," 9 March 1930, Redfield Papers, box 6, folder 17.

[67] Robert Redfield, "Culture Changes in Yucatan," *American Anthropologist* 36 (1934): 57–69; reprinted in *Human Nature and the Study of Society*, 160–172, on 164, 165, 167; Robert E. Park to Robert Redfield, 23 January 1932, Redfield Papers, box 1, folder 8.

[68] Redfield, "Culture Changes in Yucatan," 167–172.

Morgan, Émile Durkheim, and Ferdinand Tönnies. Redfield's challenge lay in determining the "relation" among the "variables" – the independent variables of isolation and homogeneity, and the dependent variables of cultural disorganization, secularization, and individualization. In Yucatan, Redfield concluded, increasing contact and communication between the folk culture and civilization had resulted in heterogeneity, cultural disorganization, secularization, and individualization.[69]

Redfield's conclusion, however, did not account for what Sol Tax, a research associate for the Carnegie Institute, had found in his fieldwork among the Maya of the Guatemalan Highlands in the mid-to-late 1930s. The Maya, Tax reported, were folk-like in their naiveté and lack of sophistication. But far from being "integrated" or simple, Maya culture seemed to Tax just as rife with conflict and complexity as the culture of "a rural community of ten thousand in Illinois." For this reason, Tax could not place the Maya on the folk–urban continuum, for they represented "neither culture nor civilization, but a combination of both." Tax's findings, confirmed by Redfield's own fieldwork in Guatemala in the late 1930s, revealed a fundamental limitation of the folk–urban continuum: it could not predict a cause-and-effect relationship among the variables that obtained everywhere. Tax's findings forced Redfield to admit that there was "no single necessary cause for secularization and individualization." If, in Yucatan, increase of contacts with the city was the necessary cause, in Guatemala, it was the spread of commerce and a money economy.[70]

Redfield's use of ideal types, borrowing of sociological concepts, and refusal either to consult documentary sources or to avail himself of his informants' knowledge of the past dismayed some of his professional peers. In George Peter Murdock's opinion, Redfield's treatment of cultural change in Yucatan as "an apparently inevitable transition from one conceptual pole to its opposite" smacked of discredited nineteenth-century evolutionary theory. Julian Steward wondered how far the "inferred history" of *The Folk Culture of Yucatan* corresponded with "known events."[71] Robert Lowie and the geographer Carl O. Sauer echoed these criticisms in confidential assessments solicited by the Rockefeller Foundation after the Carnegie Institution of Washington decided to

[69] Redfield, "The Folk Society and Culture," 736–737; Robert Redfield, *The Folk Culture of Yucatan* (Chicago: University of Chicago Press, 1941), x, 344.
[70] Redfield, *The Folk Culture of Yucatan*, 369; Sol Tax to Robert Redfield, 19 March 1935, in *Doing Fieldwork: The Correspondence of Robert Redfield and Sol Tax*, ed. Robert A. Rubinstein (Boulder: Westview, 1991), 92–94; Sol Tax, "Culture and Civilization in Guatemalan Societies," *Scientific Monthly* 48 (1939): 463–467, on 466–467; Sol Tax, "World View and Social Relations in Guatemala," *American Anthropologist* 43 (1941): 37; Robert Redfield, "Primitive Merchants of Guatemala," *Quarterly Journal of Inter-American Relations* 1 (1939): 42–56; reprinted in *Human Nature and the Study of Society*, 200–210.
[71] George Peter Murdock, review of *The Folk Culture of Yucatan*, *American Anthropologist* 45 (1943): 133–136; Julian H. Steward, review of *The Folk Culture of Yucatan*, *Journal of American Folklore* 57 (1944): 146–148.

terminate its support for Redfield's Middle American researches. Lowie thought that Redfield's conclusions were "precisely what one would infer *a priori*." While not unaware of the historical approach, Redfield "deliberately eliminated or restricted it." Sauer criticized Redfield's approach as "book-keeping" in which the "techniques of recording" were "overelaborate[d]" and the "curiosity" of fieldworkers "consistently repressed." "Why," Sauer asked, "this persistent repression of the creative and inquisitive impulses in order to embroider something that everybody already knows?"[72]

The folk–urban continuum came in for even more scathing criticism in 1951 when Oscar Lewis published *Life in a Mexican Village*. Assisted by his wife, the psychologist Ruth Maslow Lewis, who helped him administer projective tests to villagers, and by a dozen Mexican research assistants, who distributed questionnaires, Lewis engaged in fieldwork in Tepoztlán for seven months in 1944 and for shorter seasons in 1947 and 1948. In the beginning, Lewis viewed his fieldwork as a "continuation" of Redfield's work, but he quickly changed his mind. Far from being as homogeneous and integrated a village as Redfield depicted it, Tepoztlán, Lewis came to believe, was characterized by "individualism," "lack of cooperation," "schisms," and "fear, envy, and distrust in interpersonal relations." Lewis began to suspect that Redfield had gone to the village with a "preconceived notion" – the folk–urban continuum – that blinded him to "the great range of custom and belief" found there. Although he dedicated *Life in a Mexican Village* to Redfield, Lewis criticized him for glossing over "evidence of violence, disruption, cruelty, disease, suffering, and maladjustment." Stung by Lewis's criticisms, Redfield denied that he had been guilty of romanticizing village life. He did acknowledge, however, that during his fieldwork in Tepoztlán he had glimpsed "certain good things," including the villagers' "sense of conviction . . . as to what life is all about" and the "richness" of their "expressive life."[73]

REDFIELD'S TURN TO HISTORY

Ironically, even as he was being taken to task for his ahistorical approach, Redfield had begun to turn toward history. His historical turn stemmed from the impact of the Second World War, the wartime development of area

[72] Robert Redfield to Louis Wirth, 7 July 1947, Redfield Papers, box 41, folder 7; Robert Redfield to Joseph H. Willits and David H. Stevens, 24 January 1945, folder 2034, box 299, series 216, RG 2–1945; Robert H. Lowie to Joseph H. Willits, 18 February 1946, folder 2278, box 336, series 216, RG 2–1946; Carl Sauer to Joseph H. Willits, 5 August 1945, folder 2034, box 299, series 216, RG 2–1945, Rockefeller Foundation Archives, RAC.

[73] Oscar Lewis, *Life in a Mexican Village: Tepoztlán Restudied* (Urbana: University of Illinois Press, 1951), 428–430, 432; Robert Redfield, *The Primitive World and Its Transformations* (Ithaca: Cornell University Press, 1953), 155–156; Robert Redfield, *The Little Community: Viewpoints for the Study of a Human Whole* (1955; repr., Chicago: University of Chicago Press, 1960), 136. See also Philip K. Bock, "Tepoztlán Reconsidered," *Journal of Latin American Folklore* 6 (1980): 129–150.

studies, and the influence of archaeologists at the University of Chicago Oriental Institute.[74]

The Second World War troubled Redfield. In his eyes, American use of the atomic bomb against the Japanese at Hiroshima and Nagasaki threatened the destruction of the world's agriculture. "Is anything more important, to work on," Redfield asked his daughter Lisa in August 1945, than "the problem of the control of this exploded technology, this cancer-cell of human invention?"[75]

Redfield also turned to history out of interest in the emergent field of area studies. In a paper that he contributed to a conference held in Philadelphia in March 1944 to discuss the conversion of wartime area studies programs into peacetime general studies programs, Redfield proposed that "area institutes" be established at institutions across the country to study the "great world cultures," those "traditional way[s] of life that had maintained a distinguishing character over a long time, to great consequence for mankind." By combining textual analysis with fieldwork, the area institutes Redfield envisioned would promote not only collaboration between humanists and social scientists, but also convergence between humanistic culture as "enlightenment through mental and moral training" and anthropological culture as "a way of life." In addition, they would enhance students' ability "to look at [their] own culture with the fresh understanding given by acquaintance with another way of life." Americans needed to be exposed to "well-integrated" cultures because they did not have a well-integrated culture of their own.[76]

The third and most important reason why Redfield turned to history was his newfound appreciation for archaeology, a practice he had earlier dismissed as "bones and stones."[77] In the wake of Japan's surrender, the Anthropology Department at the University of Chicago began to retool its curriculum to accommodate the flood of veterans returning to school on the GI Bill. Charged with developing a year-long course on "Human Origins," Sol Tax, the physical anthropologist Wilton Krogman, and the archaeologist Robert Braidwood consulted a number of specialists, among them the British prehistorian V. Gordon Childe, who had succeeded in synthesizing European prehistory around two

---

[74] Robert Redfield to Roger F. Evans, 23 September 1955, folder 225, box 35, series 200, RG 2–1955, Rockefeller Foundation Archives, RAC; Milton Singer, "Robert Redfield: Anthropologist, 1897–1958," *Man in India* 39 (1959): 88–89.

[75] Robert Redfield to Lisa Peattie, 19 August [1945], Redfield Papers, box 90, folder 9.

[76] Robert Redfield, "Area Programs in Education and Research," Redfield Papers, box 60, folder 11; Robert Redfield, "The Study of Culture in General Education," *Social Education* 11 (1947): 259–264; reprinted in *The Social Uses of Social Science: The Papers of Robert Redfield*, vol. 2, ed. Margaret Park Redfield (Chicago: University of Chicago Press, 1963), 107–117, on 114.

[77] Redfield to Margaret Park Redfield, 10 July [1928]. On Redfield's previous lack of interest in archaeology, see Paul S. Martin, "Early Developments in Mogollon Research," in *Archaeological Researches in Retrospect*, ed. Gordon R. Willey (Cambridge: Winthrop, 1974), 4; James B. Griffin, quoted in "Discussion: American Ethnology: The Role of Redfield," in *American Anthropology: The Early Years*, ed. John V. Murra (St. Paul: West, 1976), 142–143; Richard S. MacNeish, *The Science of Archaeology?* (North Scituate, Mass.: Duxbury Press, 1978), 46–47.

"revolutions": the Neolithic ("food-producing") Revolution, in which fishing and hunting gave way to settled agriculture, and the Urban Revolution, in which villages gave way to cities.[78] Exposure to Childe's synthesis and contact with Braidwood and other archaeologists at the University of Chicago Oriental Institute, which had been founded as "a laboratory for the study of the rise and development of civilization," spurred Redfield to substitute "civilization" for "urban" at one pole of the folk–urban continuum and to conceive of civilization as an ideal type of society defined by "characteristics opposite to those [that had] characterized all societies in very ancient times." If the properties of the folk society remained for Redfield isolation, homogeneity, absence of literacy, self-sufficiency, simple technology, and a limited division of labor, civilization now signified their displacement.[79]

Redfield's historical turn can be seen in *A Village that Chose Progress: Chan Kom Revisited* (1950). In this "biography" of Chan Kom, which in 1948 he visited for the first time since 1931, Redfield told the story of how the villagers, having "committed themselves to progress and civilization," proceeded to make Chan Kom into "the recognized and authoritative community of an area fifty miles across." Yet, while remaining favorably disposed toward "proposals of reform," they now harbored reservations about "progress," and, in several instances, had even reverted to "a more traditional manner of life." Perhaps the most notable of these reversions was the villagers' "retreat to Catholicism." Soon after Redfield completed his fieldwork in 1931, many villagers, attracted by the Protestant emphasis upon hard work and sobriety, had converted to Protestantism. Yet, bridling at the Protestant proscription of candles, saints, and dancing, and ruing the "great schism" their apostasy had precipitated in their village, many of the converts returned to the Catholic fold. By 1948, there was, among Catholic and Protestant villagers alike, a new self-consciousness in which once taken-for-granted religious beliefs and practices had become "matter[s] to talk about, to take into practical consequence, to think over." By then, too, village leaders had grown worried about moral declension among the young.[80]

Although Redfield feared that the villagers' embrace of new technology and commercial practices would eventually lead to the unraveling of their culture as "a web of meaning," he did not see any alternative to their

---

[78] William J. Peace, "Vere Gordon Childe and American Anthropology," *Journal of Anthropological Research* 44 (1988): 422–423; Andrew Sherratt, "V. Gordon Childe: Archaeology and Intellectual History," *Past and Present* 125 (1989): 151–185; Bruce Trigger, *Gordon Childe: Revolutions in Archaeology* (New York: Columbia University Press, 1980).

[79] Robert Redfield, "The Birth of Civilization: A Definition of the Problem" (1947), Redfield Papers, box 72, folder 9; James Henry Breasted, *The Oriental Institute of the University of Chicago: A Beginning and a Program* (Chicago, 1922), quoted in Bruce Kuklick, *Puritans in Babylon: The Ancient Near East and American Intellectual Life, 1880–1930* (Princeton, N.J.: Princeton University Press, 1996), 112.

[80] Robert Redfield, *A Village that Chose Progress* (Chicago: University of Chicago Press, 1950), 16–24, 88–112.

"[going] forward with technology, with a declining religious faith and moral conviction, into a dangerous world." Insofar as their religious beliefs and practices, tastes and manners, and conceptions of the "good life" were becoming "more varied" and "less exclusively fixed by village tradition," the villagers increasingly "identifie[d] their interests with those of people far away." Reflecting his own ambivalence toward civilization, Redfield regretted that "none of the aesthetic sensibility of Latin culture" that so delighted him in Tepoztlán had yet "found lodgment" in Chan Kom. Although undergraduates at the University of Chicago commonly referred to Redfield's book as "The Little Village That Could," Redfield worried that the villagers, in becoming increasingly practical and commercial at the expense of "art and faith," were repeating "the characteristic mistakes of Western civilization."[81]

THE SOCIAL ANTHROPOLOGY OF CIVILIZATIONS

After 1945, Redfield's interests shifted from Middle America to the historic civilizations of Asia. In October 1948, he went with his wife and son to National Tsing Hua University in Beijing. Together with Park's student Fei Xiaotong, Redfield hoped to study Chinese peasants, but the Communist advance on Beijing forced his family to leave on one of the last flights out of the city in December. After a brief stay at Lingnan University, near Canton, the Redfields resettled in Europe.[82] In April 1949, Redfield delivered five lectures at the University of Frankfurt, Germany, in which he emphasized the humanistic roots of anthropology. Among them were anthropologists' interest in "expressive documents," use of "sympathetic understanding" (or empathy) in understanding their informants, the element of "art" in their work, and "humanity" as their subject matter.[83]

Upon his return to the University of Chicago, Redfield decided to seek external funding for an Institute of Cultural Studies that would foster the study of the "more important values" of the world's civilizations and cultures, bring humanists and social scientists together to compare Western civilization with other civilizations, and probe "the nature of human nature." Although

[81] Redfield, *A Village that Chose Progress*, 178; Ralph W. Nicholas, afterword to *General Education in the Social Sciences: Centennial Reflections on the College of the University of Chicago*, ed. John J. MacAloon (Chicago: University of Chicago Press, 1992), 283–284; Robert Redfield to John U. Nef, 21 September 1948, John U. Nef Papers, Special Collections Research Center, University of Chicago, box 36, folder 5.

[82] Robert Redfield, "Visit to China," *University of Chicago Magazine* 42 (1949): 9, 19–20; Burton Pasternak, "A Conversation with Fei Xiaotong," *Current Anthropology* 29 (1988): 643.

[83] "Chicago in Frankfurt," *Time*, 12 April 1948, 83; Robert Redfield, "The Logic and the Functions of Social Science," "Social Science among the Humanities," "Social Science as an Art," "Social Science and Values," and "Social Science as Morality," in *Human Nature and the Study of Society*, 31–98.

University of Chicago Chancellor Robert Hutchins believed that the Institute would counter hitherto "futile efforts to make the work of the intellectual count for good in American civilization and international relations," Redfield's proposal fell on deaf ears at both the Rockefeller Foundation and the Carnegie Corporation, perhaps because of the large sum of money – one million dollars over the next five years – that Redfield requested.[84]

Prospects for Redfield's proposed institute, however, brightened after Hutchins left Chicago to become associate director of the Ford Foundation, then the richest of all the philanthropic foundations. In August 1951, the Ford Foundation awarded Redfield $75,000, the first in a series of grants totaling $375,000, for a "Program in Intercultural Studies."[85] Because intercultural studies was not yet "a well established discipline or science but a congeries of efforts in different disciplines," Redfield planned "to put money where it can help the study of the 'great traditions' and other cultures to develop toward greater comparability." Well aware that he could not achieve this aim alone, he enlisted the assistance of the philosophers Milton Singer and Eliseo Vivas.[86]

Milton Singer had come to Chicago in 1936 to study philosophy with the logical positivist Rudolph Carnap. After earning his Ph.D. in 1940, he stayed on as member of the college staff that mounted the introductory sequence in social science for undergraduates. When David Riesman reorganized the sequence around the theme of culture and personality, Singer proposed a "federated project" on the American character. Unable to secure external funding for this project, Singer turned his attention to exploring the "methodological problems" involved in studying complex cultures.[87]

[84] Robert Redfield, notes beginning "What is this thing concerned with?" [1949], Redfield Papers, box 4, folder 16; Robert Redfield, "Proposal for an Institute of Cultural Studies," 1 November 1950, Redfield Papers, box 15, folder 4; Robert M. Hutchins to Chester Barnard, 23 November 1949, Robert M. Hutchins to Charles Dollard, 23 November 1949, Ford Foundation Cultural Studies Program Records, Special Collections Research Center, University of Chicago (hereafter Ford Foundation Cultural Studies Program Records), box 5, folder 10.

[85] Robert Redfield to Robert M. Hutchins, 7 June 1951, Ford Foundation Cultural Studies Program Records, box 5, folder 10. Between 1951 and 1966 the Ford Foundation doled out more than $300 million to thirty universities under the auspices of its program on International Training and Research. Richard H. Davis, *South Asia at Chicago: A History* (Chicago: University of Chicago Committee on Southern Asian Studies, 1985), 66; Robert Bendiner, "Report on the Ford Foundation," *New York Times Magazine*, 1 February 1953, 12–13, 25, 27; Francis X. Sutton, "The Ford Foundation: The Early Years," *Daedalus* 116 (1987): 41–91.

[86] Robert Redfield to Evon Z. Vogt, 28 April 1950, Redfield Papers, box 39, folder 1; Robert Redfield to Fred Eggan, 14 June 1950, Redfield Papers, box 8, folder 5; Redfield to Hutchins, 7 June 1951.

[87] Milton Singer, "A Program for the Interdisciplinary Study of Culture and Character," n.d., Ford Foundation Cultural Studies Program Records, box 2, folder 13; Redfield to Hutchins, 7 June 1951; Milton Singer, "Robert Redfield's Development of a Social Anthropology of Civilizations," in *American Anthropology: The Early Years*, 187–260, on 197, 201–202.

Eliseo Vivas, who then taught at Northwestern University, was interested in developing a "definition of man" that would compensate for philosophers' lack of interest in man as both "a culture-building animal" and "a religious, scientific, and cognitive being." Vivas was also an outspoken critic of the untrammeled cultural relativism of the interwar period.[88]

Although Vivas soon drifted away from the Program in Intercultural Studies, Singer not only became Redfield's right-hand man but retooled himself as an anthropologist. In 1953–54, he studied with the Sanskritist W. Norman Brown at the University of Pennsylvania and with the Indian anthropologist David Mandelbaum at the University of California in preparation for fieldwork in Madras, India.[89]

Redfield and Singer used some of their grant from the Ford Foundation to purchase release time for themselves and for some of their colleagues. While they established "lines of communication" and "intellectual relations" with American and European scholars, Vivas studied "the universal modes of apprehension of reality," Professor of Italian G. A. Borgese compared the Indian and Chinese "ethical relationships to Christian teaching" in an effort to bridge Western and "Oriental" thought, and Professor of Arabic and Austrian émigré Gustave von Grunebaum renewed his ties to European Islamists. Ford money also supported the medievalist Helen Mims's comparative study of communalism in medieval and modern Europe, the historian R. H. Tawney's studies of seventeenth-century English life and institutions, and Marshall Hodgson's dissertation on Islamic sects. In addition, Ford money brought scholars from Italy, Turkey, and the Gold Coast to the University of Chicago for training in "intercultural studies."[90] Finally, Ford money sponsored five conferences – two each on Chinese intellectual history and Islamic civilization, and one on the relationship between language and culture – the proceedings of which Redfield and Singer published as "progress reports" in their monograph series, Comparative Studies of Cultures and Civilizations.[91] Small wonder that in his irreverent

[88] Robert Redfield to Eliseo Vivas, 4 July [1951]; Eliseo Vivas, undated project description, Redfield Papers, box 38, folder 9. Redfield claimed to have "learned much" from his discussions with Vivas "about the aesthetic experience and the nature of art." Vivas, in turn, credited Redfield with teaching him that man had "never been known to create a culture which did not include a more or less well defined hierarchy of values." Robert Redfield, "Art and Icon," in *Human Nature and the Study of Society*, 472n; Eliseo Vivas, "Literature and Knowledge," in *Creation and Discovery: Essays in Criticism and Aesthetics* (New York: Noonday Press, 1955), 126–127, 287n, 289n.

[89] Milton Singer, *When a Great Tradition Modernizes: An Anthropological Approach to Indian Civilization* (London: Pall Mall, 1972), xii–xiii, 55–59.

[90] Tullio Tentori, Ali Othman, and Georges Creppy, respectively.

[91] *Studies in Chinese Thought*, ed. Arthur F. Wright (Chicago: University of Chicago Press, 1953); *Chinese Thought and Institutions*, ed. John K. Fairbank (Chicago: University of Chicago Press, 1957); *Studies in Islamic Cultural History*, ed. Gustave E. von Grunebaum ([Menasha, Wisc.]: American Anthropological Association, 1954); *Unity and Variety in Muslim Civilization*, ed. Gustave E. von Grunebaum (Chicago: University of Chicago Press, 1955); *Language in Culture*, ed. Harry Hoijer (Chicago: University of Chicago Press, 1954).

history of the early years of the Ford Foundation, Dwight Macdonald likened Redfield and Singer's Program in Intercultural Studies to "an academic W.P.A."[92]

At the core of the Program in Intercultural Studies was Anthropology 342, the continuing faculty and student seminar directed by Redfield and Singer. Topics in the seminar varied from the "methodological problems" involved in characterizing and comparing cultures, to the applicability of the concept of "worldview" to "folk cultures" in the process of transformation, to a comparison of Islamic and Western civilizations.[93] In the spring of 1954, seven anthropologists examined the "relation" of the villages in which they had done fieldwork to India as a cultural whole. As what Redfield termed a "culture-civilization," a "literate civilization" that had been "built upon a local popular culture," India offered a promising site on which to test the relationship he posited between the "little tradition" (the worldview and ethos of the villagers) and the "great tradition" ("classical, philosophic or religious learning"). In his paper, McKim Marriott characterized the religious outlook of the villagers of the village he had studied as a product of two "continuous processes of communication": the first "universalization," the carrying forward of elements of a little tradition into a great tradition, and the second "parochialization," the transformation of the contents of a great tradition into a form more congenial to the villagers.[94]

Anthropology 342 also gave Redfield and Singer the opportunity to develop a mid-twentieth-century version of the Enlightenment project of "philosophical anthropology," an inquiry into "the inherent capabilities and limitations of man."[95] Integral to their philosophical anthropology were the transformations wrought in the primitive world by the coming of civilization – transformations that Redfield described in the Messenger Lectures at Cornell in the spring of 1952. Published the following year under the title *The Primitive World and Its*

[92] Robert Redfield to Robert M. Hutchins, 16 January 1953, Ford Foundation Cultural Studies Program Records, box 5, folder 10; Robert Redfield to Cleon O. Swayzee, 5 July 1954, Ford Foundation Cultural Studies Program Records, box 5, folder 16; Robert Redfield to R. H. Tawney, 30 June 1952, Ford Foundation Cultural Studies Program Records, box 18, folder 4; Dwight Macdonald, *The Ford Foundation: The Men and the Millions* (New York: Reynal, 1956), 164–165.

[93] Redfield to Hutchins, 16 January 1953; Milton Singer to Robert Redfield, 12 February 1952, 13 July 1953, Ford Foundation Cultural Studies Program Records, box 3, folder 6; Robert Redfield to Everett C. Hughes, 24 July 1952, Redfield Papers, box 14, folder 13; Robert Redfield to A. L. Kroeber, 12 November 1952, Redfield Papers, box 17, folder 2; Milton Singer to Robert Redfield, 13 November 1952, Redfield Papers, box 72, folder 28; Milton Singer to Robert Redfield, 24 January 1952, Singer Papers, box 97.

[94] McKim Marriott, "Little Communities in an Indigenous Civilization," in *Village India: Studies in the Little Community*, ed. McKim Marriott (Chicago: University of Chicago Press, 1955), 171–222, on 211–212.

[95] Robert Redfield to Milton Singer, 14 May 1952; Milton Singer to Robert Redfield, 23 May 1952, Singer Papers, box 97; Milton Singer to Robert Redfield, 2 February 1953, Redfield Papers, box 72, folder 28; Wolf, *Anthropology*, 9.

Transformation, Redfield's lectures sketched the "career" of "the human race." Drawing on the work of specialists at the Oriental Institute on towns in the Ancient Near East, Redfield collapsed Gordon Childe's Neolithic and Urban revolutions into one great "transformation," the transformation of folk society into civilization. As his substitution of transformation for revolution implied, Redfield saw urban development as much more gradual than did Childe.[96]

In his earlier work, Redfield had seen the expansion of the "technical order," that order arising "from mutual usefulness, from deliberate coercion, or from the mere utilization of the same means," advancing at the expense of the moral order.[97] Now, in *The Primitive World and Its Transformations,* he redefined the relationship between the two orders. Although the coming of civilization could "confuse" villagers, throw them "into disbelief," and sometimes even deprive them of their "will to live," it could also stimulate them to greater "moral creativeness" and give birth to new "states of mind" in which individuals took "charge" of the moral order and made it "more inclusive." As an example, Redfield cited the "conscious reform" that had made life in the village of Chan Kom "so different a thing from precivilized thinking." Such deliberate efforts at reform seemed to Redfield "a conception of civilized man, [and] perhaps only of modern man."[98]

To Redfield's mind, the transformation of ethical judgment by the advent of civilization was of even greater moment than the way in which the moral order had been taken in charge. Recoiling from the untrammeled cultural relativism of the interwar period, he contended that cultural relativism enjoined "ethical neutralism," not "ethical indifference." The notion "that we ought to respect all systems of value," Redfield observed, did not necessarily follow from "the proposition that values are relative." Indeed, "we might just as well hate them all."[99] Insisting that "standards of truth and goodness" were relative to the "great *historic* cultural difference" between "uncivilized and civilized peoples," Redfield asserted that the "more decent and humane measure of goodness" accompanying civilization required him as an anthropologist to look "at the cultures of other peoples in the light of civilized ethical judgment." But he confessed that he was no longer able to separate the "feeling man" from the "objective anthropologist." Redfield, who had long held that anthropologists could understand other cultures only through what the sociologist Charles Horton Cooley had called "sympathetic introspection," or empathy with their informants, declared that he would henceforth employ a double standard of ethical judgment when evaluating the conduct of "primitive peoples": at the same time that he judged their behavior in terms of their professed ideals, he

[96] Redfield, *The Primitive World and Its Transformations,* x–xi, 77, 24, 102–103, 111–113, 7, 16.
[97] Redfield, *The Primitive World and Its Transformations,* 26–53.
[98] Redfield, *The Primitive World and Its Transformations,* 50, 77, 81, 83, 111–138.
[99] Redfield, *The Primitive World and Its Transformations,* 146–147. In *Man and His Works: The Science of Cultural Anthropology* (New York: Knopf, 1949), Melville J. Herskovits wrote that "A basic necessity of ethnographic research is the exercise of scientific judgment, which in turn calls for rigid exclusion of value judgments" (p. 80).

would also judge their behavior in terms of historic "conceptions" of "what human beings ought to be."[100]

In *The Primitive World and Its Transformations*, Redfield endorsed Alfred Kroeber's attempt to rehabilitate the doctrine of progress, which anthropologists had largely abandoned earlier in the twentieth century as they distanced themselves from evolutionary theory. According to Kroeber, there had been cumulative development over the course of recorded history not only in technology and science but also in moral refinement. As examples, he cited waning belief in magic and superstition and the decline of "infantile obsession with the outstanding physiological bases of human life." To these measures of progress Redfield now added the universalization of the moral order. Echoing the philosopher Alfred North Whitehead, Redfield proclaimed that the ideas in history that had "the most force" were those "that speak for everyone." Ideas such as "permanent peace" and "universal human responsibility," Redfield believed, were "possible only in civilization."[101]

In 1954, with Singer's help, Redfield linked the distinction between the moral and technical orders to three other distinctions: the first, between "orthogenetic" and "heterogenetic" cities; the second, between "primary" and "secondary" civilizations; and the third, between "literati" and the "intelligentsia." Orthogenetic cities arose in primary civilizations such as China and India in which literati – clerics, astronomers, theologians, and the like – developed a great tradition out of a little tradition by "carrying forth" an older culture "into systematic and reflective dimensions." Heterogenetic cities, by contrast, arose in secondary civilizations such as the Americas in which the intelligentsia, many of them foreigners or cosmopolitan figures, created "original modes of thought" that had either "authority beyond" or were "in conflict with old cultures and civilizations." These new states of mind, in turn, weakened or even supplanted little traditions.[102]

[100] Redfield, *The Primitive World and Its Transformations*, 157, 164–165 (emphasis in original); Redfield, "Social Science among the Humanities," in *Human Nature and the Study of Society*, 53.

[101] A. L. Kroeber, *Anthropology: Race, Language, Culture, Psychology, Prehistory* (New York: Harcourt, 1948), 296–304; Redfield, *The Primitive World and Its Transformations*, 155–165. In *Adventures of Ideas* (New York: Macmillan, 1933), Whitehead had asserted that "the growth of the idea of the essential rights of human beings, arising from their sheer humanity, affords a striking example in the history of ideas. Its formations and its effective diffusion can be reckoned as a triumph – a chequered triumph – of the later phase of civilization" (p. 15). Both Redfield and Kroeber were influenced by renewed interest in evolution among anthropologists in the 1950s and early 1960s. In 1964, Eric Wolf hailed the "new American evolutionism" as heralding "the achievement of a degree of scientific maturity." As it turned out, however, interest in evolution peaked around the Darwinian Centennial in 1959 and was already receding in 1964. Wolf, *Anthropology*, 31; Stocking, "Do Good, Young Man," 185–189.

[102] Robert Redfield and Milton Singer, "The Cultural Role of Cities," in *Economic Development and Social Change* 3 (1954): 53–73; reprinted in *Human Nature and the Study of Society*, 326–350, on 332. Redfield and Singer wrote this paper for a conference on "The Role of Cities in Economic Growth and Culture Change" organized by the economic historian Bert F. Hoselitz.

Although he was becoming ever more interested in civilization, Redfield never severed the deep attachment he felt to village life that originally brought him into anthropology. In lectures at Sweden's Uppsala University in 1953, which were published in 1955 under the title *The Little Community: Viewpoints for the Study of a Human Whole*, he argued on holistic grounds for the continuing relevance of the "little community," or village, as the primary site of anthropological work. "Of all the conspicuous enduring forms in which humanity occurs," he explained, the village was "the most nearly self-sufficient and the most nearly comprehensible in itself alone." Moreover, the study of villages and other "human wholes" lay in "the borderland between science and art."[103]

In 1955, Redfield essayed the "enlargement of anthropological thinking" that ensued from anthropologists' taking up the study of communities that were "parts of larger and compound societal and cultural wholes." In the Cooper Lectures at Swarthmore College, published in 1956 under the title *Peasant Society and Culture*, Redfield characterized peasants as a "generic type" of mankind uniform over space and time.[104] Peasants were rural dwellers in old civilizations who not only controlled and cultivated land "for subsistence and as part of a traditional way of life," but also looked to, and were influenced by, "gentry or townspeople whose way of life is like [theirs] but in a more civilized form."[105] Invoking "the social organization of tradition," Redfield argued that anthropologists could not understand what was going on in peasants' minds without knowing something of what was going on at the same time in the minds of the literati – the "remote teachers, priests, or philosophers" – of the civilizations of which the peasants were parts. Indeed, peasant culture depended on "continual communication to the local community of thought originating outside of it." Peasant culture, moreover, had an "evident history" that the anthropologist needed to know something about. Far from being local, this history was "the history of the civilization of which the village culture [was] but one local expression."[106]

Redfield's attempts to arrive at a generic characterization of the peasant's "worldview," or "attitude toward the universe," prompted the German émigré F. G. Friedmann, then teaching philosophy at the University of Arkansas, to organize a "symposium by correspondence" in which twenty-nine participants compared the peasantries of Italy, Spain, Syria, and other countries. Observing

[103] Redfield, *The Little Community*, 157, 163.
[104] Robert Redfield to the Ford Foundation, 29 June 1955, copy in folder 225, box 35, series 200, RG 2-1955, Rockefeller Foundation Archives, RAC; Robert Redfield to Richard Brandt, 24 November 1954, Ford Foundation Cultural Studies Program Records, box 1, folder 20; Robert Redfield, *Peasant Society and Culture: An Anthropological Approach to Civilization* (1956; repr., Chicago: University of Chicago Press, 1960), 3.
[105] Redfield, *Peasant Society and Culture*, 5–22. Redfield emphasized "the importance in peasant life of the contrast between his life and that of the townsman or gentry." Robert Redfield to Irwin T. Sanders, 16 November 1954, Redfield Papers, box 10, folder 2b.
[106] Redfield, *Peasant Society and Culture*, 40–59.

that "today more peasants are made as Indian or Chinese civilization moves into the communities of tribal peoples," Redfield distinguished "secondary peasantry," such as the villagers of Chan Kom, whose Mayan cultural roots differed from those of Spanish "invaders," from "primary peasantry" who shared cultural roots with gentry and townsmen. He also ventured a "vague and impressionistic" statement of peasant values. These included "an intense attachment to native soil; a reverent disposition toward habitat and ancestral ways; a restraint on individual self-seeking in favor of family and community; a certain suspiciousness, mixed with appreciation, of town life; a sober and earthy ethic."[107]

In 1954, when Robert Hutchins left the Ford Foundation to become president of the Fund for the Republic, foundation officers decided to terminate their support for the Program in Intercultural Studies. In response, Redfield and Singer decided to concentrate on India as "a concrete and detailed example of developed method for at least one civilization."[108] In the fall of 1955, Redfield and his wife departed for India for fieldwork in the eastern region of Orissa, where, Redfield thought, "the whole range of human civilizations" – everything from primitive forest dwellers to peasants to townspeople and "modern intellectuals" – could be found. Soon after arriving in India, however, Redfield fell ill and was advised to return immediately to Chicago, where his illness was diagnosed as lymphatic leukemia.[109]

With any further fieldwork now out of the question, Redfield devoted the remainder of his life to refining his social anthropology of civilizations. In 1957, he delivered the keynote address at a conference held at the University of Chicago to discuss undergraduate courses in Indian Civilization. Three years earlier, a faculty committee that included Milton Singer had recommended that the University of Chicago add year-long courses on "non-Western civilizations" to its undergraduate curriculum. Modeled on the university's Western Civilization survey, these courses were designed to "sharpen and deepen" students' understanding of their own culture by exposing them to "a contrasted great civilization." Redfield's suggestion that civilizations be construed as "continua" comprising all cultures, including the most primitive, rather than as discrete

[107] Redfield, *Peasant Society and Culture*, 60–79; E. L. K. Francis, "The Personality Type of the Peasant According to Hesiod's Works and Days: A Culture Case Study," *Rural Sociology* 10 (1945): 275–295; Robert Redfield to F. G. Friedmann, 28 February, 16 March 1952; F. G. Friedmann to Robert Redfield, 4 March 1952, in *The Ethnographic Moment: Robert Redfield and F. G. Friedmann*, ed. David A. Rees (New Brunswick, N.J.: Transaction Publishers, 2006), 24–30. Among the participants in the symposium by correspondence was Eric Wolf, who went on, after Redfield's death, to become the foremost anthropological student of peasants.

[108] After external consultants reviewed the Program in Intercultural Studies program, Ford Foundation officers decided that Redfield and Singer's project would not contribute "directly to the early realization of a world community." Wilcox, *Robert Redfield and the Development of American Anthropology*, 143.

[109] Redfield to Evans, 23 September 1955.

and exclusive "classes," reflected just how far his thought had evolved beyond the polarities of the folk–urban continuum.[110]

In the spring of 1958, while in residence at the Institute for Advanced Study, Redfield drafted three chapters of a manual on comparing cultures and civilizations that Singer and he had long talked about writing. In one chapter he combined his conception of the little community with Kroeber's conception of the ecumene to conceive of civilization as a persisting "historic structure" in which great and little traditions interacted over long periods of time.[111] In another chapter, he traced anthropologists' interest in studying modern communities as primitive isolates to representative microcosms, to parts of a "societal system," and, finally, to classes in typologies.[112] In the third chapter, Redfield discussed the worldviews of civilizations as "structure[s] of tradition."[113]

Redfield said his last word on "civilization" in an entry for *Collier's Encyclopedia* completed shortly before his death. He described how, since 1500, Europe, once "isolated, peripheral, and culturally dependent on the Mediterranean," had carried out "a revolutionary transformation of most of the world," in the process "substantially destroy[ing]" the great traditions of "Aboriginal America" whose "more reflective and creative elites" had been "decapitat[ed]." To his mind, Europe's "radical expansion," and the "often violent repercussions" it was producing, did not constitute so much "Americanization," or even "Westernization," but "modernization." For technological improvement, secularization, and the other processes then transforming the world were going on "almost everywhere 'of themselves.'"[114] Unlike Kroeber, who looked forward to the coalescence of an international pool of styles, Redfield worried about such far-reaching change in "the nature and arrangement of civilization." In the past, primary civilizations had "expanded and matured in relative isolation" over long periods of time. But the "world civilization" then emerging seemed to Redfield "another kind of thing." Arising less from tradition than from such

[110]   Richard E. Streeter and Chauncy D. Harris, foreword to *Introducing India in Liberal Education: Proceedings of a Conference Held at the University of Chicago, May 17, 18, 19, 1957*, ed. Milton Singer (Chicago: University of Chicago Press, 1957), iii–vi; Robert Redfield, "Thinking about a Civilization," ibid., 3–15; Davis, *South Asia at Chicago*, 46–50. Until it was reorganized by McKim Marriott in 1966–68, the year-long course on Indian civilization at Chicago took as its starting point Redfield's conception of India as "a living, organic entity characterized by a distinctive culture and social organization." Redfield's keynote address, "Thinking about a Civilization," was often the initial reading assignment in the course.

[111]   Singer, "Robert Redfield's Development of a Social Anthropology of Civilizations," 221–222; Robert Redfield, "Civilizations as Things Thought About," in *Human Nature and the Study of Society*, 364–375.

[112]   Robert Redfield, "Civilizations as Societal Structures? The Development of Community Studies," in *Human Nature and the Study of Society*, 375–391.

[113]   Robert Redfield, "Civilizations as Cultural Structures?" in *Human Nature and the Study of Society*, 392–395.

[114]   Robert Redfield, "Civilization," in *Collier's Encyclopedia* (1960); reprinted in *Human Nature and the Study of Society*, 413–414.

"new things" as science, technology, and standardization, this emergent world civilization threatened to obliterate the "local and traditional." By the late 1950s, the "two conditions of civilization" – "arrangement into ancient great civilizations" and "new widespread modernity" – coexisted. Redfield feared that if modernity ever came to predominate, it would usher in an era of "post-civilization."[115]

After Redfield's death, Milton Singer brought the Program in Intercultural Studies to an end. He also continued his fieldwork in Madras, and, in 1972, published *When a Great Tradition Modernizes: An Anthropological Approach to Indian Civilization.* Combining textual study with fieldwork, Singer's book focused on the interaction between the great tradition of Sanskritic Hinduism and modern life. It paid special attention to the "adaptive strategies" of leading Madras industrialists, who defused potential conflict between ritual duty and business acumen by "compartmentalizing" their religion. Hinduism, Singer concluded, did not impede modernization in India. Rather, Indian civilization was "becoming more 'modern' without becoming less 'Indian.'"[116]

THE ECUMENE AND THE GREAT TRADITION OF WORLD HISTORY

The convergence between Kroeber's natural history approach and Redfield's social anthropological approach to the study of civilizations paved the way for the emergence of world history, a field that American historians and anthropologists played key roles in developing.[117]

In *The Rise of the West: A History of the Human Community* (1963), William H. McNeill emphasized the mode and character of communication within the matrix of an Eurasian ecumene. Twenty-six years earlier, as a graduate student at Cornell, McNeill had conceived the idea of writing a world history after he had been "transported" by the "poetic" genius of the first three volumes of Arnold Toynbee's *Study of History.* Oswald Spengler's "Germanic thought-world" and "numerology" put McNeill off, but Toynbee's world history opened "new vistas" and convinced him of "the global scope of the meaningful past." Years later, McNeill met Toynbee, who arranged for him to spend the years from 1950 to 1952 in England. When McNeill tried to interest Toynbee in anthropology, he failed, because Toynbee, like Spengler before him, refused to take diffusion into account, assuming that "separate civilizations borrowed nothing of importance from one another." Upon his return to the

---

[115] Redfield, "Civilization," 414.

[116] Singer, *When a Great Tradition Modernizes.*

[117] According to Anthony Molho and Gordon Wood, "American historians virtually invented the concept of 'world history.'" Anthony Molho and Gordon S. Wood, introduction to *Imagined Histories: American Historians Interpret the Past,* ed. Anthony Molho and Gordon S. Wood (Princeton, N.J.: Princeton University Press, 1998), 10. I would amend Molho and Wood's statement to include anthropologists such as Eric R. Wolf.

United States, McNeill set out to "buttress" Toynbee's "edifice" with the help of diffusion and other concepts borrowed from anthropology.[118]

McNeill's interest in anthropology stretched back to his undergraduate days at the University of Chicago when he sat through Redfield's lectures on the "folk society." Quickly realizing that Redfield's folk–urban continuum lacked time depth, McNeill began "to explore the missing time dimension of social change as Redfield envisaged it." He was also influenced by Clark Wissler's writings, which revealed "how contact with the Spanish and their array of new skills tempted or allowed Plains Indians to borrow 'culture traits' from the newcomers."[119]

McNeill's exposure to anthropology convinced him not only that borrowing was a "normal human reaction of an encounter with strangers possessing superior skills," but also that "separate civilizations were not nearly as impervious to outside influences – especially technological improvements – as Toynbee claimed." Indeed, encounters between peoples, which anthropologists termed "culture contact" or "acculturation," seemed to McNeill to be "the principal motor of social change within civilized and simpler societies alike."[120] Anthropology, moreover, whetted McNeill's interest in "pattern recognition," which he eventually came to regard as the "chef d'ouevre of human intelligence."[121]

Organizing his narrative around "modes of transport and communication," McNeill identified the "center of highest skills" for each civilization, then described the reaction of "neighboring peoples" to "pattern[s] of cultural flow." The history of civilization thus became the "history of the expansion of particularly attractive cultural and social patterns through the conversion of barbarians to modes of life they found superior to their own."[122] According to McNeill, the spread of agriculture from its Middle Eastern hearth throughout Eurasia paved the way for the emergence of three other culture areas in India, China, and Mediterranean Europe. Then, in the second century B.C.E., the opening of the silk road created an ecumene, a continuous chain of civilizations stretching from China to Gibraltar. Although each of the four culture areas within this Eurasian ecumene resisted "aping" the ways of the others, cultural interchange was common. A "decisive change," however, occurred around the year 1500, when Europeans, after gaining naval control of the Indian Ocean,

---

[118] William H. McNeill, "Arnold J. Toynbee," in *Mythistory and Other Essays* (Chicago: University of Chicago Press, 1986), 187–188, 190, 194, 184. McNeill tried later to rehabilitate Toynbee's reputation among professional historians in *Arnold J. Toynbee: A Life* (New York: Oxford University Press, 1989).

[119] William H. McNeill, *The Pursuit of Truth: A Historian's Memoir* (Lexington: University Press of Kentucky, 2005), 22–26.

[120] William H. McNeill, "The Rise of the West as a Long-Term Process," in *Mythistory and Other Essays*, 57.

[121] McNeill, "The Rise of the West as a Long-Term Process," 55; William H. McNeill, "Mythistory, or Truth, Myth, History, and Historians," in *Mythistory and Other Essays*, 5.

[122] McNeill, "The Rise of the West as a Long-Term Process," 57, 62.

breached the autonomy of the other culture areas. Since then, European colonization had transformed the Eurasian ecumene into a global web.[123]

In emphasizing the role of diffusion and in placing the Eurasian ecumene at the heart of the "history of the human community," McNeill provided an alternative to Spengler's, Sorokin's, and Toynbee's "disregard of time and space." The publication of *The Rise of the West*, moreover, ensured that the rise and fall of civilizations would no longer be treated as "isolated and self-sufficient events."[124] Then, too, McNeill's book left Europe, in the words of one reviewer, "so far out on the periphery (especially after the classical period) that it [was] scarcely visible."[125]

One of McNeill's colleagues at the University of Chicago, the Islamist Marshall Hodgson, went even further in decentering European history. While working on a dissertation directed by Gustave von Grunebaum, Hodgson had been employed as a research associate for the Program in Intercultural Studies. When Anthropology 342 compared Islamic and Western civilizations in the fall of 1954, Hogdson suggested that a "civilizational pattern" could be construed in terms of "a constant and changing 'dialectic' between the orthodox and heterodox interpretations of the pattern." In his struggle against the "Europeocentrism" of much Western historical scholarship on Islam, Hogdson sketched an "interregional" history that cast the history of civilization as an Asia-centered history. Europe figured in Hodgson's "Afro-Eurasian Oikoumene," a band of "agrarian cited societies" spanning the entire landmass from China to the Mediterranean, as the site of "The Great Transmutation," the general cultural transformation that "culminated" in the industrial and the French revolutions. Holding that world history could not be "reduced to the history of the West" just "because industrialism first spread there," Hodgson detected a "whiff of Eurocentrism" in McNeill's *The Rise of the West*. In his magnum opus, the three-volume *Venture of Islam: Conscience and History in a World Civilization*, published six years after his death in 1968 at the age of forty-six, Hodgson left Eurocentrism behind by situating Islamic civilization in the context of the history of mankind – for Hodgson, the intelligible unit of history.[126]

---

[123] McNeill, *The Rise of the West*, passim; J. R. McNeill and William McNeill, *The Human Web: A Bird's-Eye View of World History* (New York: Norton, 2003).

[124] L. P. Stavrianos, review of *The Rise of the West*, *American Historical Review* 69 (1965): 715.

[125] Joseph R. Strayer, review of *The Rise of the West*, *Journal of Modern History* 36 (1964): 185.

[126] Marshall G. S. Hodgson, *The Order of Assassins: The Struggle of the Early Nizari Isma'ilis against the Islamic World* (The Hague: Mouton, 1955); Marshall G. S. Hodgson to Robert Redfield, 23 September 1954, Ford Foundation Cultural Studies Program Records, box 8, folder 1; Marshall G. S. Hodgson, "Hemispheric Interregional History as an Approach to World History," *Cahiers d'histoire mondiale/Journal of World History* 1 (1954): 715–723; Marshall G. S. Hodgson, "The Great Western Transmutation," *Chicago Today* 4 (1967): 40–50; Marshall G. S. Hodgson, "The Interrelations of Societies in History," *Comparative Studies in Society and History* 5 (1963): 227–250; McNeill, *The Pursuit of Truth*, 73–74; Marshall G. S. Hodgson, *The Venture of Islam: Conscience and History in a World Civilization* (Chicago: University of Chicago Press, 1974); Edmund Burke III, "Islam and World History: The Contributions of Marshall Hodgson," *Radical History Review* 39 (1987): 117–123.

Encouraged by the challenge that McNeill's *The Rise of the West* posed to Spengler's and Toynbee's "civilizational monads," and by Hodgson's attempt "to deal with the Islamic world in all its geographic and temporal dimensions [while avoiding] many of the ethnocentric biases of other Western historians," Eric R. Wolf incorporated the history of peoples long regarded as without history by both anthropologists and historians into the history of European expansion since 1400. "The people without history," Wolf argued in *Europe and the People without History* (1982), were as much agents in world history as they were its victims. Even in 1400, before Europe began to expand, "populations existed in interconnections"; even then, if there were "any isolated societies," they "were but temporary phenomena." Both historians and anthropologists, Wolf contended, had tended to "falsify reality" by failing to treat the world as "a totality of interconnected processes." Although critical of what he regarded as Alfred Kroeber's positivism, Wolf acknowledged that he could not have written his "analytic history" without building on Kroeber's efforts to develop "a global culture history" emphasizing the "process of cultural connections." Wolf, moreover, had studied with Kroeber's student Julian Steward, whose anthropology, he once suggested, should be understood as a reaction to Kroeber's lack of interest in "causality." Wolf had also "learned much from" Robert Redfield, "both in agreeing with him and, perhaps even more, in defining [his] differences from him."[127]

Interestingly enough, historians were divided in their opinions of Wolf's *Europe and the People without History*. Eric Hobsbawn welcomed it as "exemplifying" Karl Marx's "living influence" in the centenary year of his death. While "heartily embrac[ing] Wolf's 'working hypothesis' of the universality of human contact and influence," William McNeill condemned *Europe and the People without History* as "an exercise in Marxist piety," and Wolf's vision of history as "a vain, if valiant, effort to reaffirm truths that seemed self-evident in his youth." Philip Curtin, however, thought that *Europe and the People without History* "deserve[d] a wide reading by historians" as "a most interesting venture in world history." Indeed, in his presidential address to the American Historical Association in 1983, Curtin held up Wolf's book as "a useful example, by an anthropologist, of the kind of broad synthesis" that historians "should be doing."[128]

Generally speaking, American historians felt more comfortable in learning from anthropologists' microscopic analyses than from their macroscopic ventures, which smacked of metahistory. At the Wingspread Conference in

---

[127] Eric R. Wolf, *Europe and the People Without History* (1982; repr., Berkeley: University of California Press, 1997), 194, xvi, 19, 71, 395–396; Wolf, "Alfred L. Kroeber," 45; Eric R. Wolf, "Robert Redfield," in *Totems and Teachers*, 178.

[128] Eric Hobsbawm, "The Movement of Capitalism," review of *Europe and the People without History*, *TLS*, 28 October 1983, 1182; William H. McNeill, review of *Europe and the People without History*, *Journal of Interdisciplinary History* 14 (1984): 660–661; Philip Curtin, review of *Europe and the People without History*, *American Historical Review* 89 (1984): 89–90; Philip Curtin, "Depth, Span, and Relevance," *American Historical Review* 89 (1984): 1–9, on 4.

December 1977, convened to chart new directions in American intellectual history, the convener John Higham noted "the influence of anthropology," "the increasing affinity" that intellectual historians had recently felt for anthropology, and the anthropologists, most notably Clifford Geertz, whom the conferees thanked in their footnotes for enriching their "grasp of the meanings expressed in symbol, ritual, and language." In 1980, Raymond Grew, then editor of *Comparative Studies in Society and History*, the journal that Sylvia Thrupp had established with Alfred Kroeber's encouragement and of which Eric Wolf served as co-editor, commented that the phrase "Comparative History" suggested "first of all the comparison of civilization, comparison on the grandest scale in the manner of Spengler, Sorokin, and Toynbee." Although "stimulating and provocative," the metahistorians' "search for the morphology of history" was "not intimately related to what most practicing historians really do."[129]

AMERICA AND ITS CULTURE

At the same time that anthropologists and historians were developing the field of world history, American intellectuals were revising their attitudes toward American culture, its relationship to Europe, and its place in the world. As William Phillips and Philip Rahv pointed out in their introduction to the 1952 *Partisan Review* symposium, "Our Country and Our Culture," American intellectuals no longer regarded America as hostile to art and culture, felt "disinherited," or accepted "alienation" as their "fate in America." No longer thinking of themselves as "rebels and exiles," they wanted "to be a part of American life." Perhaps even more important, they were redefining America's relation to Europe. If, by the early 1950s, Europe had become dependent, militarily and economically on the United States, was it not becoming culturally dependent as well?[130]

By 1952, American intellectuals, almost without exception, embraced the "intrinsic and positive value" of American democracy, but they felt less sure about the democratization of culture. In particular, they worried that an emergent "mass culture," the "outgrowth of political democracy under conditions of modern industrial development," would undermine the position they had so laboriously fashioned for themselves by converting culture into a commodity and separating them from their "natural audience[s]." Could a political democracy, they wondered, "nourish great art and thought"? Or would democratization necessarily undermine "intellectual and aesthetic values traditional to Western civilization"?[131]

---

[129] John Higham, introduction to *New Directions in American Intellectual History*, ed. John Higham and Paul K. Conkin (Baltimore: Johns Hopkins University Press, 1979), xvii–xviii; Raymond Grew, "The Case for Comparing Histories," *American Historical Review* 85 (1980): 763–778, on 764, 768.
[130] "Editorial Statement," in *America and the Intellectuals*, 1, 3.
[131] "Editorial Statement," in *America and the Intellectuals*, 4–5.

4 *Anthropologists and the Rediscovery of America*

None of the participants in the symposium disagreed with the point that intellectuals had dramatically revised their attitudes toward both America and American culture. Allan Dowling contrasted the situation in 1932, when, as an American expatriate living in France, he had looked on America as "completely materialistic" and "without respect for the artist," with the situation twenty years later, when he saw America as "the chief hope for the future of the world in this century." The French émigré Jacques Barzun attributed the dramatic reversal in intellectuals' attitudes toward America to "the combined impact of the First World War and the Depression." Together, they had acted "like the extension and contraction of a vast heart," "pump[ing] Americans to Europe and then [drawing] them back." As a result, "a kind of cosmopolitan spirit" had begun "to replace the provincial, complacent attitude" about which European and American critics had long complained. Arthur Schlesinger, Jr., agreed. After the Depression stimulated the "revaluation of America," the "rise of fascism abroad thrust the problem of American culture into a new dimension. Next to Himmler, even Babbitt began to look good." By then, too, as Philip Rahv observed, the passage of time had "considerably blunted the edge of the old Jamesian complaint as to the barrenness of the native scene."[132]

Nevertheless, participants in the symposium, as public intellectuals, voiced a number of complaints about America and its culture. Some were familiar. "Culturally speaking," America remained, in James Burnham's opinion, "a 'semi-barbarian superstate of the periphery,' dependent still on the older spiritual soil [of Europe] in spite of new roots." William Barrett deplored the "widespread drift" of postwar America "toward conformism." Even while acknowledging the "new [American] hospitality to serious writing," Richard Chase lamented the "sometimes terrifying thinness and discontinuity" of American culture, and the "disjunction between professed and practical belief."[133]

A new complaint, though, centered on the democratization of culture, which, in the eyes of some observers, necessarily led to vulgarization. According to Irving Howe, America had "entered the stage of kitsch, the mass culture of the middle-brows," in which literature and art were now "estimable commodities." Arthur Schlesinger, Jr., warned that the more the mass media presupposed that Americans constituted a uniform audience, the more they tended "to strike at the roots of democracy" by manufacturing such an audience. C. Wright Mills insisted that his conception of a democratic society did not "include status uniformity or intellectual equality." Neither did Louis Kronenberger's conception, which was "surely away from democratization, from leveling off," toward "the classic pyramidal structure" that could still be found in Europe. What made any evaluation difficult, according to David Riesman, was that America's "class-mass culture" comprised "a series of audiences, stratified

---

[132] Allan Dowling, in *America and the Intellectuals*, 30–31; Jacques Barzun, ibid., 12–15; Arthur Schlesinger, Jr., ibid., 100–101; Philip Rahv, ibid., 89.

[133] James Burnham, in *America and the Intellectuals*, 25; William Barrett, ibid., 8; Richard Chase, ibid., 27.

by taste and class, each large enough to constitute, in psychological terms, a 'mass.'"[134]

Regardless of their feelings about mass culture, the symposium's participants viewed America's relation to Europe in a new light. "The end of the American artist's pilgrimage to Europe," Leslie Fiedler reminded his fellow participants, had always been "the discovery of America." To Jacques Barzun, it was Europe, and not America, that now appeared provincial. By 1952, as Barzun pointed out, America had become not only *"the* world power," but also "the center of world awareness." The situation had changed so much from the 1920s that, as Horace Gregory put it, the American artist who went to Europe no longer felt that he had left home. If "a painter, his pictures must be sold in New York"; if "a writer, his books must be published by New York publishers." Yet American intellectuals still had a lot learn from Europe. So long as one did not "confuse political democracy with majority rule in cultural matters," Joseph Frank suggested, democratization would not "necessarily lead to a leveling of culture." Intellectuals, added James Burnham, could hardly "affirm America without reaffirming Europe and the West," for Europe was their past.[135]

Finally, participants in the symposium affirmed "the tradition of critical non-conformism." To Richard Chase, "sustained dissent from and commitment to America" was "fundamentally, our *only* useful 'tradition.'" Intellectuals were necessary, Delmore Schwartz thought, "to sustain the traditional forms of culture amid the rank and overpowering growth of mass culture." To Arthur Schlesinger, Jr., "the only answer to mass culture" lay in "the affirmation of America, not as a uniform society, but as a various and pluralistic society, made up of many groups with diverse interests." In America's new intellectual elite, Lionel Trilling beheld a "countervailing condition" to the "threat" posed by mass culture. Indeed, the "rediscovery of America [could] go hand in hand with the tradition of critical non-conformism."[136]

So convinced were intellectuals of the existence of an American high culture that they enlisted in the postwar campaign of American cultural diplomats to project this high culture abroad. Deeply resentful of European condescension and generously supported by philanthropic foundations and federal agencies, American cultural diplomats struggled to disabuse Europeans of their views of America as a civilization without culture. To this end, the Rockefeller Foundation, the Ford Foundation, the Congress for Cultural Freedom (with covert support from the CIA), the United States Information Agency, and other organizations dispatched plays, art, orchestras, and other samples of American high culture to Europe. In the process, they embraced E. B. Tylor's complex whole as

---

[134] Irving Howe, in *America and the Intellectuals*, 54; Arthur Schlesinger, Jr., ibid., 102; C. Wright Mills, ibid., 76; Louis Kronenberger, ibid., 60; David Riesman, ibid., 98.

[135] Leslie Fiedler, in *America and the Intellectuals*, 33; Jacques Barzun, ibid., 15 (emphasis in original); Horace Gregory, ibid., 44; Joseph Frank, ibid., 39; James Burnham, ibid., 26.

[136] Richard Chase, in *America and the Intellectuals*, 28 (emphasis in original); Delmore Schwartz, ibid., 108; Arthur Schlesinger, Jr., ibid., 102; Lionel Trilling, ibid., 117.

"the indigenous American concept of culture." As Harry Levin pointed out in 1949, "along with our products" (everything from "jeeps and jukeboxes" to "CARE packages and foreign-language editions of the *Reader's Digest*") "we export our culture – 'culture' not in Matthew Arnold's terms, but in Ruth Benedict's patterns."[137]

Yet the influence of American high culture in postwar Europe paled in comparison with that of American popular culture. While American cultural diplomats sought to convince skeptical Europeans that American high culture was at least as good as the more historic European cultures, a generation of younger Europeans created their "own image" of America against "the background of the pictures of Hollywood and the soundtrack of rock'n'roll, jazz, blues, soul, and rhythm & blues." To these younger Europeans, American popular culture "signified an amalgam of freedom, fun, modernity, wealth, mobility, and youthful rebellion."[138]

Where, then, did postwar American culture stand in relation to European culture? Alfred Kroeber emphasized the fact that American culture was "historically derivative from West European culture." But derivation did not necessarily mean lack of creativity. On the contrary; not only had "the center of power and wealth productivity" in Kroeber's opinion "definitely moved out of western-central Europe to the peripheral East and West," there were even indications that the Russian and American peripheries "may come to dominate in creativity also."[139] For William McNeill, America figured as an appendage of Europe and a bit player on the world scene until the fateful year of 1917, when America entered the First World War and the Bolsheviks seized power in Russia. Since then, Europe had been eclipsed as "the undisputed center and arbiter of Western civilization." To McNeill, the rise of America and Russia to "world pre-eminence" was "only another instance" of the "familiar world phenomenon" of "the migration of military-political power from more anciently civilized but less effectively organized heartlands to regions nearer the frontier."[140] Arnold Toynbee also regarded America as an appendage of Europe. When

---

[137] Volker R. Berghahn, *America and the Intellectual Cold Wars in Europe* (Princeton, N.J.: Princeton University Press, 2001), xii–xiv, 88, 172, 290; John R. Everett, "American Culture in the World Today," *American Quarterly* 6 (1954): 245–252; Harry Levin, "Some European Views of Contemporary American Literature," *American Quarterly* 1 (1949): 264; Leila Zenderland, "Constructing American Studies: Culture, Identity, and the Expansion of the Humanities," in *The Humanities and the Dynamics of Inclusion since World War II*, ed. David A. Hollinger (Baltimore: Johns Hopkins University Press, 2006), 273–313.

[138] Reinhold Wagnleitner, "The Irony of American Culture Abroad: Austria and the Cold War," in *Recasting America: Culture and Politics in the Age of Cold War*, ed. Lary May (Chicago: University of Chicago Press, 1988), 285–301; Reinhold Wagnleitner, *Coca-Colonization and the Cold War: The Cultural Mission of the United States in Austria after the Second World War*, trans. Diana M. Wolf (Chapel Hill: University of North Carolina Press, 1994), xiii; Rob Kroes, *If You've Seen One You've Seen the Mall: Europeans and American Mass Culture* (Urbana: University of Chicago Press, 1996).

[139] Kroeber, *A Roster of Civilizations and Culture*, 33, 29.

[140] McNeill, *The Rise of the West*, 794.

considered in the light of his definition of a civilization ("the smallest unit of historical study at which one arrives when one tries to understand the history of one's own country"), American history was "unintelligible" until placed in "the intelligible unit of social life" of which it is a part, "call it Western Christendom, Western Civilization, Western society, or the Western world."[141]

Yet, as Alfred Kazin pointed out, the cultural relationship between America and Europe had been dramatically altered since the 1920s. No longer imbibers of European culture, Americans had become "the main event."[142] When F. O. Matthiessen visited Europe for the first time as a Yale freshman in 1920, he went in quest of culture to be imbibed. In 1947, by contrast, he carried American high culture to Europe in lectures on American literature at the Salzburg Seminar and Prague's Charles University. Agreeing with Delmore Schwartz that "Europe is still the greatest thing in North America," Matthiessen felt it was "particularly urgent" to close "the wide gap" that had opened between a Europe that had "undergone fascism and destructive war at first hand" and an America that had "come out of the war richer and more powerful than ever before."[143]

Matthiessen's concern about closing the gap between America and Europe ran through the early issues of the *American Quarterly*, which began publication in 1949 with the intention of "giving a sense of direction in the culture of America, past and present."[144] Writing in the first issue of the *American Quarterly*, the Oxford lecturer Max Beloff declared that "mutual comprehension" between America and Europe was "a vital need of civilization." Only Americans, he said, could "answer [European] misrepresentations of America."[145]

Over the course of the 1950s, the gap between culture and civilization narrowed considerably in the field of American studies. When a small group of literary scholars, historians, and intellectuals met in 1951 to organize the American Studies Association, "business went briskly" until they began to argue about whether to call the new organization the "American Civilization Society" or the "American Studies Association."[146] When Richard H. Huber

---

[141] Arnold J. Toynbee, *A Study of History*, abridgment of Volumes VII–X, by D. C. Somervell (1957; repr., New York: Oxford University Press, 1987), 321–322; Arnold J. Toynbee, "Encounters between Civilizations," *Harper's*, April 1947; reprinted in *Civilization on Trial and the World and the West* (New York: Meridian, 1958), 195–196.

[142] Alfred Kazin, "Carrying the Word Abroad," *American Studies International* 26 (1988): 62–66; Alfred Kazin, *New York Jew* (New York: Knopf, 1978), 170–171, quoted in Richard Pells, *Not Like Us: How Europeans Have Loved, Hated, and Transformed American Culture since World War II* (New York: Basic Books, 1997), 108–109.

[143] F.O. Matthiessen, *From the Heart of Europe* (New York: Oxford University Press, 1948), 3, 13–16, 22–25; F. O. Matthiessen, "The Responsibilities of the Critic," in *The Responsibilities of the Critic: Essays and Reviews by F. O. Matthiessen*, ed. John F. Rackliffe (New York: Oxford University Press, 1952), 12.

[144] Heinig Cohen, preface to *The American Experience: Approaches to the Study of the United States*, ed. Hennig Cohen (Boston: Houghton Mifflin, 1968), v.

[145] Max Beloff, "The Projection of America Abroad," *American Quarterly* 1 (1949): 27–29.

[146] Carl Bode, "The Start of the ASA," *American Quarterly* 31 (1979): 349; Janice Radway, "What's in a Name?" *American Quarterly* 51 (1999): 3–4.

advanced "a theory of American studies" in 1954, he used the terms "American studies" and "American civilization" interchangeably.[147] Also in 1954, Edward F. Grier noted that programs that called themselves programs in American civilization, as opposed to programs in American studies, did so to emphasize the fact that they were dedicated to the study of "higher culture." For "civilization," he reminded the readers of the *American Quarterly*, designated "a special aspect of more advanced cultures."[148]

Educated Europeans, however, continued to express skepticism about the existence, let alone the quality, of American civilization. The English hosts of Louis Filler, a Fulbright lecturer in England in 1955, introduced his lectures on American civilization with the "remark, uttered without guile and with almost no malice, that 'many of us have wondered if there is such a thing as American Civilization.'" Filler disarmed his audiences by saying that many Americans were asking themselves the same question. Indeed, America seemed to Filler "almost unique among nations" in the "palpable division of opinion among its literate classes on whether or not, and in what sense, it [possessed] a 'civilization.'"[149]

Publication of Max Lerner's book *America as a Civilization* in 1957 set off a running debate between Lerner and Arnold Toynbee over the existence of a distinctive American "civilization-pattern."[150] Unconvinced by the enormous amount of evidence Lerner marshaled, Toynbee continued to view America as "an extension of [European] civilization flowering in a new way and under new conditions."[151] Lerner countered by pointing out that what had once been the "Europeanization of America" had, since 1945, become the "Americanization of Europe." The result was that America now bore "something of the same relation to Europe that European civilization in its own day bore to the classical world." Even though Americans had borrowed a lot from Europe, they had developed those borrowings "with such intensity as to make them universal."[152]

Toynbee's and Lerner's essays provoked Marshall Fishwick to organize a symposium on American civilization in the literary journal *Shenandoah* in 1958. Princeton's Willard Thorp set the tone for the symposium when he asked, "If America is not a civilization, why are so many scholars engaged in studying something called American Civilization?" Convinced of the existence of an American "high culture," Thorp pointed to the proliferation of cultural institutions in postwar America – universities, libraries, museums, orchestras, and

[147] Richard M. Huber, "A Theory of American Studies," *Social Education* 18 (1954): 269–270.
[148] Edward F. Grier, "Programs in American Civilization," *Journal of Higher Education* 25 (1954): 179-190, on 184, 186-187.
[149] Louis Filler, "The Interdisciplinary Factor in American Civilization," *School and Society*, 9 June 1956, 199.
[150] Max Lerner, "Notes on Literature and American Civilization," *American Quarterly* 11 (1959): 215.
[151] Arnold Toynbee, "Is America a Civilization?" *Shenandoah* 10 (1958): 5–10.
[152] Max Lerner, "Is America a Civilization?" *Shenandoah* 10 (1958): 10–13.

theaters – that guaranteed that no "man of talent" would languish in the provinces. "No other high or national culture (or civilization)," Thorp claimed, had "accomplished" such an extension of high culture from metropolitan centers to the peripheries.[153]

Brown's William Jordy had a different interpretation of Thorp's statistics. To his mind, they demonstrated less the American "ability to create" a high culture than the "will to consume" it. Although America remained in Jordy's eyes an appendage of Europe, it now appeared to be "the most creative country in the world in the visual arts" – a "surprising development" that as recently as the Depression could not have been foreseen. Moreover, by 1958, a "healthy balance" characterized "the American's attitude toward his European background": no longer did the man of superior gifts flee America "in chagrin at the crudeness of [its] frontier culture," or "overcompensate," as Constance Rourke had done, "by burrowing into [American] provincialities in search of their 'uniquely American' flavor." To Jordy, the greatest challenge now facing educated Americans was not to establish a high culture, but rather to cope with the democratization of culture. A "surge for higher education" was swelling the ranks of those who would "at least provide enthusiastic support for" American culture, if not "become its creators." Yet, "where quantity reigns supreme," Jordy asked, "can quality survive outside the coterie?" Jordy did not share John Everett's optimism that access to America's high culture would offset any tendency toward cultural leveling.[154]

David Potter, then teaching at Stanford, found himself hard-pressed to determine the "ratio" between such "distinctively American factors" as rapid technological change, a "social revolution" that had made Americans "the most mobile, most adaptable, and most rootless people on the planet," their rejection of "European ideas of hierarchy," and unprecedented affluence, on the one hand, and the factors producing "homogeneity within Western culture" on the other. Potter predicted that until American Studies scholars could agree on some "criteria for cultural measurement," "civilization" would remain a subjective term in their usage, "implicitly boasting a degree of excellence or a degree of independence." In America, "a society in its origins derivative [and] in its character very extensively adapted," those who spoke of an autonomous American civilization "den[ied] the derivation," while those who continued to regard America as an appendage of Europe "den[ied] the adaptation."[155]

Although Berkeley's Henry Nash Smith viewed American civilization as an "extension" of Western civilization, he denied that American myths and symbols were indistinguishable from those of Europe. To be sure, American myths and symbols had "come out of a [common] past which America and Europe

[153] Marshall Fishwick, "Is America a Civilization? *Shenandoah* 10 (1958): 3; Willard Thorp, "Is America a Civilization?" ibid., 15–18.
[154] William Jordy, "Is America a Civilization?" *Shenandoah* 10 (1958): 32–36.
[155] David M. Potter, "Is America a Civilization?" *Shenandoah* 10 (1958): 18–22.

share," but "the new conditions of life" on this side of the Atlantic had given them "different emphases." Thus the three myths Smith treated in *Virgin Land* – the Passage to India, the frontiersman as Noble Savage, and America as the Garden of the World – were all of European provenance, but each of them had acquired a recognizable American flavor over the course of the nineteenth century.[156]

The English-born Marcus Cunliffe had the last word in the *Shenandoah* symposium. In his opinion, America did not yet "constitute a separate major civilization." Although Western civilization exhibited "a great deal of regional variation," the commonalities between America and Europe outweighed the differences. Although "far from negligible," the American contribution to Western civilization did not seem to Cunliffe yet "so dominant" as to over-shadow the European "endowment." Still, Cunliffe admitted, there were numerous American "customs and attitudes that [owed] nothing directly to Europe" and that could be "understood only with close reference to the actualities of the American scene." Even more telling, ever since the American Revolution, millions of Americans had believed in the "uniqueness" of their country. "What matter that much of their culture was derivative?" Cunliffe asked. "Few Americans realized it." What did matter was that what Americans "had absorbed became American, and was steadily transformed."[157]

Whether or not America should be considered a civilization in its own right remained a "pressing question" to the American Studies scholars who gathered in Wilmington, Delaware, in 1963 for a conference on "New Frontiers in American Studies." All agreed that "the relation between the United States and Europe" remained a "great theme of American history."[158] In 1964, Harvard's Howard Mumford Jones reaffirmed "the profound and central truth that American culture [arose] from the interplay of two great sets of forces – the Old World and the New." Americans were thus "related to Europe by alternations of attraction and repulsion."[159]

Given the postwar concern about the existence of American high culture, it is hardly surprising that one of the arguments advanced for the establishment of the National Endowment for the Humanities in 1965 was to strengthen America's claim to world leadership by heralding the coming of age of its high culture.[160] By 1968, the taunts of skeptical Europeans such as the Reverend Sydney Smith about the lack of American masterpieces seemed "quaint" to the University of Pennsylvania's Hennig Cohen. Yet the "current counterpart" of

---

[156] Henry Nash Smith, "Is America a Civilization?" *Shenandoah* 10 (1958): 22–23.

[157] Marcus Cunliffe, "Is America a Civilization?" *Shenandoah* 10 (1958): 36–39.

[158] Marshall W. Fishwick, "New Frontiers in American Studies," *American Studies* 6 (1963): 1, 3–4.

[159] Howard Mumford Jones, *O Strange New World. American Culture: The Formative Years* (New York: Viking, 1964), vii–viii, 390–391.

[160] *Report of the Commission on the Humanities* (New York: American Council of Learned Societies, 1964), 4–6; James M. Banner, Jr. "At 25, the Humanities Endowment Faces New Perils," *Chronicle of Higher Education*, 16 May 1990, A48.

Smith's taunt – "Is there an American civilization?" – continued "to plague" American Studies scholars.[161]

By the mid-1960s, then, American intellectuals recognized that American culture had its own patterns. Although much of American culture might consist of borrowed elements (many of European provenance), it remade these elements along its own distinctive lines. Americans now boasted a high culture that had attained a rough equality with the more historic cultures of Europe. It was this high culture, defined broadly as a "complex whole," that American cultural diplomats were then trying to export to Europe. The United States had become Europe's protector and economic benefactor; had not Americans become custodians of Europe's cultural heritage as well? Whether America represented a civilization in its own right, or whether it remained a variant of European civilization, remained an open question. What was no longer at issue was whether Americans had to continue to apologize for the relative scarcity of American masterpieces. By the 1960s, the broad denotation of culture that Americans had embraced as the indigenous American concept of culture rendered the question of American masterpieces moot.

Thanks, in part, to the efforts of anthropologists, American culture had been reconciled with American civilization. This reconciliation owed a debt not only to the way in which anthropologists broadened the American understanding of culture from the Arnoldian emphasis on refinement and sophistication to culture as a complex whole. It also owed a debt to the way in which Alfred Kroeber emphasized collective cultural creativity as measured by "style" and Robert Redfield organized seminars that brought humanists and social scientists together to study the culture-civilizations of Asia. In the course of taking a historical turn after 1945 and taking up the study of civilizations, anthropologists had partially redefined "culture" to mean both refinement and civilization and way of life.

Yet, in democratizing culture, anthropologists had unleashed an impulse that they could not control. As we shall see in the Epilogue, scholars who once turned to anthropology when they were interested in culture began instead to turn to cultural studies. One of the reasons why they did so was because cultural studies gave them greater purchase on American popular culture, which even in the 1950s appears to have exercised more influence in Europe, at least among the young, than the high culture American cultural diplomats were then exporting.

[161] Cohen, preface to *The American Experience*, vi.

Epilogue

Between the First World War and the 1950s, anthropologists and like-minded social scientists recast a number of perennial concerns: they democratized culture, recognized the existence of social classes on the American scene, rid the American character of its racialist associations, formulated new American values, and reconciled American culture and civilization.

As we have seen, culture in its anthropological sense was far broader, and less elitist, than humanistic culture. For Matthew Arnold, the pursuit of culture required self-discipline, a considerable length of time, and, in many cases, leisure. The culture concept, by contrast, made culture a birthright, conferring culture on groups into which people were either born or assimilated. By the 1950s, American culture was no longer confined to masterpieces but had come to be seen as a "complex whole" that included behavior and artifacts as well as aesthetic and intellectual pursuits. Anthropology offered an alternative to the then-prevailing conception of the humanities: the notion, as Edward Said put it, that "humanism was a special attainment that required the cultivating or reading of certain difficult texts and, in the process, the giving up of certain things, like amusement, pleasure, relevance to worldly circumstances, and so on."[1] The broad conception of culture that anthropologists popularized helped Americans answer the taunts of skeptics about the rarity of American masterpieces by emphasizing popular access to cultural institutions. As Americans increasingly conceived of culture as a complex whole, they began to think in terms of cultural forms, cultural crisis, cultural trend, cultural analysis, and culture context. In short, as Jacques Barzun announced in 1956, "our culture" had become "an entity to reckon with."[2]

As the locus of culture shifted from the individual to the group, anthropologists and like-minded social scientists challenged men of letters as its

---

[1] Edward W. Said, *Humanism and Democratic Criticism* (New York: Columbia University Press, 2004), 16.

[2] Jacques Barzun, "Cultural History as a Synthesis," in *Varieties of History*, ed. Fritz Stern (New York: Meridian, 1957), 387–388, 390.

custodians. Ethnographies of the American scene came to rival both the novel of manners and the foreign visitor's travelogue as a source of authoritative insight into American manners and morals and furthered anthropologists' claim to the custody of culture. Inaugurated by Robert and Helen Lynd in 1929, and developed by W. Lloyd Warner and his many associates, the ethnography of the American scene called into question the vaunted American classlessness. By reorienting attention from production toward consumption and leisure, and by subordinating gains in occupation and income to lifestyle and social acceptance, Warner and his associates recast the way in which a generation of Americans thought about social class. By making class distinctions more resistant to changes in income, they raised doubts about the so-called middle-classification of postwar America. By delineating a culture of inequality in which class membership exposed one to snobbery and humiliation, they suggested that, in this respect, America was not so different from Europe.

Thanks to their collaboration with psychiatrists and others interested in culture and personality, anthropologists also became parties to the long-standing debate about the making of Americans by writing about national character in a new way that emphasized nurture more than nature and socialization instead of blood. At the heart of their inquiries into culture and personality was curiosity about what made a Frenchman a Frenchman, a Russian a Russian, or an American an American. Such a broad, nongenetic definition of who is an American expanded American nationality well beyond the native-born white Protestants who had staked exclusive claims to it in the nineteenth century. Although the controversy surrounding some of the national character studies published after 1945 tarnished culture and personality in the eyes of many social scientists, interest in delineating the American character spilled over into American history and American studies. In its new incarnation, the American character held considerable appeal to consensus historians and to members of the myth-symbol school of American studies, who wished to emphasize the commonalities among Americans and the continuities of American history.

In the late 1940s, Clyde Kluckhohn turned his attention from culture and personality to the scientific study of values. Modeling anthropology on linguistics, he searched for the cultural equivalents of the phoneme. Discovery of the basic units of cultures, Kluckhohn believed, would not only enable anthropologists to compare cultures, but also reveal common humanity amid human diversity. For Kluckhohn, the scientific study of values continued Edward Sapir's and Ruth Benedict's inquiries into the selectivity of cultures. In his attempts to chart changing American values, he extended Sapir's notion of "drift" from the linguistic to the cultural realm. Values, Kluckhohn held, were affective as well as cognitive; they added a deeply felt, nonrational, dimension to E. B. Tylor's "intellectualistic" definition of culture. As the organizing principles of implicit culture, values explained why culture had organization, or structure, as well as content. Values spoke to Kluckhohn's involvement in the postwar American quest for national purpose. By explaining why human behavior was neither random nor determined, values also anchored morality. In studying values, anthropologists were moving into an area – debate over what constituted the good life – that had been abandoned by American philosophers.

As anthropologists expanded their horizons beyond North America after the Second World War, they increasingly turned their attention to peasantries, complex societies, and historic civilizations. Leading the way were Alfred Kroeber, a macro-anthropologist who approached civilizations from the top down, and Robert Redfield, a student of contemporary change who approached civilizations from the bottom up. The convergence between Kroeber's and Redfield's approaches helped pave the way for the development of both global anthropology and world history. As anthropologists began to study such historic high cultures of the world as China and India, they decisively rejected Oswald Spengler's fatalistic notion that civilization marked the terminal stage of culture, a notion that many of them had shared between the wars. By the early 1960s, the terms "culture" and "civilization" had become nearly synonymous.[3]

HUMANISTS AND THE CULTURE CONCEPT

The emphasis that anthropologists had placed on patterning and valuation since Ruth Benedict's *Patterns of Culture* enabled some prominent American and English humanists "to climb aboard the culture wagon" during and after the Second World War. Finding the breadth and holism of the culture concept especially appealing, these humanists explored ways in which they could appropriate the broad, inclusive definition of culture that anthropologists had propagated for their own purposes.[4]

One humanist who climbed aboard the culture wagon was Lionel Trilling. Throughout his career, Trilling wrote for the "intellectual middle class" as a disciple of Matthew Arnold who viewed literature as the criticism of life. In *The Liberal Imagination* (1950), Trilling treated liberalism, more of "a large tendency" than "a concise body of ideas," in its relation to "the politics of culture"; that is, to the end of improving "the quality of human life." In his 1965 collection of essays, *Beyond Culture*, Trilling acknowledged the "semantic difficulties of the word culture." By 1965, "everyone," he wrote, was "conscious of two meanings of culture." There was its inclusive meaning – culture as comprising "a people's technology, its manners and customs, its religious beliefs and organization, its system of valuation, whether expressed or implicit" — and there was its narrower meaning as "that complex of activities which

[3] Felix Gilbert, "Cultural History and Its Problems," *Comité International des Sciences Historiques*, Rapports (1960) 1:40–41; E. H. Gombrich, *In Search of Cultural History* (Oxford: Clarendon Press, 1969), 1–2.

[4] Robert F. Berkhofer, Jr., "Clio and the Culture Concept: Some Impressions of a Changing Relationship in American Historiography," in *The Idea of Culture in the Social Sciences*, ed. Louis Schneider and Charles Bonjean (Cambridge: Cambridge University Press, 1973), 81–82; Roger Sandall, "When I Hear the Word 'Culture,'" *Encounter*, October 1980, 90.

includes the practice of the arts and of certain intellectual disciplines." When Trilling placed Sigmund Freud both "within" and "beyond" culture, it was in the context of the broader, more inclusive meaning of the word. Culture, he said, had become "a kind of absolute." Cultures were "thought of as self-contained systems not open to criticism from without." But Trilling, who wanted to harness literature "to liberate the individual from the tyranny of his culture" and thereby "permit him to stand beyond it in an autonomy of perception and judgment," gave Freud more credit than any anthropologist for the ubiquity of "the idea of culture" in its "modern sense." By at once situating the self within culture and setting it against the culture, Freud "made it apparent to us how entirely implicated in culture we are."[5]

On the other side of the Atlantic, the Anglo-American poet and literary critic T. S. Eliot explored how to keep culture as "the whole complex of behavior, thought, and feeling," distinct from, "but always in relation" to, the humanistic notion of culture. First, Eliot declared in 1943 that "there is no 'culture' [culture as refinement and sophistication] without 'a culture.'" Then, in his 1948 book, *Notes towards the Definition of Culture*, he attempted to reconcile these two conceptions of culture by distinguishing the culture of an individual and of a group or class from the culture "of a whole society." In Eliot's opinion, a lot of "men of letters and moralists" erred when they isolated the culture of the individual or the group from the culture of a whole society. "Our notion of 'perfection,'" he insisted, "must take all three senses of 'culture' into account at once." Updating Matthew Arnold, Eliot identified mid-twentieth-century English culture with the "characteristic activities and interests" of the English people, with everything from "Derby Day" and "dog races" to "boiled cabbage cut into sections" and "the music of Elgar."[6] In adopting such a broad conception of culture, Eliot broke ranks with Arnold's disciple F. R. Leavis, who not only construed culture more narrowly but also entrusted it to the safekeeping of that minority upon whom the "discerning appreciation of literature depends."[7]

The English critic Raymond Williams pushed Eliot's broad conception of English culture even further so that it included "steelmaking, touring in motorcars, mixed farming, the Stock Exchange, coalmining and London Transport." As a scholarship boy from the border country between Wales and England who matriculated in Cambridge University on the eve of the Second World War,

---

[5] Lionel Trilling, "The Situation in American Writing" (1939), quoted in Thomas Bender, "Lionel Trilling and American Culture," *American Quarterly* 42 (1990): 88; Lionel Trilling, *The Liberal Imagination: Essays on Literature and Society* (1950; repr., Garden City, N.Y.: Doubleday, 1953), viii–ix; Lionel Trilling, preface to *Beyond Culture: Essays on Literature and Learning* (New York: Viking, 1965), xi; Lionel Trilling, "Freud: Within and Beyond Culture," ibid., 105–107.

[6] T. S. Eliot, "Notes towards a Definition of Culture," *Partisan Review* 11 (1944): 145–157, on 145; T. S. Eliot, *Notes towards the Definition of Culture* (1948; repr., New York: Harcourt, 1949), 19, 22, 30. Eliot's essay appeared first in the *New England Weekly* in 1943.

[7] F. R. Leavis, *Mass Civilization and Mass Culture* (Cambridge: Gordon Fraser, 1930), 3–4, 6.

Williams heard "culture" used in two traditional senses: first, as "the preferred word for a kind of social superiority"; and second, as "an active word for writing poems and novels, films and painting, and working in theaters." Upon his return to Cambridge after wartime military service, Williams heard "culture" used in two new senses: in literary study, to refer to "some central formation of values"; and, in "more general discussion," to indicate "a particular *way of life*." The last usage, which had been popularized by anthropologists and other American social scientists, piqued his curiosity about the etymology of culture in English usage. In his 1958 book, *Culture and Society, 1780–1950*, Williams traced the development of culture to Romantic writers who had invoked it while grappling with the ugliness, poverty, and despair of the Industrial Revolution. As "culture" eventually came to be detached from "society" in English usage, it came to be seen as an ideal realm of value offering an escape from the horrors of industrialism. Borrowing from Marxists the notion that England was a "class-dominated culture," and from F. R. Leavis the notion that the "old, mainly agricultural England" was "a traditional culture of great value," Williams set out to "extend" English culture so that it encompassed the working classes and became "almost identical with our whole common life." Williams's aim was to show that culture was not only "ordinary" but also that it denoted a meaningful, inclusive way of life.[8]

ANTHROPOLOGY AND THE HUMANITIES

At the same time that prominent humanists on both sides of the Atlantic were climbing aboard the culture wagon, prominent American anthropologists were reclaiming the humanistic roots of anthropology and reaffirming their status as scientific humanists. As we have seen, Ruth Benedict called attention to the common ground that anthropology shared with the humanities and the compatibility of the "scientific" and "humanistic" traditions in her 1947 presidential address, "Anthropology and the Humanities," before the American Anthropological Association.[9] Similarly, Robert Redfield promoted the reconciliation of the humanities and anthropology in the five lectures he delivered at the University of Frankfurt, Germany, in the spring of 1949 by emphasizing the common interest in culture that anthropologists shared with humanists. To be

[8] Raymond Williams, *Culture and Society, 1780–1950* (1958; repr., New York: Harper, 1966), 234, 256; Raymond Williams, *Keywords: A Vocabulary of Culture and Society* (New York: Oxford University Press, 1976), 9–11 (emphasis in original); Raymond Williams, "Culture Is Ordinary," in *Conviction*, ed. Norman Ian MacKenzie (London: MacGibbon and Kee, 1958), 74–92; Alfred Kazin, "What's Wrong with Culture?" review of *Culture and Society, 1780–1950*, *Reporter*, 23 July 1959, 43–44.

[9] Ruth Benedict, "Anthropology and the Humanities," in *An Anthropologist at Work: The Writings of Ruth Benedict*, ed. Margaret Mead (Boston: Houghton Mifflin, 1959), 459–470; Sidney W. Mintz, "Ruth Benedict," in *Totems and Teachers: Key Figures in the History of Anthropology*, 2nd ed., ed. Sydel Silverman (Walnut Creek, Calif.: AltaMira Press, 2004), 116–117.

sure, they came at culture from different directions. Humanists, interested in "the thoughtful, deliberate, original, and creative aspect[s] of a people's life," came upon culture "from the top," whereas anthropologists, interested in "the spontaneous, common, average, and less original aspects" of a people's life, began "at the bottom, where the ordinary people work out their ways of life without benefit of books or Socrates." Yet both anthropologists and humanists studied culture. As we have seen, one of the goals of the seminars that Redfield organized with Milton Singer's help at the University of Chicago in the 1950s was to bring together humanists interested in texts with anthropologists and other social scientists interested in context.[10]

Presiding over the Wenner-Gren international symposium, "Anthropology Today," in 1952, Alfred Kroeber assigned anthropologists the task of introducing "a naturalistic point of view" into the humanities. For too long, he observed, humanists had claimed an "exemption from nature," regarding the human spirit as "something outside [natural] laws." But it was this exemption that prevented humanists from being able to weld their aesthetic judgments into "an intellectually satisfying coherence." The introduction of a naturalistic point of view into the humanities, Kroeber predicted, would make them at once "more broadly comparative," "less selective," and certainly "not normative."[11]

In his valedictory, a series of lectures that he delivered at Brown University in the spring of 1960 published posthumously under the title *Anthropology and the Classics*, Clyde Kluckhohn drew on his training in the classics to trace "the lineage of anthropological thought" to Greek culture, "the first man-centered culture." He went on to pronounce the postulates and categories of anthropology to be closer to those of both the natural sciences and the humanities than to those of the social sciences. For both the natural sciences and the humanities "worked in depth" and treated values "as *ta onta* – things as they are." Neither approach was characteristic of the social sciences.[12]

The convergence that these prominent anthropologists promoted between their discipline and the humanities helps to explain why, in a 1964 appraisal of anthropology commissioned by the Princeton Council of the Humanities, Eric Wolf stressed both anthropology's "distinctive interdisciplinary role" and the "premium" that anthropologists placed upon "intellectual synthesis."[13] It also

[10] Robert Redfield, "Social Science among the Humanities," in *Human Nature and the Study of Society: The Papers of Robert Redfield*, vol. 1, ed. Margaret Park Redfield (Chicago: University of Chicago Press, 1962), 51, 55–56.

[11] A. L. Kroeber, "Concluding Review," in *An Appraisal of Anthropology Today*, ed. Sol Tax, Loren C. Eiseley, Irving Rouse, and Carl F. Voegelin (1953; repr., Chicago: University of Chicago Press, 1976), 358–361. Kroeber repeated these sentiments in "Critical Summary and Comments," in *Method and Perspective in Anthropology: Papers in Honor of Wilson D. Wallis*, ed. Robert F. Spencer (Minneapolis: University of Minnesota Press, 1954), 273–299.

[12] Clyde Kluckhohn, *Anthropology and the Classics* (Providence: Brown University Press, 1961), 27, 23–24.

[13] Eric R. Wolf, *Anthropology* (1964; repr., New York: Norton, 1974), x.

helps to explain why the sociologists Gertrude Jaeger and Philip Selznick proposed in 1964 that "high culture" be placed at the center of "the study of culture
in the social sciences." As their contribution to bringing about a rapprochement
between the "selective" and "evaluative" humanistic conception of culture and
the "non-selective" culture concept, Jaeger and Selznick enumerated criteria
with which social scientists could evaluate, or distinguish the "better" from
the "worse."[14]

THE NEH AND THE TWO CULTURES

The postwar rapprochement between the anthropology and the humanities lay
behind the drive for a humanities foundation that culminated in the establishment of the National Endowment for the Humanities (NEH) in 1965. The
foundation's proponents, many of whom organized under the aegis of the
American Council of Learned Societies (ACLS), argued that the humanities
purveyed such "enduring values" as freedom, beauty, and truth; promoted
democracy by enhancing the "wisdom" of the average American; promised
to fill the "abyss of leisure" in an affluent society; heralded the coming-of-age
of American "high civilization"; disabused foreigners of the notion that Americans were "skilled only in gadgeteering" and "interested only in the material
aspects of life"; and strengthened America's claim to world leadership in its
Cold War struggle against the Soviet Union. Above all, proponents hoped that
the establishment of a national humanities foundation would redress the imbalance between the lavish federal support for the natural sciences since the establishment of the National Science Foundation in 1950 and the relative neglect of
the humanities. This imbalance, they contended, made it increasingly difficult
for humanists to realize their "full capacities" and to recruit "first-rate individuals" into their ranks.[15]

   In its campaign for a national humanities foundation, the ACLS emphasized
the humanities' "enrichment," qualitative judgment, breadth, and "excellence."
Such emphasis, however, did nothing to close C. P. Snow's "gulf of mutual
incomprehension" between the culture of scientists, who "had the future in
their bones," and the culture of literary intellectuals, "natural Luddites" who
refused to accept either the industrial or the scientific revolution. Snow could
characterize both groups as "cultures" precisely because the term referred at
once to the "intellectual development of the mind" and to a group whose

---

[14] Gertrude Jaeger and Philip Selznick, "A Normative Theory of Culture," *American Sociological
Review* 29 (1964): 653–669; Berkhofer, "Clio and the Culture Concept," 81n.
[15] *Report of the Commission of the Humanities* (New York: American Council of Learned Soci-
eties, 1964), 4–6; James M. Banner, Jr., "At 25, the Humanities Endowment Faces New Perils,"
Chronicle of Higher Education, 16 May 1990, A48; Roger L. Geiger, "Demography and Cur-
riculum: The Humanities in American Higher Education from the 1950s through the 1980s," in
The Humanities and the Dynamics of Inclusion since World War II, ed. David A. Hollinger
(Baltimore: Johns Hopkins University Press, 2006), 59–60.

members "without thinking about it . . . respond alike."[16] The sharp distinction that Snow drew between the two cultures, as John Higham pointed out, became "one of the constitutive ideas" that "frame[d]" American "intellectual life" in the 1960s.[17]

Controversy over Snow's two cultures induced *The Reader's Guide to Periodical Literature* to establish a new subject heading, "Science and the Humanities," in 1961.[18] It also led the American Academy of Arts & Sciences to convene a conference on "Science and Culture," the proceedings of which were published in a special issue of *Daedalus* in 1965. As the journal's editor, Gerald Holton, explained, the time had come for the term "culture" to be reexamined "in each of its multiple senses." The time had also come to examine "the place of science in our culture." Could "culture," Holton asked, be defined "in such a way that the sciences are not automatically thought to be a disturbing component in our culture"? Was it also possible to have "a unified culture in which the philosopher and the engineer communicate often and easily about each other's work"?[19]

To the conferee Harry Levin, the dispute between Snow and his critics revolved around "the implication that science can stand by itself as a culture." In his paper on the "Semantics of Culture," Levin noted how close Alfred Kroeber and Clyde Kluckhohn had come to "capturing" for social science the term "culture," which humanists had traditionally regarded as "our term." In the stress that they placed on "the collective at the expense of the individual," anthropologists and like-minded social scientists played down the older emphasis on culture as self-cultivation or improvement. As a result, culture had come to be seen as "a *donnée* to be passively accepted" rather than "a goal to be strenuously achieved." Rejecting the traditional western view of "high culture" as "the proud possession of an elite" and as "the mark of a caste," anthropologists had popularized the usage of culture in the plural. They had also "relativized" the term. In the process, culture had become a descriptive term rather than a prescriptive term. As a result, such locutions as "beauty culture" could be found in the third edition of the *Merriam-Webster's Third New International Dictionary.*[20]

The American Anthropological Association (AAA) lent it support to the ACLS campaign for a national humanities foundation. The AAA's statement pointed to both the "social ties" that anthropologists shared with humanists (such as membership in the American Folklore Society and the Linguistic Society of America) and the "logical ties of scholarly interests" (such as common

[16] C. P. Snow, *The Two Cultures* (1959; repr., Cambridge: Cambridge University Press, 1998), 4, 17; C. P. Snow, "The Two Cultures: A Second Look," ibid., 62, 64.

[17] John Higham, "The Schism in American Scholarship," in *Writing American History: Essays on Modern Scholarship* (Bloomington: Indiana University Press, 1970), 6.

[18] Higham, "The Schism in American Scholarship," 176*n*.

[19] Gerald Holton, introduction to "Science and Culture," *Daedalus* 94 (1965): vi, vii, xiv.

[20] Harry Levin, "Semantics of Culture," *Daedalus* 94 (1965): 8–9, 12–13.

interest in "culture, human nature, and creativity"). It also called attention to the postwar convergence between anthropology and the humanities as anthropologists took up the study of complex societies and historic civilizations and humanists drew "a wide comparative net" in their studies of "man's work and thought." To be sure, anthropology differed from the humanities in at least four key respects: it was rooted in natural history, commonly classified as a social science, unusually broad in its range of interests, and holistic in its insistence that the "biological, social, and cultural aspects of man [all] be viewed together." Still, anthropologists felt just as keenly as humanists the "imbalance" between sciences and the humanities. "No matter how rigorous [their] scholarship," few of the qualitative or the historical projects they proposed to the National Science Foundation were funded.[21]

In support of its contention about the convergence between anthropology and the humanities, the AAA's statement cited *The Teaching of Anthropology*, a volume of essays published in 1963. In one of the essays, Ethel Albert asserted that anthropology, as "the scientific study of the human," had "a corrective effect on the pernicious dichotomy of science and humanism dignified by C. P. Snow under the rubric 'the two cultures.'" In another essay, David Mandelbaum pointed out how, in their fieldwork, anthropologists customarily looked "closely, clearly, and dispassionately at what people are actually doing," and listened not only to what those people "say they're doing" and but also to "what others say about them." It was for this reason that anthropologists did not equate "social science" with either "theoretical models" or "statistical compilations." In yet another essay, Charles Leslie declared that "in a civilization divided by the two cultures," anthropology's value for general education lay in its being "a field of learning in which the naturalist tradition of scientific culture takes human nature and the varieties of human culture for its subject matter." In a fourth essay, McKim Marriott discussed how, in the two-semester survey of Indian civilization that he taught at the University of Chicago, he reconciled the anthropologist's "relativism," "disregard for excellence," interest in "comparison," and focus on "context" with the humanist's "preference for universalistic evaluation," interest in "the unique phenomenon," and focus on "text."[22]

But the nonscientific rationale advanced by the ACLS for a national humanities foundation eroded the middle ground staked by anthropologists who, defining themselves as scientific humanists, emphasized the overlap between culture in its anthropological sense and the venerable humanistic conception of culture; employed intuition and empathy in their fieldwork; admired generalists

[21] Alexander Spoehr, Eric R. Wolf, and Stephen T. Briggs, statement of the American Anthropological Association, in *Report of the Commission on the Humanities*, 62–70.

[22] Ethel M. Albert, "Value Aspects of Teaching Anthropology," in *The Teaching of Anthropology*, ed. David G. Mandelbaum, Gabriel W. Lasker, and Ethel M. Albert (Berkeley: University of California Press, 1963), 578; David G. Mandelbaum, "The Transmission of Anthropology," ibid., 5–6; Charles Leslie, "Teaching Anthropology and the Humanities," ibid., 487; McKim Marriott, "An Indian Civilization Course," ibid., 210.

who rose above specialization; and construed science more in terms of "ethos" or "moral code" than in terms of method.[23] In the meantime, the National Science Foundation's policy of funding only those social scientists whose research employed "objective methods" and promised to "yield verifiable results" widened the gulf between the sciences and the humanities. So, too, did the National Endowment for the Humanities' policy, following its founding in 1965, of funding "those aspects of the social sciences which have humanistic content and employ humanistic methods."[24]

RETHINKING THE CULTURE CONCEPT

The middle ground between anthropology and the humanities also eroded because of the new "rigorism" that swept through the social sciences after the Second World War. Modeling their disciplines on the natural sciences, physics in particular, social scientists sought to replace "soft" approaches with "hard" ones, description with analysis, looseness with precision, empathy with value-free neutrality, and subjectivity with objectivity.[25] From this scientistic perspective, the culture concept, as defined by Kroeber and Kluckhohn, looked awfully loose, artificially bounded, and spuriously homogeneous – in sum, too humanistic.

The diffusiveness of the culture concept not only made it hard to "operationalize," but also weakened its analytical and explanatory power.[26] Accordingly, two of Kluckhohn's students, Clifford Geertz and David Schneider, set out to "turn" the culture concept "into a less expansive affair." Geertz and Schneider attempted to do so by building on the entente reached between Alfred Kroeber and Talcott Parsons in 1958 that restricted the meaning of "culture" to "values,

[23] Mark A. May, "The Moral Code of Scientists," in *The Scientific Spirit and Democratic Faith*, ed. Eduard C. Lindeman (New York: King's Crown Press, 1944), 40–45; David A. Hollinger, "The Knower and the Artificer, *with* Postscript 1993," in *Modernist Impulses in the Human Sciences, 1870–1930*, ed. Dorothy Ross (Baltimore: Johns Hopkins University Press, 1994), 26–53.

[24] Higham, "The Schism in American Scholarship," 6.

[25] Carl E. Schorske, "The New Rigorism in the Human Sciences, 1940–1960," in *American Academic Culture in Transformation: Fifty Years, Four Disciplines*, ed. Thomas Bender and Carl E. Schorske (Princeton, N.J.: Princeton University Press, 1998), 309–329; Higham, "The Schism in American Scholarship," 18. The new rigorism even affected the practice of intellectual history. John Higham noted "the insistent demand for rigor and precision" that participants at the Wingspread Conference in 1977 voiced "even more strongly in the conference discussions than in [their] papers." John Higham, introduction to *New Directions in American Intellectual History*, ed. John Higham and Paul K. Conkin (Baltimore: Johns Hopkins University Press, 1979), xvii; Arthur M. Schlesinger, Jr., "Intellectual History: A Time for Despair?" *Journal of American History* 66 (1980): 891.

[26] For complaints about the looseness of the culture concept voiced in the 1950s, see Douglas G. Haring, "Is 'Culture' Definable?" *American Sociological Review* 14 (1949): 26–32; John W. Bennett, "Interdisciplinary Research and the Concept of Culture," *American Anthropologist* 54 (1954): 169–179. Complaints like these multiplied over time.

ideas, and [symbols]" while allowing the "social system" (or "society") to designate "interaction" and "social action."[27]

Geertz began by distinguishing "culture" as an "ordered system of meanings and of symbols" from "social system" as the "pattern of social interaction itself." Next, he likened culture to "a set of control mechanisms." Finally, in his 1973 book, *The Interpretation of Cultures*, Geertz conceived of culture in terms of cultural performances that could be analyzed by employing the techniques of close reading, as if they were texts. Culture was public, Geertz contended, because meaning was public. This meant that instead of continuing to rely on empathy to get inside their informants' heads, anthropologists now had to learn how to interpret their informants' "constructions of what they and their compatriots are up to."[28]

Objecting to the "all-embracing quality" of Kroeber and Kluckhohn's definition of culture because it attempted to explain too much, David Schneider adopted a narrower conception derived from Talcott Parsons. Culture, Schneider insisted, did not consist of "patterns . . . of and for behavior"; rather, it consisted of "symbols and meanings." As "norms" and "rules of actions," patterns of and for behavior properly belonged to the "social system." In his 1968 book, *American Kinship*, Schneider analyzed kinship in the United States as "a symbolic system purely in its own terms," making no attempt systematically to relate cultural symbols "to the social and psychological systems."[29]

Despite the best efforts of Geertz, Schneider, and other anthropologists to cut it down to size, the culture concept remained awfully loose. In 1973, Louis Schneider remarked that culture, as a "complex whole," included even "the proverbial kitchen sink." In 1974, Roger Keesing complained that Kroeber and Kluckhohn's "holistic, humanistic view of culture" still included too much and remained "too diffuse." The prevailing "global" conception of culture, Walter Goldschmidt observed in 1976, lacked "analytic power."[30]

[27] Clifford Geertz, "Passage and Accident: A Life of Learning," in *Available Light: Anthropological Reflections on Philosophical Topics* (Princeton, N.J.: Princeton University Press, 2000), 13; A. L. Kroeber and Talcott Parsons, "The Concepts of Culture and of Social System," *American Sociological Review* 23 (1958): 582–583; Talcott Parsons, "Culture and Social System Revisited," in *The Idea of Culture in the Social Sciences*, 33.

[28] Clifford Geertz, "Ritual and Social Change: A Javanese Example" (1959), in *The Interpretation of Cultures: Selected Essays* (New York: Basic Books, 1973), 143–144; Clifford Geertz, "The Impact of the Concept of Culture on the Concept of Man" (1966), ibid., 44; Clifford Geertz, "Thick Description: Toward an Interpretive Theory of Culture," ibid., 3–30.

[29] *Schneider on Schneider: The Conversion of the Jews and Other Anthropological Stories*, ed. Richard Handler (Durham: Duke University Press, 1995), 78–83; David M. Schneider, "Notes toward a Theory of Culture," in *Meaning in Anthropology*, ed. Keith H. Basso and Henry A. Selby (Albuquerque: University of New Mexico Press, 1976), 197–220; David M. Schneider, *American Kinship: A Cultural Account*, rev. ed. (Chicago: University of Chicago Press, 1980), 118–137, 1, 1n.

[30] Louis Schneider, "The Idea of Culture in the Social Sciences: Critical and Supplementary Observations," in *The Idea of Culture in the Social Sciences*, 119; Roger M. Keesing, "Theories of Culture," *Annual Review of Anthropology* 3 (1974): 73; Walter R. Goldschmidt, "Anthropology and America," *Social Science Quarterly* 57 (1976): 175–176.

As anthropologists increasingly moved away from Kroeber and Kluckhohn's humanistic conception of culture, they placed ever greater reliance on "society."[31] In 1964, after noting American anthropologists' preference for "culture," as opposed to "society" or "civilization," Eric Wolf expressed the hope that the "concept of society," "how men *claim* to be," might yet "gain over that of culture," "what they *are*." In addition to criticizing anthropologists for thinking of cultures as bounded, static, coherent entities, isomorphic with societies, Wolf insisted on distinguishing culture, as "historically developed forms," from society, as "human maneuver."[32]

Sidney Mintz also emphasized the element of maneuver. Without it, he believed, culture amounted to nothing more than "a lifeless collection of habits, superstitions, and artifacts." But when the element of maneuver was included, culture became a "repository of historically derived beliefs [and] values" on which a society could "draw, particularly for symbolic purposes."[33]

In 1982 and 1985, respectively, Wolf and Mintz published the influential historical works *Europe and the People without History* and *Sweetness and Power*.[34] This turn toward history "historicized" the culture concept. As Wolf commented, "the notion of the static primitive isolate [could] be sustained only as long as one abjures any interest in history." Anthropologists' belated recognition that many of the traditions they customarily studied were not ancient, but recent, reinforced their increasing inclination to see culture as invented or constructed.[35]

In the meantime, anthropologists began to question whether cultures depended upon shared values among their carriers. Anthony F. C. Wallace led the way. Asserting that "cognitive non-sharing" was more characteristic of cultures than shared values, Wallace urged anthropologists to turn their attention from the "replication of uniformity" to the "organization of diversity."[36] As other anthropologists followed Wallace's lead, they began to see culture as "unequally distributed."[37]

---

[31] Wolf, *Anthropology*, ix.

[32] Wolf, *Anthropology*, 18–19 (emphasis in original); Eric R. Wolf, "Specific Aspects of Plantation Systems in the New World: Community Subcultures and Social Classes" (1959), in *Pathways of Power: Building an Anthropology of the Modern World* (Berkeley: University of California Press, 2001), 225.

[33] Sidney Mintz, *Caribbean Transformations* (1974; repr., New York: Columbia University Press, 1989), 18, 325.

[34] Sherry B. Ortner, "Theory in Anthropology since the Sixties" (1984), in *Culture/Power/History: A Reader in Contemporary Social Theory*, ed. Nicholas B. Dirks, Geoff Eley, and Sherry B. Ortner (Princeton, N.J.: Princeton University Press, 1994), 386, 402.

[35] Eric R. Wolf, "Culture: Panacea or Problem?" (1984), in *Pathways of Power*, 310; Nicholas B. Dirks, Geoff Eley, and Sherry B. Ortner, introduction to *Culture/Power/History*, 6.

[36] Anthony F. C. Wallace, *Culture and Personality* (New York: Random House, 1961), 39, 26–29.

[37] Regna Darnell, "Editor's Introduction," in *American Anthropology, 1971–1995: Papers from the "American Anthropologist," 1971–1995*, ed. Regna Darnell (Lincoln: University of Nebraska Press, 2002), 20; Theodore Schwartz, "Where Is the Culture? Personality as the Distributive Locus of Culture," in *The Making of Psychological Anthropology*, ed. George D. Spindler (Berkeley: University of California Press, 1978), 422–424.

VICTIMS OF THEIR OWN SUCCESS

Anthropologists' campaign to make Americans more culture-conscious succeeded all too well. As the culture concept became, by the early 1950s, more
or less identical with the indigenous American notion of culture, practitioners
in a number of disciplines learned to appreciate the analytical usefulness of
culture, and they viewed anthropologists as its custodians. Such deference
proved short-lived. The erosion of anthropologists' control over the concept
of culture began in the 1970s. By the turn of the twenty-first century, "culture"
in its broad anthropological sense was heard almost everywhere, at home and
abroad, but in usages and for purposes that often made anthropologists uncomfortable. Anthropologists also lost proprietorship over ethnography, their characteristic literary genre. They had, it increasingly appeared, become "victims of
[their own] success."[38]

What ended as appropriation had begun as flattering imitation as, in the
1970s and 1980s, historians, literary critics, and other scholars took the cultural turn. When the social historian William H. Sewell, Jr., wanted to learn
more about culture, he turned to the works of symbolic anthropologists like
Clifford Geertz. What particularly attracted Sewell was the anthropologists'
emphasis on "meaning," which, he felt, had been "marginalized" in social
history. Sewell also found attractive Geertz's stress on meaning as public, to
be gotten at by close reading rather than through empathy and intuition.[39]
Geertz's emphasis on meaning appealed to intellectual historians as well.
Indeed, he became "virtually the patron saint" of the Wingspread Conference
convened in 1977 to revitalize intellectual history.[40] In anthropologists' ethnographies of the masses of historical actors who had left no written record,
intellectual historians found clues about how to read "the rituals, iconography,
and popular 'languages' and signs of past cultures."[41] By shifting attention
from the literate thinkers with whom historians customarily were concerned
to "ideation," to "thinking" as a public activity, Geertz's work collapsed one of
"the barriers between social and intellectual history."[42] Literary critics similarly
found appealing Geertz's extension of close reading to "the flotsam and jetsam

---

[38] Ulf Hannerz, "When Culture Is Everywhere: Reflections on a Favorite Concept," *Ethnos* 58
(1993): 95–111, on 96.

[39] William H. Sewell, Jr., *Logics of History: Social Theory and Social Transformation* (Chicago:
University of Chicago Press, 2005), 152–153, 40–43, 180–181. On social historians' turn to
anthropology and cultural history, see Lynn Hunt, "History beyond Social Theory," in *The
States of "Theory": History, Art, and Critical Discourse*, ed. David Carroll (New York: Colum-
bia University Press, 1990), 95–111; Geoff Eley, *A Crooked Line: From Cultural History to the
History of Society* (Ann Arbor: University of Michigan Press, 2005).

[40] Higham, introduction to *New Directions in American Intellectual History*, xvi.

[41] Gordon S. Wood, "Intellectual History and the Social Sciences," in *New Directions in American
Intellectual History*, 29.

[42] Ronald G. Walters, "Signs of the Times: Clifford Geertz and Historians," *Social Research* 47
(1980): 547–548.

in his fieldnotes," emboldening the New Historicist Stephen Greenblatt "to venture out to unfamiliar cultural texts."[43]

As anthropologists moved toward history, and as historians and literary critics moved toward anthropology, genres blurred. In what Geertz termed "the refiguration of social thought," anthropologists and like-minded social scientists increasingly turned away from the natural sciences toward the humanities. As they reconsidered their allegiance to a value-free, objective, natural scientific conception of their disciplines, the formerly sharp line between the social sciences and the humanities blurred.[44]

The increasing permeability of disciplinary borders accelerated centrifugal impulses within anthropology. So, too, did the sheer growth in the number of practitioners and the proliferation of subdisciplines. By 1980, most of the sub-disciplines that had appeared within anthropology boasted not only their own specialized organizations, but their own specialized publications as well. Long gone were the days when anthropology constituted a face-to-face community, the four-field approach that Franz Boas installed at Columbia encompassed most anthropological activity, and anthropologists "achieved unity" under the aegis of the culture concept. What Eric Wolf described as "a church of believers in the primacy of Culture" was fast becoming "a holding company of diverse interests."[45]

Increasingly pulled apart by diverse interests, anthropologists faced a formidable challenge to their custody of culture and ownership of the ethnography from cultural studies scholars. A transdisciplinary field that did not so much cross disciplinary boundaries as dissolve them, cultural studies originated in the efforts of Raymond Williams, Richard Hoggart, E. P. Thompson, and other British leftists to "take culture seriously."[46] Cultural studies scholars applied close reading and other techniques of textual analysis to television, the movies, and other forms of popular culture that flourished in modern, industrial societies and that anthropologists had largely neglected. While conceiving of culture broadly, as a whole way of life, cultural studies scholars repudiated the "great divide" between "high" and "low" culture that once bulked large in both

[43] Stephen Greenblatt, "The Touch of the Real," in *The Fate of "Culture": Geertz and Beyond*, ed. Sherry B. Ortner (Berkeley: University of California Press, 1999), 19–20.

[44] Clifford Geertz, "Blurred Genres: The Refiguration of Social Thought" (1980), in *Local Knowledge: Further Essays in Interpretive Anthropology* (New York: Basic Books, 1983), 19–35; Peter Novick, *That Noble Dream: The "Objectivity Question" and the American Historical Profession* (New York: Cambridge University Press, 1988), 546–547.

[45] Eric R. Wolf, "They Divide and Subdivide, and Call It Anthropology," *New York Times*, 30 November 1980, E9; Darnell, "Editor's Introduction," 1–2. The historical profession also fragmented, owing to sheer growth, "diffusion of concerns," and the increasing number of non-historians such as Eric Wolf and Sidney Mintz who published "historical studies of considerable breadth and power." Novick, *That Noble Dream*, 581, 584–587.

[46] Carolyn Steedman, "Culture, Cultural Studies, and the Historians," in *Cultural Studies*, ed. Lawrence Grossberg, Cary Nelson, and Paula A. Treichler (New York: Routledge, 1992), 613; Richard Handler, "Interpreting the Predicament of Culture Theory Today," *Social Analysis* 41 (1977): 77.

British and American thought.[47] Cultural studies thus reflected the "new sensibility" heralded by Susan Sontag in the mid-1960s. She located this sensibility in a "new non-literary culture" whose bearers – everyone from painters to social planners, to electronic engineers – not only rejected the hoary distinction between high and low levels of culture, but, in what might be regarded as long overdue homage to Thorstein Veblen, no longer drew an invidious distinction between unique, or one-of-a-kind, objects, and those that were mass-produced, or machine-made.[48]

Cultural studies appealed to a younger generation of more politically active, and theoretically self-conscious, American scholars.[49] The strong emphasis that British leftists placed on social class, however, did not carry over to the United States.[50] Cultural studies scholars in the United States proved to be much more interested in race and ethnicity, reflecting the "ethnic revival" that had been under way in the United States since the late 1960s. While Euro-Americans reclaimed the symbols of ethnicity that Lloyd Warner and other commentators had expected them to discard, Americans of non-European descent, frequently disadvantaged or marginalized, demanded that their identities and heritages be recognized in what came to be known as "identity politics."[51]

At the heart of identity politics lay what the Canadian philosopher Charles Taylor termed a "demand for recognition." Such recognition was deemed essential to collective identity. Also lying at the heart of identity politics was "authenticity," a notion that has run through anthropology (and the cognate discipline of folklore) since the days of Johann Gottfried von Herder. For the exponents of identity politics, enlarging the common culture became less a matter of ensuring "a broader culture for everyone," as it was for Raymond

---

[47] Stuart Hall, "Cultural Studies: Two Paradigms," *Media, Culture and Society* 2 (1980): 57–72; Stuart Hall, "The Emergence of Cultural Studies and the Crisis of the Humanities," *October* 53 (1990): 11–22; Stuart Hall, "Race, Culture, and Communications: Looking Backward and Forward at Cultural Studies," *Rethinking Marxism* 5 (1992): 10–18; Lawrence Grossberg, "The Formations of Cultural Studies: An American in Birmingham," *Strategies* 2 (1989): 114–149.

[48] Susan Sontag, "One Culture and the New Sensibility," in *Against Interpretation, and Other Essays* (New York: Farrar, 1966), 293–304.

[49] Michael Schudson, "Paper Tigers: A Sociologist Follows Cultural Studies into the Wilderness," *Lingua Franca*, August 1997, 50; Michael Lambeck and Janice Boddy, "Introduction: Culture in Question," *Social Analysis* 41 (1977): 3; Handler, "Interpreting the Predicament of Culture Theory Today," 76–77. Among American anthropologists, the "activist tide" receded after 1970. Darnell, "Editor's Introduction," 2.

[50] John Higham, "Multiculturalism and Universalism: A History and Critique" (1993), in *Hanging Together: Unity and Diversity in American Culture*, ed. Carl J. Guarneri (New Haven, Conn.: Yale University Press, 2001), 221–239; Jay Mechling, "Some [New] Elementary Axioms for an American Cultur[al] Studies," *American Studies* 38 (1997): 12–13; Handler, "Interpreting the Predicament of Culture Theory Today," 76–77; Renato Rosaldo, "Whose Cultural Studies?" *American Anthropologist* 96 (1994): 525–526.

[51] Will Kymlicka, *Multicultural Citizenship: A Liberal Theory of Minority Rights* (Oxford: Clarendon Press, 1995), 61, 55, 66.

Williams, than of giving "due recognition to the hitherto excluded."[52]
To the extent that identity politics involved the attribution of unique properties
to groups, it suggested that the rise of the culture concept had irrevocably
relocated culture from the individual to the group or collective. By the
1980s, however, the postwar emphasis on the universals and near universals
of culture had given way to an emphasis on difference. Indeed, many
cultural studies scholars were highly suspicious of anything that smacked of
"universalism."[53]

A number of things about cultural studies annoyed anthropologists. First
and foremost, cultural studies scholars did not look to anthropologists for
guidance about how to deploy the culture concept.[54] Second, the "culture" of
cultural studies – "evaluative," predominantly textual, and often detached from
society – struck anthropologists as a new iteration of culture in its humanistic
sense.[55] Anthropologists also missed in cultural studies the attention to context
that had run through anthropology, from Franz Boas's emphasis on historical
and geographical setting, to Alfred Kroeber's descriptive integration, to Robert
Redfield's attempt to bring together textual and contextual studies, to Clifford
Geertz's declaration that "culture is a context." Context, it appeared, took a
back seat to text. Indeed, critics often complained about the way in which
cultural studies obliterated "the social."[56] Fourth, the ethnographies that cultural studies scholars produced were more often based on market surveys than
on fieldwork. When they did engage in fieldwork, it rarely involved what James
Clifford once referred to as "deep hanging out."[57] Finally, insofar as they
identified culture as the fundamental property of ethnic or racial groups,

[52] Charles Taylor, *Multiculturalism and "The Politics of Recognition"* (Princeton, N.J.: Princeton University Press, 1992), 25, 30, 68; Regina Bendix, *In Search of Authenticity: The Formation of Folklore Studies* (Madison: University of Wisconsin Press, 1997).
[53] Alan Wolfe, "Social Science and the Moral Revival: Dilemmas and Difficulties," in *In Face of the Facts: Moral Inquiry in American Scholarship*, ed. Richard Wightman Fox and Robert B. Westbrook (Cambridge: Cambridge University Press, 1998), 242.
[54] Handler, "Interpreting the Predicament of Culture Theory Today," 76–77; Richard Parker, "Why Do Multiculturalists Ignore Anthropologists?" *Chronicle of Higher Education*, 4 March 1992, A52. In Britain, where cultural studies scholars taught either in the newer, "red brick" universities or outside the universities altogether, cultural studies "barely touched" anthropol-ogy, which was "almost entirely confined to the older, research-based, elite universities." Jonathan Spencer, "British Social Anthropology: A Retrospective," *Annual Review in Anthro-pology* 29 (2006): 6; Steedman, "Culture, Cultural Studies, and the Historians," 614.
[55] Roger H. Keesing, "Theories of Culture Revisited," in *Assessing Cultural Anthropology*, ed. Robert Borofsky (New York: McGraw-Hill, 1994), 303; Lawrence Grossberg, Cary Nelson, and Paula A. Treichler, introduction to *Cultural Studies*, 4.
[56] Schudson, "Paper Tigers," 50–51; Victoria Bonnell and Lynn Hunt, introduction to *Beyond the Cultural Turn: New Directions in the Study of Society and Culture*, ed. Victoria Bonnell and Lynn Hunt (Berkeley: University of California Press, 1999), 11; Eley, *A Crooked Line*, 194.
[57] Richard Handler, "Anthropology Is Dead! Long Live Anthropology!" review of *Cultural Stud-ies*, ed. Lawrence Grossberg, Cary Nelson, and Paula A. Treichler, *American Anthropologist* 95 (1993): 993; James Clifford, quoted in Clifford Geertz, "Deep Hanging Out," *New York Review of Books*, 22 October 1998, 69.

cultural studies scholars reified cultures and overemphasized their internal homogeneity at a time when anthropologists were playing down their boundedness and coherence.[58]

What also dismayed anthropologists is that practitioners of other disciplines had begun to look to cultural studies to get their bearings on culture. This was certainly true of the generation of American studies scholars who came of age in the 1970s and 1980s.[59] Thus George Lipsitz turned to cultural studies because its practitioners were more self-conscious than were anthropologists about culture, long an "undertheorized" concept in American studies.[60] To Michael Denning, the questions posed by cultural studies scholars – "what is culture?" and "what are its forms and how is it related to material production?" – were far more theoretically fruitful than the perennial question of American studies, "what is American?"[61] Then, too, as a transdisciplinary field closely linked to political activism, cultural studies addressed two problems with which American studies scholars had long wrestled: Was American studies an interdisciplinary field, or did it constitute a discipline in its own right? And how was the scholarship of American studies scholars related to their cultural politics?[62] Cultural studies offered American studies scholars a better purchase on mass and popular culture; it also spoke to Americans who did not share F. O. Matthiessen's concern about participating on equal footing with European intellectuals in transatlantic discourse. Nor were American studies scholars still concerned with reconciling the humanistic concern for value and text with the social scientific concern for fact and context.

It is no wonder that, by the late 1980s, Clifford Geertz detected a "pervasive nervousness" among anthropologists. This nervousness stemmed from several sources. Since the late 1950s, the breakup of European empires had drastically altered anthropologists' relations to the peoples they studied. Anthropologists were no longer "sheltered by colonialism." Their informants were no longer "colonial subject[s]," but "sovereign citizen[s]."[63] What was more, the natives now talked back. They not only read what anthropologists wrote about them, but, much in the manner of John P. Marquand's challenge to Lloyd Warner, they

[58] Terence Turner, "Anthropology and Multiculturalism: What Is Anthropology That Multiculturalists Should Be Mindful of It?" *Current Anthropology* 8 (1993): 411–412.
[59] Norman R. Yetman, introduction to "American Studies: From Culture Concept to Cultural Studies?" *American Studies* 38 (1997): 5–6.
[60] George Lipsitz, "Listening to Learn and Learning to Listen: Popular Culture, Cultural Theory, and American Studies," *American Quarterly* 42 (1990): 617.
[61] Michael Denning, "'The Special American Conditions': Marxism and American Studies," *American Quarterly* 38 (1986): 360.
[62] Barry Shank, "The Continuing Embarrassment of Culture: From the Culture Concept to Cultural Studies," *American Studies* 38 (1997): 96–97.
[63] Clifford Geertz, *Works and Lives: The Anthropologist as Author* (Stanford: Stanford University Press, 1988), 132; George W. Stocking, Jr., "Postscriptive Prospective Reflections," in *The Ethnographer's Magic and Other Essays in the History of Anthropology* (Madison: University of Wisconsin Press, 1992), 366.

also claimed that their knowledge as insiders trumped anthropologists' interpretations as disinterested outsiders.[64]

Yet another source of the pervasive nervousness among anthropologists was
the "crisis of representation" that beset anthropology and other observational
sciences in the 1980s. Publication of Edward Said's *Orientalism* and Derek
Freeman's *Margaret Mead and Samoa* in 1979 and 1983, respectively, raised
questions about the accuracy and transparency of ethnography as a mode of
representation. Yet, even as anthropologists questioned their ability to repre-
sent other cultures, the practice of ethnography was quickly spreading to other
disciplines.[65]

As anthropologists reconsidered both the culture concept and the practice of
ethnography, they heard the word "culture" uttered all around them. In 1993,
Henry Lewis Gates, Jr., noted the "avalanche of books" with "culture" in their
titles that had been published in the United States over the preceding fifteen
years.[66] By 1997, it had gotten "to the point" in American usage that every time
he heard the word "culture," Kwame Anthony Appiah "reach[ed] for [his]
dictionary."[67] In Adam Gopnik's opinion, culture had become the term that
Americans invoked "to explain things that resist explanation." Where the
Enlightenment had Fate and the Victorian Age History, fin-de-siècle America
had Culture.[68]

Culture-consciousness was spreading abroad as quickly as it was at home.
Marshall Sahlins called to how "imperialism's erstwhile victims" invoked culture, or "some local equivalent," to assert their right to "their own cultural
space in the global scheme of things" – a phenomenon that Sahlins labeled the
"indigenization of modernity." As an example, Sahlins cited the Kayapo of the
Amazon Basin, who, reported Terence Turner, were invoking "the Portuguese
word 'cultura'" to confer honor and meaning on their traditional way of life.
The Kayapo illustrated what Sahlins considered the "surprising paradox of our
time: that localization develops apace with globalization, differentiation with
integration; that just when the forms of life are becoming more homogeneous,

[64] Renato Rosaldo, *When Natives Talk Back: Chicano Anthropology since the Late Sixties*
(Tucson: University of Arizona Mexican American Studies and Research Center, 1986);
Caroline B. Brettell, "Introduction: Fieldwork, Text, and Audience," in *When They Read
What We Write: The Politics of Ethnography*, ed. Caroline B. Brettell (Westport, Conn.:
Bergin and Garvey, 1993), 1, 3; Handler, "Interpreting the Predicament of Culture Theory
Today," 76.
[65] Geertz, *Lives and Works*, 131–132; Adam Kuper, *Culture: The Anthropologists' Account* (Cam-
bridge, Mass.: Harvard University Press, 1999), 223; George E. Marcus and Michael M. J.
Fischer, *Anthropology at Cultural Critique: An Experimental Moment in the Human Sciences*
(Chicago: University of Chicago Press, 1986); James Clifford, "Introduction: Partial Truths," in
Writing Culture: The Poetics and Politics of Ethnography, ed. James Clifford and George E.
Marcus (Berkeley: University of California Press, 1986), 1–26.
[66] Henry Louis Gates, Jr., "The Weaning of America," *New Yorker*, 19 April 1993, 113, 116.
[67] K. Anthony Appiah, "The Multiculturalist Misunderstanding," *New York Review of Books*, 9
October 1997, 30–31.
[68] Adam Gopnik, "Comment: Culture Vultures," *New Yorker*, 24 May 1999, 27–28.

the peoples are asserting their distinctiveness." The world, according to Sahlins, was becoming a "Culture of cultures."[69]

In the 1990s, culture consciousness even spread to political conservatives. No longer relying on discredited racial rhetoric, they adopted anthropologists' old "habits of talk" to reify cultures as "compact, bounded, [and] localized," root "nationality and citizenship" in "shared cultural heritage," and emphasize the "incommensurability" of cultures to oppose immigration and cross-racial adoptions.[70]

The ubiquity of culture and the uses to which it was put worried anthropologists who realized, as Renato Rosaldo acknowledged in 1994, that they had "lost their monopoly on the concept of culture." Marilyn Strathern agreed. In becoming "a global phenomenon," culture had acquired for many laymen "a taken-for-granted status." In 1995, Annette Weiner devoted part of her presidential address to the American Anthropological Association to the "discontent" anthropologists felt "about the proprietary 'takeover' of the culture concept by other disciplines."[71] Sidney Mintz worried that the "ever-widening currency" of culture – which, by 2000, had become "synonymous with 'someplace where somebody does something'" – was vulgarizing the concept's meaning and draining its content.[72] Marshall Sahlins agreed. The word "culture," he said, was "at a discount" everywhere in the English-speaking world, designating "social categories and groups of every shape and form."[73]

In response, some anthropologists engaged in what Robert Brightman described as "lexical avoidance behavior." Although they continued to use the adjective "cultural," they placed the term "culture" in quotation marks or substituted such terms as "hegemony" and "discourse."[74] Sidney Mintz, however, regretted that anthropologists were abandoning culture at the same time that non-anthropologists were adopting it in a "wholesale" and "somewhat

[69] Marshall Sahlins, "Goodbye to *Tristes Tropes*: Ethnography in the Context of Modern World History" (1993), in *Culture in Practice: Selected Essays* (New York: Zone Books, 2000), 474, 493; Terence Turner, "Representing, Resisting, Rethinking: Historical Transformation of Kayapo Culture and Anthropological Consciousness," in *Colonial Situations: Essays on the Contextualization of Ethnographic Knowledge*, ed. George W. Stocking, Jr. (Madison: University of Wisconsin Press, 1991), 304.

[70] Verena Stolcke, "Talking Cultures: New Boundaries, New Rhetorics of Exclusion in Europe," *Current Anthropology* 36 (1995): 1, 12, 4, 8; Michel-Rolph Trouillot, *Global Transformations: Anthropology and the Modern World* (New York: Palgrave Macmillan, 2003), 113.

[71] Rosaldo, "Whose Culture Studies?" 526–527; Marilyn Strathern, "Foreword: Shifting Contexts," in *Shifting Contexts: Transformations in Anthropological Knowledge*, ed. Marilyn Strathern (London: Routledge, 1994), 2, 3, 11; Annette B. Weiner, "Culture and Its Discontents," *American Anthropologist* 97 (1995): 14, 18–19.

[72] Sidney W. Mintz, "Sows' Ears and Silver Linings: A Backward Look at Ethnography," *Current Anthropology* 41 (2000): 169–170, 177.

[73] Marshall Sahlins, "'Sentimental Pessimism' and Ethnographic Experience: or, Why Culture Is Not a Disappearing 'Object,'" in *Biographies of Scientific Objects*, ed. Lorraine Daston (Chicago: University of Chicago Press, 2000), 158, 159n.

[74] Robert Brightman, "Forget Culture: Replacement, Transcendence, Relexification," *Cultural Anthropology* 10 (1995): 510; Sewell, *Logics of History*, 154.

opportunistic" manner. Mintz worried that anthropologists' "near-abandon-ment" of the culture concept would deprive anthropology of "a voice of its own" in which anthropologists could continue to speak to non-anthropologists.[75]

Still other anthropologists, especially practitioners of subdisciplines such as biological anthropology, archaeology, and linguistics, continued to view culture as the unifying thread of their increasingly specialized, fragmented discipline.[76] The culture concept might be "a deeply compromised idea," but it was not yet one that the historian James Clifford or a number of anthropologists felt that they could "do without."[77] Still other anthropologists, however, concluded that the word "culture" was "lost to anthropology for the foreseeable future."[78]

Since the end of the Second World War, anthropologists had reconceived culture as they came to terms with what Clifford Geertz described as a "world in pieces." Decolonization and the disintegration of the Soviet empire had shattered the "larger coherences" of the post-1945 world into "smaller ones, uncertainly connected with one another." In the closing decades of the twentieth century, anthropologists increasingly had to address such questions as "what is a culture if not a consensus?" and "what is a country if not a nation?"[79] More than ever before, anthropologists had to learn how to study what Sidney Mintz described as "human groups *in motion*," the hallmark of an increasingly "transnational" world.[80] No longer the premier students of culture to whom others interested in culture looked for guidance, anthropologists still saw considerable value in their insistence on observation, ethnographic field-work, and cosmopolitanism. It was their insistence on observation that, as Eric Wolf pointed out, "allowed" anthropologists "to separate norms from behavior and to see the relation between the two as problematic," to be "professionally suspicious of nomothetic abstractions about what people do," and to continue to practice an "integrative science" that "crosses the boundaries of different domains and resists the dismemberment of relations and contexts."[81] For Sidney Mintz, ethnographic fieldwork was the main reason for anthropology's continuing existence. Indeed, it was precisely "in accordance with the quality, honesty, and reliability of [their] fieldwork" that anthropologists' theories "acquire[d] their strength, elegance, and conviction."[82] Clifford Geertz also believed that "the anthropological way of looking at things" still had something

[75] Mintz, "Sows' Ears and Silver Linings," 170, 177.
[76] Sydel Silverman, foreword to *Anthropology beyond Culture*, ed. Richard G. Fox and Barbara J. King (New York: Berg, 2002), xvii.
[77] James Clifford, The *Predicament of Culture: Twentieth-Century Ethnography, Literature, and Art* (Cambridge, Mass.: Harvard University Press, 1988), 10.
[78] Trouillot, *Global Transformations*, 115.
[79] Clifford Geertz, "The World in Pieces: Culture and Politics at the End of the Century," in *Available Light*, 221, 246.
[80] Sidney W. Mintz, "The Localization of Anthropological Practice: From Area Studies to Trans-actionalism," *Critique of Anthropology* 18 (1998): 117.
[81] Eric R. Wolf, "Anthropology among the Powers" (1990), in *Pathways of Power*, 79–80.
[82] Mintz, "Sows' Ears and Silver Linings," 177.

to offer. Although anthropology's "patent on the study of cultural diversity, if it ever had one, [had] long since expired," the world still needed anthropologists' cosmopolitanism and "determination" to "look beyond" the "familiar," "received," and "near at hand."[83]

Amid anthropology's evident disarray at the dawn of the twenty-first century, it is important to recall the discipline's accomplishments over the previous century. What Henry James said about Matthew Arnold, that although Arnold did not "invent" culture, he "made it more definite than it had been before – he vivified and lighted it up," applies just as well to Franz Boas and his successors, who popularized in American usage an inclusive, pluralistic, relativistic, and holistic conception of culture.[84] Culture in this sense was far broader than the refinement and sophistication denoted by humanistic culture. Indeed, breadth or inclusiveness was the first property that came to mind when many non-anthropologists thought of the culture concept.[85] Boas and his successors also popularized the term "cultures," culture in the plural, to designate "what peoples had and held in common."[86] As Harry Levin pointed out in 1965, it was just a short step from demonstrating the existence of a plurality of cultures to insisting upon "relativism of standards."[87] This had long been true of German usage, where, from the late eighteenth century on, Germans had invoked cultures in the plural to reject normative and hierarchical traditions of culture.[88] Finally, culture in its anthropological sense was holistic. Indeed, anthropologists taught non-anthropologists to "look for connections," in Eric Wolf's words, or, as David Riesman put it, to see "what goes together with what."[89] By the 1950s, thinking of culture holistically had given the expression "our culture" new meaning.

The culture concept, as we have seen, countered racialist thought; provided American intellectuals with the remove from which to criticize America and to propose schemes for social engineering; encouraged humanistic approaches that resisted being made rigidly scientific, systematic, quantitative, or even empirical; resolved the paradox of Americans' disdain for culture as a feminine pursuit with their willingness to pour millions of dollars into cultural institutions; and reinforced the growing conviction among American intellectuals that the United States did possess a national "high" culture that was the equivalent of the more historic cultures of Europe.

[83] Geertz, "The World in Pieces," 251.
[84] Henry James, "Matthew Arnold" (1884), quoted in John Henry Raleigh, *Matthew Arnold and American Culture* (Berkeley: University of California Press, 1961), 37.
[85] Barzun, "Cultural History as Synthesis," 392–393; Carl E. Schorske, "History and the Study of Culture," *New Literary History* 21 (1990): 409, 415.
[86] Levin, "Semantics of Culture," 8; Geertz, "The World in Pieces," 249.
[87] Levin, "Semantics of Culture," 8.
[88] Q. v. "culture," *Oxford English Dictionary*, online.
[89] Wolf, "Culture: Panacea or Problem?," 308; David Riesman, memo to Kansas City Research Committee, 1 November 1952, Havighurst Papers, box 19, folder "Kansas City Research Plans."

Arguably, the Americanization of culture (a term that Americans borrowed from German thought, proceeded to make their own, and then sought to export after 1945), represented one of the supreme intellectual achievements of American civilization. Its history from the 1880s on illustrates one of the points that Merle Curti made in 1953 in assessing twentieth-century American scholarship. By then, according to Curti, the "long tradition of debtor-creditor relationships between American and European scholarship" had been reversed. "The totalitarian onslaught" of the 1930s and 1940s, which spurred the immigration of thousands of European intellectuals to the United States, followed by "the breakdown of Europe in the midst of dislocation and war," had made the United States "the chief center of learning in the world." If the United States was "thought of as essentially European in culture," then perhaps this geographical shift was "of no great point." But if the United States was "regarded as the center of a new civilization," as Max Lerner was to do in his 1957 book, *America as a Civilization*, then "the widely recognized prestige of American scholars could be rightly considered as a major factor in modern cultural history."[90]

Thanks to the wide currency that culture in its broad anthropological sense had gained in American usage by the 1950s, Americans convinced themselves that they possessed a national culture of some worth. With that question answered in the affirmative, new questions arose about the content, levels, and worth of American culture. Over time, the middlebrow and popular levels of American culture became more salient than high culture. As culture became even more popular and accessible, distinctions between its levels (particularly that between high and low) blurred if they were not obliterated. By democratizing culture, by rendering it a birthright rather than the goal of self-improvement, anthropologists made it all the more likely that culture would slip out of their control.[91]

Much as historians now have to cope with the "democratization" of the past in what David Lowenthal has called the "heritage crusade," as all sorts of people, not just elites, have come to take history seriously, so, too, have anthropologists had to cope with the enormous popularity of culture, a popularity they did so much to promote. They have also had to cope with the stubborn persistence of habits of talking about culture – thinking in terms of one culture per society, emphasizing the separation and isolation of cultures, and seeing cultures everywhere – that they themselves once engaged in but have since largely repudiated. Culture, much like heritage, now belongs to everyone. It has become truly popular as educated Americans have become culture-conscious.[92]

[90] Merle Curti, "The Setting and the Problems," in *American Scholarship in the Twentieth Century*, ed. Merle Curti (Cambridge, Mass.: Harvard University Press, 1953), 5–6.
[91] Sidney W. Mintz, "Culture: An Anthropological View," *Yale Review* 71 (1982): 499.
[92] John R. Gillis, introduction to *Commemorations: The Politics of National Identity*, ed. John R. Gillis (Princeton, N.J.: Princeton University Press, 1994), 17; David Lowenthal, *The Heritage Crusade and the Spoils of History* (1996; repr., Cambridge: Cambridge University Press, 1998).

Index

value and, 3
"Culture, Genuine and Spurious," 48–50
culture-consciousness, 3, 14, 57, 60, 62
Cunliffe, Marcus, 155, 248
Curti, Merle, 64, 271

Daedalus, 257
Dalhousie Review, 48
Danilevsky, Nikolai, 215
Davis, Allison, 94–96, 132
Davis, David Brion, 196
Davis, Elizabeth, 95
"Declaration of Interdependence, A Creed
  for Americans as World Citizens,"
  190
Decline of the West, The, 57, 206–207
Deep South, 96
Della Vida, G. L., 207
Democracy in Jonesville, 102
Denney, Reuel, 151, 155–156
DePauw University, 51
Depression, 60
  American values, changing of, 192–193
  class struggle and, 73
  cultural nationalism and, 201
  democratization of culture and,
    242–243
  Muncie, impact on, 84–85, 87
  Newburyport during, 116
  social persistence and, 94
DeVinney, Leland C., 182
Dewey, John, 33, 48, 62, 80, 145, 183
Dial, 22, 46, 48, 121
Dicks, Henry, 137
Dilthey, Wilhelm, 57
Dobu, 58–59, 128, 152
Dollard, John, 133
  Kardiner and, 134
  Kluckhohn and, 161, 163
  life history and, 123, 131–132
  Mead and, 129
  psychoanalysis and, 125
  Sapir and, 128
  Warner and, 131
Driver, Harold, 205–206
Du Bois, Cora, 134–135
Duffus, R. L., 81, 87
Dundes, Alan, 197
Durkheim, Émile, 91, 93, 217

Early Civilization, 38
ecumene, 209, 218, 236–237, 238–239
Elias, Norbert, 14–15
Eliot, T. S., 13, 202, 253
Ellwood, Charles A., 39, 41
Elmtown's Youth, 103
Embree, John, 138
"Emergence of the Concept of Personality
  in a Study of Culture, The," 126
Emerson, Ralph Waldo, 17–18
Encyclopedia of the Social Sciences, 7, 45,
  126–127, 162
Enlightenment, 14–15
EP. *See* Evaluated Participation
Erikson, Erik, 137, 150–151
Escape from Freedom, 130, 136
Eskimo, 28
Ethical Record, 31
eugenics, 35
Europe
  American cultural independence
    from, 14
  American inferiority to, 2, 16–18
  changing American view of, 202,
    241–243
  export of American culture to,
    243–244, 249
  postwar gap between America and,
    244–245
  World War II and, 271
Europe and the People without History,
  240
Evaluated Participation, 101–102
Everett, John R., 2, 67, 247

Fahs, Charles B., 184
Fallers, Lloyd, 115–116
Family and Community in Ireland, 95
Faris, Ellsworth, 40–41
Faris, Robert E. L., 111
Feudalism in History, 213
fieldwork
  anthropology, essence of, 269–270
  cultural studies and, 265
  psychiatric concepts and, 167–168
  psychoanalysis and, 125–126
  rise of, 34
  World War II and, 119, 136
Filler, Louis, 194, 246